S0-BDP-828

essentials

Regulation of the Legal Profession

Editorial Advisors

ASPEN PUBLISHERS

essentials

Regulation of the Legal Profession

Stephen Gillers
Emily Kempin Professor of Law
New York University School of Law

Wolters Kluwer
Law & Business

AUSTIN   BOSTON   CHICAGO   NEW YORK   THE NETHERLANDS

About Wolters Kluwer Law & Business

Wolters Kluwer Law & Business is a leading provider of research information and workflow solutions in key specialty areas. The strengths of the individual brands of Aspen Publishers, CCH, Kluwer Law International, and Loislaw are aligned within Wolters Kluwer Law & Business to provide comprehensive, in-depth solutions and expert-authored content for the legal, professional, and education markets.

CCH was founded in 1913 and has served more than four generations of business professionals and their clients. The CCH products in the Wolters Kluwer Law & Business group are highly regarded electronic and print resources for legal, securities, antitrust and trade regulation, government contracting, banking, pension, payroll, employment and labor, and healthcare reimbursement and compliance professionals.

Aspen Publishers is a leading information provider for attorneys, business professionals, and law students. Written by preeminent authorities, Aspen products offer analytical and practical information in a range of specialty practice areas from securities law and intellectual property to mergers and acquisitions and pension/benefits. Aspen's trusted legal education resources provide professors and students with high-quality, up-to-date, and effective resources for successful instruction and study in all areas of the law.

Kluwer Law International supplies the global business community with comprehensive English-language international legal information. Legal practitioners, corporate counsel, and business executives around the world rely on the Kluwer Law International journals, loose-leafs, books, and electronic products for authoritative information in many areas of international legal practice.

Loislaw is a premier provider of digitized legal content to small law firm practitioners of various specializations. Loislaw provides attorneys with the ability to quickly and efficiently find the necessary legal information they need, when and where they need it, by facilitating access to primary law as well as state-specific law, records, forms, and treatises.

Wolters Kluwer Law & Business, a unit of Wolters Kluwer, is headquartered in New York and Riverwoods, Illinois. Wolters Kluwer is a leading multinational publisher and information services company.

Table of Contents

Briefly, By Way of Introduction …

The word *essentials* is in the title of this book. It fairly describes the content. This is not a treatise, not a heavily footnoted law review article, not a law professor's extended excursion into the intellectual or historical explanations for the subject. The book *is* a reflective introduction to the major and minor rules and themes in the law and ethics governing the behavior of American lawyers. As its guide, it uses the American Bar Association Model Rules (where ethics rules are the subject) and cases from various jurisdictions. Material on the legal liability of lawyers relies on case law. The endeavor required selection, and selection always requires judgment. What to include. What to omit. I have tried to balance the interest in coverage and depth against the goal of avoiding excessive detail.

Each of the chapters discusses a discrete area of legal ethics. More or less. Choosing the focus of each of the chapters itself required judgment. I don't expect that most readers will read the book from beginning to end, though some will. More likely, readers will look at one chapter or another as their own interest directs them at the time. For that reason, I have cross-referenced chapters. Subtitles to each chapter identify the chapter's main themes. There is minor duplication across chapters when a subject could properly be raised in more than one place. Footnoting is light but sufficient, I hope, to enable a reader who wants to pursue a question to begin further research.

I have tried to make the book conversational, personal, and accessible. Much legal writing is just the opposite, reasonably so, perhaps, given the differences in purpose or audience. This assignment, however, offered a chance for a casual and distinct voice — even the first-person singular when useful — and I have taken advantage of the opportunity.

Readers are invited (indeed urged) to drop me a note if there are issues not addressed here, or not adequately addressed, in their view. Should the book go into a second edition, all suggestions will receive serious consideration.

Stephen Gillers
New York University School of Law
stephen.gillers@nyu.edu

New York City
August 2009

~ 1 ~

What Are Legal Ethics?

Who Makes the Rules?

Why Do We Need Them?

Why Do We Want Them?

The Competing Interests in the Ethical Rules

Legal Ethics and the Administration of Justice

Legal ethics have something of an image problem. Maybe that's too polite. Let's just say the subject gets relatively little respect. But even that may put it too mildly. The truth is that quite a few lawyers and law students treat legal ethics with an attitude approaching passive hostility. And no wonder. Law students at most schools are required to take a course called Legal Ethics (or The Legal Profession, or Professional Responsibility, but they all amount to the same thing).[1] Right off, the subject gets a bad rap simply because it is required. By the time a student is in her second or third year of law school, *required* may be a dirty word.

Lawyers may not love legal ethics for their own good reasons — *good* as they perceive it. Ethics rules can hurt business. Conflict rules limit a lawyer's ability to accept new clients or new matters from current clients.[2] Other rules may prevent lawyers from certain tactics in representing clients.[3] Sometimes, the rules may even require a lawyer to betray a client, at least as the lawyer may see it.[4] If all that were not bad enough, ethical rules have lately become potent weapons in the arsenals of lawyers and law firms that sue other lawyers and law firms for malpractice, breach of fiduciary duty, or aiding a client's fraud (among other theories of liability).[5] When that happens, lawyers for the plaintiffs find legal ethics quite congenial, so the subject is not entirely without friends, even if they are fair-weather friends. Last, the rules are getting quite complicated, which, when added to their inescapable vagueness, can cause many a lawyer, in moments of frustration, to wonder whether it is even possible to find a secure balance between the desire to stay out of trouble on one hand, and on the other hand, the duty to protect and advance the goals of clients and the wish, perfectly laudable, to raise one's market appeal and public profile (in a good way).

What about the public? Does it believe that ethical rules for lawyers actually have teeth, that they require lawyers to behave in ways they would rather not, or not to behave in ways they would like to behave? (They have to do one or the other, or else why have them? We don't need rules to tell people they can do whatever they want.) Probably, the public does not much think about it, which is just as well, because if it did, a general cynicism about the bar (don't forget all those lawyer jokes) could make the term "legal ethics" sound, even more than it now does, like a joke or a public relations ploy, not a serious endeavor. It could even sound downright elitist. Who ever heard of carpenter ethics? Do bankers fret over a code of banker ethics? (Of late, we wish they did.)

Which leads us to ask, Why bother? The sky won't fall without a set of ethical rules for lawyers. The American Bar Association (ABA) did not adopt the first such set until 1908. The nation managed to grow and prosper quite nicely for more than 125 years without ethical rules for lawyers. And the 1908 Canons of Legal Ethics (as they were named) weren't all that impressive when you take a close look at what the document actually had to say. For example, the Canons tell lawyers that "it is unprofessional for a lawyer to volunteer advice to bring a lawsuit, except in rare cases where ties of blood, relationship or trust make it his duty to do so." In other words, if a casual friend or acquaintance has been mistreated, you're not supposed to tell him he could probably sue because "[s]tirring up strife and litigation is . . . unprofessional" and may even be criminal (Canon 28). That's ethics?[6]

But back to the question: Why bother? What if there were no ethics rules for lawyers? Who is served by having these rules, especially as they often get such little regard, including from the profession itself?

The fact is that we could probably get along quite nicely if we just left the regulation of lawyers to the law — case law, statutes, administrative agency rule making — which is how most everyone and everything else is regulated. Actually, as we'll see, many of the rules governing the behavior of lawyers do in fact come to us not from a code of ethics but from court decisions (in the areas of malpractice, fiduciary duty, tort, and agency law, among others), legislation, and agency rules. In other words, *the law*. So-called codes of ethics (by whatever name) are just one part, though not a minor part, of the regulatory architecture for lawyers. But the point here is that we could have left it all to other sources entirely. That would deny lawyers the ability to boast that they are part of a profession with a code of ethics (or of professional conduct or professional responsibility) — a code of ethics being what a profession is

expected to have, part of the very definition of a profession —
but what of it? What would be lost? Well, the boast might be
lost, and that has currency, at least for lawyers. It makes them
special in some way, part of a small fraternity of traditional
professionals that includes doctors, teachers, and the clergy.
It makes them, in the view of some lawyers certainly, different
from (say) accountants.

While the ability to make that boast might seem to some (viz,
the cynical public again) little more than public relations, there's
another way to look at it. Having the rules not only allows lawyers
to *claim* that they are part of a profession, but it also *reminds*
them that they are part of a profession. Don't underestimate the
symbolic value of a separate document purporting to establish
rules of ethics. Much angst has beset the bar in the last 30 or so
years over whether the practice of law is merely a business or
also a profession. Of course, these are not mutually exclusive
categories. Law can be both. In truth, law must be both. A law
firm that didn't conduct itself like a business — didn't apply
all of the methodologies and financial controls of a traditional
business — would not be around very long, and that is especially
true for large modern law firms. It's a question of degree.

Or, to put it another way: To what extent does the fact that
law is a profession, not just a business, restrain the conduct of
lawyers from acting in a situation as businesspeople might act,
and properly so? The fact of the existence of ethics rules and
their content help us identify a proper balance between the
business and the professional sides of doing the work of a
lawyer. So, too, does the inevitable debate that accompanies
adoption of new rules or amendment of old ones. Not only the
bar, but the rule of law and the administration of justice benefit
from establishing professional identity in this way. Doing so
acts as a constraint on purely commercial or market behavior.
Or one might say a check on unrestrained greed.[7]

But while all of this is true, there are other truths as well.
None of this is simple. To varying degrees, depending on the

state, but to a significant degree everywhere, judges claim the right to make the rules that govern lawyers. Sometimes this claim is based on explicit language in the state's constitution. Sometimes it relies on the court's inherent power and separation-of-powers principles. That's because lawyers are part of the administration of justice, which is the job of the judiciary, at least primarily.[8] Sometimes the court's power is just assumed without a felt need to defend or explain it. But once we accept that judges have the power to make the rules governing the bar, even if in partnership with lawmakers, there is a certain pressure for them to do so. The pressure comes from at least two places. First, if the judges claim the power but do nothing, the legislature and executive may decide to fill that particular vacuum. Judges won't like that, but it would be hard for them to discourage or forbid those efforts if judges remain passive. So this first influence is defensive. Protect your turf. Second, pressure will come from the fact that other state courts have adopted lawyer ethics rules. The impulse to do so is catching. As a result, the business of promulgating ethics rules gets wrapped up in the judiciary's sense of professional identity. It's what judges do, or at least one thing they do.

Once we accept as inevitable that state courts (usually the highest state court) will produce a document containing rules regulating how lawyers must behave, must not behave, and may behave, a whole new set of incentives come into play. These rules by whatever name are *law*, as that term is usually understood. That is, they come from a government body with rulemaking authority. They compel, permit, or forbid behavior. Ignoring them can have serious legal consequences in (among other ways) professional discipline, in identifying a forbidden conflict of interest, or, as we shall see in Chapter 24, in civil lawsuits against lawyers for damages. So they do matter. The label "ethics" should not lull us into thinking that we are talking about piffle.

Now, because the rules matter, lawyers don't want to be left out as the judiciary goes about drafting them. They want to participate. (Who knows what the court might say if it were left to its own devices, uneducated by the bar!) Courts, for their part, are willing to bring the bar into the enterprise for several reasons. First, judges are busy enough as it is. They value the free help. Second, judges were once lawyers and so come from a professional culture in which the courts and the bar have long partnered in this effort. In other words, it's tradition. We underestimate the importance of tradition in law at our peril. Third, judges would not actually be *delegating* the regulatory power to the very lawyers the rules will govern. No foxes and chicken coops here. The judges would only be seeking advice from the bar. This shows collegiality, not abdication. Nothing will become final until the judges say so, and judges don't have to approve anything they don't like. They remain in control. That's what it means to be a judge. And last, as noted above, it is generally recognized that part of the definition of what it means to be regarded as a profession is that its members are trusted with participation in the heavy lifting of self-regulation.[9] Even if self-regulation doesn't extend as far as giving lawyers the *final* say on the content of the professional conduct rules, it at least means that lawyers will be part, often an influential part, of the process formulating its content.

Now we have to put another player on the stage — the American Bar Association. Remember, the ABA first adopted an ethical code, called the Canons of Legal Ethics, back in 1908, more than a century ago. Today, it promotes something called the Model Rules of Professional Conduct. Gone from the title is the word *canons*, which over time, some came to think, implied excessive grandeur, if not religiosity. (But lawyers, even young ones, still talk about the "canons" as in "I've got to check the canons." Old habits, etc.) Gone, too, is the word *ethics*, which should tell us that the profession views the rules we are discussing as about something hard and real, the law, not ethics, or not *just* ethics, which can seem soft and penumbral, akin to etiquette.

Between the Canons and the Rules, from 1970 to 1983, the ABA was promoting a different document, called the Model Code of Professional Responsibility. Its short life attests to its many inadequacies. (By 1977, only seven years after the ABA approved the Code, its president appointed a commission to write a new document meant to correct the deficiencies.) In its 1983 adoption of the Model Rules, the ABA did away with the words *code* and *responsibility* just as the title of the Code had tossed out the word *ethics.* You have to watch for these subtle shifts in word choice. They don't go out of the way to call attention to themselves, but they can signify fundamental shifts in ideology.

Probably, it was inevitable that the ABA would turn out to be the dominant player in the development of rules for lawyers. It has the resources — money and volunteers — to do so. It has more than 400,000 members from all areas of the country and all varieties of practice settings. And because its membership is diverse in these and other ways, it has credibility with judges. Many judges are members. Conversely, it would hardly make sense for each of the nation's bar associations separately to develop rules of conduct for lawyers from scratch, even if they had the resources to do so, which many do not. So everyone is pleased to let the ABA spend the time and money needed to do the research, hold the hearings, write the drafts, and propose a model — but only a model.

The ABA is a private organization. It has no power to tell any lawyer how to behave. All it has is its credibility as an honest broker, its willingness to devote time and resources to the effort, and the hope that its recommendations will be persuasive on the merits. That is why the title "Rules of Professional Conduct," like the Code, its immediate predecessor, is preceded by "Model." The ABA presents its work for the consideration of the nation's courts. Starting with the ABA's model, courts can make whatever changes they wish as they assess the policy choices. And they do make changes, sometimes small ones, occasionally large ones. Differences from the ABA model and differences between the states themselves are especially prominent in the following areas, among others: exceptions to the lawyer's duty to protect client confidences,[10] the conflict-of-interest rules,[11] and rules governing lawyer advertising and solicitation.[12] And one state, California, has never fully embraced the Model Rules (nor did it fully embrace the Code), although it does borrow a good deal from the ABA's work. Another state, New York, retained the form and most of the language of the 1970 ABA Code for more than 25 years after the ABA abandoned the Code in favor of the Rules, although it cherry-picked language from the Model Rules as well. Effective April 1, 2009, New York adopted new rules, which follow the format of the ABA Model Rules but in many respects diverge. Some of the new rules are substantively the old New York rules with new numbers. Because of these differences, large and small, among the states (which includes the District of Columbia), it became necessary to have a choice-of-rule rule for representations that touch on more than one jurisdiction, as increasingly many do (*see* Rule 8.5.).

Here is a paradox of sorts: As the work of the bar has become more national (indeed, international), the rules have become more dissimilar from place to place (at least when measured against the near uniformity prior to 1983, California excepted). Lawyers rarely think twice about crossing state boundaries in serving clients or meeting with potential clients. And even when they don't travel in person, they travel virtually, via e-mail, fax, telephone, and video conferencing. All this has made the choice-of-rule rule more important because many a representation can touch on two or more jurisdictions. It has also led to questions about unauthorized practice of law because a lawyer from Virginia (say) is not a lawyer in neighboring Maryland. If Virginia lawyers travel to Maryland to work on a client matter, are they violating Maryland's rule against unauthorized practice? We discuss this problem in Chapter 23. For now, it is sufficient to recognize the disconnect between cross-border law practice, physical or virtual and aided by easy travel and modern communications systems, on the one hand, and variations in state rules in a system of local licensure and regulation, on the other.

I wrote above that we would not be bereft of rules regulating lawyers even if there were no canons or codes or rules purporting to do so, although without them it would be harder for the bar to present itself as a profession. We have statutory law, common law, agency rules, and (especially for government lawyers, including prosecutors) the Constitution. If there were no ethics rules, we might expect some of these sources of law to be even more detailed than they now are, but as it is, they occupy a good part of the jurisprudence of professional regulation. And here's another interesting phenomenon: The ethics rules and the other sources of law reinforce each other. They enact a kind of pas de deux. The ethics rules are drafted and revised against the backdrop of the other sources of law. They can't contradict them, of course. Nor can they merely restate them, or they would be redundant (although on quite a few issues they do no more than that, such as Rule 3.4(a), which says lawyers should not "unlawfully obstruct another party's access to evidence"). The law for its part develops with awareness of the ethics rules. For example, in addressing the scope of a lawyer's civil liability, courts may look to ethics rules for guidance and content.[13] So the dialogue operates in both directions. Ethics and law are in a symbiotic relationship, each taking cognizance of and reinforcing the other, including the changes over time.

It is surely a fool's errand to think we can state a single overarching theory that will guide the proper resolution of all policies reflected in the law of lawyer regulation. But here is one perspective that may help guide your understanding.

Issues become issues only if the interests of two or more constituencies clash or potentially clash. If everyone benefits from a particular policy, it will not be controversial (it might not even appear as a rule). So we must ask, What interests are implicated in the world of lawyer regulation? They are easier to list than reconcile.

First, and perhaps foremost, are the interests of clients — for example, to confidentiality, to competent service, to lawyers who have no conflicting interests. Second are the interests of lawyers. Many interests of a lawyer will overlap the interests of his or her clients. Both have an interest in achieving the client's goals. But some may be in opposition. For example, lawyers may have an interest in permissive conflict-of-interest rules to maximize professional freedom, while clients may be alarmed that permissive rules will threaten (or appear to threaten) their lawyers' devotion to their interests. Then there are the interests of opposing clients. They have an interest, for example, in rules that limit the tactics an opposing lawyer may employ or in rules that impose a duty to speak if others (like the lawyer's own client) have lied in a negotiation. Courts, too, have an interest, mainly in preventing lawyers from participating or acquiescing in misconduct that impedes the institutional purpose of the tribunal and, as we will see, in requiring lawyers to speak up when others so behave (see Chapter 16). Finally, there is a less focused interest in the proper operation of the profession generally. The lawyer advertising and solicitation rules mean to ensure that clients are not misled when choosing a lawyer. The rules governing bar admission ensure that those licensed to practice law are competent to do so. Keep these varying interests in mind as you read the ensuing chapters. Almost always, any difference of opinion about the best policy on a particular issue will entail a debate over the proper resolution of two or more competing interests.[14]

Whether or not you identify a grand design for all or most of the rules regulating the bar — a theory of (nearly) everything—and you should certainly be encouraged to try, keep in mind that while a theory can be a thing of great clarity and beauty, a theory is not self-executing. The law is very much a retail product with a distribution system all its own. People have access to law through lawyers, the intermediaries or translators between legal rules (and the theories that inform them) and their application. Without these messengers, the law is an idea. It should be clear, then, that the quality of our justice— the success of even the most irresistible legal theory—will partly depend on how rules regulating the bar require, permit, or forbid lawyers to act in representing their clients. Legal ethics are part of the ether through which the rule of law comes to us.

Researching Legal Ethics Researching legal ethics issues is much like researching any other area of law. But there are also differences. The part that's the same addresses the case law, statutory law, constitutional law, and agency regulations. The part that's different comprises the rules of ethics themselves. Once upon a time, discovering these rules could be a challenge. But today they're all a click or two away on any computer. A terrific source for primary and secondary authority is the Web site of the Center for Professional Responsibility of the American Bar Association—*www.abanet.org/cpr*. Follow the links to the subject of interest. Many state bar association sites contain their jurisdiction's rules and the bar association ethics opinions. Westlaw and LEXIS have all the U.S. jurisdictions' ethics codes and post updates to them soon after adoption. They both also have the ABA and some of the state and local bar committee ethics opinions (with LEXIS having the most because it contains the National Reporter on Legal Ethics and Professional Responsibility, which includes nearly every jurisdiction). These opinions construe the respective jurisdiction's ethics rules when lawyers pose questions or when the committees themselves see an emerging issue of interest.

It could take an entire chapter to discuss secondary authorities in the field, but let me mention three. First, the American Law Institute's *Restatement of the Law Governing Lawyers* was a 13-year project that produced two volumes of black letter rules, comments, and notes on nearly any question that may arise in the field of lawyer regulation. Second is the multivolume *Lawyer's Manual on Professional Conduct*, jointly published by the Bureau of National Affairs and the ABA and which includes a biweekly newsletter of important case law, ethics opinions, and reportage for anyone who wants to stay aware of trends and recent decisions. Last is the *Georgetown Journal of Legal Ethics*, started more than 20 years ago by Georgetown law students and is the brainchild of their advisor, Father Robert Drinan.

ENDNOTES

1. This is a result of an American Bar Association rule (Standard 302(a)(5) of the ABA Standards for Approval of Law Schools), which provides:

> A law school shall require that each student receives substantial instruction in . . . the history, goals, structure, values, rules and responsibilities of the legal profession and its members.

Because nearly every state requires graduation from an ABA-accredited law school, every law school that wants its graduates to be eligible for admission in these states must satisfy this Standard. Most law schools do so by requiring a course in legal ethics or other study that is substantially the equivalent.

2. *See, e.g.*, Model Rule (MR) 1.9(a), further discussed in Chapter 12.

3. *See, e.g.*, MR 4.1(a), which forbids a lawyer to "make a false statement of material fact or law to a third person."

4. *See, e.g.*, MR 3.3, further discussed in Chapter 16, which sometimes requires a lawyer to reveal a client confidence to prevent a fraud on a tribunal.

5. See Chapter 24.

6. But of late, the Canons of Ethics have enjoyed some modicum of renewed respect. *See, e.g.*, James Altman, *Considering the A.B.A.'s 1908 Canons of Ethics*, 71 Fordham L. Rev. 2395 (2003). *See also* Norman Spaulding, *The Myth of Civil Republicanism: Interrogating the Ideology of Antebellum Legal Ethics*, 71 Fordham L. Rev. 1397 (2003); Russell Pearce, *Rediscovering the Republican Origin of the Legal Ethics Codes*, 6 Geo. J. Legal Ethics 241 (1992). Justice O'Connor was especially articulate on this point. See her dissenting opinion in *Shapero v. Kentucky Bar Assn*, 486 U.S. 466 (1988).

7. See Justice O'Connor's dissent in *Shapero v. Kentucky Bar Assn*, 486 U.S. 466 (1988). She wrote, "Imbuing the legal profession with the necessary ethical standards is a task that involves a constant struggle with the relentless natural force of economic self-interest."

8. *See, e.g.*, State ex rel. *Fiedler v. Wisconsin Senate*, 454 N.W.2d 770 (Wis. 1990) (striking down legislation imposing continuing education requirements on lawyers who wish to be appointed as guardians); *Irwin v. Surdyk's Liquor*, 599 N.W.2d 132 (Minn. 1999) (invalidating statutory limits on attorney fee awards as a violation of separation of powers).

9. ABA Commission on Professionalism, *A Blueprint for the Rekindling of Lawyer Professionalism*, 112 F.R.D. 243, (1986), quoting sociologist Eliot Freidson, a commission member, that one part of the definition of a profession is that it "is self-regulating — that is, organized in such a way as to assure the public and the courts that its members are competent, do not violate their client's trust, and transcend their own self-interest."

10. MR 1.6.

11. MR 1.7, 1.8, 1.9, and 1.10.

12. *See* Article 7 of the Model Rules.

13. See Part II. In evaluating Sixth Amendment claims of ineffective assistance of counsel, the Supreme Court has looked to professional conduct norms. *Strickland v. Washington*, 466 U.S. 668 (1984).

14. For a general discussion of the competing interests, *see* Stephen Gillers, *What We Talked About When We Talked About Ethics: A Critical View of the Model Rules*, 46 Ohio St. L. J. 243 (1985).

part I

The Attorney-Client Relationship

What Lawyers Owe Clients: An Introduction

Clients Are Not Customers

Lawyers Are Not Merchants

How Does the Relationship Begin and End?

Episodic and Virtual Clients

To say that lawyers are not merchants is simply meant to bring home the fact that the lawyer-client relationship is not, as the term goes, at arm's length. As soon as you have a client, the rules governing lawyers impose a web of obligations enforced mainly through discipline, disqualification, and civil liability. You get power—the power to act for the client in the wide world of law, to make decisions that may affect the life of another person (or a company, which is a collection of people) in dramatic ways—but the power comes with responsibility and constraints on how you employ it.

A *Fiduciary Relationship* The lawyer's relationship to the client is fiduciary, which broadly speaking means that the interests of others or the lawyer's own interests cannot be permitted to impede or compromise fulfillment of the lawyer's duties to the client. (All agents are fiduciaries, and lawyers are agents of their clients, who are the principals, but courts treat lawyers as super-fiduciaries, with obligations above and beyond those that attend plain-vanilla fiduciaries.[1]) The lawyer-client relationship partakes of other attributes as well, which we will discuss throughout this book. These mainly emanate from the position of trust and confidence that is the cornerstone of fiduciary status. If I were asked to list in everyday (i.e., not legal) language what lawyers owe clients as professionals and fiduciaries, I would say solicitude for, candor toward, and tenacity on behalf of the client *within the scope of the work the lawyer has been hired (or appointed) to do*. Fiduciary status is further discussed in Chapter 6. Now here's what may seem to some (especially clients) to be the odd thing. I don't include affection for the client in the above list. You can dislike your client as a person — some clients are really unpleasant people or worse, as are some lawyers — but that's neither here nor there (unless your animosity compromises your representation, in which case you should not accept, or you should withdraw from, the matter).

Defining the *Scope of the Work* You noticed the italicized qualifier in the prior paragraph. I added it because as imposing as a lawyer's obligations to a client may be, they are nonetheless bounded by the scope of the matter. For example, the duties of a lawyer retained to negotiate an employment contract for a corporate client hiring a new chief financial officer (CFO) are defined with reference to that task. The lawyer has no professional duty to help the client with its corporate tax return or its breach of contract claim against another company. The lawyer's scope of work also determines the breadth of the conflict-of-interest rules arising out of the relationship. For example, the client may not be happy if the lawyer's partner represents the client's main competitor in negotiating an employment contract with *its* new CFO, but the firm can usually take that job, as we'll see when we take up conflicts of interest in Chapters 10 and 12.

Rule 1.2(c) permits lawyer and client to agree reasonably to limit the scope of a representation. Of course, merely by defining the scope of work, they necessarily exclude tasks outside that scope. But Rule 1.2(c) permits the lawyer to make it clear what service is *not* within that scope, where a client might otherwise believe it is. For example, a lawyer who agrees to defend a civil claim might explicitly exclude appeals from final judgments, an exclusion that might not otherwise occur to the client. Or consider a client with a claim against companies *A, B, C,* and *D.* A lawyer may be willing to take the matter only against *A, B,* and *C,* but not *D* because of a conflict. If the client can get complete relief from *A, B,* and *C,* if dropping *D* does not prejudice the client's case, that explicit limitation may also be reasonable. But if *D* is the "deep pocket," the primary wrongdoer, or a key source of discovery, any limitation may be unreasonable.

How the Relationship Begins   Lawyers traditionally get clients in two ways. Most often, a person or company becomes a client because it retains the lawyer to perform a defined service. Transfer title to my house. Represent me in a divorce. Negotiate my employment contract. Take my company public. And so on. The relationship is formed by a contract, which may be in writing (some states require that retainer or fee agreements be in writing) or oral, express or implied.[2] Even a casual conversation can be enough. A friend of a friend of an IP lawyer calls for advice about the scope of the fair use exception to copyright. The lawyer, generously, gives that advice. The call takes five minutes. Has the caller become a client? Probably. It will depend on how specific the advice is.

In one case, a former client called a lawyer to ask if likely amendments to the tax law affected the advice the lawyer's firm had given the former client years earlier. They didn't, said the lawyer, but if that changes, the lawyer promised to alert the former client. (These at least were the allegations in the ensuing civil action.) The legislation was changed and the changes did alter the validity of the earlier tax advice. But the lawyer did not call, and the former client acted on the assumption that the advice was still good (not having heard to the contrary) and got socked with a very big tax bill. The court held that the lawyer's alleged promise to alert the client if a new tax law altered the validity of the earlier advice created a duty and potential liability if the lawyer failed to do what he said he would do.[3] This was true even if the lawyer would not otherwise have had a continuing obligation to the former client. The moral: Be careful what you promise, and deliver if you do.

Courts will find a lawyer-client relationship if under the circumstances a person reasonably could conclude from the lawyer's words and conduct that the lawyer had agreed to represent her but the lawyer reads it differently. In other words, there's been a failure of communication. Courts will resolve ambiguity against the lawyer if the client's resolution of the ambiguity is reasonable. On recommendation of a friend, Marsha Moss calls Diana Todd, an expert in commercial leases, after Marsha's negotiation with the owner of her office building has become heated and she is served with a court summons. Diana says, "Fax me the summons, and meanwhile I'll check to see if I'm able to handle it and let you know." Diana means, "I'll let you know if I am able to handle it." Marsha hears, "I'll let you know if I'm not able to handle it." When Diana checks, she discovers that a conflict of interest will prevent her from accepting Marsha as a client. So Diana doesn't let Marsha know because she has equated silence with rejection. Meanwhile, Marsha has equated silence with acceptance. A court could easily find that Marsha's inference is reasonable and that Diana became Marsha's lawyer. See Restatement §14, which recognizes that a lawyer may form a lawyer-client relationship not only by manifestation of consent but also by failing to deny consent when the lawyer knows or should know that the putative client "reasonably relies on the lawyer to provide the services." In other words, in case of possible uncertainty, it is best for the lawyer to clear it up.

The other way lawyers get clients is through court assignment, ordinarily to represent a criminal defendant who cannot afford counsel. There is no contract here, as conventionally understood. The court's assignment creates the relationship. Unlike a client who retains a lawyer, the client with an assigned lawyer cannot readily fire the lawyer and get a new one. (If he wants to represent himself, he may have the right to do so.[4]) Nonetheless, the panoply of duties and authorities that apply in the private attorney-client relationships also apply here — except, of course, those surrounding the fee agreement, since the assigned lawyer's client by definition is not paying a fee.

As we'll see when we come to Chapter 21 on what I call "virtual clients," these two categories — retention and assignment — do not define the universe. Courts have held that even people and companies that are not clients in the traditional sense — no court assignment; no contract, express or implied — may have the right to claim that a lawyer's representation adverse to them violates conflict-of-interest rules or that his conduct creates liability to them. One court has used the term "vicarious clients" to describe some clients in this group.[5] No matter what the label, the lesson is the same. Sometimes, when the question is whether or not XYZ or Ms. Jones is or was a client, the answer may have to be: For what purpose are you asking? In any event, the notion that a person cannot become a client unless, with that aim, he comes to your office or otherwise makes contact is not realistic (and probably never was). Or as Judge Arthur Sprecher presciently wrote in a 1978 opinion, "The client is no longer simply the person who walks into a law office."[6] Amen. Not by a long shot. Given the obligations lawyers assume when they have a client, it behooves them to be aware of all the ways the professional relationship or (some) professional obligations might also arise.

How the Relationship Ends Clients don't stay clients forever. When the relationship ends, so do many of the obligations lawyers have to current clients under legal ethics rules. The fiduciary relationship also ends.[7] On the other hand, some obligations continue, including to avoid certain kinds of conflicts of interest and to protect confidential and privileged information, as discussed in Chapter 12. But because the law imposes fewer duties on a lawyer (and on other lawyers in his or her firm) when a client becomes a former client, it is important to be able to say when that happens. And lawyers who want to free themselves and their office colleagues from the heightened obligations that lawyers and firms owe to *current* clients may want to make it clear that a client has moved from "current" to "former" status as soon as that can properly occur. (Perhaps, of course, for business reasons a firm may choose *not* to do so, preferring to have the client consider the lawyer as still "my lawyer," notwithstanding the greater professional obligations that status entails.)

Just as the attorney-client relationship usually begins by agreement, so too can it end by agreement. If the matter is in litigation and the client changes lawyers or the lawyer has a valid reason to withdraw from the case, a judge's order substituting new counsel will end the professional relationship with the first lawyer (assuming she is handling no other matter for the client). Otherwise, if nothing is said, the relationship will be deemed over when the lawyer has completed the work she has been hired to perform. The scope of work described in the retainer agreement (if there is one) can tell us when that happens, which makes it prudent to have such an agreement, and put it in writing, even if the jurisdiction's rules do not require it.

But sometimes lawyers discover to their dismay that a matter or a relationship that they thought was over was not over, even though nothing further seems to be required in the matter or because the firm has done no work for the client in years. This kind of surprise can befall a firm in two ways. First, the firm may have concluded that the work was done (bill paid), but the client reasonably thinks otherwise, perhaps because under the circumstances a settlement or agreement could become undone. That happened in a federal case in Washington.[8] The second reason is that even though the law firm is doing absolutely no work for the client at the time and no concluded work is likely to come undone, the *pattern* of the firm's occasional work for the client makes the client an *episodic client*, which means it remains a client *between* assignments, even when there is no current work. Both reasons are further discussed in Chapter 10.

ENDNOTES

1. *Milbank, Tweed, Hadley & McCloy v. Boon*, 13 F.3d 537 (2d Cir. 1994) (lawyers occupy a "unique position of trust and confidence" toward clients). *See also, Matter of Cooperman*, 633 N.E.2d 1069 (N.Y. 1994) ("ultimate trust and confidence").

2. *See, e.g.*, Calif. Bus. & Prof. Code §6148. Most states require contingent fee agreements to be in writing. So do the Model Rules (MR). MR 1.5(c).

3. *Lama Holding Co. v. Shearman & Sterling*, 758 F. Supp. 159 (S.D.N.Y. 1991).

4. *Faretta v. California*, 422 U.S. 806 (1975).

5. *Glueck v. Jonathan Logan, Inc.*, 653 F.2d 746 (2d Cir. 1981) (referring to companies that are members of a trade group client).

6. *Westinghouse Electric Corp. v. Kerr-McGee Corp.*, 580 F.2d 1311 (7th Cir. 1978).

7. *See, e.g., In re Marriage Pagano*, 607 N.E.2d 1242 (Ill. 1992) (no "confidential relation" exists either before "the attorney undertakes the business of the client" or in regard to "dealings which take place after the relation has been dissolved").

8. *Jones v. Rabanco, Ltd.*, 2006 U.S. Dist. LEXIS 53766 (W.D. Wash. 2006).

~ 3 ~

What Lawyers Owe Clients: Competence

What Is the Standard for Competence?

The Difference Between Errors and Incompetence

Incompetence as a Basis for Malpractice

The Centrality of Competence   I would wager that if you polled every law firm's clients in the United States on any given day (or a statistically reliable sample), and asked them to name the most important quality they want in a lawyer, competence would be among the two most frequent responses. Honesty would be high on the list, too, but on reflection competence would likely be cited first because honesty would be assumed. Or it would be a tie. And when clients mentioned "honesty," they would mean honesty in a lawyer's relations with them. A lawyer can be the nicest and most honest person in the world, but if he or she is not competent, the client's interests are in jeopardy. Other qualities would also show up on an expanded list. You might get answers like "professionalism," "intelligence," or "commitment." These overlap competence and honesty. Few clients would say "loyalty" or "the ability to keep my secrets," although for lawyers those obligations are the bedrock of professional identity. Some clients might say "judgment" and "discretion." Some might even say "ethical."

Let me amend what I just wrote. Clients might find the word *competence* insufficient to describe what they most want to see in their lawyers. After all, how comfortable would you be if, searching for a new doctor, you asked a friend if Dr. Allbetter was "good" and your friend assured you that that there was no need to worry because all who knew her found her "competent." You would probably keep looking. So clients would in all probability use a word more substantial than *competence*, a stronger version of the same quality. They might toss out a string of adjectives and synonyms: *smart, resourceful, imaginative, experienced,* and "knows what she's doing." These are simply higher gradations of the basic idea of competence.

But competence, just competence, is all that ethics rules and civil law require, or if the lawyer holds himself out as a specialist (or with an equivalent word), then the particular competence we expect of specialists will be required. Just as well. We can't all be at the top of the game or better than average. Nor can we label lawyers below the top incompetent, or they would soon be out of business, victims of malpractice lawsuits or client flight. In any profession, there will inevitably be a range of aptitudes among the members. Everyone wants the best, but not everyone can afford the best or knows how to identify it. Yes, clients can hire the best lawyers they can afford. Or try to. The lay public is not generally equipped to judge the quality of professionals, whether doctors, lawyers, or architects, which makes shopping for one a challenge. *Consumer Reports* does not rank lawyers, although there are the occasional magazine articles (of mixed reliability) with titles like "The Best Lawyers In. . . ." Mostly, though, clients have to rely on their judgment and recommendations from friends.

Too often, they might just open the Yellow Pages (or nowadays, go to Google). Furthermore, it won't always make sense for clients to hire the best lawyers they can afford. A person charged with a felony might do that. So might a person negotiating a complex commercial contract. But a client who wants to buy a condo or sign a simple will is likely to conclude that good enough is good enough. Mere competence will do.

What Is Competence?   We can offer a general definition for starters. The Model Rules describe it as requiring "the legal knowledge, skill, thoroughness, and preparation reasonably necessary for the representation."[1] California uses the terms "diligence," "learning and skill," and "mental, emotional, and physical ability" in describing what a lawyer must bring to a representation.[2] Omitted here is the term "judgment," which I think is key and which you sometimes find in court opinions describing what a lawyer must reasonably exercise in order to avoid malpractice liability. Competence is not only an ethical mandate; lack of competence is a basis for liability in malpractice (see Chapter 24). In fact, lawyers are rarely disciplined for incompetence. Instead, we rely on the threat of civil liability to ensure a minimum level of quality. Reasonable judgment should be added to the list of qualities that define competence because it is different from skill, knowledge, and thoroughness. Judgment is a quality a lawyer brings to a problem after the other qualities have done their work. Judgment is displayed in a lawyer's informed prediction based on experience about the risks and advantages of different courses of action. (Or inaction. Elihu Root, the U.S. Secretary of State in the first decade of the twentieth century, said that "[a]bout half of the practice of a decent lawyer is telling would-be clients that they are damned fools and should stop."[3])

When a lawyer is judged to have behaved incompetently, it does not necessarily mean that he or she lacks the ability to perform the particular service well. Rather it means only that in this instance the work was below par, perhaps because the lawyer was handling too much at once and lacked the time needed to do the work adequately. But it could also mean that the lawyer lacked the skill to handle the matter, even with preparation, and should not have tried to do so, at least not alone. A lawyer can gain that skill in two ways — by formal study or by associating on the matter with a lawyer who has it. Newly minted lawyers, lacking experience, are (paradoxically?) by definition often incompetent to handle all but the simplest legal matters by themselves. For that reason, despite the great strides made by clinical law courses, legal education does not generally enable a law school graduate to practice law despite bar passage. We rely on law offices, public and private, to continue the training and bring the new hires past the starting line.

Once we agree on the *qualities* that competence requires, the next question is how much of those qualities do we expect? By definition, not every lawyer can be in the top half. So against what standard should we measure a counsel's performance? Here's where things get fluid. The standard cannot be quantified. We certainly cannot say that lawyers must be as competent as the average lawyer — the lawyer at the median of a spectrum, assuming we could even create one — because that would immediately put half the state's lawyers at risk. We can only describe competence generally and then deal with each allegation of incompetence in the particular factual context of the matter the lawyer was called upon to handle. The Model Rules say that the lawyer must exhibit the listed qualities as "reasonably necessary for the representation." We have to know about "the representation" to judge the quality of the work.

Competence and Malpractice   Malpractice cases, another source of information for us to analyze, ask how reasonably competent lawyers in the same state would perform. This gets a bit circular, even when the court does not use the word *competent* to define competence. In *Chapman v. Bearfield*, a typical case, the Tennessee Supreme Court held that an

> attorney practicing in Tennessee . . . must exercise the ordinary care, skill, and diligence commonly possessed and practiced by attorneys *throughout* the state. Indeed, while there may be local rules of practice within the various judicial districts of our State, there are no local standards of care. There is only one standard of care for attorneys practicing in Tennessee: a statewide standard.[4]

To my mind, the key word in this quote is *commonly*. It hides a lot. What does it mean? To some statistically significant (but impossible to specify) degree, if lawyers in the state performing the same service will ("commonly") do X or not do Y, where the lawyer who has been sued either failed to do X or did Y, then the service was incompetently performed absent some contrary persuasive explanation.

When former clients do sue lawyers for malpractice, how do they prove it? Chapter 24 delves into the elements of a malpractice action, but one oddity (or at least what lawyers may see as an oddity) should be highlighted here. First, some conduct is self-evidently incompetent. Failing to do any factual investigation before trying a case is one example. When representing the purchaser of land, failure to record the title is another example. A third example is when a client loses his claim because a lawyer misses a statute of limitations. Juries will be allowed to find such obvious defaults negligent without need for an expert witness to testify how competent lawyers behave. But often, juries, which are composed mainly of nonlawyers, won't know if the lawyer's actions or failures to act constitute negligence (which is the civil law's other word for the lack of competence that will subject a lawyer to liability). Jurors won't be able to say, from their own experience, whether the lawyer has failed to "exercise the ordinary care, skill, and diligence commonly possessed and practiced by attorneys throughout the state." Nor will they ordinarily know if a particular representation subjected the lawyer to a conflict of interest forbidden by the state's ethics rules.

Who knows the answer to these questions? Other lawyers, of course, and each side to the malpractice litigation will likely call one or more experts to say that the defendant lawyer did or did not exercise the requisite level of care, skill, and diligence or did or did not have a disabling conflict of interest. Then the judge will instruct the jury on what the plaintiff must prove to win the malpractice claim, and a jury of nonlawyers will be asked to decide which side's expert witness is correct.[5] (True, today, the jury may include a lawyer or two, but this is statistically unlikely and, if one did happen to show up as a potential juror, we can be pretty sure that one of the parties, probably the plaintiff, would try to remove him.)

One final point, implied above, warrants emphasis. The fact that a lawyer is found to have done incompetent work on a matter speaks only about that matter. It is not meant to say anything about the lawyer's professional character or ability across the board. There are many reasons why a lawyer may slip up in a particular representation. It does not mean that he or she will do so the next time or indeed ever again. You do sometimes hear lawyers or clients talking about a lawyer as "walking malpractice," by which they mean to say, I think, that the subject of their conversation will almost surely mishandle nearly any matter he or she is allowed to touch. But this is rare. At least it will be rare so long as lawyers know their own limits and refrain from accepting clients whose work demands experience and knowledge they simply do not have.

ENDNOTES

1. Model Rule 1.1.
2. Rule 3-110, California Rules of Professional Conduct. New Hampshire may go the furthest in describing the requirement of competence. New Hampshire Rule 1.1(b) and (c) provide:

(b) Legal competence requires at a minimum:

(1) specific knowledge about the fields of law in which the lawyer practices;

(2) performance of the techniques of practice with skill;

(3) identification of areas beyond the lawyer's competence and bringing those areas to the client's attention;

(4) proper preparation; and

(5) attention to details and schedules necessary to assure that the matter undertaken is completed with no avoidable harm to the client's interest.

(c) In the performance of client service, a lawyer shall at a minimum:

(1) gather sufficient facts regarding the client's problem from the client, and from other relevant sources;

(2) formulate the material issues raised, determine applicable law and identify alternative legal responses;

(3) develop a strategy, in consultation with the client, for solving the legal problems of the client; and

(4) undertake actions on the client's behalf in a timely and effective manner including, where appropriate, associating with another lawyer who possesses the skill and knowledge required to assure competent representation.

3. Root is quoted, among other places, in *Hill v. Norfolk & Western Railway Co.*, 814 F.2d 1192 (7th Cir. 1987).

4. 207 S.W.3d 736 (emphasis in original).

5. For a collection of cases in which expert testimony either was or was not required to prove legal malpractice, *see* Annot., Admissibility and necessity of expert evidence as to standards of practice and negligence in malpractice action against attorney, 14 A.L.R. 4th 170.

What Lawyers Owe Clients: Confidentiality

Confidential and Privileged Information Distinguished

Permissive and Mandatory Exceptions

Confidentiality and the Prospective Client

Confidential and Privileged Information   In the course of a representation, lawyers learn a great deal of information about a client and about the matter that the client has entrusted to the lawyer. Some of it they learn from the client herself or, if the client is a company or an organization, they learn the information from its agents (its CEO, its accountants, its managers, its sales people, the receptionist, etc.). But a lot of information lawyers need in their work they gather on their own — talking to witnesses, to consultants, to a client's neighbors and friends.

Think about a lawyer representing a client on a complicated tax issue. She learns quite a lot about the client's financial picture, possibly more than even the client knows. Much of this will come from the client, but some will come from third parties. Or what about a lawyer handling a corporate client's effort to buy another company? The lawyer learns about the client's business objectives and financial resources from the client itself, but also, from others, she learns information about the commercial and financial situation of the target company. Last, consider a lawyer whose client is charged with a crime or who is in a custody battle. His investigation will require him to talk to many people other than the client to gather details about the client's life. You get the picture.

Yet another kind of information a lawyer gets are the fruits of the legal research she does in working out how to advise the client or to achieve its objectives. Information the lawyer gathers about the law may be protected as the lawyer's work product, but it is not the sort of information the rules and law define as a client's privileged or confidential information. The lawyer can reuse it for other clients. She does not have to retrace her steps to "relearn" the law.

I have so far elided the difference between privileged information and confidential client information. The category we call confidential client information and the information that falls within the attorney-client privilege share many features. So the two doctrines — confidentiality and privilege — can be confused, and often are, even by experienced lawyers. But there are also critical differences between them. *Similarities first:* The focus of each doctrine is information lawyers learn in representing their clients. Both doctrines have as their purpose *the protection of information* against revelation except if the client chooses to reveal, or let the lawyer reveal, the information or if the doctrines themselves allow or require it, perhaps even over the client's objection. A policy behind both the confidentiality rule and the attorney-client privilege is to encourage clients to be candid with their lawyers by assuring them that their lawyers cannot reveal protected information except to advance the client's goals.[1] Lawyers often tell new clients that anything "you tell me stays in this office. It's confidential." Or words to that effect. This assurance is meant to encourage the client to be forthcoming. It overstates the level of protection the law affords to the client's information, but in most cases, as a practical matter, not by much. That is, although there are circumstances that may allow or require the lawyer to reveal, over objection, what a client has said "in this office," as an empirical matter those circumstances are the exception. And it would be a formidable challenge to give the client a tutorial on the exceptions to the privilege or confidentiality. Such a caution would, in the view of some, also inhibit candor when in fact the preconditions for the exceptions to confidentiality are most unlikely to occur.

Now for the *differences* between the two doctrines. They are important.

The Sources of the Information   As will be more fully explained shortly, but worth emphasizing at the outset and remembering forever, is this: Even though both the attorney-client privilege and the ethical duty of confidentiality are concerned with protecting information, the **privilege protects** communications *between lawyers and clients* (or the representatives of either), whereas the **duty of confidentiality protects** that information *plus information the lawyer learns from others* in representing the client. So we might imagine two concentric circles with the inner one containing all privileged information (i.e., information from the client or agent) and the outer one, which *includes* the inner one, containing all confidential information (i.e., information from anyone in connection with the representation).

The Sources of the Doctrines: Privilege   The attorney-client privilege is a doctrine in the law of evidence. It is a creature of statute or case law, although given the Sixth Amendment right to counsel in criminal cases, it has a constitutional dimension in those cases as well on the theory that the constitutional promise would be hollow if the defense lawyer could be required to reveal what the client tells him.[2] When the privilege applies, it permits the client, and the lawyer on behalf of the client, to refuse to give information despite process (e.g., a court order) from a court or other governmental body demanding the information. The doctrine does not permit the client or lawyer to refuse to respond to the process — say, a grand jury subpoena or a deposition notice. They must show up. Rather, privilege can be asserted as a valid legal basis to refuse to answer those questions that call for privileged information. Ordinarily, a refusal to answer questions in these circumstances would be a contempt of court (or of another body, perhaps a legislature, that issued a subpoena) because as is sometimes said, "The law is entitled to every person's evidence." But privilege is a shield against contempt.

The attorney-client privilege is, of course, not the only privilege known to the law of evidence. Communications with other professionals — traditionally doctors and the clergy — also enjoy privilege. And many states and the federal law extend privilege to others as well, including (depending on the jurisdiction) nurses, social workers, accountants, and psychologists. Beyond professionals, all jurisdictions recognize a privilege of some scope for spousal communications. Last, of course, the U.S. Constitution's Fifth Amendment and equivalent provisions in state constitutions recognize a privilege against self-incrimination, which entitles a person to refuse to answer questions if the answer might be incriminating. This is not the place to talk about the other privileges except to recognize that the attorney-client privilege is not unique, although judges (usually former lawyers, after all) do seem to be more protective of attorney-client communications than of those protected by other privileges.

The Sources of the Doctrines: Confidentiality   Confidentiality obligations derive from doctrinally distinct sources. They are present in the law of agency and the law of fiduciary duty. All agents are fiduciaries, although not all fiduciaries are agents (a doctor may have a fiduciary duty to a patient but is not the patient's agent). All agents have confidentiality obligations.[3] Lawyers are the agents of their clients before the law and so they stand in a fiduciary relationship to clients. Even if nothing were said about confidentiality in the lawyers' ethics codes, lawyers would still be bound by duties of confidentiality as agents and fiduciaries, although perhaps then the confidentiality rules for lawyers would have developed differently. We will never know. Every set of ethics rules for lawyers contains provisions addressing confidentiality or exceptions to it; but the language of these provisions and the scope of the exceptions are hotly debated. It reveals something of the profession's deep interest, especially in the exceptions to the duty of confidentiality, that the provisions vary a good deal among U.S. jurisdictions.[4]

If lawyers would have confidentiality duties as agents and fiduciaries even if their ethics codes said nothing about confidentiality, why bother to debate them or even include them in lawyer ethics codes? For four reasons, I think. *First*, lawyers do not want to leave their obligations and authority to the same generic legal rules that govern all other agents. They want the greater clarity that can come from capturing the scope of the duty and its exceptions in a text written especially for lawyer-agents. *Second*, having a text gives the bar the assurance that judges and lawyers will be on the same page about the boundaries of the doctrine as it affects lawyers (remember the rules must eventually have the blessing of courts). *Third*, since lawyers are part of the rule-generating process, the bar will have a greater opportunity to influence the content of confidentiality rules than if it were left to common law development, one case at a time. *Fourth*, and perhaps most important, while lawyers and other kinds of agents may stand in similar legal relationships to the principals they serve, there are differences, too. Legal services are unique (or so lawyers believe). The bar's ethics rules on confidentiality may be seen as a specific application of the generic confidentiality duties in the law of agency, with adjustments that are meant to focus on the particular attributes of the lawyer-client relationship and the specialized services that lawyers provide to clients.

None of this is to say that lawyers are a better or more important kind of agent, only that they are different from, say, a company's salesperson, an accountant, or a corporate manager and that the generic confidentiality rules in the substantive law of agency will not adequately address that difference. That, anyway, is the claim. To be sure, the generic rules continue to govern lawyers as agents and fiduciaries. The confidentiality rules in the ethics rules don't displace them entirely, although in the event of a direct inconsistency, the more specific lawyer ethics rules will likely prevail in court.

What the Doctrines Do: Privilege   As stated, the privilege has one purpose. It shields the client's (or the client's agent's) communication with counsel or her agent from forced revelation through process and thereby is meant to encourage open communication between lawyer and client. Of course, not everything a person says to another person who happens to be a lawyer is privileged. People talk to lawyers as friends, even as advisers on a whole host of issues, but that doesn't necessarily create a professional legal relationship. But where the client's purpose is to get legal advice or representation, and he communicates with the lawyer in confidence (i.e., not in the presence of strangers to the relationship as described shortly), then absent an exception to privilege, his communications with the chosen lawyer (or those who help the lawyer) will be privileged, with the consequence identified. So if a person who is a lawyer's client happens to ask the lawyer's advice on how to invest a bonus he received at work, the conversation will not be privileged because it was not connected to a request for legal advice, only financial advice. On the other hand, if the client asked the lawyer to tell him how the tax code characterizes his bonus, the conversation would be privileged because the client is asking for legal advice. A classic definition of the privilege, nearly 60 years old but still often cited, appears in the endnotes.[5]

Note, however, the important limitation implied in the prior paragraph. The communication (oral or written) must be between the client (or the client's representatives) and the lawyer or those who work with the lawyer to provide the legal service. In the latter category is everyone who works in the law office — secretaries, paralegals, computer technicians, messengers, accountants, librarians — so long as their access to the privileged information is for the purpose of facilitating the lawyer's work for the client. Also in this category are persons the lawyer might retain specifically to better understand the client's matter — for example, an economist if the matter is antitrust, a structural engineer if the matter is liability for a building collapse, a private investigator for criminal defense lawyers. Lawyers cannot be expected to be experts in these other fields, yet they need the knowledge of those experts to figure out how best to serve the client's legal needs.[6]

Privilege Protects Communication, Not Information

Courts often say that the privilege protects communication with counsel but does not protect the underlying information.[7] This is an important distinction. Let's say a prosecutor is trying to learn what Jones said to Smith on a particular day. Perhaps the prosecutor thinks this information will help identify a person who committed a crime (who may be Jones or a third person). Smith knows that Jones is under investigation and is worried about her own legal exposure. She goes to a lawyer and tells the lawyer what Jones told her. The lawyer assures her that she has nothing to worry about. Smith is then subpoenaed to a grand jury (or elsewhere). The prosecutor wants to ask two questions: "What did you tell your lawyer Jones said to you?" and "What did Jones say to you?" Smith can assert privilege to refuse to answer the first question because it calls on her to reveal a communication with her lawyer. If Smith's lawyer is called before the grand jury, he can assert privilege, too, and ordinarily must do so unless Smith wishes to waive the privilege. But Smith cannot cite the attorney-client privilege to refuse to answer the second question because *the underlying information* is not protected by the privilege. It does not become privileged simply because Smith repeated it to her lawyer.

What the Doctrines Do: Confidentiality   The confidentiality rules have a different objective. Remember that these rules define as a client's confidences *any* information that the lawyer learns in representing the client (the precise language may vary from place to place, but not the idea), regardless of the source of the information. Unlike privilege, the sources need not be the client or the client's representatives. They can be witnesses, neighbors, or people who work in the particular industry of a corporate client and to whom the lawyer has spoken, because their experience can shed light on the client's legal problem. And so on. And even when the source is the client or the client's representatives, the communication may not be privileged because, for example, a third person unconnected to the lawyer's representation was present during it. Ordinarily, the presence of (or revelation to) a third person who is not someone working on the client's matter with the lawyer or the client's agent will destroy the privilege. Say a young adult has a legal problem and his father comes with him to the lawyer's office. The father's presence during the conversation with the lawyer is likely to mean that the communications with the lawyer are not privileged. For this reason, the lawyer may tell the father to stay in the waiting room. But let's assume that does not happen and the father is present for some or all of the meeting. Although the communications in the father's presence are not privileged, they are still protected as confidential.[8]

What does it mean to say that a communication is not privileged but is nonetheless confidential? First, it means that the shield of the privilege will not entitle lawyers and clients to refuse to reveal the communication if a judge orders them to do so. If they refuse, they will be in contempt of court, like anyone else (unless they have another valid excuse, like work product protection), and can be jailed. But information that is confidential (whether or not privileged, too) has another protection. A lawyer may not reveal it unless the client explicitly or implicitly authorizes the lawyer to do so or an exception (discussed below) applies. Implicit permission can be inferred from the circumstances. A lawyer may reveal confidential information to help achieve the client's goal if in her professional judgment the lawyer believes that doing so will advance the goal and the client has not explicitly forbidden revelation of the information. In addition to this general prohibition on revealing confidential information, a lawyer may not *use* a client's confidential information (even if she does not reveal it) if the lawyer's use of the information will disadvantage the client. For example, a lawyer who knows that a client, a land developer, needs to buy particular acreage for a still-secret second home community it plans to build, cannot advise another client to buy the acreage first (even without revealing why), or buy it himself, in the expectation of a large profit if the developer client will pay a premium for the land.

Or, to put it another way: Information a lawyer learns in representing a client, whether or not privileged, might be said to be held "in trust" for the client, which again means that the lawyer may not reveal it at all, except for the client's benefit, and may not use it in a manner that harms the client. So, the confidentiality rules are protection against certain voluntary disclosures or use while the privilege (a smaller category) is a shield that gives the lawyer and client the right to refuse to reveal the privileged information when served a subpoena from a court or other government body with subpoena power. Because privilege is a smaller category, all privileged information will (as a practical matter) be confidential, but much information that is confidential will not be privileged.

Duration of Privilege and Confidentiality Absent an exception, the duty of confidentiality in the American Bar Association's rules continues forever, even after the client's matter is long over and indeed even after the client is dead. One exception is where the "information has become generally known." If indeed this is so, it makes no sense to prevent the lawyer from revealing or using the generally known information.[9] But notice that the phrase is "generally known." It is not "capable of being discovered." The fact that an assiduous investigator might be able to unearth the information through an extensive search — in a county clerk's archives, for example — will not satisfy the "generally known" test.

As for the privilege, every jurisdiction recognizes that it survives the conclusion of the lawyer's work (otherwise it could not achieve its purpose of encouraging candor). The privilege even survives the death of the client in most jurisdictions, which would also seem to be necessary to encourage candor. Clients are not likely to be forthcoming with embarrassing information if their lawyers can be forced to reveal the information after they are dead, hurting their posthumous reputation and perhaps the value of their estates. The most famous case so holding is the Supreme Court's decision recognizing a lawyer's claim of privilege for communications between a private lawyer and Vincent Foster, who was deputy White House counsel in the Clinton administration and a Clinton confidante from Arkansas. Foster killed himself during the Whitewater investigation. Before his suicide, he confided in the lawyer about the investigation. Kenneth Starr, the Whitewater prosecutor, then subpoenaed the lawyer before a grand jury to learn what Foster had told him. Starr argued that the privilege should give way in light of Foster's death because there was no other source for the information. But the Supreme Court held that Foster's privilege survived his death.[10] By contrast, the California Supreme Court has held that when a person dies, the privilege holder becomes the personal representative in charge of his estate and once the estate is distributed and the representative is discharged, the privilege ends because there is no one available to assert it.[11]

Prospective Clients   Just as the duty of confidentiality and the privilege may survive the death of the client, so too may they arise even before the client formally becomes a client. People with legal problems may interview several lawyers before deciding which one to retain (or before they find one willing to accept their matter). This is a good thing. Clients should be encouraged to shop for lawyers just as they shop for other important purchases. Clients need to know if they feel comfortable with the lawyer, whether they have confidence in him or her, and if the quoted fee is competitive. Lawyers have to decide if they are interested in the client's matter. They may also need to ascertain whether any of the lawyer conflict rules may prevent them from accepting the matter. In an initial meeting with a lawyer, therefore, the client will likely have to give the lawyer information about his or her legal problem. That information will be privileged and confidential unless the lawyer and client have a contrary understanding at the outset (which some lawyers may want in order to avoid the conflict of interest problems that can arise even if no formal relationship ensues; see Chapter 12). If privilege and the confidentiality duty attached only if the client retained the lawyer, the client would be in an obvious bind. To protect her information, a client would be pressured to retain the first lawyer to whom she talked; or she would need to refrain from giving the lawyer the full story because then, if no retention came to pass, the information would not be protected, and the lawyer himself would have no confidentiality duty.[12]

Exceptions to Privilege and Confidentiality There are exceptions to both the privilege and the duty of confidentiality. These are not uniform nationwide, although for privilege they are largely so. For confidentiality, as stated above, the exceptions vary significantly because of differences in each jurisdiction's lawyer ethics rules.

Privilege As stated above, privilege will be lost if a third person not reasonably necessary to the provision of the legal service is present during the communication or if the client or the lawyer (with explicit or implied authorization) reveals an oral or written communication between lawyer and client to a third person ("My lawyer said. . . ."). In other words, if for some reason the client or lawyer decides that it will be beneficial to reveal their communications to a third person who has no role to play in the representation, they may do so, but they cannot then protect the information through a claim of privilege when someone else comes looking for it.

A client will not be allowed to assert privilege if there is a dispute between the client and the lawyer (say, over fees or in a malpractice action) and the lawyer needs to use or reveal the privileged information in order to defend himself or prove his claim. Most places, the same is true if the lawyer is charged with wrongdoing arising out of the work for the client — by a prosecutor, a plaintiff in a civil case, or a disciplinary authority — and the lawyer needs to disclose the privileged information to defend himself. The client will not be able to prevent that disclosure by asserting privilege.[13] Last, the privilege is lost if the client's purpose in hiring the lawyer was to facilitate a crime or fraud, although the lawyer may not have been aware of that purpose and even if the crime or fraud is not consummated. This is called the crime/fraud exception to the privilege, and it operates from the assumption that if the client was intent on committing a crime or fraud and hired the lawyer to advance that effort, there was never a valid attorney-client relationship to begin with (since we don't recognize criminal or fraudulent goals as legitimate reasons to hire a lawyer) and so no privilege.[14]

Confidentiality   As stated above, the exceptions to the duty of confidentiality — that is, the preconditions to the authority to reveal or adversely use a client's confidential information — vary from state to state, much more so than do the exceptions to the attorney-client privilege. The variations can be explained in several ways. First, remember that the bar participates in decisions about the confidentiality exceptions through its work in advising courts on the jurisdiction's ethics rules. Although the courts are the final arbiters, they do listen to the bar's recommendations both as a matter of institutional identity (the judges were once lawyers) and tradition. The scope of the privilege's exceptions, on the other hand, is determined by legislatures or by the courts in the context of a litigated case. The bar's institutional influence is less prominent in these venues. Further, lawyers have diverse views among themselves, sometimes dramatically diverse, on the importance of confidentiality and the comparative importance of particular exceptions. Those views surface and may compete as lawyers in a jurisdiction weigh in on what rule to recommend to the courts. The diversity of views helps explain the disparity among jurisdictions.

Lawyers who strongly favor broad confidentiality duties and narrow exceptions stress the need for client trust and candor. Only if a lawyer can learn everything relevant about a client's matter, they argue, will he or she be optimally able to serve the client. If clients become aware of broad exceptions to their lawyer's confidentiality obligation, they may hold back information that they consider harmful to their interests because they are unsure whether the lawyer will be free to, or required to, reveal the information. Even if revelation would not actually harm their legal or economic interests, the client may fear shame or embarrassment if the information were to become known. Lawyers who favor strong confidentiality duties and narrow exceptions stress that they are more likely to learn about a client's illegal, fraudulent, or embarrassing conduct — and be in a position to dissuade the client from continuing to engage in the conduct if it is still prospective — if the client knows that the lawyer is bound to keep even confessions of unlawful conduct confidential.

Opponents of broad exceptions to confidentiality also cite a normative reason as well as these practical ones. They argue that respect for the autonomy and personhood of clients demands that society afford them a safe place where they can confide in an expert in order to get advice about a legal terrain often much too complicated for nonlawyers to understand without help.

Proponents of broader exceptions to confidentiality doubt that these will actually affect a client's willingness to be candid with counsel, especially if the lawyer explains that keeping the lawyer ignorant may damage her ability to represent the client competently. The client's opponent and his lawyer may know (or eventually learn) what the client is not telling her own lawyer, who will then not be prepared to deal with the surprise. Proponents of broad exceptions also point out that much confidential information comes not from the client but from third parties, so even if the exceptions do inhibit client candor somewhat (which proponents will not concede), they will in any event not impede the lawyer's ability to get information from third parties (unless knowledge of the identity of the third parties is itself dependent on client candor).

Protecting Others But the main reason that proponents of broader exceptions give for their position is that the effect on client candor is not as important as countervailing interests. From the perspective of wise social policy, they say, the exceptions they favor reach the correct balance between the value of client trust and candor and the valid interests of others. This is especially so, they claim, for exceptions that allow the lawyer (or even require her) to warn victims of a client's intended fraud or crime when the lawyer has unwittingly helped advance the client's unlawful objectives, or to reveal that a client has committed a fraud on a tribunal in the course of the lawyer's representation. As for the normative argument — respect for client autonomy and personhood — the proponents of broader exceptions acknowledge the importance of this value but question why the profession should afford that respect where the client is bent on unlawfully harming others or obstructing justice and won't back off when his lawyer warns him against the behavior. Those who support broader exceptions to the duty of confidentiality are not unanimous in what these should be. Even within this group, differences exist. It is convenient to talk about proponents and opponents of exceptions to confidentiality, but realistically we're dealing with a continuum of positions.

State Variations   So, as we see, the debate over the appropriate balance between encouraging client trust, on the one hand, and the interests of other persons and the courts, on the other, relies both on empirical and normative claims. The empirical claims have not been tested. It might seem to be impossible to design an experiment in the real world to learn if clients vary in their level of candor with counsel depending on whether the jurisdiction has broad or narrow confidentiality exceptions (let alone all the intermediate possibilities). But as next shown, we do have a sort of "natural" laboratory already in place. Some jurisdictions have very limited exceptions; others have very broad ones. Many are in between. No study has yet reported whether lawyers experience differences in the willingness of their clients to speak candidly depending on the scope of the confidentiality exceptions in their jurisdictions. It would be interesting to construct one.

Let's take three examples. These address the exceptions to prevent harm to a third person, not a tribunal. We discuss fraud on a tribunal in Chapter 16. Our examples are from California, a state with a very limited confidentiality exception; New Jersey, which has many exceptions; and the Model Rules provisions, whose exceptions lie between California and New Jersey and which have been influential nationwide. In addition to the language of the exceptions themselves, a separate issue, of great importance to the question under discussion, is whether the revelation of confidential information under the particular exception is permissive (i.e., up to the lawyer) or mandatory.

The **California** rule provides:

(B) A member may, but is not required to, reveal confidential information relating to the representation of a client to the extent that the member reasonably believes the disclosure is necessary to prevent a criminal act that the member reasonably believes is likely to result in death of, or substantial bodily harm to, an individual.

(C) Before revealing confidential information to prevent a criminal act as provided in paragraph (B), a member shall, if reasonable under the circumstances:

(1) make a good faith effort to persuade the client: (i) not to commit or to continue the criminal act or (ii) to pursue a course of conduct that will prevent the threatened death or substantial bodily harm; or do both (i) and (ii); and

(2) inform the client, at an appropriate time, of the member's ability or decision to reveal information as provided in paragraph (B).

(D) In revealing confidential information as provided in paragraph (B), the member's disclosure must be no more than is necessary to prevent the criminal act, given the information known to the member at the time of the disclosure.

(E) A member who does not reveal information permitted by paragraph (B) does not violate this rule.[15]

So the California exception as contained in its professional conduct rules is limited to prevention of criminal acts reasonably likely to cause death or substantial bodily harm. The act does not have to be the client's but it does have to be a crime, which is likely if it will cause physical harm or death. But it is not inevitable. Think, for example, about a corporate lawyer who discovers that his client has (perhaps innocently) put a dangerous product on the market and refuses to recall it. Is that failure a crime or just immoral? Further, the California exception is permissive. A California lawyer who knows that his client, armed and dangerous, plans to commit an imminent violent crime is not ethically obligated to call the police or warn the intended victim.

New Jersey, by contrast, has many exceptions to confidentiality, and some of them are mandatory. The New Jersey rule provides:

(b) A lawyer shall reveal such information to the proper authorities, as soon as, and to the extent the lawyer reasonably believes necessary, to prevent the client or another person:

(1) from committing a criminal, illegal or fraudulent act that the lawyer reasonably believes is likely to result in death or substantial bodily harm or substantial injury to the financial interest or property of another;

(2) from committing a criminal, illegal or fraudulent act that the lawyer reasonably believes is likely to perpetrate a fraud upon a tribunal.

(c) If a lawyer reveals information pursuant to RPC 1.6(b), the lawyer also may reveal the information to the person threatened to the extent the lawyer reasonably believes is necessary to protect that person from death, substantial bodily harm, substantial financial injury, or substantial property loss.

(d) A lawyer may reveal such information to the extent the lawyer reasonably believes necessary:

(1) to rectify the consequences of a client's criminal, illegal or fraudulent act in the furtherance of which the lawyer's services had been used;

(2) to establish a claim or defense on behalf of the lawyer in a controversy between the lawyer and the client, or to establish a defense to a criminal charge, civil claim or disciplinary complaint against the lawyer based upon the conduct in which the client was involved; or

(3) to comply with other law.

(e) Reasonable belief for purposes of RPC 1.6 is the belief or conclusion of a reasonable lawyer that is based upon information that has some foundation in fact and constitutes prima facie evidence of the matters referred to in subsections (b), (c), or (d).[16]

If we focus solely on the part of the exception whose goal is to prevent future harm, we see an ethical duty to prevent anyone, client included, from acting illegally or fraudulently (even if not criminally) if serious physical harm or harm to financial interests or property, or a fraud on a court, will likely result. This is one of the broadest exceptions in the nation not only because of the scope of the harm it aims to avoid (physical as well as financial) but also because lawyers have no discretion to remain silent. The verb phrase is "shall reveal."

In the middle are the exceptions in the **Model Rules** (Rule 1.6(b)),[17] all of which are permissive as in California (except where there has been fraud on the court, discussed in Chapter 16); but the Model Rules, unlike the California rules, address financial harm as well as physical harm when, in addition, the lawyer's services have been used to advance the criminal or fraudulent conduct causing the financial harm. The rule provides:

(b) A lawyer may reveal information relating to the representation of a client to the extent the lawyer reasonably believes necessary:

(1) to prevent reasonably certain death or substantial bodily harm;

(2) to prevent the client from committing a crime or fraud that is reasonably certain to result in substantial injury to the financial interests or property of another and in furtherance of which the client has used or is using the lawyer's services;

(3) to prevent, mitigate or rectify substantial injury to the financial interests or property of another that is reasonably certain to result or has resulted from the client's commission of a crime or fraud in furtherance of which the client has used the lawyer's services;

(4) to secure legal advice about the lawyer's compliance with these Rules;

(5) to establish a claim or defense on behalf of the lawyer in a controversy between the lawyer and the client, to establish a defense to a criminal charge or civil claim against the lawyer based upon conduct in which the client was involved, or to respond to allegations in any proceeding concerning the lawyer's representation of the client; or

(6) to comply with other law or a court order.

An Objective Test Note another requirement in each of these rules. Whether revelation is permissive or mandatory, the rules require the lawyer to behave "reasonably," which means the lawyer's decision to reveal is tested by an objective standard. A lawyer who in subjective good faith reveals a client confidence, but acts unreasonably in reaching her conclusions about the need to do so, is technically subject to discipline or to a civil action for breach of fiduciary duty (or malpractice) since, as discussed earlier in this chapter, the substantive law of agency and fiduciary duty also recognizes the duty of confidentiality and will provide a remedy for its violation. Now, it is highly unlikely that a lawyer who conscientiously concludes that revelation is needed or permitted would ever be disciplined (unless there was some self-serving or other improper interest that motivates the decision). Lawyers are so disinclined to harm a client by revealing confidential information that the decision to do so is almost certainly one that the lawyer reaches with great anguish and reflection, making it quite likely that the disclosure was also reasonable based on the information available to the lawyer. Even if the lawyer's prediction of harm turns out to be wrong, discipline will not ensue if it was reasonable. But even so, a client may still sue the lawyer. "You guessed wrong. It was just a guess. You had no reasonable basis for thinking I was going to _____. You blabbed my secrets and I'm paying the price." That claim may ultimately fail, but the incentives in civil litigation are different from those that operate in discipline. The risk of a lawsuit is greater, if still not great, than the risk of discipline.

The Risk of Civil Liability to the Victim   One reason a lawyer might be inclined to reveal client confidences if permitted is to avoid potential liability to the client's intended victim if the lawyer remains mute. For example, a lawyer who has been representing a corporate client in connection with substantial bank loans, and who discovers to his surprise that the security for the loans is fictitious, might fear that the banks will sue the lawyer for any losses the banks could have avoided if warned. The banks' theory would be that the lawyer had a duty to warn once he discovered the fraud because the lawyer had represented the client in connection with the loans. Even if the lawyer was unaware of the client's bad conduct at the outset, the fact that he had facilitated it, and may even have unwittingly confirmed the existence of the security, obligated the lawyer to warn once he discovered the truth. By authorizing the lawyer to do so, the argument would run, the exception in the ABA confidentiality rule frees the lawyer from a need to choose between breaching a confidence to avoid civil liability (but at the expense of possible discipline), on one hand, and remaining silent to avoid discipline (but running the risk of civil liability), on the other.

This very dilemma actually faced a New York firm and led to the adoption first of a comment to the Model Rules, and eventually to the explicit exception, that allows lawyers to reveal client fraud where the client has used the lawyer's services to advance the fraud.[18] The lawyers in the New York case consulted their own outside counsel and were told that under the New York rules at the time, they could not warn the banks. They didn't, but eventually (too slowly, some say) they withdrew from the representation. The banks meanwhile continued to lend money in the belief that the collateral for the loans was real. When the banks discovered the fraud, they sued the law firm and settled for many millions of dollars. This case — called the OPM case, after the company committing the fraud — is further discussed in Chapter 19.

Noisy Withdrawal   Today, as a result of the OPM case, the New York Code of Professional Responsibility has an explicit exception that would allow lawyers in this position to alert the banks, thereby freeing them from having to choose between risk of discipline and risk of civil liability. Exceptions in Rule 1.6(b)(2) and (3) permit the same. But the New York rule differs from the Model Rules in one way. The New York rule would allow the lawyer only to give notice of withdrawal from the representation and to withdraw any oral or written statements the lawyer may have made, without actually revealing his knowledge of the fraud that has led to his withdrawal.

This is called a noisy withdrawal (which the Model Rules also recognize in comments to Rules 1.2 and 4.1).[19] However, even a noisy withdrawal — assuming there is in fact a statement for the lawyer to withdraw — should ordinarily guarantee that the recipient realizes that there's something "smelly" that requires investigation. The Model Rules go further and allow actual revelation of confidential client information when the preconditions are met.

We shall again discuss the confidentiality obligation when we come to the subject of fraud on the court (in Chapter 16) and a lawyer's duty to correct it even if doing so will reveal a client's confidences (this is not the rule everywhere). As we shall see, in the Model Rules, prevention of fraud on a court (as opposed to fraud on a person) is deemed more important than client confidentiality, so the duty to reveal client information is mandatory if no other remedy is available.[20] Another place where the need to protect confidential information comes up is in the various conflict-of-interest doctrines (see Chapter 12). The goal of protecting confidential information (and assuring clients and former clients that the information *is* protected) is one justification for rules that, absent waiver, will sometimes forbid a lawyer to accept a matter adverse to a current or former client.

Summary Two concepts protect information a lawyer learns in representing a client or in meeting with prospective clients: privilege and confidentiality. Privilege is part of the law of evidence. Confidentiality derives from the law of agency and fiduciary duty. Privilege protects the lawyer-client communication but not the underlying information. All privileged information is also confidential, but much confidential information — that is, information learned from third persons — is not privileged. If privileged, lawyer and client can refuse to reveal the communication even if served with a subpoena from a court or other government body with subpoena power. But that is not so if the information is only confidential (unless some other doctrine, like work product, protects it). Both privilege and confidentiality have exceptions. For privilege, that includes waiver by revealing the lawyer-client communication to others, the lawyer's need to reveal the communication in self-defense, and the crime-fraud exception. For confidentiality, the exceptions vary greatly depending on the jurisdiction. Some places, revelation may be mandatory for some exceptions; elsewhere, revelation may be forbidden or only permissive. A noisy withdrawal allows a lawyer to "take back" anything he or she said or wrote when withdrawing, thereby presumably warning the other side of a problem without actually providing the details.

ENDNOTES

1. *Upjohn Co. v. United States*, 449 U.S. 383 (1981) (privilege), Model Rule (MR) 1.6 cmt. [2].

2. In the federal system, Federal Rule of Evidence 501 instructs courts that privilege "shall be governed by the principles of the common law as they may be interpreted by the courts of the United States in light of reason and experience." In effect, this statute leaves the development of the attorney-client privilege, as well as other privileges, to common law development. Most states, however, define the privilege by statutes. *See, e.g.*, California Evidence Code §954. Federal Rule of Evidence 501 requires federal judges to use state privilege law if the issue before the court is governed by state substantive law (as in diversity cases). For the constitutional dimension of the privilege in criminal cases, *see People v. Johnson*, 999 P.2d 825 (Colo. 2000).

3. Restatement (Third) of Agency §1.01 (all agents are fiduciaries). The Restatement §8.05 provides: "An agent has a duty . . . (2) not to use or communicate confidential information of the principal for the agent's own purposes or those of a third party." Comment c would seem to go beyond Rule 1.6 by requiring agents to protect a principal's information even if it is not related to the purpose of the agency:

> An agent's relationship with a principal may result in the agent learning information about the principal's health, life history, and personal preferences that the agent should reasonably understand the principal expects the agent to keep confidential. An agent's duty of confidentiality extends to all such information concerning a principal even when it is not otherwise connected with the subject matter of the agency relationship.

4. For examples of the many variations, *see* Stephen Gillers, Roy Simon, and Andrew Perlman, *Regulation of Lawyers: Statutes and Standards*. This annual

publication, published by Aspen, identifies significant state variations in legal ethics rules, along with many other documents in the field.

5. A famous definition of the preconditions to the privilege appears in Judge Wyzanski's opinion in *United States v. United Shoe Machinery Corp.*, 89 F. Supp. 357 (D. Mass. 1950). Judge Wyzanski wrote:

> The privilege applies only if (1) the asserted holder of the privilege is or sought to become a client; (2) the person to whom the communication was made (a) is a member of the bar of a court, or his subordinate and (b) in connection with this communication is acting as a lawyer; (3) the communication relates to a fact of which the attorney was informed (a) by his client (b) without the presence of strangers (c) for the purpose of securing primarily either (i) an opinion on law or (ii) legal services or (iii) assistance in some legal proceeding, and not (d) for the purpose of committing a crime or tort; and (4) the privilege has been (a) claimed and (b) not waived by the client.

6. *See, e.g., United States v. Alvarez*, 519 F.2d 1036 (3rd Cir. 1975) (therapist).

7. *Upjohn Co. v. United States*, 449 U.S. 383 (1981).

8. *Lynch v. Hamrick*, 968 So.2d 11 (Ala. 2007).

9. MR 1.9(c) forbids revelation or adverse use of confidential information of a former client unless the information "has become generally known." *See also* Rule 1.9 cmt. [8].

10. *Swidler & Berlin v. United States*, 524 U.S. 399 (1998).

11. *HLC Properties, Ltd. v. Superior Court*, 105 P.3d 560 (Cal. 2005).

12. For the proposition that the attorney-client privilege attaches to preliminary interviews, see *Restatement of the Law Governing Lawyers* §15. Communications with prospective clients can also create problems under the lawyer conflict rules. This subject, including MR 1.18, which permits firms to screen lawyers in order to avoid a conflict that would otherwise arise from a preliminary interview, is discussed in Chapter 12.

13. *See, e.g., Apex Municipal Fund v. N-Group Securities*, 841 F.Supp. 1423 (S.D. Tex. 1993) (exception to privilege). MR 1.6(b)(5) recognizes parallel exceptions to confidentiality.

14. *See, e.g., In re Grand Jury Proceedings*, 87 F.3d 377 (9th Cir. 1996); *United States v. Doe*, 429 F.3d 450 (3d Cir. 2005). Depending on the court, the privilege will be lost if there is "a reasonable basis for believing that the [client's] objective was fraudulent" or criminal, *In re Grand Jury Subpoena Duces Tecum*, 731 F.2d 1032 (2d Cir. 1984); or if the opponent of the privilege can prove the criminal or fraudulent purpose by a "preponderance of the evidence." *In re Napster*, 479 F.3d 1078 (9th Cir. 2007). On the ability of the judge to review the allegedly privileged information in deciding whether or not the crime/fraud exception has been proved, see *United States v. Zolin*, 491 U.S. 554 (1989) (holding that the judge may do so upon "a showing of a factual basis adequate to support a good faith belief by a reasonable person . . . that in camera view of the materials may reveal evidence to establish the claim that the crime/fraud exception applies") (internal quote omitted).

15. California Rule of Professional Conduct 3-100.

16. New Jersey Rule of Professional Conduct 1.6.

17. Chapter 19 on negotiation expands on the Model Rules confidentiality exceptions and on noisy withdrawal (summarized below in this chapter) in the context of transactional work.

18. MR 1.6(b)(2) and (3).

19. New York Rule 1.6(b)(3) permits a lawyer to reveal client information

to the extent implicit in withdrawing a written or oral opinion or representation previously given by the lawyer and believed by the lawyer still to be relied upon by a third person where the lawyer has discovered that the opinion or representation was based on materially inaccurate information or is being used to further a crime or fraud.

20. MR 3.3.

～ 5 ～

Privilege and Confidentiality for Organizational Clients

Who Controls Privilege and Confidentiality?

Whose Communications with Counsel Are Privileged?

Miranda Warnings to Constituents

Upjohn and Its Tests

The Control Group Test

Special Privilege and Confidentiality Issues for Organizations Organizational client-like corporations enjoy the same level of respect for their confidential information as do individuals. Model Rule 1.6 does not distinguish between biological and entity clients in this regard, although, as we'll see, another rule (1.13) does recognize an *exception* to confidentiality when a client is an organization that is inapplicable when the client is an individual (see Chapter 20).[1] However, organizations do present a special issue when the question is the attorney-client privilege. Where the client is an organization — say, a company — the following questions arise: Whose communications with the company's counsel are protected as privileged? Those of any employee? Only communications with an officer? Some other category? And who owns the privilege and the right to waive it where there is one? The last question can also be asked about the duty of confidentiality.

Here's a common situation. Let's say that at request of management, a company lawyer is investigating an allegation that a midlevel manager made racially discriminatory comments to a subordinate. If so, the conduct can subject the company to substantial damages and reputational loss. But is it so? Here's whom the lawyer interviews: the manager, the person making the charge, corporate employees who may have overheard the comments, corporate employees who have worked with the manager or with the accuser but were not witnesses to the alleged incidents, the manager's supervisors, and former employees of the company who once worked with the manager. The lawyer conducts all the interviews in person and writes a memorandum to the CEO detailing the information she learned in each interview and offering her analysis. She labels each memo "Privileged and Confidential."

Our questions are, first, to the extent any of these communications are privileged — and on these facts they would be privileged — whose privilege is it? The interviewees' or the company's? The answer of course is that the privilege belongs to the company, which is the client.[2] That means it has a right to receive the information the lawyers learned, and it can also waive the privilege if it wishes, even over the objections of an interviewee, who may have said things that can expose him or her to liability (even criminal liability, in some situations), loss of a job, loss of promotional opportunities, or simply great embarrassment. The company, as the lawyer's client, is also owed the lawyer's duty of confidentiality with regard to whatever the lawyer learns in the investigation. No interviewee can claim that his conversation was confidential to him.

Corporate Miranda Warnings   In the interest of fairness, the American Bar Association (ABA) rules require that when interviewing an organizational "constituent" (like an officer or employee) the lawyer must "explain the identity of the client" if he knows or should know that the company's interests "are adverse" to those of the interviewee.[3] Another reason the lawyer will be inclined to give this caution to the interviewee is to avoid the risk that a court will later say that the constituent reasonably believed that the lawyer was working for him, too, a decision that could lead to a finding of conflict of interest or even liability; this risk is heightened if no caution is given if the circumstances could reasonably imply that the constituent was also a client.

Corporate lawyers doing internal investigations have come to call these preliminary cautions "corporate Miranda warnings" after the Supreme Court's *Miranda* opinion. (Some call them Upjohn warnings, after the *Upjohn* case below.) To be sure, the need for a warning is still infrequent because ordinarily there is no reasonably apparent potential adversity between the lawyer's client and the interviewed constituent. So in our hypothetical, the only interviewee who should *clearly* get this caution would be the manager whose conduct is in question. The warning goes something like this: "I want to talk to you about [SUBJECT]. You should understand that I represent COMPANY and not you or anyone else. Only COMPANY is my client. Anything we discuss will be privileged and confidential but the privilege belongs to the company only, which means it can choose to waive the privilege or waive confidentiality in what you tell me. And of course, because the company is my client, I will share with company officials the results of all my interviews, including this one. Do you have any questions?"

Whose Communications Are Privileged? Once we establish that the company owns the privilege, we must next ask whether indeed an organizational lawyer's communications with a *particular* corporate constituent are subject to privilege. I suppose an antecedent question is whether organizations enjoy the protection of the attorney-client privilege at all. We've been assuming that they do, and that is true in every U.S. jurisdiction, although very briefly, many years ago, that principle was put in doubt.[4] Which of our hypothetical lawyer's communications with the various individuals she interviewed are within the company's privilege? Remember that if the information is not privileged, an opponent will be able to seek it in discovery. A grand jury may subpoena it. Although other protections may be available, most obviously the qualified protection for an attorney's work product, the attorney-client privilege is about as much protection as the law ever affords a communication and is certainly stronger than protection in the work-product doctrine. For example, imagine that in the eventual discrimination litigation, the plaintiff's lawyer asks for the company lawyer's memos, figuring they'll have a lot of juicy information about the manager's bad behavior. The attorney-client privilege will give the company the greatest protection — indeed, on these facts virtually absolute protection — against disclosure.

The Upjohn Tests At this point, the law varies among jurisdiction. (Remember that the privilege is a creature of the law of evidence, whose definition and exceptions are either statutory or made by courts or both). In federal courts, where the issue is governed by federal law, the federal privilege will cover communications between the company's counsel and its employees that "concer[n] matters *within the scope of the* *employees' corporate duties"* where the purpose of the communications is so "that the corporation could obtain legal advice." (If the dispute arises under state law, Federal Rule of Evidence 501 requires the court to use state privileges.) The quoted language comes from the Supreme Court's influential opinion in *Upjohn Co. v. United States.*[5] At a second point, the Court described the preconditions to privilege with words that were even less demanding. There, the Court said that the communications were privileged because they were made "by Upjohn employees to counsel for Upjohn acting as such, at the direction of corporate superiors in order to secure legal advice from counsel."[6] Omitted is the reference to the "matters within the scope of" of the employee's duties.

Does this matter? It might. Is it within the scope of the duties of the plaintiff's coworkers to notice discriminatory comments of a supervisor? Or is it just something they might happen to witness? Probably the latter if we look at a job description, which means the communications with the coworkers would not be protected under the attorney-client privilege if the stricter reading of *Upjohn* controlled. On the other hand, perhaps it suffices that the interview itself is "within the scope of [their] duties." Or perhaps it is enough that the information the employee provides was acquired during (i.e., within the *temporal* scope of) their workday. Of course, company lawyers would prefer the broadest interpretation, and they have generally succeeded in persuading courts and other authorities that this is the right policy, even when the interviewee is a former, not a current, employee or officer of the company.[7]

The second quoted test from *Upjohn* is quite likely to cover all the communications our hypothetical lawyer is conducting with corporate constituents. They all have the purpose of enabling the company to "secure legal advice from counsel."

The Control Group Test   Many state courts have accepted *Upjohn's* definition of the breadth of an organization's attorney-client privilege. But as stated, the privilege can vary from state to state, so we should not be surprised to discover that some courts have adhered to a narrower "control group" test (as the lower court in *Upjohn* did). Under this test, only communications between company counsel and higher echelon officers of the company — those who "control" the company and direct counsel — are privileged.[8] *Upjohn* rejected this test for federal courts adjudicating federal claims as providing inadequate guidance and protection. Some courts that have followed *Upjohn* have nonetheless read it *not* to protect communications from employees who just happen to be witnesses to an event, although they may have witnessed the event while on the job. In this view, the interviews with the discrimination plaintiff's coworkers would not be protected by the attorney-client privilege since what they tell counsel would not be seen as information acquired within "the scope of [their] duties." Their job description does not obligate them to observe and record discrimination.[9] Functionally, they would be seen as witnesses.

Comparing the Tests The control group test may be seen as inadequate because it is both overinclusive and underinclusive. It is overinclusive because it would privilege a communication with a high-ranking officer even if she were simply a casual witness to an incident while on a day off. It is underinclusive because it would not privilege communications with those corporate constituents who are not in the control group but whose own conduct may have given rise to the organization's liability. An example is the truck driver who went through a red light and caused an accident. *Upjohn* purports to plow a middle ground. But as shown, its scope is somewhat ambiguous. Which version of *Upjohn* should we favor? Imagine that the company lawyer interviews Sally, a receptionist. Sally says she never saw the manager exhibit any discriminatory behavior or heard him make such comments while on the job. But she says that while having lunch at a nearby restaurant during the work week, she overheard him at the next booth making highly disparaging comments about the plaintiff, using racially charged language. Should this communication be privileged to the company? On the one hand, it is made to the company lawyer while Sally is employed. On the other hand, Sally overheard the comments while she was on her lunch break and what she heard is outside the scope of her employment because her job does not include responsibility to enforce the company's antidiscrimination policy.

Extending *Upjohn* to cover the interview with Sally because of the fortuity that she is employed by the company may go too far. The same interview with a witness in the restaurant who overheard the same comment but had no relationship to the company would not fall within the attorney-client privilege. The fortuity of Sally's employment would seem a weak justification to reach a different conclusion. On the other hand, a proponent of a broad privilege might argue that Sally has incentive to cooperate with the company's counsel because she represents her employer and that fact should give her interview greater protection than would be true for a mere witness.

In Chapter 7, we will discuss a closely related but distinct issue. It is the scope of the no-contact rule in the corporate or organizational setting.[10] Essentially, this rule forbids a lawyer with a client in a matter from knowingly communicating with the *client* of another lawyer in the matter about the matter, with some exceptions. In other words, lawyers have to work through lawyers. But when the opposing client is a big organization, which of its constituents are covered by the no-contact rule? To whom can the opposing lawyer *not* talk? As you will see, broadly speaking the big policy issue on the scope of the no-contact rule is much like the big policy issue here — namely, finding an appropriate balance between protecting information on one hand and avoiding excess corporate secrecy on the other hand. But the reasons for the privilege and the reasons for the no-contact rule are fundamentally different. So it will be important to realize that a jurisdiction's answer to the "*Upjohn* question" will not determine the measure by which it will answer the questions we raise in discussion of the no-contact rule in Chapter 7.

ENDNOTES

1. Model Rule (MR) 1.13(c).
2. *Commodity Futures Trading Comm'n v. Weintraub*, 471 U.S. 343 (1985). *Weintraub* holds that a company in bankruptcy is controlled by its trustee, who in turn controls its privilege on behalf of the company. Former officers and directors of the company have no claim to assert the privilege of the company.
3. MR 1.13(f).
4. *Radiant Burners, Inc. v. American Gas Assn.*, 207 F. Supp. 771 (N.D. Ill. 1962), *rev'd*, 320 F.2d 314 (7th Cir. 1963).
5. 449 U.S. 383 (1981) (emphasis added).
6. *Id.* at 394.
7. *Surles v. Air France*, 2001 WL 815522 (S.D.N.Y., 2001) (collecting cases).
8. Most notably, California is less protective of the attorney-client privilege in a corporate context than are federal courts. *D.I. Chadbourne, Inc. v. Superior Court*, 388 P.2d 700 (Cal. 1964).
9. For a thoughtful opinion taking a narrower view of *Upjohn, see Samaritan Foundation v. Goodfarb*, 862 P.2d 870 (Ariz. 1993). The Arizona Supreme Court would not have recognized a corporate lawyer's communications with corporate employees, who are effectively mere witnesses to an incident, as privileged. The Arizona legislature overruled this decision, but only for civil cases. *Roman Catholic Dioceses of Phoenix v. Superior Court*, 62 P.3d 970 (Ariz. App. 2003).
10. MR 4.2(a).

~ 6 ~

What Lawyers Owe Clients: Other Attributes of the Attorney-Client Relationship

The Lawyer as Agent and Fiduciary

The Requirement of Diligence

The Duty to Inform and Client Autonomy

Although competence and confidentiality may be the two of the three constituents of the attorney-client relationship that get most of the attention (with loyalty, a foundation of the conflict of interest rules discussed in Chapters 9, 10, and 12, being the third), they are not exclusive. The lawyer, as stated earlier, is also an agent and assumes all of the traditional duties that agents of any kind owe their principals. As a fiduciary, the lawyer's relationship to the client is not "arm's length"; rather, the lawyer is there to serve the client, to make the client's lawful goals within the scope of the retention the lawyer's own professional goals. Inherent in the obligations of an agent and fiduciary is the requirement of diligence in pursuing the client's objectives. And finally, and getting a great deal of attention of late but often slighted, is the duty to keep the client informed about developments in the client's matter entrusted to the lawyer and to respond promptly to the client's request for information or a status report. We consider these aspects of the professional relationship *seriatim* but must recognize that they are interdependent. A lawyer who is not diligent, for example, is unlikely to be keeping the client informed of her lack of diligence or the status of her case.

Lawyer as Agent: Obligations   We can approach the lawyer's status as agent from two perspectives. The first perspective is to ask what the status requires of the lawyer. Confidentiality is one obligation, as we saw in Chapters 4 and 5. Fiduciary treatment, next discussed, is another. Avoidance of conflicts of interest (in part because they may threaten confidences or compromise loyalty and fiduciary duty) is a third responsibility of a lawyer-agent. As stated, agents must also be diligent and keep the principal informed; discussed below is their application to lawyers.

Lawyer as Agent: Powers   The second perspective from which we must approach the meaning of the agency relationship looks not at what the lawyer-agent owes to the client-principal but at the *authority* of the lawyer to say and do things with regard to others that will affect the legal relationships of the client, for better or worse. While this book cannot delve into the intricacies of the law of agency, one aspect of that law is that an *actual, inherent, or apparent agency authority* empowers the agent to alter the principal's legal position. For example, a purchasing agent for a corporation can bind the company to a contract to pay for a product that is within the actual authority of the agent to buy. (That authority may be explicit, as in a job description, or it may be implied from the circumstances.) One person may authorize another to enter a contract on the first person's behalf, and when that happens, the principal is legally obligated as though he had signed the contract himself. The commercial and much of the noncommercial worlds could not operate without agents and the assurance that third persons may deal with the agent, with the same confidence in the enforceability of any agreement, or the binding effect of a representation, as if they were dealing with the principal himself.

A lawyer is an agent who represents the client in his or her *legal* relationships — with others or with courts and government agencies. (Of course, a lawyer may also have additional nonlawyerly responsibilities. Many in-house lawyers are also officers of their corporate clients.) An attorney *at law* is an agent for the client in the legal system. An attorney *in fact* is an agent authorized to do certain things for the principal in other contexts (like sell property or invest money) and, of course, an attorney in fact need not be a lawyer at all.

Statement of Agents: Effect on Clients   If a lawyer makes a factual statement in negotiating a transaction for a client, it has the same legal effect as if the client had made the same statement.[1] A lawyer who takes a position for a client in the courtroom or in a pleading, or who fails to do so, ordinarily binds the client to that position, or to the consequences of the failure, to the same extent as if the client had said or failed to say the same things. The judge and opponent may rely on the position. As for statements made outside the litigation system, the law of evidence recognizes that the statement of an agent (or employee, who is one kind of agent), within the scope of the agency and while the agency is in existence, can be offered against the principal as an exception to or exclusion from the rule against hearsay.[2] Statements of lawyer-agents outside of court are included. These vicarious admissions, as they are called, do not bind the client in court, meaning that the client can always challenge their accuracy in court. But they are admissible in evidence against the client.[3] This rule would also admit against the client any factual concession a lawyer may make in the course of discussing settlement of a claim, but in many jurisdictions a special rule excludes those concessions from use in court. The policy for exclusion is to encourage settlement by allowing free-ranging discussion without fear that one or another lawyer may "slip" and say something that comes back to harm the client. If it weren't for this rule, careful lawyers would have to begin many of their statements in settlement negotiations with the words "hypothetically, let's suppose that" or "even assuming for the sake of argument that," or the like.[4]

A lawyer may misuse her agency authority, most commonly through negligence, in which case the client may have a malpractice claim, but the third party who relies on the lawyer's act or statement on behalf of the client will be entitled to do so as long as the lawyer had actual or apparent authority to act for the client (we discuss the different kinds of authority below). For example, if a lawyer chooses not to assert a particular defense to civil or criminal charge against the client, the opponent can rely on that failure. In *Taylor v. Illinois*, a case that reached the Supreme Court, a criminal defense lawyer intentionally did not reveal an alibi witness in violation of a state law that required notice of a planned alibi defense. The trial judge refused to let the lawyer call the witness. After conviction, the defendant wanted to challenge the trial judge's decision, claiming that he should not be bound by the lawyer's conduct because he was not party to the strategy and knew nothing about it. The Supreme Court disagreed:

> The argument that the client should not be held responsible for his lawyer's misconduct strikes at the heart of the

attorney-client relationship. Although there are basic rights that the attorney cannot waive without the fully informed and publicly acknowledged consent of the client the lawyer has — and must have — full authority to manage the conduct of the trial. The adversary process could not function effectively if every tactical decision required client approval. . . . Putting to one side the exceptional cases in which counsel is ineffective, the client must accept the consequences of the lawyer's decision to forgo cross-examination, to decide not to put certain witnesses on the stand, or to decide not to disclose the identity of certain witnesses in advance of trial.[5]

In civil cases, similarly, courts have bound clients to the consequences of a lawyer's discovery failures. Or a client may lose a claim or defense for failure of the lawyer to prosecute (meet deadlines) or to assert the defense.[6]

Malpractice by Lawyer-Agents As stated, if a client does lose the right to assert a claim or defense in a litigation, or suffers a loss in a transaction, because of her lawyer's act or omission, whether negligent or intentional, the lawyer may be exposed to malpractice liability. In civil cases, the client will have to prove that the negligence proximately caused her loss, which means that she would have done better in the underlying negotiation or lawsuit (gotten more or had to pay less) absent the lawyer's negligence (see Chapter 24). In criminal cases, the situation is more complicated. Causation issues differ (also as discussed in Chapter 24). Merely proving that a criminal accused would likely have been acquitted if the lawyer hadn't erred will not entitle the client to sue the lawyer in most jurisdictions. Nor will it necessarily entitle the client to a new trial. One exception, as the *Taylor* excerpt recognizes, is that a client can (if rarely) avoid a defense lawyer's error (or improper conduct) if he can establish that the failure amounted to constitutionally ineffective assistance of counsel.[7]

Scope of Authority What is a lawyer's authority as an agent? Simply put, the lawyer has authority to act for the client in the area of (i.e., within the scope of) the representation. A handy test is to say that a lawyer, by virtue of retention, has the authority to choose the means for achieving the client's legal goal while the client has the right to decide on what the goal will be. Model Rule 1.2(a) puts it this way:

> Subject to paragraphs (c) and (d), a lawyer shall abide by a client's decisions concerning the objectives of representation and, as required by Rule 1.4, shall consult with the client as to the means by which they are to be pursued. A lawyer may take such action on behalf of the client as is impliedly authorized to carry out the representation. A lawyer shall abide by a client's decision whether to settle a matter. In a criminal case, the lawyer shall abide by the client's decision, after consultation with the lawyer, as to a plea to be entered, whether to waive jury trial and whether the client will testify.

That this ends/means distinction, while useful, is not entirely satisfactory is revealed in the comments to Rule 1.2, which provide in part:

> [1] Paragraph (a) confers upon the client the ultimate authority to determine the purposes to be served by legal representation, within the limits imposed by law and the lawyer's professional obligations. The decisions specified in paragraph (a), such as whether to settle a civil matter, must also be made by the client. See Rule 1.4(a)(1) for the lawyer's duty to communicate with the client about such decisions. With respect to the means by which the client's objectives are to be pursued, the lawyer shall consult with the client as required by Rule 1.4(a)(2) and may take such action as is impliedly authorized to carry out the representation.
>
> [2] On occasion, however, a lawyer and a client may disagree about the means to be used to accomplish the client's objectives. Clients normally defer to the special knowledge and skill of their lawyer with respect to the means to be used

to accomplish their objectives, particularly with respect to technical, legal and tactical matters. Conversely, lawyers usually defer to the client regarding such questions as the expense to be incurred and concern for third persons who might be adversely affected. Because of the varied nature of the matters about which a lawyer and client might disagree and because the actions in question may implicate the interests of a tribunal or other persons, this Rule does not prescribe how such disagreements are to be resolved. Other law, however, may be applicable and should be consulted by the lawyer. The lawyer should also consult with the client and seek a mutually acceptable resolution of the disagreement. . . .

A lawyer's reliance on the ends/means distinction to assume authority to make decisions without client consultation, even if technically correct so far as the ethics rules and agency law are concerned, can make for bad client relations. The fact that a question can be defended as one about means, not ends, and therefore within the lawyer's jurisdiction to resolve, may not impress clients, especially sophisticated clients, who expect to be (and are accustomed to being) consulted on any nonemergency question of even medium import to their matters. As far as court matters are concerned, however, unless a client explicitly withholds particular authority, a lawyer will have implicit (but still actual) authority to act to further the goals the client hired the lawyer to achieve.[8] In transactional matters including negotiations, persons with whom the lawyer deals will draw the same inference. These inferences reflect the fact that the decision about *how* to achieve the client's goals ordinarily belongs to the lawyer, although conscientious lawyers will routinely confer with the client before taking significant action. The inference is generally justified. After all, the reason the client went to the lawyer in the first place was to get help in achieving a goal (for the client to identify) with the benefit of the lawyer's legal knowledge and experience.

Then there is a concept called *apparent authority.* Even where the lawyer does *not* have authority in fact, whether implicit or explicit, he or she may appear to third persons to have it. Reliance on apparent authority will be honored. A lawyer has apparent authority when a client (or any principal) says or does something that gives others a reasonable basis to believe that the lawyer does have the particular authority. In other words, if a client by action or inaction encourages others to assume a lawyer has authority, that's enough for others to rely on it, even if the client has privately instructed the lawyer that he has no such authority.[9]

Authority to Settle   A final recurrent issue concerns settlement of claims. By hiring a lawyer, does a client give the lawyer actual authority to settle on terms the lawyer deems reasonable? Or must the lawyer get the client's consent? The Model Rules view settlement as an objective of the representation and for the client either to accept or not (although the client can delegate that decision in whole or in part to the lawyer, as she might by saying, for example, "I'm willing to pay up to $10,000, but get the best deal you can" or "Get whatever you think is the most they'll pay").[10] Merely by hiring a lawyer, a client does not impliedly gives the lawyer the power to settle on terms the lawyer deems just.[11] In any event, good lawyers will not settle without first going back to the client unless explicitly instructed otherwise. It is, after all, the client's money.

The Indiana Supreme Court has briefly set out the scope of a lawyer's various authorities (not only to settle). A lawyer had settled a client's claim in the course of mediation. The client refused to accept the settlement, which it said it had not authorized. The question was whether the lawyer's act bound the client. Notice in the following that although the court concludes that a client does not give a lawyer settlement authority simply by hiring the lawyer, the answer is different when the client sends the lawyer into a tribunal (which can include alternate dispute resolution or ADR) if the rules of the tribunal require the parties to appear by representatives with settlement power.

If an attorney settles a claim as to which the attorney has been retained, but does so without the client's consent, is the settlement binding between third parties and the client?

The answer to this question is the same as to many others: it depends. An attorney's authority may be derived from the conduct of the client, either with respect to the third parties who deal with the attorney or with respect to the attorney. It may also derive from the nature of the proceedings in which the attorney represents the client and enters into a settlement agreement. In order to bind the client the attorney must have either express, implied, or apparent authority, or must act according to the attorney's inherent agency power. For the reasons explained below, we conclude that the sole act of retaining an attorney does not give the attorney the implied or the apparent authority to settle or compromise a claim in an out of court proceeding. Specifically, retention in and of itself neither confers the implied authority to settle a claim, nor is it a manifestation by the client to third parties such that the attorney is clothed with the apparent authority to settle. However, under longstanding Indiana authority, retention does equip an attorney with the inherent power to bind a client to the results of a procedure in court. We hold that for purposes of an attorney's inherent power, a procedure governed by Indiana's Rules for Alternative Dispute Resolution (the "ADR rules") is a procedure "in court" if the parties are expected to appear by representatives with authority to resolve the matter. Accordingly, in the absence of a communication of lack of authority by the attorney, as a matter of law, an attorney has the inherent power to settle a claim when the attorney attends a settlement procedure governed by the ADR rules.[12]

"Inherent authority," mentioned in the quote, is an agency concept (recognized in some but not all jurisdictions) that posits that there "inheres" in the nature of the attorney-client (or other agency) relationship certain powers for the lawyer even if the client does nothing to create that power or to cause others to believe the lawyer has it.[13]

Fiduciary Duty   While all agents are fiduciaries and lawyers are the agents of their clients, it is obvious that courts consider lawyers to be something like *super*-fiduciaries, with an obligation of faithful conduct toward a client that is higher than what the law expects from any other fiduciary (or at least as high as the highest). Consider the language courts use. Lawyers are in a "unique position of trust and confidence," the Second Circuit Court of Appeals wrote in one case. In another case, the New York Court of Appeals also talked about a "unique fiduciary reliance." The definition of *unique* is one of a kind — in a class by itself — and the context of these two cases (the first involving a firm's loyalty, the second involving exorbitant fees) leaves no doubt about the meaning of the perceived uniqueness. Lawyers are held to the highest standards.[14]

But does the fiduciary duty carry obligations in addition to the other (ethical) attributes of the professional relationship studied here: competence, confidentiality, diligence, the duty to keep a client informed, the duty to put the client's interests above one's own, and so on? Probably fiduciary status adds no *additional* duty, encompassing all of them; it is instead meant to drive home the point that we expect lawyers to observe their obligations fully and without reservation. Any lawyer who seeks to lessen or qualify the degree of his or her duties to a client must expect to be met with the response that the claim is inconsistent with the lawyer's fiduciary status. The word *fiduciary* has a nice ring to it. It is a foreboding and constant reminder. And more than that, unlike its components as preserved in ethical rules (though not necessarily with the same terms as in case law), fiduciary duty is a *legal concept* so that violation of the duty carries enforceable civil law remedies.

It is worth recalling why lawyers are given these demanding duties. The lawyer-client relationship is not a relationship between equals. The client needs help, is perhaps in some trouble that can change her life, possibly irrevocably. As she sees it, the law is a mystery with its own language and procedures, traps, and tricks. Her lawyer is the person who must guide her through it to safety, if possible. She cannot protect herself in this strange world. Even if she knew how, the emotional toll would likely limit her objectivity and judgment. She needs an advisor who is there for her as against the world, or at least against anyone who would do her harm, who would take advantage. This is not a business deal where the parties are understood to be out for themselves. The client is by definition unable to be looking out for herself at this time, in this place. It is the stark differential in knowledge, in distance and objectivity, in vulnerability between lawyer and client that explains why the law deems the relationship fiduciary with all that entails.

Diligence   This is at once one of the most important obligations, looked at from the client's point of view, yet one of the most slighted and least enforceable. Wealthy clients need not worry quite so much about lack of diligence. A moneyed client has the means to fire the lawyer and hire another. Lawyers know that.

What do we mean by diligence? One definition is conscientious attention to a client's matter and pursuit of his goals. Model Rule 1.3 uses the word *promptness* and the comment suggests that "procrastination" may be the "shortcoming . . . most widely resented" by clients. Often, when lawyers fail in this duty it is because they have too much work and can't get to it. That's no excuse. The antidote is not to take on the work.

It is no wonder that lack of diligence should be a common complaint, particularly when the client is an individual or small company. From the client's point of view, delay in resolving a legal problem can take an emotional toll and disturb the equilibrium of the client's life (or business) even if no limitations period is missed and no legal rights are compromised. Where a lawyer represents a plaintiff who has been injured, the client may need money for medical bills or to cover lost income during recovery. Delay may push the client toward bankruptcy. But from the lawyer's point of view, delay may not be seen as problematic as long as the client's legal position is protected. The lawyer may not think about non-legal consequences of inaction, and that's a professional mistake.

It is difficult to make sure that lawyers behave diligently. How would we police it? A client is unlikely to have a malpractice action for delay if no legal rights or opportunities have been lost, if the only harm is living with uncertainty and anxiety. Besides, a client will not be eager to sue her lawyer for delay alone, even assuming that she could find (and pay) another lawyer to do so. Further, doing so will force her to hire a new lawyer for the original matter as well because the lawyer she sued can no longer represent her. The client can complain to the disciplinary authorities, of course, but may fear doing even that because it will antagonize the very person on whom she's relying to vindicate her legal rights.[15]

So the lack of diligence in legal representation, which the least powerful of clients are most likely to suffer, lacks an effective remedy except in extreme cases, such as when the delay causes the client to lose her right to sue or a defense.

The Duty to Inform   Even when a lawyer is diligent in working on the client's matter, it may not give the client much solace if he is not told what is happening in the matter or, if for good reason nothing is happening, telling the client at least that, with an explanation. Often the only way the client can learn about progress in the matter is from his lawyer. Clients may try to reach their lawyers to learn "what's happening in my case," but often they complain that the lawyer is unavailable, or in a conference, or in court, or at a meeting, and then they wait in vain for the lawyer to call back. This can happen through repeated calls. When I was in practice, my rule was always to return phone calls within one business day unless for some reason (like a trial or a vacation) I was unable to do so, in which case I asked a colleague or my secretary to call for me and explain my unavailability and when I would be able to return the call. I told new clients my one-business-day rule, and I commend it to my students. I tell them to imagine their anxiety about a medical problem and a doctor who fails to respond to their calls. This is just human decency, as far as I'm concerned, in addition to being an absolute requirement of professionalism (and good business).

The Duty to Inform and the Ends/Means Distinction A less client-centered way to look at the scope of a lawyer's duty to keep her client informed of the status of and developments in the matter is to say that the client only needs to know those things that bear on the decisions that clients are entitled to make. As we saw above, a traditional view had it that a client's decisions were few, mainly dealing with the objectives of the representation in a civil matter (including whether to settle a claim, whether to accept the terms of a deal), and in a criminal case limited to decisions whether to plead guilty, accept a plea bargain, testify, and appeal. Indeed, for many lawyers, especially in high-volume practices, that is the only time they feel obligated to confer. Lawyers may defend noncommunication by citing the time it takes, and therefore the expense, when there's nothing really to say and there's nothing for the client to decide.

This is quite wrong in my view. It is also not a good way to win the confidence of clients and build a practice, at least not if reliance on client recommendations are any part of a lawyer's business plan. And today, at least, it is also improper under governing ethics rules.

Even where clients do not have the authority to make decisions in a matter, they understandably want to know what is happening, or not happening. It is *the client*, after all, who will have to live with the result. Peace of mind is compromised by uncertainty and ignorance. Beyond that, as we saw above, the view that clients must defer to the choices of their lawyers on all questions except a few is no longer accepted, if it ever was. The ends/means distinction — where the lawyer alone chooses the means to achieve the client's ends — has never proved truly workable. For example, the decision whether a criminal accused will testify is, strictly speaking, a decision about means toward the end of an acquittal, yet it is a decision for the accused. The decision whether to assume an unusually large expense to search for information that may prove marginally helpful in a civil litigation is a decision about means, but since the expense will be paid by the client, he or she should decide, not the lawyer. And as we saw earlier, in this chapter, the comment to Model Rule 1.2, which sets out a nonexclusive list of decisions that belong to clients, recognizes that the ends/means decision is only a generalization and that the substantive law may give to the client the power to make decisions about certain means.

Conscientious lawyers, lawyers who exhibit the solicitude for the client's comfort and autonomy that we should expect from fiduciaries and professionals, will go out of their way to keep their clients informed about the status of their matters, to consult where time permits on significant strategic decisions, and to respond with dispatch to a client's request for information. Indeed, although the lawyer is the expert on the law, all legal problems emanate from a factual context (a business, a marriage, various kinds of relationships). The client is much more likely to understand the details of and the personalities of others in that factual context than is the lawyer. Seeking the client's participation in choices, even those that belong to the lawyer, is therefore likely to lead to the best decisions as a practical matter, in addition to being the appropriate way to behave.

Model Rule 1.4 requires as much. It is a significant advance over the language of the rule before the 2002 amendment. The earlier version of the rule, in paragraph (a), only required lawyers to "keep a client reasonably informed about the status of a matter and promptly comply with reasonable requests for information." (Paragraph (b), which is unchanged, required and still requires a lawyer to "explain a matter to the extent reasonably necessary to permit the client to make informed decisions regarding the representation.") This was not a particularly demanding duty, not least of all because of the wording: "reasonably," "reasonable," and "to the extent." The word *necessary* is begrudging. No wonder that lawyers might have read Rule 1.4, as originally adopted, as imposing only the most modest of duties.

Today, the Rule is more demanding. Paragraph (a) requires a lawyer to

(1) promptly inform the client of any decision or circumstance with respect to which the client's informed consent . . . is required . . . ;

(2) reasonably consult with the client about the means by which the client's objectives are to be accomplished;

(3) keep the client reasonably informed about the status of the matter; [and]

(4) promptly comply with reasonable requests for information. . . .

Paragraph (1) would encompass conflicts of interest that arise in the course of a representation. "Informed consent," referenced in paragraph (1), is defined expansively in Rule 1.0(e) to require "adequate information and explanation about the material risks of and reasonable alternatives to the proposed course of conduct." Paragraphs (2) and (3) reject the view that the client only needs to know information when the client has to make one of the few decisions reserved for clients. The soft word *reasonable* still populates the rule.

Of course, no one wants to require lawyers to do things that are *unreasonable*. But it might have been better if the comment had instructed lawyers to evaluate reasonableness from the viewpoint of the (often worried) client, not what the busy lawyer may conclude the client reasonably needs to know.

Autonomy of Lawyer and Client   Truth be told, the autonomy issue is not, strictly speaking, an "attribute" of the attorney-client relationship (a word used in the title of this chapter) in the same way as are confidentiality, fiduciary duty, and the other concepts discussed here. It may be more accurate to see autonomy as a moral imperative that can help us describe the lawyer's authority consistent with the claim to client self-determination that inheres in an enlightened concept of personhood. We have been identifying the various duties lawyers owe clients and their power as agents to affect the client in his or her relationship to rest of the world. Clients go to lawyers because they have problems or objectives requiring a knowledge of law that clients do not usually have. (Even if the client is a lawyer, he or she will lack the distance from the situation that dispassionate analysis will always demand.)

To put it starkly, a client wants something. Knowledge of the law is either helpful or required to get what the client wants. And so the client needs a lawyer to be his interpreter, guide, and perhaps advocate before the law. The law can be a dangerous place, and the client needs the lawyer to get him in and out of its powers in one piece.

For her part, the lawyer is trained to do just that. She has specialized knowledge. She is charged to exercise *independent professional judgment*. Each italicized word is important. Sometimes, the most important quality a lawyer can bring to a representation will be good *judgment*, which we may define (at least in part) as the capacity, based on experience, to make accurate predictions and correct choices from among several alternative courses of action, all in the face of often imperfect information. *Independence* is important because we want professionally disinterested lawyers to look for and see the situation in a way that a client, due to inexperience or stress or lack of knowledge, may not be able to do. Independence also informs the duty to avoid conflicts of interest.[16] And *professional* is part of the equation because it reminds us that the lawyer is bound by a set of ethical rules, is skilled, and is there to serve the client.

While it is well and good to emphasize the client-centered nature of this relationship — to say that the client is the principal, that the lawyer is an agent, that the lawyer is there only to serve the client — we must also remain cognizant of the fact that the lawyer as a professional needs to have discretion. Except for the simplest legal tasks, there is not only one single way to do things. The lawyer must choose from among alternatives, sometimes many alternatives. If a representation is a kind of journey from point *A* to point *B*, the lawyer can expect to come to many forks in the road. He must choose which to take. He is not a puppet or a mouthpiece. The lawyer may be the client's agent, but he is not a subordinate of the client whose only job is to do what he is told.

Finding the Proper Balance   So how do we reconcile that truth, as it certainly is, with respect for the client's personhood. One ingredient of personhood — if we're talking about a competent adult — is control over the decisions that affect your life. An autonomous person has the right to make choices about her life and to pursue them. That means trivial choices (which movie to see), momentous choices (whom to choose as a mate), choices in between (whether to take a gap year after college to live in Australia, whether to *move* to Australia). A person's choices may not be the same ones others — including the lawyer — might make, but that's irrelevant. Your choices may not be the wisest, but if they are not illegal and you're prepared to accept the consequences of your decisions (or realize that you'll have to accept them whether or not you're prepared), it's your call.

Hiring a lawyer necessarily limits a client's autonomy. Clients must cede some degree of control over their legal problems. If the problem is significant (a divorce after many years, a large financial dispute, the legal work incident to opening a business, the defense of a serious criminal charge), the lawyer will be making many decisions that can affect a client's life in profound ways. The challenge is to identify how much of the client's autonomy is appropriately ceded to the lawyer's domain as a professional. That domain constitutes the lawyer's autonomy.

The question of the scope of the autonomy of lawyer and client does not often arise in court. But in one case, the Supreme Court said that a lawyer representing a convicted man on appeal does not have to follow the client's instructions with regard to the points to argue in the appeal brief. The client wanted the lawyer to add arguments that the lawyer thought would detract from the strength of other arguments, although they were not frivolous. So he refused to add them. The Supreme Court held that the lawyer's refusal was not the ineffective assistance of counsel under the Sixth Amendment. Similarly, no court or disciplinary body would find it unethical to decline to add the client's arguments, although Justice Blackmun did write, in concurrence, that as an "ethical matter, a lawyer should argue on appeal all non-frivolous claims upon which his client insists." True, it is the client who would remain in prison if the appeal failed (which it did), not the lawyer, but the lawyer's autonomy entitled him to make this strategic decision, at least as far as the Sixth Amendment right to counsel was concerned. That doesn't mean the lawyer was obligated to reject the client's request. Many lawyers would defer to the client's wish after trying to talk him out of it by explaining why it was a really bad idea. But the fact that a lawyer could let the client's instruction control does not mean that she must.[17]

How to find the right balance between the lawyer's professional autonomy and the client's personal autonomy (which the lawyer partly controls when he decides how much to tell a client and when to seek the client's participation in a decision) is a real challenge. Factors that influence the decision are the legal complexity of the issue, the sophistication of the client, the client's preferences, the need for speed, the consequences of the decisions, and whether in the lawyer's view contrary decisions are plausible. Good lawyers, in my experience, err in favor of conferring with their clients when the question is in doubt even if, in the end, they may be prepared to "overrule" the client on a particular decision. Generally, the concern expressed by the act of conferring will encourage the best decision. The client might relent. The lawyer might learn new facts that change his position. The object is to avoid a situation where a tribunal somewhere will have to decide whether the lawyer crossed a line by usurping the client's right to decide. Lawyers who understand their instrumental role — that the matter is not "about them" — will respect the client's autonomy not only when they have to do so, but also because conferring, and often deferring, is the right and respectful thing to do.

ENDNOTES

1. *Brown v. Hebb*, 175 A. 602 (Md. 1934) (debt to doctor admitted when patient's lawyer offered to settle "for the services rendered"). *See also Fed R. Evid.* 801(d)(2)(C), admitting as a vicarious admission any out of court statement of an agent authorized to speak for a principal.
2. Fed R. Evid. 801(d)(2)(D).
3. *United States v. McKeon*, 738 F.2d 26 (2d Cir. 1984) (opening statement by lawyer at former trial admissible against client); *Dugan v. EMS Helicopters, Inc.*, 915 F.2d 1428 (10th Cir. 1990) (prior inconsistent pleadings admissible in evidence). These statements are admissible but not binding on the client, who is free to challenge them. But statements characterized as judicial admissions are binding. These include stipulations and opening statements to the jury in the case on trial. *DiLuglio v. Providence Auto Body, Inc.*, 755 A.2d 757 (R.I. 2000).
4. *See, e.g.*, Fed. R. Evid. 408.
5. *Taylor v. Illinois*, 484 U.S. 400 (1988).

6. *Cotto v. United States*, 993 F.2d 274 (1st Cir. 1993).

7. *Kimmelman v. Morrison*, 477 U.S. 365 (1986).

8. *The Restatement of the Law Governing Lawyers* §26.

9. *Id.* at §27. *United States v. International Brotherhood of Teamsters*, 986 F.2d 15 (2d Cir. 1993).

10. MR. 1.2(a). *The Restatement of Law Governing Lawyers* agrees in §22(1).

11. *Koval v. Simon Telelect, Inc.*, 693 N.E.2d 1299 (Ind. 1998).

12. *Id.*

13. *Id.*

14. *Milbank, Tweed, Hadley & McCloy v. Boon*, 13 F.3d 537 (2nd Cir. 1994); Matter of Cooperman, 633 N.E.2d 1069 (N.Y. 1994).

15. *In re Brown*, 967 So.2d 482 (La. 2007), is an example of discipline for neglect.

16. Numerous cases emphasize the importance of an attorney being able to exercise independent professional judgment, an ability that is compromised if the attorney allows the interests of others, including other clients, to influence his or her representation. *See, e.g., In re Rumsey*, 71 P.3d 1150 (Kan. 2003). *See also In Re Disciplinary Proceedings Against Felli*, 718 N.W. 2d 70 (Wis. 2006).

17. *Jones v. Barnes*, 463 U.S. 745 (1983).

~ 7 ~

How the Law Protects the Attorney-Client Relationship

The Rule Against Communicating with Opposing Clients

Special Issues for Entity Clients and Prosecutors

Protection of Privilege in Cases of Accidental Disclosure

What with all of the ethics rules and laws we've developed to safeguard the attorney-client relationship against abuse by lawyers and to encourage clients to trust their lawyers, you would expect to see other rules and laws that operate to protect that relationship against what we might call invasion or spying by outsiders. Of course, laws protecting privacy generally — such as those that make electronic eavesdropping, hacking into a person's computer, theft, and trespass a crime — protect lawyers and clients like everyone else. But you might expect to see something focused particularly on the attorney-client relationship. And you would be right. In several ways, the law and rules do operate to keep the attorney-client relationship free from meddlers.

The No-Contact Rule Probably the best known of these rules is called the "no-contact" or "anti-contact" rule. It is an infelicitous tag but now firmly embedded in the jurisprudence. It does what it says. It forbids contact between a lawyer and someone else's client under specified circumstances. The basic rule is concisely phrased and present in all U.S. jurisdictions. The American Bar Association (ABA) version (Rule 4.2) says, "In representing a client, a lawyer shall not communicate about the subject of the representation with a person the lawyer knows to be represented by another lawyer in the matter. . . ." The rule is not limited to situations where the represented person is the direct opponent of another client. It applies where two clients have exactly the same interests, as might two defendants in a civil or criminal case or two plaintiffs in a civil matter, but separate lawyers. And the rule is not limited to litigation or disputes. It applies in transactional matters, too.

The rule has two exceptions. The other lawyer can authorize the communication with his or her client, and substantive law or a court order may override the rule.

Preconditions for the No-Contact Rule Note the several prerequisites for the rule to apply. *First,* the contacting lawyer has to be representing a client "in the matter" for the rule to apply. A lawyer without a client in the matter can communicate with another lawyer's client about the subject of that client's representation. So Lawyer Jones can talk to Lawyer Smith's client about the matter Smith is handling if Jones has no client in that matter. This is important. It allows clients who are unhappy with their lawyers, or who just want a second opinion, to consult a second lawyer without getting permission from their current one, whom perhaps they would prefer not to tell.

Second, the rule does not apply unless the communication is on the subject of the other lawyer's representation. So even if Jones is representing Ann in negotiating a deal with Clare, whom Smith represents, Jones does not violate the rule by communicating with Clare about anything other than the deal (say the weather or the Yankees).

Third, of course, the other person must have a lawyer in the matter. The rule does not apply if Clare is unrepresented, although another rule does apply, specifically Rule 4.3, which sets down some fairness requirements when a lawyer is dealing with an unrepresented person.

Fourth, for the rule to apply, the first lawyer (Jones) must *know* that Clare has a lawyer in the matter. Knowledge means actual knowledge, which can be inferred from the circumstances.[1] Belief is not enough. Nonetheless, it will sometimes behoove the careful lawyer who does not know that the other person has a lawyer in the matter to inquire before moving on to talk about the subject of the representation. While an affirmative answer will end the conversation, it also protects the inquiring lawyer, who may be overly optimistic in concluding that he does not "really and truly know." A tribunal may later conclude otherwise.

Fifth, the rule only forbids "communication." In one case, a court held that lawyers who set up a video camera outside a retail establishment to record how employees treated minority customers were not communicating within the meaning of the rule, just taking pictures.[2]

Violation Through Intermediaries and Waiver   Here are two other things to know about the rule: First, lawyers may not do through a third person what they may not do directly.[3] Often, lawyers use investigators to gather facts. The lawyer may not instruct or allow an investigator to do what he or she may not do. And to ensure that the investigator behaves as the lawyer must, the rules in all jurisdictions require lawyers to supervise "non-legal" personnel, including investigators.[4] "Don't ask, don't tell" won't cut it. Even a negligent failure to supervise investigators or other non-legal personnel can get a lawyer into trouble.[5] Second, and what might seem astonishing at first glance, the no-contact rule is not one that a client can waive. If a client, on his or her own, calls or drops in on the opposing lawyer, perhaps because he thinks he might able to achieve a resolution that his own lawyer has failed to effect, the first lawyer must refuse to talk to him (and, as a matter of prudence, should then call the other lawyer, recount what happened, and tell her to tell her client to cut it out).

The rule is obviously paternalistic. Listed below are the policies behind the rule, but essentially the rule means to protect clients from opposing lawyers. Clients need this protection whenever a communication is directed at the subject of the representation, which includes whether to waive protection *of the rule itself*. In other words, the rule operates on the assumption that clients need the advice of counsel before they can decide to proceed without the advice of counsel.

Reasons for the No-Contact Rule   As stated, the rule's purpose is to protect the represented client from another client's lawyer. Protecting the client is the lawyer's job, of course, but she cannot do so effectively if the opposing lawyer is free to communicate with the client directly. What might a lawyer achieve in a direct contact with an opposing client? She can try to learn historical facts or obtain documents that she could not otherwise get because of privilege or for another reason. She could seek to learn the other lawyer's strategy or the client's bottom-line settlement or negotiating position. She could use the opportunity to undermine the client's confidence in his case or his lawyer. The questioned client may make a damaging statement admissible against him at trial. Or the client may reveal a fact that will lead to adverse evidence. The premise here is that lawyers have the training and experience to get people to talk or reveal facts, even otherwise sophisticated people, when their lawyers are not present to protect them. The premise seems intuitively correct, which doesn't mean that a lawyer will always succeed in such efforts.

Unpopularity of the Rule   Oddly enough, many lawyers and clients don't like this rule, at least not in its absolute form, but not because the lawyers want to try to take advantage of other lawyers' clients. They see it as highly inefficient (not to mention expensive) to have all communications go through opposing lawyers even when there is no risk they will be able to or even want to take advantage of the opposing clients. Very often, the clients are highly sophisticated and will give nothing away. I am told that common practice in some industries is for lawyers routinely to communicate directly with clients of other lawyers. Music and entertainment lawyers sometimes say this. Labor lawyers and mergers-and-acquisition lawyers do, too. Lawyers who structure big-ticket deals (lots of zeroes) tell me things move too quickly to deal with the no-contact issues, and besides, they don't even know when the deals begin who'll be part of it as it proceeds. So deal lawyers say there is a "Wall Street exception" to the rule. But there isn't.

I hear these and other complaints at legal ethics continuing legal education (CLE) talks. It would drive up the costs for clients if they could not talk to other clients' lawyers directly, I'm told. The particular area of business would be seriously hobbled. What can I answer? Perhaps this is all true, but the rule is the rule. Anyway, there is an easy solution, at least on paper. Have each lawyer sign on to an e-mail chain giving blanket authorization for each other lawyer to communicate with his or her client. Somehow, though, my audiences do not find this solution satisfactory.

The lawyers who argue for a less airtight rule for *their* kind of practice would probably agree that the rule makes a great deal of sense when the clients are unsophisticated in the use of lawyers, especially in litigation. They emphasize that their clients — businesspeople, union officers, entertainment agencies — are not pushovers, know a lot, and can protect themselves. In this critique we see a fundamental problem with the ethics rules, present elsewhere, too. The text of the rules does not explicitly differentiate between sophisticated and unsophisticated clients, although to some extent the comments do.[6] If we think of lawyer ethics rules as mainly a consumer protection document, with the clients the consumers and the lawyers the merchants, the rules presume that all clients are equally in need of protection, absent contrary agreement. In other words, the "going in" presumption is that the client in every matter is most in need of protection, not least in need. This may be wise as a matter of policy even if it is not empirically true. It would be hard to draft a document that had different rules depending on client sophistication because it would be hard to define the precise boundary between the sophisticated and unsophisticated client. This is so because it would be hard to define *sophisticated*, a category that may vary in meaning depending on the nature of the matter.

So the rules err on the side of protecting the little guy on the assumption that the big guys can displace the no-contact rule (and many other rules) simply by agreeing to do so through their lawyers. But even if the decision to assume that all clients are unsophisticated in the first instance is wise, it does create the resistance that I encounter at CLE lectures.

Client-to-Client Contact   Sometimes two clients will want to discuss their matters — even two clients who are opponents in a negotiation or litigation. They may believe that they can "get to yes" faster than their lawyers seem to be able to do. And of course, they may be right. They're free to try. The rule only binds their lawyers. But either client may also ask his or her lawyer for guidance before making an overture. Or the lawyer may want to broach with his client the idea of talking to the other client and provide the guidance about how to do so. Is this allowed? Or will the lawyer be violating the rule that says you cannot do through a third person (here the client) what you cannot do directly? For a long time, the answer to this last question was either that it is not allowed (it would be a violation) or the answer was unclear and varied from place to place. It may still vary from place to place somewhat, but the ABA has decided that a lawyer may raise the idea and may provide the guidance. Comment [4] to Rule 4.2 states, "Parties to a matter may communicate directly with each other, and a lawyer is not prohibited from advising a client concerning a communication that the client is legally entitled to make."

There is one exception to the ability of clients to communicate with each other. If one of the clients is a lawyer (or if a lawyer is representing herself), then some courts have said the rule applies to that lawyer, too, although literally she is in the role of client.[7]

The No-Contact Rule for Organizations: Who Is the "Client"?   The rule is reasonably easy to apply when the other clients are individuals. But when a client is an organization, say a corporation, it becomes dramatically more challenging. With whom, then, can a lawyer not communicate? The person actually represented (the client) is the company, not any of its agents or employees. So can a lawyer freely communicate with the employees, managers, and officers of another lawyer's corporate clients? A yes answer would seem to deprive the company of all of the protection the rule offers by denying it the protection of its lawyer. The employees and agents of the company, if questioned outside the presence of corporate counsel, might reveal privileged or strategic information or even make damaging statements that the jurisdiction's evidence rules will admit against the company. But if *every* company employee and agent is out of bounds, won't that excessively expand corporate secrecy and control of information as well as impede informal (and cheaper) information gathering in favor of more expensive and often less productive formal discovery? Yes, it surely will.

The challenge has been to identify *which* organizational agents cannot be questioned. That is, who will be deemed the equivalent of the corporate client for purposes of this rule? These questions are not unlike a question we addressed in Chapter 5 — namely, the identity of those employees and agents of an organizational client whose communications with corporate counsel will be privileged. There may be temptation to say that if under *Upjohn* a particular employee's conversation with a company's lawyer is privileged (albeit with the company holding the privilege), then it should follow that the same employee should be seen to be within the scope of the no-contact rule. The two categories should be congruent in that view. But the policies behind the scope of the corporate attorney-client privilege are different from the policies behind the no-contact rule. Should that matter?

Judicial Reaction Courts have gone all over the place in deciding which organizational employees and agents cannot be contacted by another client's lawyer. One court said every agent and employee is the client for purposes of the no-contact rule.[8] Another went further and said that even *former* agents and employees are deemed clients.[9] Either holding is rather broad. The first no longer enjoys general acceptance, and the second has been rejected.

Most courts have employed narrower definitions, but not always by much. Today, three categories of employees and agents are clearly within the rule. First, it is generally agreed that high officials are clients for purposes of the rule because they can say or do things that legally bind or commit the company to a particular position.[10] (This makes sense but will often be irrelevant since persons in management's higher echelon are unlikely to talk to lawyers for opponents anyway.) Another generally accepted category includes those employees and agents of the company whose actions or failure to act may be imputed to the company for liability purposes.[11] This is the most important category. So, for example, where the charge against the company is an antitrust violation, the manager who negotiated the arrangement alleged to constitute the violation cannot be contacted because her conduct may form at least part of the basis for the company's potential liability. Also, where the claim is that the company's truck driver went through a red light, the driver could not be contacted because the liability of the company will depend on the company's vicarious liability for the driver's alleged negligence. The manager and the driver are deemed represented persons within the meaning of the no-contact rule. (One interesting wrinkle is that if the manager or driver hires his own lawyer on the matter, the no-contact rule still applies, but it is now *that* lawyer, not the company lawyer on the matter, who can consent to the contact. In fact, the company lawyer would then be bound by the no-contact rule not to communicate with the manager or driver on the subject of the representation without permission.)

The final generally accepted category, quite a narrow one, is to bring into the rule's protection those persons at a company who are directing or helping the company's lawyer on the matter.[12] The notion here is that the persons *instructing* counsel and those *helping* counsel (secretaries, investigators, paralegals) have significant access to protected information, which would be at risk if other lawyers could communicate with them outside the presence of company counsel.

Using the Vicarious Admission Rule as a Measure   The category that has caused the most trouble and still does consists of persons who are not in any of the other three categories but whose statements would be admissible against the company under the jurisdiction's vicarious admission rule in its law of evidence. Now, the vicarious admission rule is quite broad most places. A broad version appears in the Federal Rules of Evidence and has been highly influential in state evidence rules.[13] The federal rule allows in evidence as a hearsay rule exception (or to be precise as non-hearsay) statements by agents and employees of a party to a dispute if these statements are made within the scope of the agency or employment relationship and during its existence.[14] If we go back to our example of the truck driver in the accident, we saw that the driver could not be contacted because his conduct can be imputed to the company. But how about the company employee sitting next to the driver and who is there to help load and unload the truck? Assume that no one is alleging that this passenger was negligent, so his conduct will not be imputed to the company for the purpose of proving liability. But perhaps, under the jurisdiction's vicarious admissions rule, his statements about what he witnessed while on the job could be introduced in evidence against the company. If so, we can all see that the company would have an interest in bringing that person within the scope of the rule so that the opposing lawyer (or his investigator) would be forbidden to talk to him informally and get such a statement — just what the opposing lawyer would love to do.

On the other hand, if we read the rule to encompass persons who are mere witnesses, like the truck passenger, who happen coincidentally to be employees or agents of the entity, aren't we unduly expanding the number of people from whom information cannot be informally sought and therefore corporate secrecy? Besides, even if the employee says something against the company's interest and admissible in evidence, the company is free to challenge its accuracy. It's not *bound* by what he says. And remember, the employee doesn't have to talk to the other lawyer. In fact, the company's lawyer can encourage him not to do so. Rule 3.4(f)(1) lets the company lawyer "request" that the employee "refrain from voluntarily giving relevant information to another party." Last, we might ask why a jurisdiction's vicarious admission rule in its law of evidence — whatever sense it might make in the law of evidence — should determine the scope of its no-contact rule in the law governing lawyers. The two rules have different policies.

Nonetheless, many courts have used the vicarious admission rules as the measure of the no-contact rule when a client is an organization.[15] That approach seems now to have receded, though not eliminated, by three developments. First, the New York Court of Appeals rejected it in a case called *Niesig v. Team I*.[16] What's odd here is that New York law does *not* subscribe to a broad vicarious admission rule in the first place (it has not adopted the federal standard), so its refusal to extend its no-contact rule to, for example, the coworker of the truck driver who runs the light makes a lot of sense. Such coworkers could not make a vicarious admission under New York's narrow rule. But then courts in jurisdictions that *did* have a broad vicarious admissions rule followed *Niesig* anyway, essentially deciding (wisely) to unyoke the law of evidence from the law of lawyer ethics.[17] The next thing that happened was that the *Restatement of the Law Governing Lawyers* also refused to bring agents and employees within the no-contact rule simply because their statements could be vicarious admissions of their employers.[18]

And finally, the ABA, whose rule on the issue once used the vicarious admission rule as one measure of the scope of the no-contact rule, changed its mind and agreed with *Niesig* and the *Restatement*.[19] While the three sources — *Niesig*, the *Restatement*, and the ABA — use somewhat different language in stating their positions, their positions are essentially the same.

How Do You Know Whom You Can't Talk to Before You Talk to Them? One problem a lawyer may have in deciding whether he is free to request an informal interview with an organization's employee is that the lawyer may not know whether the employee falls within any of the three established categories for defining client identity under the no-contact rule. While the answer will likely be known for two of the categories, high officials and persons directing or implementing the advice of counsel, it will often be less clear for the last category — persons whose conduct may be imputed to the organization for liability purposes. Sometimes you can't know whose conduct you mean to impute to the company until you're well into investigation of the case. The lawyer may have to make an educated guess, assessing the risk. The same risk is present in jurisdictions that define as off-limits employees who can make vicarious admissions. Is the employee in a position to make vicarious admissions? How can the lawyer know in advance? A lawyer who wants to play it safe in any jurisdiction — and don't we all — can ask the judge for a ruling,[20] but unless that is allowed ex parte, doing so tips the lawyer's hand to the opposing lawyer. Alternatively, the lawyer can proceed with the interview but precede it by trying, through preliminary questions, to ascertain whether the employee is within any of the forbidden categories.

Identify Yourself When lawyers communicate informally with an organization's employees or former employees, or indeed with anyone else, some authority suggests that lawyers (or their investigators) should reveal their true status and purpose. The *Niesig* court "assume[d]" that the lawyer would do this. Is that the correct rule even when the lawyer and investigator are not making affirmatively false statements? In some situations, it would be silly to require this disclosure. Let's say a lawyer enters a (represented) retail establishment to see if it is passing off inferior goods as manufactured by its client. The lawyer wants to ask the salesperson for her client's product and see what happens. Requiring the lawyer to reveal his identity and purpose would defeat the effort. Besides, the lawyer is not saying anything untrue or even anything misleading and is certainly not seeking to learn information that is not freely shared with all customers. She is merely asking what any customer might ask.[21] Nonetheless, is the lawyer's conduct misrepresentation? Is it deceptive? She is not really a customer. And Rule 8.4(c) forbids "dishonesty," "fraud," and "misrepresentation." Is this the sort of thing the rule is getting at? Unlikely, on these facts. As it happens, there has been much debate of late about when lawyers or those working for them should be allowed to engage in deception or misrepresent their purpose in order to gather information. This topic is further addressed a little later in the chapter. Whether or not the investigation is allowed, however, a lawyer should not seek to elicit privileged information or other legally protected information from the source.

The No-Contact Rule in Law Enforcement The debate over the reach of the no-contact rule is of special interest to government lawyers, mostly prosecutors, whose job is law enforcement. These lawyers (and let us talk of prosecutors) often supervise investigators, and, indeed, we may want them to do so in the hope that lawyers will be able to restrain abusive and possibly illegal tactics. But it is in the nature of investigation that sometimes investigators misrepresent their purpose or identity in order to gather information. Sometimes, investigators and the lawyers who supervise them rely on an undercover informant who, perhaps as part of an exchange of cooperation for a lower sentence or nonprosecution, will try to get information or incriminatory admissions from targets who don't know that they have "turned." Sometimes the undercover person is a law enforcement person. The informant or investigator may be "wired" to preserve the target's admissions. And, finally, sometimes the individuals to whom the investigator or informant talks are known to have legal counsel on the matter. Can a prosecutor supervise such conduct without running afoul of the no-contact rule?

For a long time, the courts avoided this question. Then the Second Circuit Court of Appeals, applying the New York version of the no-contact rule, said the answer was no — prosecutors could not do this — which caused massive tremors in the U.S. Justice Department and state prosecutorial offices.[22] The Justice Department fired back with the claim that its lawyers were not subject to state ethics rules, not even in the states in which they were admitted or practiced, so long as they were enforcing federal law. The ABA challenged this claimed exemption. The battle of words escalated. To buttress its position, Justice purported to adopt rules governing contacts with persons or parties represented by counsel — rules that, as you might imagine, permitted most such conduct — and to argue that with these rules in place, the contacts fell within the "authorized by law" exception to the no-contact rule because the rules were "law."

The McDade Amendment The Eighth Circuit rejected that claim on the ground that the Justice Department had no statutory authority to adopt the rules in the first place.[23] Congress had either to do so or to give the Justice Department the authority to do so, and Congress had done neither. Congress did then act, but not in the way the Justice Department wished. It adopted a law, called the McDade Amendment after Joseph McDade, its sponsor and a member of Congress whom the Justice Department had unsuccessfully prosecuted. The McDade Amendment obligated a government lawyer to comply with the "State laws and rules, and local Federal court rules" in the jurisdictions in which "such attorney engages in that attorney's duties, to the same extent and in the same manner as other attorneys in that State," even while enforcing federal law. And it directed the attorney general to adopt rules "to assure compliance" with the new law.[24]

One may question the wisdom of this law. Why subject federal lawyers, who are after all enforcing a uniform law nationwide, to the disparate ethics rules and court interpretations in each U.S. jurisdiction? Shouldn't the rules that govern a U.S. Attorney in Maine be the same as those that bind a U.S. Attorney in Texas? But that is not what McDade says, and it's the law.

"Authorized . . . by Law" Despite these setbacks, state courts seem willing to allow lawyers engaged in law enforcement greater freedom than private lawyers;[25] and if a state court (or a local federal court rule) allows it, McDade permits the conduct for federal lawyers working in the particular state or court. In the language of Rule 4.2, if the state or court permits the conduct, it is "authorized . . . by law" and outside the restriction of the Rule. Oregon has amended its ethics rules specifically to address the special case of lawyers in law enforcement and even private lawyers who claim a need to engage in deceptive practices.[26] Nonetheless, a federal lawyer like his or her state counterparts must be careful before authorizing or supervising undercover operations (where the target is known to have a lawyer on the matter) to make sure that the state or court in which he or she works will permit the conduct.

The No-Contact Rule and Private Lawyers What about private lawyers? Are there any special circumstances that will lead courts to relax the no-contact rule for their conduct even when a state's rules do not do so explicitly? The jury is still out on this question, but we have a few answers. There is sentiment in the profession that the conduct should be allowed in two kinds of cases. They are when the lawyer is investigating discrimination and when the lawyer believes that someone is violating her client's intellectual property rights.

Regarding discrimination, lawyers argue that the only way to prove it (short of admission or statistical sampling) is to send applicants with equal credentials to the employer or landlord (or other covered person). One applicant is white and the other is a member of a protected class. Their conversations are then secretly recorded to see if the decoys are treated differently.

With regard to intellectual property cases, a federal judge in New York refused to apply the rule where a lawyer suspected that a wholesale furniture business was violating his client's intellectual property rights. He sent investigators (one was his secretary) to the wholesale establishment posing as buyers. They recorded the salespeople's answer to questions they asked as "buyers," questions that a real buyer would ask, and the recorded answers (and their testimony) were later offered in court.

The judge rejected a motion to suppress the fruits of this investigation on the grounds that the no-contact rule was not intended to reach it, explaining that there was no other effective way to detect such conduct, that the questions of the salespeople did not overreach (they were not, for example, asked about communications with counsel), and that in any event the court was not obligated to suppress the evidence even if the rule had been violated.[27] While this decision is warmly embraced by many intellectual property lawyers, there is some inconsistent (if not contradictory) authority.[28]

Note that the use of undercover investigators or informants raises two other issues under ethics rules. First, by definition, the tactic involves deception, and, as stated, a lawyer is ordinarily forbidden to engage in deceit or misrepresentation directly or through another (and is obligated by Rule 8.4(a) to supervise non-legal personnel to ensure that they don't act in ways forbidden to the lawyer). Second, where the communication with a target is recorded, a question arises whether the secret recording is permissible even if legal (as it is under federal and many state laws if done with the permission of at least one participant to the communication). The deceit and recording did not trouble the New York federal judge in the case discussed above, where the goal was detecting violation of intellectual property rights. And the deceit, such as it was, consisted solely of pretending to be a buyer. But in other contexts, or even in other courts on the same facts, the answer may be different. So even where the no-contact rule is not an issue because the target of the contact is not known to have a lawyer in the matter, the deception that accompanies undercover work or other varieties of misrepresentation, and the proprietary of secret recording, must still be addressed.[29] Secret recording, in particular, requires attention. Even when legal, some local bar ethics committees say it is deceitful. The ABA, reversing a longstanding position, has concluded that the Model Rules do not forbid secret recording that does not violate law.[30]

Confidential Information Accidentally Revealed
Another prominent way in which legal and ethical rules protect the attorney-client relationship is to recognize that sometimes privileged information may be revealed accidentally, not intentionally, and when that happens it may not be appropriate to treat the event as a waiver of privilege. On the other hand, sometimes an accident is so careless that law and ethics will not step in to protect the client and lawyer from the conduct. The debate over this issue became particularly focused with the advent of facsimile transmissions, and then the debate continued with the introduction of e-mail. Either technology can easily result in a mistake, and both are instant or nearly instant, so there is little or no time to retract a mistake. For example, a secretary may punch the wrong number on the facsimile machine, sending a document intended for a client or co-counsel to the opposing lawyer instead or in addition. Or a lawyer may send an e-mail intended for co-counsel to an opponent by mistake. The danger of a misdirected e-mail is heightened because of address books that fill in names of intended recipients and because of "reply all" options.

Another way in which allegedly privileged information may reach an unintended recipient is in document discovery. Today, substantial litigation can encompass discovery of hundreds of thousands, even millions, of pages of documents, generally in electronic format. Even taking care, a law firm might let some privileged documents slip through as part of a document production. But whatever the particular context, the profession inevitably had to confront the same issue: Where communications claimed as privileged are erroneously sent to a third person, usually an opponent, will the privilege be lost, or will the sender be able to call it back? And what about a lawyer who receives the document and perhaps has started to read it before recognizing that it may have been sent in error? What is her responsibility? What do we do about the fact that she may have learned privileged or protected information in good faith, before realizing the mistake?

Promptly Notify After much consideration and some changes of mind, the ethical rule now seems to be this: The recipient under ABA Rule 4.4(b) must call the sender "promptly" if she knows or "reasonably should know" that the document was "inadvertently sent." Exactly how it can be expected that the recipient will notify the sender if she doesn't know but "should know" is unclear. Will failure to notify in those circumstances subject the recipient to discipline for not knowing what she should know as well as for failing to call the sender even though she is ignorant of the fact that creates the duty to call? It would seem so. In any event, the ABA rule imposes no other duty. Before the addition of Rule 4.4(b), the ABA read other provisions of the Model Rules to require the recipient to cease reading the document and to return it if requested or, if the recipient believed that the inadvertent transmission waived any privilege the sender claimed in the document, or that the document was in any event not privileged to begin with, the recipient could present that claim to the court.[31]

That additional responsibility is now gone. Today, the ABA's view is that whether the recipient of a misdirected facsimile or e-mail or material inadvertently included in response to discovery must do more than "promptly" notify the sender, that duty must come from law, not the ethics rules. But some state and local ethics committees continue to require more than just prompt notification, including the responses the ABA formerly required and now does not.[32] In any event, authorities agree that if the recipient has read any or all of the material prior to the time she knew or reasonably should have known (for example, from the context) that it was inadvertently sent, she is not foreclosed from using what she learned. In that instance, the problem stems entirely from the inadvertence (or even negligence) of the sender. The recipient will have done nothing wrong. Of course, this resolution depends on an honorable recipient, who might be sorely tempted to read the entire document and claim ignorance of the error.[33]

Metadata   Oddly enough, when it comes to another kind of accident — mistaken transmission of metadata — the ABA has refused to say whether Rule 4.4(b) even requires a recipient lawyer to notify the sender. (Metadata is content in an electronic document that the author has attempted to delete and which is not visible in the document but which can be revealed with various programs.) Some local bar committees have disagreed with the ABA on this point.[34]

Federal Rules   The problem of accidental transmission of allegedly privileged information has also engaged the law of discovery, at least at the federal level. Rule 26(5)(B) of the Federal Rules of Civil Procedure provides:

> If information is produced in discovery that is subject to a claim of privilege or of protection as trial-preparation material, the party making the claim may notify any party that received the information of the claim and the basis for it. After being notified, a party must promptly return, sequester, or destroy the specified information and any copies it has and may not use or disclose the information until the

claim is resolved. A receiving party may promptly present the information to the court under seal for a determination of the claim. If the receiving party disclosed the information before being notified, it must take reasonable steps to retrieve it. The producing party must preserve the information until the claim is resolved.

The Federal Rules of Evidence now have a parallel rule, which enables the sender to avoid loss of privilege.[35] Even where no procedural rule so provides, lawyers often enter into stipulations to the same effect.

ENDNOTES

1. See the definition of *knows* in Model Rule (MR) 1.0(f).
2. *Hill v. Shell One Co.*, 209 F. Supp. 2d 876 (N.D. Ill. 2002).
3. *See* MR 8.4(a).
4. *See* MR 5.3.
5. *In re Industrial Antitrust Lit.*, 1986 Westlaw 1846 (N.D. Ill. 1986), *vacated*, 1986 Westlaw 68509. The duty of reasonable care is also implicit in MR 5.3(e) and (b) which requires lawyers with managerial authority or direct supervisory responsibility over other lawyers to "make reasonable efforts to ensure that the firm has in effect measures giving reasonable assurance" that the nonlawyer personnel act compatibly with the lawyer's professional obligations.
6. *See, e.g.*, MR 1.7 cmt. [22] (dealing with prospective waivers of conflicts of interest.
7. *Matter of Haley*, 126 P.3d 1262 (Wash. 2006).
8. *Niesig v. Team I*, 545 N.Y.S.2d 153 (2d Dept. 1989), *reversed*, 558 N.E.2d 1030 (1990).
9. *Public Service Elec. & Gas Co. v. Associated Elec. & Gas Ins. Services, Ltd.*, 745 F. Supp. 1037 (D. N.J. 1990). This holding has now been universally repudiated, including in the New Jersey Rules of Professional Conduct.
10. MR 4.2 cmt. [7]; *Restatement of Law Governing Lawyers* §100. *See also Niesig v. Team I*, 558 N.E.2d 1030 (1990).
11. *Id.*
12. *Id.*
13. Federal Rule of Evidence 801(d)(2)(D) admits as an exception to the rule against hearsay "a statement by the party's agent or servant concerning a matter within the scope of the agency or employment, made during the existence of the relationship."
14. *Id.*
15. *See, e.g.*, *Midwest Motor Sports v. Arctic Cat Sales, Inc.*, 347 F.3d 693 (8th Cir. 2003).
16. *Niesig v. Team I*, 558 N.E.2d 1030 (1990).

17. *See, e.g., Messing, Rudavsky & Weliky, B.C. v. President and Fellows of Harvard College,* 764 N.E.2d 825 (Mass. 2002).

18. *Restatement* § 100.

19. MR 4.2 cmt. [7].

20. MR 4.2 cmt. [6].

21. The lawyer or investigator would still have to comply with M.R. 4.3, which concerns communication with unrepresented persons.

22. *United States v. Hammad,* 858 F.2d 834 (2d Cir. 1988).

23. *United States ex rel. O'Keefe v. McDonnell Douglas Corp.,* 132 F.3d 1252 (8th Cir. 1998).

24. 28 U.S.C. § 530B.

25. *See, e.g., United States v. Grass,* 239 F. Supp. 2d 535 (M.D. Pa. 2003).

26. *See, e.g.,* Oregon Rule 8.4(b), which permits lawyers to supervise "covert activity in the investigation of violations of civil or criminal law or constitutional rights," provided a lawyer's conduct otherwise complies with the Rules of Professional Conduct. As another exception, some state rules explicitly, and the ABA by construction of its rules, have concluded that the anti-contact rule does not apply to the same extent when the adversary is the government. See ABA Opinion 97-408; *Restatement* § 101.

27. *Gidatex, S.r.L. v. Campaniello Imports, Ltd.,* 82 F. Supp. 2d 119 (S.D.N.Y. 1999).

28. *Midwest Motor Sports v. Arctic Cat Sales, Inc.,* 347 F.3d 693 (8th Cir. 2003).

29. In a related area, the D.C. Bar's ethics committee has concluded that a government lawyer who authorizes deception in an investigation is not violating the ethics rule that prohibits false or deceptive statements because the lawyer is not acting in a representative capacity (for a client) but in an enforcement capacity. See D.C. Opinion 323 (2004). Whether the D.C. Bar's distinction will be embraced for the no-contact rule is another matter.

30. ABA Opinion 01-422 (taping permitted); NYC Opinion 03-02 (routine taping not permitted with exceptions).

31. ABA Opinion 92-368, now superseded by ABA Opinion 05-437. For an example of an inadvertent disclosure in the course of informal discovery where the judge found that the lawyer's sloppiness led to loss of privilege, *see SEC v. Cassano,* 189 F.R.D. 83 (S.D.N.Y. 1999).

32. *See, e.g.,* NY City Opinion 2003-04.

33. *Id.*

34. ABA Opinion 06-442. Compare N.Y. Opinion 749 (2001).

35. Federal Rule of Evidence 503.

~ 8 ~

Lawyers and Money

The Market for Legal Services

What Rules Govern the Size of Legal Fees?

Special Issues for Contingent Fees

In criminal cases, indigent defendants are constitutionally entitled to free counsel. Some statutes provide for counsel for indigent parties in civil cases. But these avenues aside, lawyers charge fees and clients pay them. In certain cases, a statute will provide that the opposing party can be ordered to pay a lawyer's fee where the lawyer prevails through trial or settlement. Civil rights, antitrust, and some intellectual property cases are in this category.[1] In class action cases and common fund cases (where a lawyer produces a fund to be shared by a large group), a judge will determine the amount of the lawyer's fee, which may be paid by the adversary or from the recovery for the class.[2] Sometimes lawyers work for nothing, of course. They help out a friend or a friend of a friend. More often, they do work *pro bono publico* ("for the public good"), representing, for example, an indigent civil plaintiff, an asylum seeker, or a nonprofit or community group. Larger law firms, which can more readily afford to do free work, often stress their pro bono contributions in part because it helps them recruit new lawyers.[3] State and federal governments provide some money for civil representation even though they are not generally required to do so. But representation in civil matters, whether for free or paid by someone else, is much the exception. Overwhelmingly, if you want to hire a lawyer, you pay. To make a will. To sell your house. To get divorced. Even when the fee is contingent on the outcome of the matter, as it is for most personal injury plaintiffs, clients pay by giving the lawyer what in effect is an interest in their claim and a portion of the recovery if successful.

The Market in Legal Services Of interest here are the rules that govern the permissible size of a fee and other requirements for fee agreements. But before we even discuss those rules, it bears emphasis that the single most important factor influencing the amount of a legal fee is the market for legal services. In other words, supply and demand. If a prospective client and a lawyer agree on a fee, rarely will a court upset it or, still more rarely, will a disciplinary committee find it to be unethical based on size.[4] Market control is of no special concern — indeed it is healthy — when the client is as knowledgeable as the lawyer in what different legal services are worth and the relative value of lawyers, which in turn will depend on their specialty and experience and the geographical market in which they practice. (Hourly rates in New York and Los Angeles will be higher than those in St. Louis and Omaha for the same work.)

Equal knowledge and bargaining power will be true for corporate and other organizational clients that routinely retain lawyers and which may even negotiate the fee arrangement through in-house counsel. But it is not true for those individuals or small companies who rarely need to hire a lawyer. The client who wants to be a knowledgeable consumer can somewhat correct for the imbalance in market savvy by shopping around and getting different "quotes" for a matter. That strategy — wise, but too often ignored — will provide comparative numbers. But it will be a real challenge, and probably impossible for most occasional users of legal services, to evaluate worth or value. That is, the lawyer who charges $300 hourly may provide better value than the lawyer who charges $200 per hour either because the first lawyer will do a better job or because she'll do it faster, and so more cheaply. But maybe not. It will be the rare client without current experience in the legal marketplace who is able to compare and predict quality with anything approaching precision let alone monitor the work. It is hard enough for those in the know.

The Ethics of Fees   What do the rules say? We now turn to the rules governing legal fees. The Model Rules (like the Model Code before it) contain a list of factors to evaluate when judging whether a fee is too high.[5] What is too high? At one time, a fee was not too high for the ethics rules unless it was "clearly excessive," and it was clearly excessive only if "a *lawyer* of ordinary prudence would be left with *definite and firm* conviction that the fee is in excess of a reasonable fee"[6] (emphasis added). The profession took a lot of criticism for the italicized modifiers. The test was seen to present almost no limit; linguistically, it seemed to favor lawyers heavily. It is certainly not a test that a consumer protection group would ever write. American Bar Association (ABA) Model Rule 1.5(a) now tones down the rhetoric, but the effect on substance is anything but clear. The rule forbids an "unreasonable fee." (It also forbids an "unreasonable amount for expenses," which means to control the lawyer's markup for the cost of in-firm services like photocopying or electronic research.) Even though the language of the test has changed from the Code to the Rules, one thing has not changed: Each document lists eight factors to be weighed in determining whether a fee passes the test that the document prescribes. These eight factors, which have often been cited in court decisions, are:

(1) the time and labor required, the novelty and difficulty of the questions involved, and the skill requisite to perform the legal service properly;

(2) the likelihood, if apparent to the client, that the acceptance of the particular employment will preclude other employment by the lawyer;

(3) the fee customarily charged in the locality for similar legal services;

(4) the amount involved and the results obtained;

(5) the time limitations imposed by the client or by the circumstances; (6) the nature and length of the professional relationship with the client;

(7) the experience, reputation, and ability of the lawyer or lawyers performing the services; and

(8) whether the fee is fixed or contingent.

The interesting thing about a few of these factors is that they would appear to have been written (at least in part) to enable a judge or tribunal to determine an appropriate fee in retrospect. That can occur in cases where the court is called upon to set the fee (as in fee shifting cases) or where for some reason the lawyer and client did not agree on the fee at the outset and cannot agree after the work is done; as a result the dispute goes to court. For example, "results obtained" (#4) is not something a lawyer or client can evaluate at the outset. The "difficulty of the questions involved" (#1) may not be known, or well known, until the middle or at the end of the matter. Even numbers 2 and 5 may not be fully known at the outset. But the other factors can all be weighed when the fee is set in advance. Another oddity about the list is that it offers no guidance about how to weigh each factor. Is it possible for one of them, say the "amount involved" or "the experience" of the lawyer, to weigh so heavily on the scale that it can justify a very high fee even if the other factors would not? We don't know the relative weight of each factor. Probably, none can be easily identified.

The upshot is that as a practical matter one or two things will be true: Because the factors are so general and the rule does not assign them relative weight, only in the rare case will a fee be found to violate the provision; and in setting a fee, a lawyer who consciously consults the rule, where the question is close, will find it hard to predict whether his fee will be upheld. Between these two possibilities, the first is certainly true. Rarely are fees found to violate the rule. As for the second, it will be the unusual lawyer who consults the rule when setting a fee. Any consultation will more likely occur if and when the fee is challenged.

Telex v. Brobeck: A Test Case   Telex Corporation challenged the million-dollar fee of the Brobeck law firm back in the 1970s for work Brobeck did in an antitrust case.[7] The firm earned the fee under a written agreement with Telex that required it to file a certiorari petition to the Supreme Court on Telex's behalf. The Brobeck lawyer whom Telex wanted was Moses Lasky, a preeminent American antitrust lawyer. Lasky's petition persuaded Telex's opponent, IBM, to settle a case that had resulted in a large judgment against Telex, threatening it with bankruptcy. At trial, Telex had won a much larger judgment against IBM, but Telex's trial court victory had been reversed on appeal to the Tenth Circuit while IBM's judgment against Telex was affirmed. After Lasky filed his petition, days before the Supreme Court was expected to rule on it, IBM settled for a "wash" (neither party paid the other anything) to avoid the risk, however slim, that the huge trial court judgment against IBM would be reinstated.

Brobeck's fee agreement was complicated. The fee would depend on how the dispute was resolved, whether in settlement or in court. The agreement contained many permutations. The complex fee formula provided that a "wash" settlement would yield Brobeck a fee of $1 million, which Telex challenged as unconscionably high. It was certainly high. No question about that. The certiorari petition could not have required more than 200 hours of work (and probably less). Meanwhile, in 2009 dollars, the Brobeck fee would translate into about $4 million, or more than $19,000 hourly. The Ninth Circuit, which approved the fee under the very deferential California standard at the time, emphasized the risk of bankruptcy to Telex, the fact that the fee was contingent (but see below), and the fact that the fee was negotiated by in-house Telex lawyers (who wanted Lasky, had shopped around, and would be expected to know what they were doing). The court concluded, quoting California precedent, that "the contract . . . was not so unconscionable that 'no man in his senses and not under a delusion would make on the one hand, and as no honest and fair man would accept on the other.'"[8]

Brobeck's fee was not entirely contingent. The firm also got a nonrefundable retainer of $25,000. Assuming again that the work took 200 hours, that's $125 hourly. The fee agreement was reached in 1975. In 2009 dollars, that's an hourly rate of more than $500, and it was guaranteed above and beyond the contingent part of the fee.

Would a court reach the same result today after analyzing the list of factors in Rule 1.5? Almost certainly it would, despite the facially more demanding test in the Model Rule, given the sophistication of the client (a factor that now appears in the California counterpart to Rule 1.5), the fact that the fee was negotiated through lawyers, the risk facing the client (bankruptcy), the partially contingent nature of the fee, and the prominence of the lawyer. But if the client were not experienced in the legal marketplace, or the lawyer were the not the equal of Moses Lasky, or the fee were determined to be way out of line with what other lawyers of equal stature would charge for the same service, the result might have been different. And if all of these differences were present, the ruling would certainly have been different.

Timing and Writing Requirements for Fee Agreements
The Model Rules do not require that noncontingency fee agreements be in writing, although doing so is said to be preferred. It is in the interests of everyone to have a writing. It avoids misunderstanding and focuses the client's attention. The failure of the ABA to require a writing is a major shortcoming of a set of rules whose overarching purpose is client protection. Many states do require a writing, including California, Ohio, New York, and Washington, DC.[9] Exceptions are sometimes made when the fee is small or the lawyer has regularly represented the client. As for timing, it is best if the fee agreement is reached before the client formally retains the lawyer. The client has the greatest freedom to choose at that point. He can just walk away.

If the issue of fee arises only after the lawyer has started work, perhaps after the client has paid a retainer, it will be harder for the client to change lawyers if the fee demand is unacceptable. The client has less and possibly no leverage. From the lawyer's point of view, it is also best to reach the fee agreement at the outset. This is because until the lawyer is retained, he or she has no fiduciary duty to the client. The negotiation is arm's length. Fee agreements first reached or revisited after the lawyer has begun work, and therefore after the fiduciary relationship is in place, will be viewed with heightened scrutiny. Courts will impose a greater duty on the lawyer to show that these post-retainer agreements are fair. They will no longer be seen as the product of arm's-length negotiation.[10] This is in line with the courts' general suspicion of business deals between lawyers and clients that are reached during the professional relationship.[11] The ability of the lawyer to overreach in business deals with current clients, to favor her interests over those of the client who may (mistakenly) rely on the lawyer's fairness and concern for the client, leads to greater judicial scrutiny, as we shall see in Chapter 11.

Nonrefundable Fees Although the ethics rules do not address the issue of nonrefundable fees, courts have done so. A nonrefundable fee is what the name implies — a payment that the lawyer can keep no matter what happens in the case. Sometimes nonrefundable fees can result in an unethical fee, and sometimes they make a whole lot of sense. To take the first situation, imagine a lawyer who accepts a nonrefundable retainer of $15,000 for a seemingly complicated civil litigation. The amount will be applied against the lawyer's time charges but is denominated as nonrefundable. On the day of the retainer, the amount is reasonable given the nature of the dispute and the time it is expected to take. Within a day, and before the lawyer has done more than an hour or two of work, the litigation is withdrawn. Or perhaps the client decides she doesn't want that lawyer. If the lawyer gets to keep the $15,000 anyway, shouldn't we say that under the circumstances, it is too much even if it wasn't too much when paid? Also, if the client will get nothing back, it makes it hard for her to change lawyers the next day since she may not have the money to retain a second lawyer.

But what about the lawyer's interests? Is she limited to her time charges — two hours of work? She has sold something beyond time. She has promised availability and stands ready to provide it before the case ends prematurely or the client decides to change lawyers. You can even imagine a situation where a client is willing to pay for availability alone. For example, a client may be entering a deal where it may or may not need the lawyer's help but if it does need the help, it wants the lawyer to commit herself now. ("If something happens, I want to know that I can call you and you'll drop everything and take the matter.") That promise limits the lawyer's professional choices (she can't say no when the call comes, if it comes) and has value even if the lawyer, as it turns out, never spends a minute on the matter because as it happens, the work doesn't arise. And in either of these situations — where the client becomes a client for a day and then discharges the lawyer or where the client hires the lawyer only for the promise of availability—a further consequence is to limit the ability of the lawyer and her firm colleagues to accept those new matters that, under conflict rules, are precluded by the retainer. So it makes much sense to say that the lawyer is not restricted to time charges. She is selling something more and giving up something more. Nonetheless, whatever she gets to keep beyond her time multiplied by her hourly rate must still satisfy the Rule 1.5 criteria. So there is a ceiling on the size of the fee, but it's not necessarily the number on the meter, so to speak.

The New York Court of Appeals, in a somewhat unclear opinion, seems categorically to have condemned nonrefundable fees.[12] This was particularly unnecessary because the court could have reached the same result by holding that the amount of money the lawyer claimed he was entitled to keep (a lot), even after the clients discharged him within days, was far too high to be ethically tolerable, especially as the clients were unsophisticated individuals and needed a refund to hire other counsel. The opinion ignored important distinctions, used terms like "general retainer" and "minimum fee" without definitions, and all in all left the area in great doubt.

But other courts and authorities have recognized the complexity of the problem and distanced themselves from a categorical condemnation of nonrefundable fees. For example, in one case a law firm agreed to serve as national coordinating counsel for a corporate client facing multiple asbestos lawsuits around the country. The client paid a $1 million nonrefundable fee for availability and set costs, but it then fired the firm after only ten weeks. It sued to recoup some of its retainer. The Third Circuit affirmed summary judgment for the law firm. The client had paid the retainer to buy the "opportunity" to use the firm's services at capped costs. And it got what it wanted. The payment was earned when paid because it guaranteed the client the comfort of favorable rates going forward. The fact that the client ultimately chose not to utilize those services did not change the fact that it got what it wanted.[13]

Contingent Fees Discussion of the *Brobeck/Telex* case earlier in this chapter broached the often controversial issue of contingent fees, a particularly (if not a unique) American phenomenon. A contingent fee is what the name describes — a fee whose payment depends (is contingent) on an occurrence in the matter that is not certain. Because it is not certain, a lawyer who works on contingency takes a risk that he or she will not get paid if the contingency does not occur. Or not get paid as much. Fees can be blended, part contingent, and part certain, which is what happened in the *Brobeck* case. Lawyers and clients can agree on contingent fees in most any kind of case, but not in criminal cases; and most places, fees in matrimonial cases cannot be contingent on divorce or the amount the client receives in support or division of property.[14] Contingent fees are most common in personal injury (and property damage) cases, and we'll discuss them mostly in that context. First, though, a short digression to explain why public policy forbids them in criminal and matrimonial cases.

Contingent Fees in Criminal Cases In criminal cases, the explanation is pretty straightforward. A fee contingent on, say, acquittal outright, or acquittal of the most serious charges, or even on nonconviction (because of a hung jury) gives the lawyer great incentive to go to trial. Only with a trial can he bring about the contingency that will produce the payoff. What that means, in turn, is that the lawyer has a disincentive to have the client accept a plea bargain that will not trigger the contingency and produce the fee. For example, the fee agreement might provide for payment only if the client is not convicted of a felony. The plea offer may be to a low-degree felony and a short sentence where the client faces a higher degree felony and a long prison term if convicted of the higher crimes charged. How can the lawyer offer the client disinterested advice on the wisdom of accepting the offer? How can he exercise independent professional judgment? Even the most honorable of lawyers may find it hard to separate his interests from those of the client (the more so the greater the contingent fee). Perhaps he can, but we can't know. The criminal justice system itself (meaning the state) has an interest in fairness and accuracy and confidence in the eventual verdict, which may be undermined if a lawyer is tempted to look out for his own, and not only his client's, interest.

A little reflection tells us that the skewing of incentives when criminal cases are handled for a contingent fee will also arise in civil cases. Depending on the contingency and the formula for determining the fee, the chance that the lawyer's recommendations between two or more alternatives will be affected by her fee interest cannot be ignored. If we are nonetheless going to permit contingent fees in civil cases, and we do, it has to be because there are strong policy reasons to do so and because the effect on judgment will not be so potentially acute. As for the policy reasons, the state may be seen to have a stronger interest in accuracy in criminal verdicts than in civil ones. Also, in criminal cases, the state will provide a free lawyer to defendants who cannot afford one, which eliminates the client's need to use the lure of a contingent fee to attract a lawyer if he is to have a lawyer at all.

Contingent Fees in Matrimonial Cases The absolute prohibition against contingent fees in matrimonial cases, though widespread, is not universal. Virginia, for example, will allow them in "rare circumstances."[15] But most places, the prohibition is against a fee contingent on securing a divorce or a fee that is set as a percentage of the amount of alimony, support, or property awarded. Some states also expressly forbid a contingent fee in custody matters or on securing an annulment. The policy behind these prohibitions is easy to identify but perhaps less strong, at least in present times, as is the policy forbidding contingent fees in criminal matters. The rules eschew giving a lawyer a financial incentive to secure a divorce when reconciliation may be in the client's interest and perhaps better for the family unit, including children. If the fee is contingent on divorce, a lawyer may be tempted to encourage animosity to ensure that the client does not change her mind. The prohibition on a contingent fee tied to alimony, support, or property has a different focus. Even if there is a divorce, the law favors harmony where possible and especially so if there are young children. A lawyer whose fee is tied to the amount of alimony or property he can win may resort to tactics that, though legal and ethical, inflame the situation. Behind all this are rules that enable a judge to require the more affluent spouse to pay all or some of the counsel fees of the other spouse. This opportunity for fee shifting is seen as sufficient to assure the lawyer of payment even when his client is the nonmoneyed spouse. Consequently, there is no need for the incentive of a contingency fee in this view. These justifications have merit, but to some, perhaps, not so much merit as they may have had when divorce was uncommon and seen as unfortunate, to be avoided if at all possible.

We should take note of one oddity and one exception in the subject of matrimonial contingent fees. The oddity first: As we saw above, one factor in determining a reasonable fee is the "results obtained." If a judge is asked to set a fee in a matrimonial case, perhaps because the opposing spouse will pay it or because lawyer and client have for some reason failed to agree on the fee at the outset, can the judge consider and be asked to consider the results obtained, which would presumably include the alimony, support, or property recovery? If so, isn't the judge then calibrating the fee according to the value of the recovery, which gets rather close to a contingent fee? It is not a contingent fee exactly because there is no fixed percentage. Still, if the factor is permitted, it can lead to an incentive on the part of the lawyer that the prohibition against contingent fees is partly meant to avoid (i.e., inflammatory tactics to increase the recovery and therefore the fee). So if judges can weigh results obtained, and they can, could a lawyer's retainer agreement with a matrimonial client specify "results obtained" as one of a number of factors to be used in determining the final fee? The agreement, for example, might identify an hourly rate to determine the minimum fee (rate times hours) but then leave open the possibility of an increment based on "results obtained." That agreement would not seem to violate the rule (which has this very criterion) and, in fact, has been allowed.[16]

The exception to the prohibitions against contingent fees in matrimonial matters is where the lawyer is really seeking to collect a debt created by a failure to pay already secured alimony or support or where the lawyer is seeking enforcement of a property division to which the parties have already agreed. In those instances, the danger of inflaming the situation between the parties has less resonance. The parties are already divorced or separated. While it is true, aggressive tactics can then destroy whatever semblance of harmony may remain between them, the danger is reduced, and forbidding a contingent fee in this situation will prevent the spouse with the claim from using what may be her best chance to attract a good lawyer — that is, an interest in what she is owed. As with many rules, the distinctions are not neat. We see a balancing of interests, common to the law.

Arguments Pro and Con Contingent Fees   If a matter is not criminal or matrimonial, contingent fees are routinely allowed, although, as stated, they are most common in personal injury and property damage cases. This American innovation is hailed by many as a way to enable persons of moderate means to secure counsel and vindicate their rights. It is decried by others because, they say, it leads to excessive litigation by making it free to the client to sue and because it gives lawyers an interest in the client's claim that will in turn distort their independent judgment and encourage them to pursue cases, if only for the settlement value (and most claims do settle), that the legal marketplace would not otherwise support. Indeed, critics argue, even clients easily able to pay a noncontingent fee would forgo lawsuits if they could not hire a contingent-fee lawyer, thus supporting the charge that the contingent-fee regime spawns unmeritorious or weak litigation in which the lawyers are the parties who have the real (and determinative) interest.

This is not the place to resolve the dispute, fascinating though it may be. It is clear who has won, at least in the United States. Contingent fees are successfully defended on the ground that they enable persons who could not otherwise (easily) afford lawyers to hire lawyers when they have legal claims. This is an argument about access to justice. The claim may be overstated — other societies manage to satisfy the social policy, as they view it, through expanded legal aid or fee shifting — but still there is much merit to it. And it has been persuasive. Another argument in favor of contingent fees is that they are the epitome of value billing. The lawyer gets paid because the client gets value but gets nothing otherwise. The interests of the two are aligned, although, as discussed below, in some situations the interests can come into conflict. A contingent fee encourages a lawyer to fight hard for the client because she will also be fighting for herself. This is the converse of the opponents' argument that contingent fees encourage excessive litigation. A lawyer paid hourly, contingent fee opponents argue, will be objective since she doesn't have to win to get paid.

Regulating Contingent Fees The contingent fee is not going away. The only question is how to regulate it. To that question there is no single answer. The Model Rules require contingent fees to be in writing as do the rules in nearly every other American jurisdiction.[17] Rules generally require the lawyer to specify whether her contingent percentage will be applied before or after deduction of expenses (court costs, discovery, investigators). And of course the agreement must identify the contingency whose occurrence will entitle the lawyer to a fee and it must say what the contingent percentage is. In many U.S. jurisdictions, court rules establish maximum contingent percentages in personal injury cases, either with a fixed number (say, a third) or a sliding scale where the lawyer's percentage is reduced for larger recoveries. Establishing maximum percentages in personal injury cases (which courts may sometimes modify where facts warrant) is meant to protect those (many) clients who are less able to know the value of lawyer time or to predict the factors that enter into a rational determination of a fair fee.

Factors That Contribute to Determination of Contingent Percentage Whether the case is one for which the court sets a ceiling on the percentage or not, it is worth identifying the factors that a rational lawyer (and aren't all lawyers rational?) will weigh in determining whether to accept a case on contingency and the acceptable percentage. These factors are the likelihood that the triggering event (judgment or settlement) will occur, the likely recovery if it does occur, how long it will take for it to occur (reflecting the time value of money), and the amount of legal work that will be required to achieve the recovery. Once all of those factors are assessed, the appropriate percentage can be determined. For example, we would expect a lower contingent percentage if the recovery is highly likely (though not certain), would be large, would be quick, and would not require a lot of work than if the opposite were true.

Who best knows the answers to these questions, lawyers or clients? That's a rhetorical question. Because lawyers, especially those experienced in personal injury matters, deal with these issues all the time, they will be much better able to identify a "fair" percentage, or at least a fair range, on particular facts. But lawyers don't do that by and large. They quote the maximum allowed by the state's rule (if there is one) and may even encourage the client to accept that maximum by pointing out that it is, after all, in a rule adopted by the state courts. This is meant to assure the client that long before the client showed up in the law office, disinterested judges studied the issue and concluded that the number the lawyer quoted was the right and fair number for everyone. Of course, this is false. The number in the state rule is merely the maximum the lawyer can charge. But in my experience, some lawyers have allowed, and even abetted, misunderstanding of this fact, leaving the client to infer that the court percentage is obligatory.

Contingent Fees on Early Money   Despite the social utility in theory and often in practice of rules permitting contingent fees, one concern that has recently arisen must give pause to supporters of the contingent fee regime, but which does not seem to have been adequately addressed. As stated, the vast majority of cases are settled, and a great many of these have some settlement value soon after the incident giving rise to the claim occurs and before the client even shows up at the law office. Defendants and their insurers may be inclined to delay payday as long as they can, because doing so gives them the use of the money in the interim and because the longer the plaintiff has to wait for compensation, the more "realistic" she may be in her settlement demands. On the other hand, experienced lawyers and adjustors can often predict what a case is worth, at least at a minimum, and an experienced defendant (insurance company) may be prepared to pay that amount early on to avoid the cost of defending the case.

Critics of the contingent fee regime—and here I do not mean only those who would abolish it entirely—have argued that a plaintiff's lawyer does not really "earn" that minimum settlement value, that it is already on the table before he does anything at all or anything much, and that therefore the fee for securing it should be less than any maximum fee the jurisdiction may allow for contingent fees generally. Not, mind you, that plaintiffs' lawyers should get nothing from this "early" money (as we may call it), but that because the work required to get it is less than the work needed to get additional sums, and maybe quite a bit less, court rules should entitle lawyers only to a lower percentage. Another way to put this is to say that some amount of money is almost always nearly certain and much more certain than the balance of the claim. Consequently, there is little or no risk for the lawyer, little or no contingency. When a future event approaches certainty, the whole idea of a contingent fee collapses because those fees are meant to compensate the lawyer for taking the risk of getting nothing for his work.

But how can we know the amount of any money that is almost certainly on the table? And if the justification for a lower fee, however we measure it (e.g., with an hourly rate or a lower percentage), is the absence of risk, how low must the risk be before we say that the ordinary caps on contingent fees should be reduced? As it happens, critics have devised a method that will not only identify the amount of early money but will actually eliminate all risk by making the availability certain.[18] It sounds like magic, but it's really quite simple. Critics propose that within 60 or 90 days after the lawyer is retained, she must make a demand and support it with medical records, police reports, and whatever else she thinks justifies her demand. The defendant then has a designated time to reply with an offer. If no offer is made, the proposal is inapplicable and the lawyer can charge her ordinary fee. If an offer is made, the amount is considered early money and the lawyer's fee on any recovery up to that sum is limited.

Let's say the jurisdiction has a maximum of one-third for contingent fees. In this proposal, recognizing the modest amount of work required, the fee would be (say) 15 percent on the early money. Now, of course, the plaintiff may reject the early money and choose to proceed with her claim in court. Fine. But if the plaintiff wins or settles for more than the early money, the lawyer's percentage is limited to 15 percent of the amount of the early money (which was there for the taking) and her usual rate for any excess (which she went on truly to earn). In the view of its advocates, this is a consumer protection proposal. The defendant doesn't get to keep the difference between the 15 percent cap and the lawyer's usual fee. The difference goes to the client, the customer. The lawyer forgoes the difference because the early money offer was there from the beginning. The lawyer did nothing special to get it.

This proposal can be challenged in several ways. The plaintiff's lawyer may not have sufficient information in the weeks following retainer to make an informed demand. The proposal leads to one-sided discovery. The plaintiff has to submit information to generate an early offer, but the defendant will have provided no information. Without it, the plaintiff may be unable fully to evaluate the response. Perhaps the most serious objection is that the lawyer whose client rejects the early offer will have less incentive to pursue the claim. Here's why. Let's say the lawyer thinks the case is worth $500,000 and the early offer is $200,000. If the case proceeds, the lawyer figures, realistically, that the plaintiff may get between nothing and $500,000, but a minimum of $200,000 is a good bet. If the lawyer can only get 15 percent of that sum, his incentive to fight for the $500,000 is less. That is, the prospect of at least one-third of $200,000 makes it economically worthwhile to pursue a larger recovery. The lawyer has the cushion of one-third of the predicted minimum. The client may even desire that his lawyer be able to get his full percentage of the likely minimum recovery, as a way to encourage the lawyer to fight for the larger sum. Otherwise, lawyers may gravitate to those cases where there is no early offer (and they therefore get their full percentage of every dollar) or where the early offer is very low in relation to the expected recovery so the reduced compensation on the early money is not a disincentive to fight on.

Critics also argue that if a plaintiff cannot waive the "protection" of the proposal (and either she cannot or cannot without court permission under the proposal), the effect is to deny plaintiffs a resource (an interest in their recovery) they may wish to "spend" to "fund" their litigation even if it takes some money out of their own pockets. That may mean the plaintiff cannot hire the lawyer she wants. Isn't this a decision an informed and autonomous adult should be able to make? This criticism of the proposal may not persuade everyone, and perhaps it should not. For one thing, treating this as an autonomy issue ignores the fact that the plaintiff group here is not composed of experienced consumers of legal services. Most personal injury plaintiffs never or only rarely will have had a need to hire a lawyer. Furthermore, haven't we already crossed the autonomy bridge by adopting the current caps on contingent fees in personal injury cases, which deny plaintiffs total freedom to decide how to spend the interest in their potential recoveries?

Contingent Fees and Conflicts of Interest   Sometimes, a claim funded with a contingent fee will, because of the numbers involved, introduce conflicting interests between those of the lawyer and those of the client. This won't always happen, but it is always a potential risk. It depends on the numbers. Here is an example. Assume Lawyer estimates that a personal injury case is worth between $600,000 and $750,000 with a 20 percent chance of losing at trial. Lawyer's contingent fee is one-third. Here is how the case plays out.

> Scenario A: With 100 hours of work, Lawyer gets an offer of $330,000, yielding Lawyer a contingent fee of $110,000 or $1,100 hourly. Client would get $220,000.

Scenario *B*: If Lawyer puts in another 75 hours of work, experience tells him he could increase the offer to $420,000 closer to trial, in perhaps six months, yielding an hourly rate of $800 ($140,000 fee/175 hours). Client would get $280,000 instead of $220,000. That's not as good for the lawyer, but better for Client unless she needs the money now.

Scenario *C*: To go to trial would increase the time requirements an additional 125 hours (because trials are labor intensive) with a prospect of a fee of up to $250,000 if the client wins the $750,000 maximum, yielding an hourly rate of $833 ($250,000/300 hours). Client would get $500,000. But Client might win less than the maximum or nothing. If the trial produced a judgment of at least $420,000, Client is no worse off (except for lost time) than if she had accepted the offer in scenario *B*, but the lawyer will have reduced his hourly rate to $466, given the additional time.

The lesson: While going to trial carries a risk of loss for both, the upside advantage to the client is significantly greater than for the lawyer. Or to put it another way, depending on the numbers, it will sometimes be better for the lawyer, but not the client, to accept low-range early offers because doing so maximizes his hourly (and certain) compensation.

ENDNOTES

1. *See, e.g.*, 42 U.S.C. §1988 (civil rights fee shifting statute).

2. *See, e.g., Goldberger v. Integrated Sources, Inc.*, 209 F.3d 43 (2d Cir. 2000) (discussing formulas for evaluating fees in class action cases).

3. Model Rule (MR) 6.1 encourages lawyers to provide 50 hours a year of legal services "to those unable to pay." But the rule does not mandate that they do so.

4. One such case is *Matter of Fordham*, 668 N.E.2d 816 (1996), which disciplined a lawyer who charged in excess of $50,000 for time spent in defending a prosecution for DUI that could have resulted in the loss of a license. The lawyer won the case but lost the discipline.

5. MR 1.5(a). The Model Code equivalent was DR 2-106(A) and (B).

6. This is the language of DR 2-106(B).

7. *Brobeck, Phleger & Harrison v. Telex Corp.*, 602 F.2d 866 (9th Cir. 1979).

8. Today, California Rule of Professional Conduct 4-200 forbids an unconscionable fee, which would appear to be less demanding than the prohibition in

the Model Rules against an "unreasonable" fee. To the list of factors to be evaluated in determining whether a fee is "unconscionable," California adds the following: the "relative sophistication of the [lawyer] and the client," the "amount of the fee in proportion to the value of the services performed," and the "informed consent of the client to the fee."

9. Most jurisdictions that require a writing say so in their ethics rule. California does so by statute. California Business and Professions Code §6148. New York does so in Rule 1.5 and by court rule. 22 N.Y.C.R.R. Part 1215.

10. *Johnson v. Gudmundsson*, 35 F.3d 1104 (7th Cir. 1994).

11. MR 1.8(a). Some courts view post-retainer fee agreements as within Rule 1.8(a). *Matter of Hefron*, 771 N.E.2d 1157 (Ind. 2002). But in any event, fiduciary duty law will impose its own set of requirements on post-retainer fee agreements.

12. *Matter of Cooperman*, 633 N.E.2d 1069 (1994).

13. *Ryan v. Butera Beausang Cohen & Brennan*, 193 F.3d 210 (3d Cir. 1999). *See also Matter of Sather*, 3 P.3d 403 (Colo. 2000).

14. MR 1.5(d).

15. Virginia Rule of Professional Conduct 1.5(d)(1).

16. *Alexander v. Inman*, 974 S.W.2d 689 (Tenn. 1998) (fee agreement included "results obtained" in determination of a "reasonable fee" at the conclusion of the matter). Some jurisdictions have no limit at all on contingent fees in matrimonial matters, including Washington, DC, and California. MR 1.5(c).

17. MR 1.5(c).

18. Brickman, O'Connell & Horowitz, *Rethinking Contingent Fees* (Manhattan Institute 1994), offers a somewhat more complicated variation of the method outlined in the text.

part II
Conflicts of Interest

~ 9 ~

Conflicts of Interest: An Introduction

Why Do Lawyers Worry About Conflicts?

Policies Behind Conflict Rules

Types of Conflicts

Conflict Rules as Default Rules

Statistically speaking, few lawyers will ever hear from a disciplinary committee or face claims of liability to clients or to third persons for misbehavior connected to their law practice. To be sure, both of these events happen with some (and some think increasing) frequency, and if such a charge is made against you, the level of frequency is irrelevant. But the odds are pretty favorable that neither discipline nor a civil lawsuit for negligence will confront any particular lawyer in the course of a career. Even more rarely are lawyers criminally charged based on acts arising out of their practice.[1] No, what lawyers worry most about is finding themselves with a conflict of interest, and they are wise to do so. Indeed, worrying about conflicts is a good thing because it should lead to precautions that will avoid them and therefore avoid the unpleasant consequences of a finding of a conflict. These consequences can include an increased risk of civil liability to clients and also loss of a fee,[2] disqualification, a court sanction, publicity and attendant embarrassment, and bad client relations. Lawyers must pay attention to possible conflicts in order to avoid these consequences for themselves and their law offices. They can avoid these consequences in two ways. Most obviously, if they know the rules, they will recognize a conflict situation before landing in it and then decline the work that creates the conflict; or if a conflict arises while doing the work, they will withdraw from a conflicting representation. But lawyers also do not want to lose good work because a conflict forbids accepting it or continuing with it. So the second thing lawyers can do, with careful planning, is to agree with their clients that certain situations that might otherwise present a conflict will not do so. Informed client consent, in other words, can make a conflict that prevents a representation disappear, if done right. A consent, as we will later explain (see Chapter 15), allows the lawyer to stay in the conflicted matter. It does *not* allow her to ignore the duties she owes to the client or to let the conflict affect her performance.

This chapter is a general introduction to, and overview of, the conflict rules and the policies behind them. Future chapters will discuss the rules in greater detail.

Why Do We Have Specific Conflict Rules for Lawyers?

Although ethics rules for lawyers describe the conflicts lawyers and firms must avoid, even without these rules the law of agency and fiduciary duty would (and do) independently require lawyers to avoid conflicts.[3] Why bother then to have conflict provisions in the ethics rules? The answer is that the lawyer conflict rules (like the confidentiality rules discussed in Chapter 4) enable the courts, with the advice of the bar, to provide more detailed guidance to lawyers than the generic fiduciary duty law or agency law provides for everyone else. Lawyers may be agents and fiduciaries, but they work in a highly specialized world, a world that will benefit from greater clarity and precision about how the generic policies in the substantive law that governs all agents and fiduciaries operates in law practice. That is what the lawyer conflict rules do — provide the greater clarity and precision — although there is a limit to how detailed most conflict rules can be. This is because the key conflict rules are standards, not bright lines, whose interpretation and application, consequently, requires prediction and judgment. Judgment in turn depends on experience and knowledge of the case law and bar opinions in the field.

Two Goals of the Conflict Rules Conflict rules describe situations that a lawyer should not be in without informed client consent (where permitted), not because being in that situation will *necessarily* harm the client but for two other reasons. First, the forbidden situation can create an unacceptable *risk* that the lawyer will fail in his duty of loyalty or duty of confidentiality to his client even if the lawyer's intention is to do the right thing. It doesn't mean the lawyer *will* fail, only that the conflict situation creates too high a risk that he will fail, and not necessarily on purpose, because of some countervailing interest of another client, the lawyer, or a third person. The conflict rules means to avoid that risk. In this way, the rules may be seen as prophylactic or preventive. Second, we forbid the lawyer from being in particular situations because, even if doing so does not lead to any actual harm to the client as it turns out, the trust and confidence that we want clients to repose in their lawyers may be lost or diluted if clients understand that the rules allow lawyers to be in positions that, as clients may view it, pose significant threats to their interests. In other words, client comfort is a legitimate value that the rules seek to protect.

Let's illustrate these goals with four hypothetical situations.

Hypothetical One: Say you are president of a small business that manufactures kitchen equipment. You need more warehouse space to hold your inventory. After much searching, a perfect space comes on the market and you hire a lawyer to research its title, resolve environmental and land use issues, and negotiate with the seller's lawyer. A month or two goes by and the lawyer does not seem to be having much success coming to an agreement. Then you learn that the lawyer's brother has also been negotiating to purchase the same space. Or perhaps you learn that the lawyer's partner, representing a different client, has been negotiating for the space. No one told you about the parallel negotiations. Wouldn't you feel a bit put out? Maybe, if you really want that building and are perplexed at the delay given what you think is your attractive offer, you're also a little suspicious. Is your lawyer dragging her feet to give her brother a leg up? To give her partner's client an advantage? What if you also learn that the partner's client gives the firm far more business than you ever can? Might you even begin to worry whether the amount of your offer has become known to the other bidder, giving it a negotiating advantage? You are not an especially suspicious person, but you might just wonder why your effort has gone nowhere. And if it turned out that the brother or other firm client succeeded in buying the building out from under you for a few dollars more than you offered, your suspicions would likely grow. You might feel betrayed.

So you can see in this hypothetical the operation of both underlying policies: the danger that your lawyer's commitment to help you get what you want may actually have been subordinated to the interests of others. The lawyer may have failed to pursue your interests with vigor and may have failed to protect your confidential information. And even if none of that happened, even if the lawyer did the very best job any lawyer could possibly have done for you under the circumstances, even if there are innocent explanations for your loss of the building, how can you know for sure? Your suspicions may not be allayed, and that is a harm in itself, recognized by the policies underlying the conflict rules. We don't want clients to have unfounded but plausible suspicions of their lawyer's commitment to their goals as a result of other influences. That circumstance will cause clients to be less candid with and trusting of their lawyers and that in turn can affect the quality of a lawyer's services.[4] We are talking, of course, about suspicions aroused in and responses of reasonable clients. Obviously, we cannot make rules that will comfort the least trusting.

As *Hypothetical Two*, imagine you are challenging the government's broad interpretation of a tax law, which if it is a correct interpretation will cost you a cool million dollars. But if your interpretation is right, you get a refund of a million dollars. Too bad. You lose. Then you learn that your lawyer stood to gain a lot of money from the interpretation you opposed and to lose a lot of money from the one he advocated on your behalf. Or if not your lawyer, then a second (and much more important) client of the firm, who was not involved in the matter, was in the exact opposite position and several times forcefully told your lawyer that it was hoping he would lose your case and expressed its "displeasure" that "our firm" is making the argument. How do you feel about that? Well, however *you* feel, the conflict rules operate from the assumption that many clients would feel seriously put out and might wonder whether their lawyer pulled his punches for his own or his firm's other client's economic advantage. Respect for that reaction and avoiding that client discomfort is one objective of the conflict rules. And a second is to make sure your lawyer does not put himself in the position where he's tempted, even unconsciously, to sell you short because of his own interest or the interest of his firm's other client.

Now, consider *Hypothetical Three*, which is somewhat different. A lawyer represents two defendants accused of murder, Joe and Lynn. The prosecutor offers Joe a plea bargain that will allow him to get out of prison in seven years, whereas conviction on the murder charge will result in a mandatory sentence of 20 years to life. But in exchange, Joe, in addition to pleading guilty to the reduced charge, must agree to testify against his co-defendant, Lynn. The same lawyer cannot possibly give Joe objective and independent advice while also honoring his duties to Lynn. Encouraging Joe to accept the deal (perhaps because the evidence against him is strong and he's likely to be convicted if he goes to trial) is bad for Lynn because Joe's testimony will then be introduced in evidence against her. But urging Joe to reject the deal (because the lawyer wants to protect Lynn) denies Joe the independent advice of his lawyer — that is, advice based on Joe's interest only. The lawyer in this situation should be motivated solely by Joe's interest or Lynn's interest. Joe has an interest in independent advice, which includes giving serious consideration to accepting the offer, and Lynn has an interest in having their common lawyer persuade Joe to reject the offer. Their interests are directly opposed, and both are clients. The lawyer cannot be the champion of either client. We won't allow the lawyer to claim that concern for Lynn had no role in his advice that Joe should reject the deal. Maybe that's true, but we cannot be confident that it is true; indeed, not even the lawyer may be confident that it is true. An even more dramatic conflict would arise if Lynn and Joe each wanted to claim at trial that the other was the one who shot the victim. One lawyer cannot possibly argue both positions.

Finally is *Hypothetical Four*: A lawyer represents Sally, who is negotiating to buy some real property. While that's going on, a new client wants to hire the lawyer or her firm to sue Sally for breach of contract. The alleged breach has nothing whatsoever to do with Sally's bid for the real property. The lawyer may claim that her firm can go forward with the lawsuit against Sally because (let us assume) nothing that happens in the suit can affect the work the firm is doing for Sally, and none of the confidential information that the firm has learned or will learn in negotiating for Sally would be at all helpful to Sally's opponent (the firm's other client) in the contract case. Yet we will not allow the dual representation (without informed consent) because we can't really ask Sally to repose complete trust and confidence in her lawyer if that lawyer, or her firm, is also suing Sally, a starkly adversarial position. Even if the adverse matter were another negotiation, not a lawsuit, we accept that without informed consent, Sally has a legitimate interest in not seeing her lawyer or the lawyer's firm bargaining against her on behalf of an opponent while also representing her.

"It's Not About You": The Rule Is Objective   When I have suggested to lawyers that they may have a conflict, or where an adverse party makes that accusation, or a judge says as much, the response is often heartfelt and personal. "I would never compromise a client's goal for my own or some other firm client's interests. And in fact I did not. Look, I did everything humanly possible." Perhaps so. The mistake here is in failing to realize that the conflict rules are not about any particular lawyer or his actual conduct or susceptibility to improper incentives. Or as I sometimes respond, "It's not about you. It's not about whether or not you're a good person." The conflict rules are objective rules, one size fits all, lawyers who are angels and those who, well, are less than angels. The fact that a lawyer has a conflict does not mean that he or she (necessarily) succumbed or will succumb to temptation, only that there *is* temptation enough in the particular situation to which some well-meaning lawyers might succumb, consciously or not. The risk is great enough to disconcert even a trusting client, which in and of itself is a harm to avoid.

Balancing Risk Against Other Values   Finding the proper balance between tolerable and unacceptable risk — that is, how broadly to define the scope of impermissible conflicts — is made harder by the fact that a finding of conflict exacts a cost to other values. These have to be recognized when we decide what we choose to define as an impermissible conflict. One value is the lawyer's professional interest in working on a matter. That interest may not carry great weight, but respect for the lawyer's professional development does deserve some consideration. If, as is almost always so, a lawyer's client conflict is *imputed* to other lawyers with whom he or she practices — meaning that the second lawyer is deemed to labor under the same constraints as the first one — the disqualification effect will radiate to disable an entire law firm or law office from accepting the same matter. Next, and deserving more respect, are the interests of other clients who wish to hire a lawyer (or that lawyer's firm) but cannot because of the conflict. Counsel of choice is a value we embrace. Of course, for many reasons clients cannot always get the lawyer they want (too busy, too expensive, not interested, on vacation, retiring), but the professional conduct rules ought not create additional roadblocks unless justified by protection of some greater value. And that's the challenge: When is it justified? The decision that a matter presents a conflict is an exercise in balancing values and making predictions: *How great* is the risk that there will be disloyalty or breach of confidentiality? *How much* will it damage client trust if lawyers are permitted to accept the allegedly conflicting matters? How much will a particular rule infringe on values like availability of counsel of choice?

Last, we have to be aware that an allegation of conflict can be tactical. A client or former client who really has no worry about diminution of loyalty or loss of confidentiality may raise the charge for purely strategic motives — shedding crocodile tears when the real purpose is to deny an adversary a particularly able lawyer or to impose the temporal and financial costs of finding a new lawyer.[5] Or just to delay things.

Identifying the Types of Conflicts: An Overview It is useful now to describe briefly the types of conflicts of interest that we will discuss in subsequent chapters. This is preliminary as an overview.

Concurrent conflicts. As its name implies, these are conflicts between the interests of at least one client and the interests of someone else. Who else? Most often, it's another client (as in each of the hypotheticals), but it can also be the interests of the lawyer herself (Hypothetical Two), a former client, or a third person close to the lawyer, such as a relative (Hypothetical One) or a close friend. (By definition, a lawyer cannot have a current or former client conflict without at least one current or former client or a person or entity a court is prepared to treat as a client for conflict purposes.) When the rules identify a current client conflict, what they are saying is that the lawyer will have conflicting *loyalties or influences* that *may or will* detract from her duties to the current client. We need to understand each of the two italicized phrases in the prior sentence.

Why do I say *"loyalties or influences"*? A conflicting loyalty arises because of a duty to a client. That is so in Hypothetical Three above. The lawyer has a duty of loyalty to both Joe and Lynn, and they are inconsistent. But sometimes the conflict is between the interests of a client and the interests of others to whom the lawyer owes no professional duty of loyalty but whose interests may nevertheless *influence* the lawyer. That would be true in the first hypothetical, where the interests of the lawyer's brother may affect his representation of the client; and it is true in the second hypothetical, where the interests of the lawyer himself or the interests of the firm's second client may do the same. Why is there no duty of loyalty to the firm's second client in Hypothetical Two? It is because on the facts posed, the firm does not represent that other client in the tax matter. So no lawyer in the firm has a *professional* duty to it on that matter; that is, the firm has no duty to it to see that the tax matter comes out the way the second client wishes. The lawyer's duty of loyalty is circumscribed by the scope of the retainer. Nonetheless, the interests of the firm's second client (who hopes the firm loses the tax matter) may *influence* how the firm handles it, especially if the second client is an important one whom the firm will not want to offend.

In the fourth hypothetical, the conflict is somewhat different. There are no divided loyalties as such. The client suing Sally has no interest in the matter the firm is handling for Sally, and the firm has no duty to Sally in the lawsuit where it is suing her. But the existence of the lawsuit can have a doleful effect on Sally's legitimate interest in being able to work with her lawyer in an atmosphere of trust and confidence. In addition, the other client in Hypothetical Four would also have a grievance. He may worry that the firm will not be as aggressive in his lawsuit against Sally because she is a firm client, an influence that can affect the firm's willingness to be zealous in the action against her.

Why do I say "*may or will* detract from his duties to the current client," the other italicized phrase above? The contrary loyalties or outside influences *may* temper the lawyer's commitment in situations illustrated with the first, second, and fourth hypotheticals. For example, the lawyer *may* fail in his obligations to the client who wants to buy the warehouse, or to the client who wants to argue for a particular interpretation of a tax statute, as a result of other interests (of the lawyer, his brother, the other firm client), even though the lawyer owes no professional duty to advance their contrary interests. He *may* be able to avoid their influence, as he should. But he may also *not* be able to do so. A finding of conflict says that the risk is too high absent informed consent. On the other hand, a conflict *will* compromise a lawyer's duty to a client, as in Hypothetical Three above, when a lawyer represents two or more clients in the same matter and the clients have inconsistent factual or legal interests in the matter such that if the lawyer pursues the interests of one of the clients he must *necessarily* fail to pursue the interests of the other client simply because by definition he can't do both. Yet professionally he is committed to doing both. That's the conflict.

Special concurrent client conflict rules. Although the concurrent conflict rule is stated as a standard (*see* American Bar Association [ABA] Model Rule 1.7), some bright(er)-line requirements or prohibitions, preserved in Rule 1.8, focus on certain recurrent issues and attempt to resolve them categorically in so far as possible. We will discuss some of these in Chapter 11.

Successive conflicts.[6] A conflict may not only create a risk to a current client, but it may also create a risk to a former client. These are not mutually exclusive situations. A lawyer can have a current and former client conflict in the same matter. While it may at first seem strange to talk about a duty to a *former* client, in fact we have already seen in Chapter 4 one duty that survives the end of the professional relationship. Absent an exception, a lawyer may not reveal or adversely use (even without revealing) the confidential information of a former client no matter how much time has elapsed since the client ceased to be a client. So it should come as no surprise that the successive conflict rules aim to protect a former client's confidential information against the risk of revelation or adverse use. But while protection of confidences is the primary objective of the successive conflict rule, it is not the only one. Lawyers also have modest loyalty obligations to former clients — much reduced from the duties to current clients, but still important.[7]

The challenge for the courts and drafters of the professional conduct rules was easy to state but not so easy to solve. That solution can in turn be a challenge to implement. The challenge is this: After a lawyer finishes her work for a client, and the client is no longer a client, how shall we define the representations that the lawyer may not thereafter accept (absent consent) because of her work for the first client? Or to put it another way: After a representation has ended, what legitimate interests does the former client continue to have, and how should we limit the work for her former lawyer in order to protect those interests? This is the subject of Chapter 12.

Imputation of conflicts and screens. If a current or former client conflict affected only one lawyer at a time, the consequences might be significant for that lawyer but modest otherwise. Only one person would be affected. But that is not so. Welcome to the world of imputed client conflicts. (Some non-client conflicts are not imputed; others are. See Chapter 13.) The doctrine of imputation exponentially magnifies the disqualifying effects of a conflict. Debate over the wisdom of imputation, or of imputation as broad as current rules require, are common, but the doctrine has shown no sign of serious contraction. To the contrary, it has had remarkable staying power despite the growth of the modern law firm and the consequent reach of the imputed conflict. The one exception — the one place in which there have been inroads that permit firms to avoid imputation of client conflicts — is where a lawyer moves from one law office to a second law office (a lateral lawyer). About half the states and the ABA Model Rules permit a firm to erect a screen to avoid imputation of the lateral lawyer's conflict, at least some of the time (see Chapter 13). One proposed antidote against ascribing one lawyer's client conflict to another lawyer is a screen between them that is meant to interrupt the imputation. Screening (absent client consent) is not universally allowed.[8] Where recognized, it mainly avoids imputation of the conflict of a lateral lawyer. A lateral lawyer is a lawyer who moves from one law firm or law office to another. That lawyer's conflict arising from his own work will travel with him, but a screen where allowed will prevent imputation of his conflicts to his new colleagues.

For policy reasons, courts and the ethics rules uniformly permit screening of one type of lawyer so that his or her conflicts will not debilitate colleagues in a new law office. This is the government lawyer who leaves for private life (or to work in the public sphere but for a different government — say, a move from federal to state government).[9] If a former government lawyer's conflicts were routinely imputed to a new employer, without permission to screen, she might find it hard to get a job, or at least a job in her specialty, on departure, especially if she had a lot of responsibility (i.e., participated in a lot of matters) while with government. That prospect, in turn, might dissuade lawyers from going to work in government in the first place. Thus, the exception to imputation for lawyers who work for government. See Chapter 13.

Consent. Most conflicts can be waived by consent. When lawyers complain that the conflict rules are too strict or require them to give up too much business or are too hard to understand, I like to say that the conflict rules are default rules. They're what you get if you don't provide other rules by agreement with an informed client. I tell lawyers, "Except where the rules forbid consent — and that's quite rare — your firm can write its own conflict rules if the client is willing to agree." Informed client consent can make the rules less strict. The more sophisticated the client, the easier it is to adopt substitute rules, even in advance,[10] before the conflict emerges, if it ever does. Of course, the door swings both ways. Some sophisticated clients with a lot of business to throw around might demand greater restrictions on what a lawyer or firm does than the limits imposed by the default rules.

So this has been an introduction to the world of conflicts and the broad policies underlying the conflict rules. The details will be addressed in the ensuing chapters.

ENDNOTES

1. One example, where a failure to reveal a conflict of interest resulted in a criminal conviction, is *United States v. Gellene*, 182 F.3d 578 (7th Cir. 1999) (upholding perjury convictions of a large law firm partner whose sworn declaration and oral testimony to bankruptcy court failed to reveal the firm's

representation of clients with conflicting interests). *See also United States v. Ross*, 190 F.3d 446 (6th Cir. 1999), where a lawyer was found guilty of drug and money-laundering conspiracies in part for assisting clients in transferring real property and posting a cash bond. Both acts advanced a client's crimes.

2. Chapter 24 discusses the concept of fee forfeiture or disgorgement.

3. *See, e.g., Restatement (Third) of Agency* §§8.01 et seq.

4. For a discussion of this value, *see, e.g., Trone v. Smith*, 621 F.2d 994 (9th Cir. 1980) ("Both the lawyer and the client should expect that the lawyer will use every skill, expend every energy, and tap every legitimate resource in the exercise of independent professional judgment on behalf of the client and in undertaking representation on the client's behalf").

5. Courts are cognizant of this danger. *See, e.g., Bottoms v. Stapleton*, 706 N.W.2d 411 (Iowa 2005) ("a court must also be vigilant to thwart any misuse of a motion to disqualify for strategic reasons"); *Barragree v. Tri-County Elec. Co-op, Inc.*, 950 P.2d 1351 (Kan. 1997) ("whether or not a motion to disqualify has been used as a tactical device or a means of harassment should also be considered").

6. The successive conflict rules are preserved in Model Rules (MR) 1.9, 1.10, and 1.11.

7. *Sullivan County Regional Refuse Disposal Distrib. v. Town of Acworth*, 686 A.2d 755 (N.H. 1996); *Franklin v. Callum*, 782 A.2d 884 (N.H. 2001) (disqualifying law firm that had drafted a document that was the subject of the litigation).

8. MR 1.10(a) does now recognize screening in this instance.

9. MR 1.11.

10. MR 1.7 cmt. [22].

❧ 10 ❧

Current Client Conflicts

The Definition of a Current Client Conflict

Who Is a Current Client?

Issue Conflicts

Examples of Direct Adversity   As summarized in the prior chapter, a current client conflict exists when, because of some other interest or influence, the lawyer may be unable to serve the client adequately, at least as far as the rules are prepared to predict. More specifically, Rule 1.7 contains two definitions of a concurrent conflict. One definition states that a concurrent conflict exists if representation of a client is "directly adverse to another client." This definition is pretty clear. It forbids litigation or negotiation against a current client. If another party in the lawsuit is your firm's client and is taking a position inconsistent with your client's position in the action (and certainly if it's the plaintiff when you represent the defendant or vice versa), that's a direct adversity. So, too, is it direct adversity if the other party to a negotiation with an inconsistent position is your firm's client. In either situation, it doesn't matter that the other party is represented by a different firm in the lawsuit or the

147

negotiation. You're still directly adverse to a client of your firm, albeit a client that your firm represents on a different matter, perhaps a wholly unrelated matter.[1] Remember that two parties can be adverse and still be friendly and cooperative, as parties to negotiations often are. *Adversity* is a legal term of art. It means that the economic, factual, or legal positions of the parties may diverge even if they are not diametrically opposite.

"Significant Risk" and "Materially Limited" Lawyers should ordinarily have no problem following this part of the concurrent client conflict rule — they need only identify the opponent and see if it's a firm client — although as we shall see it can sometimes be a challenge to know whether a client is a current or a former client or even whether a person or entity claiming to be a client is or was ever a client within the meaning of the rule. But that challenge is modest compared to the next one. It is the second definition of a current client conflict in Rule 1.7(a) that can especially bedevil lawyers. It says that a concurrent conflict exists "if there is a *significant risk* that the representation of one or more clients will be *materially limited* by the lawyer's *responsibilities* to another client, a former client or a third person or by a personal interest of the lawyer." As you can see, the italicized terms are quite elastic. What does "significant risk" and "materially limited" mean? And although somewhat more clear, what "responsibilities" does the rule mean to identify as creating the *risk* of a threat to a representation? The answer to these questions will be highly dependent on the facts of a particular situation. It is impossible to get much beyond a general prescription and discussion without concrete facts.

Predicting Risk: A Mind Game Without focusing on the precise language of Rule 1.7 in the prior chapter, we saw four examples of situations in which it could be said that the forbidden "significant risk" was present. To illustrate the question another way, let us try to approach this mathematically. Imagine (counterfactually) that we can graph the level of risk that other interests or influences will pose to a lawyer's representation of a client. Say the graph runs from 0 to 100, where 0 is no risk and 100 is certainty of a materially limited representation. At what point on the graph will we cross the tripwire in Rule 1.7's second definition. At what point will we have created the *significant risk* of a *material limitation* on the representation? Remember, the easier that is to happen — the lower the number — the greater the restriction on the lawyer's and (because of imputation of conflicts throughout a firm) her colleague's freedom to accept new matters, and so the greater the impediment to the ability of other clients to hire the lawyers they want.

So what's your answer? You might begin at the midpoint on our imaginary graph, 50, and depending on the weight you give to the respective values, your views of human nature, and perhaps the nature of your current or intended law practice, move up or down on the scale. I'd wager that if you took a poll of all lawyers and judges in the country, the number would come out somewhere between 30 and 60, thereby tending to favor the client's interest. (These are not meant to be percentage risks, only an artificial way to measure risk tolerance.) Some will argue that concern for client trust should make any risk higher than 30 intolerable absent consent. Alternatively, others will say that 60 is the right compromise, citing the basic trustworthiness of lawyers and the interests of other clients. If we took the same poll of clients, the number might come back much lower, perhaps at 10 or 20, in order to protect the interests of current clients over the interests of prospective clients and those of the firm itself.

Although we cannot graph the issue, it would solve many problems if we could. Lawyers would not have to run a different risk — the risk of guessing wrong. This is just a mind game, but a mind game with a purpose. It is intended both to show the inherent ambiguity of the rule and to help us sort out the competing values. The ambiguity of the rule, in turn, tells us the importance of judgment and experience in evaluating whether acceptance of a matter is or is not permitted. The more immersed a lawyer is in the doctrines, the better will be his judgment. Judgment, after all, is predictive accuracy, based on experience. An informed or developed intuition, if you will. The experience that informs judgment includes constructions of the rule and its application to actual facts, in case law, bar ethics opinions, and secondary literature. What does this mean to the practicing lawyer? That he has to be able to recognize a possible conflict when it appears and either have the judgment and experience with the lawyer conflict rules to resolve the question or have access to someone who does. The second option is generally preferred.[2]

Good Predictions Require Good Records Recognizing the possibility of a conflict requires good recordkeeping, a task that computers have made exceedingly easy, although not foolproof. Sometimes information does not make it into the database (as, for example, the prior work of lateral lawyers, a growing population for many firms nowadays). So as a backup to checking a computer database of clients, a firm should also send out new business e-mails identifying the new client or matter and the scope of the work. I say "the firm" because the American Bar Association (ABA) Rules require lawyers who manage a law office to institute systems to prevent unethical conduct, which includes conflicted representations.[3] Once a lawyer (or the ethics counsel of the firm) has this information, he or she can decide whether interests of or responsibilities to others create a Rule 1.7 problem.

Conflict Rules Are Mostly Absolute Liability Rules One startling fact about Rule 1.7 is the absence from its language of any *mens rea* requirement. It does not say that a lawyer should not do such-and-such if he "knows" or if he "reasonably should know" of a fact creating a conflict. Compare other Model Rule provisions that do have an explicit state of mind component. So a lawyer can violate the rule with the best of intentions. (Some students of the subject believe that, when the issue is professional discipline, it makes sense to read the conflict rules to include a "should know" requirement anyway.) The imputation rule, Rule 1.10(a), discussed in Chapter 13, does use the word *knowingly*. What that means is that if the only reason partner Green cannot take the case is because partner Brown could not do so — perhaps because of the work Brown is doing for another client — imputation of Brown's conflict to Green depends on Green knowing about Brown's conflict. Green cannot get into disciplinary trouble if he doesn't know.

This might seem like a very handy escape hatch for Green. "What I don't know can't hurt me," Green might think. Green might in fact be encouraged to cultivate a certain level of ignorance about the work of other firm lawyers. But that would be a mistake for two reasons. The lesser reason is that it is well established in law that intentional ignorance — perhaps achieved by simply not doing a conflicts check — is a little too cute and may be the equivalent of knowledge.[4] But sometimes Green's ignorance will not be intentional. What then? Isn't Green liberated from the conflict? Not quite. Green is personally liberated from the risk of discipline for the conflict of which he was, in good faith, unaware; but the firm as an institution may still be at risk of a civil lawsuit seeking damages for breach of fiduciary duty or malpractice or for fee disgorgement (which we talk more about in Chapter 24). Disqualification also looms. And the firm's managing partners will be at risk for failing to install a conflict-checking system that would have alerted Green to the problem.

What if partner Brown's conflict arises not because she represents a client but because of Brown's personal interest, an investment, say, or the investment of her spouse? How can Green know about that? Lawyers don't record their personal interests in a firm's client database. The answer of course is that Green ordinarily cannot know of Brown's personal interest through a traditional conflicts check, although Brown might recognize the problem if notice of the new matter is e-mailed to all firm lawyers, with the client's identity and scope of work revealed, which is another reason to have this backup system to a computer check. Brown could then speak up.

But even if Green becomes aware of Brown's personal interest — an interest that would prevent Brown from working on that matter — Brown's *personal* (as opposed to *client*) conflict will not be imputed to Green if it's the kind of conflict that "does not present a significant risk of materially limiting [Green's] representation of the client," as the imputation rule (Rule 1.10(a)) puts it. So, for example, if Brown could not advocate a client's construction of a tax statute because it would significantly increase his own taxes, Green could likely do the work anyway unless there was some special relationship between the two (such as if Brown were Green's immediate boss or best friend).

A "Current" Client and a Current "Client" To have a current client conflict, by definition, a lawyer needs a current client. This sounds so obvious you might wonder why it's even worth saying. The reason is that it is not always clear when a client is *current*, rather than former; and it's not always clear whether a person or entity is even a *client* within the meaning of the current (or indeed former) client conflict rules. As discussed in Chapter 2, traditionally clients become clients by agreement or court assignment. A lawyer-client relationship can form in a minute and last five minutes, as when a person seeking advice gets it, no matter how informal the circumstances. That's unusual, of course, but it can happen; a lot depends on the details.[5] (Members of a certified class will also be deemed clients for many purposes, but that's a special case that need not concern us here.) The problem arises because in some situations a court may be willing to view a person or an entity as a client (or the functional equivalent of one) for conflict purposes even when the traditional indicia of a lawyer-client relationship are absent. See Chapter 21. Here, we talk about what makes a client current as opposed to former.

The answer is easy if a lawyer is then doing work for a client. If the matter for which the client hired the lawyer is not yet finished, the client is a client. Full stop. Lawyers don't always have the ability to conclude a matter when they want and on their own say-so. The cooperation of others — opponents, courts, lenders — may be required. A matter may drag on for months or even years. If the work is not over, the client remains a current client unless the lawyer has properly withdrawn. Firms often provide a place to indicate in client databases when a matter has "closed." That way, another lawyer doing a conflict check can determine whether a client is current. (Unfortunately, lawyers don't always bother to update databases to indicate closure, which could lead a court to deem the client current when the firm prefers the client to be former in order to enjoy the more generous former client conflict rules.)

Be Aware of Episodic Clients A client can be current even if the firm is doing no work at all for the client because no matter is open. How can that be? This question introduces us to the phenomenon of the *episodic client.* If you ask people for the name of their dentist or accountant or eye doctor, they would likely tell you Dr. Painless or Ms. Numbers or Dr. Insight, even if they haven't been to the dentist, accountant, or eye doctor for a year. Painless, Numbers, and Insight are the professionals they regularly use when they have a problem with their teeth, taxes, and vision. Clients approach their lawyers the same way and courts recognize as much. If client Barton or client Fisbee Corp. regularly goes to lawyer Mishkin whenever he or it has a particular kind of problem (or any problem), Barton and Fisbee will think of Mishkin as "my lawyer" even if they haven't spoken to Mishkin in a year because they haven't had a legal problem (or a problem of the type Mishkin handles for them) in a year. Yet if asked the name of their lawyer, they will say "Mishkin." So the upshot is that lawyers have to realize that a client can be a client between matters because of the pattern of use the client has made of the lawyer (or firm).

But what pattern is enough to trigger the episodic client doctrine? There is no bright line. Using a lawyer twice in five years for a month or two at a time is unlikely to be sufficient. Using a lawyer five times in two years, even for a month or two, will likely make the client a current client between matters — if not after the first or even the second assignment, then probably after the third. Courts look to other indicia, too. Has the firm encouraged the client to think of itself as still a client? For example, if the firm handles tax or estate matters for the client, a court might ask whether the firm sends periodic advisories to the client urging her to do some tax planning or update her estate plan in light of changes in the law. Does the firm retain the client's documents so as to be ready to assist if an issue arises? Does the firm send generic notices to the client (along with other clients), which might be said to encourage the client to think of the firm as still her law firm? Has the firm changed the designation of the client in its own files — from current to former? None of these factors may be enough standing alone to make a client a current client, but they may contribute to such a finding.[6]

Matters You Thought Were Over but Aren't   Related to the concept of the episodic client is the client who is deemed an ongoing client because although the firm may have done no work for the client for quite a while, for some reason the court finds that the matter it was handling for the client (or permutations from it) are still ongoing. Consider this case, which probably pushes the doctrine to its limits if it does not actually exceed the limits.[7] The law firm had settled a litigation for a client whom it had not previously represented. More than three years went by. It did no other work for the client or any member of its corporate family. Then it was hired to sue the client's parent. The court said the subsidiary was still a client despite the three year hiatus for three reasons: The firm was listed on the settlement documents as a party to receive a copy of any notice to the client; the firm had not marked its own records to indicate that the client's matter was closed; and the firm was storing a great many of the client's files in the matter, which would become useful in the event of a dispute over the settlement the firm had negotiated. In the court's view, the firm was positioning itself to continue to serve the client in the event of such a dispute. The firm easily could have made an effort to return the files or could have made it clear to the client that its services were concluded. The relationship remained open-ended.

So the client was still a current client. But what does that have to do with the parent, which is the defendant the firm sued in the new matter? This presents the second part of the question posed above (not "is it current?" but "is it a client?"). As we shall see, at least for conflict purposes, courts will sometimes treat another member of a client's corporate family as a firm client (see Chapter 20).

It is easy for law firms to avoid the episodic and (sometimes) the open-ended client problems simply by telling clients that they are no longer clients once the work is done. Of course, firms would phrase this message as politely as possible. Some firms in fact do this. Those that do not wish to deliver the news when the matter is concluded (say, along with the final bill) may do so in the retainer letter, by adding a paragraph that says, in effect, that the attorney-client relationship will end when the work is completed. But at other times a lawyer may not want to make this statement, either before or at the end of a matter, because the firm and client have such a longstanding relationship that it would be bizarre to say anything of the kind. Or the firm may be handling a dozen matters for the client so the end of one matter does not end the lawyer-client relationship. Alternatively, a firm may not wish to declare the relationship over because it *wants* the client to think of itself as a current client. That makes it more likely that the client will return when it again needs a lawyer. Fine. A firm can make that decision as a *business judgment* but then it may have to accept the possibility, maybe even the likelihood, that the client will later be deemed a current client, when the firm would prefer otherwise, because a potential new client has a matter adverse to the still current client.

Issue Conflicts Issue conflicts are one specific type of current client conflict that attracted a good deal of attention for a while but now seem to be more theoretical than real, although not entirely. The idea cannot be wholly dismissed. Imagine a firm whose lawyers are asked to argue for a particular legal rule in one court while other firm lawyers are arguing for an inconsistent rule in another court on behalf of a different client. Success in the first court could influence the second court to rule against the second client (or vice versa). In fact, the first court's decision might even be precedent that binds the second court. The particular legal issue on which the decision will be influential or binding may either be central to the second client's matter or peripheral, with little effect on the outcome. But still, the firm will be advocating for inconsistent positions on the same issue. The consequence of victory in either tribunal may hurt the client (more or less) in the other tribunal. Can the firm accept both matters?

To complicate things further, the particular problem may not be apparent when the firm is first asked to accept either client but may suddenly appear in the middle of the representations.

No one can be sure exactly how a litigation will evolve. The question may not arise when the firm is asked to accept a case. Can the firm continue in the matters even though it will have to argue for opposite positions on the same issue?

The answer turns on consideration of several factors. Rule 1.7, comment [24] asks whether "there is a significant risk that a lawyer's action on behalf of one client will *materially limit* the lawyer's effectiveness in representing another client in a different case" (emphasis added). So there is that elastic phrase again — *materially limit* — which means someone will have to make a prediction based on judgment and experience. If the firm is not confident that no material limit on its representation is at stake, it can ask the two clients for their informed consent to proceed.

The test is phrased slightly differently elsewhere. The Washington, DC, Bar asks whether the representation will "in some foreseeable and ascertainable sense, adversely affect the lawyer's effectiveness on behalf of" another client.[8] Both sources provide a checklist for consideration, as does the *Restatement.*[9] Among the factors to weigh are the following:

- What is the relationship between the two courts? If one is likely to be influential over the other, and especially if it can create precedent binding on the other, the conflict is more likely.
- How important is the issue to the client's overall matter? The more tangential the issue the less likely will there be a conflict since resolution of it will not significantly affect the result.
- Will the fact that the two firm lawyers are arguing for inconsistent positions in different courts likely lead either lawyer to soft-pedal her argument so as not to create precedent harmful to the firm's other (perhaps favored) client?

One problem firms have in the area of issue conflicts, to which courts are likely to be sensitive, is that in all but the smallest firms, it can be nearly impossible to identify an issue conflict. There is no effective way to record and preserve issues and search for them in a computer database as one can do with client names. When partner Cummings in Los Angeles has an issue before the Ninth Circuit, he is likely to be unaware that partner Gottshalk in Chicago has the other side of that issue in district court in Illinois, or even that partner Clemmons in the same Los Angeles office (assuming it's a moderately large office) has the other side of the issue in a state trial court in California. Cummings might learn of the other matter if the issue is very prominent, perhaps discussed at firm meetings, but may not hear about it otherwise.

An Example of a Real Issue Conflict   At one time, I might have dismissed issue conflicts as presenting an interesting intellectual riddle but unlikely to appear in actual practice. But while working on this book, I got a question that did reveal a forbidden issue conflict. Lawyers were representing Client *AB* in a particular court before Judge One. The answer to Issue *X* in this matter was going to determine whether *AB* was subject to liability. Issue *X* was novel. Only one judge on the busy trial court (Judge Two) had ever decided it, and she had decided it in another case adversely to *AB*'s position. The firm was not involved in that other case.

Then, while representing *AB*, another lawyer in the firm was asked to accept Client *YZ* in a new matter before Judge Two. That new matter also concerned Issue *X*. Client *YZ* and Client *AB* had opposite positions on Issue *X*. So if the firm took *YZ*'s matter, it would be asking Judge Two to reaffirm her position on Issue *X* while asking her colleague, Judge One, in *AB*'s matter to reject that position as wrong.

Now, the two judges were both trial judges, and the opinion of neither bound the other. But for *YZ*, the firm would have to argue the rightness of Judge Two's ruling on Issue *X*, perhaps strengthening the ruling's persuasiveness, which could in turn influence Judge One. At the same time, before Judge One, the firm would be obligated to show why Judge Two's reasoning was faulty. Success there could cause Judge Two to change her mind (she was free to do so). Further, the firm's opponents in each case would be certain to benefit from (and even cite) the firm's research and arguments in the other case, where the firm would be on the opposite side.

Most important, of course, the resolution of Issue X was determinative of liability in both cases. My conclusion: an issue conflict.

ENDNOTES

1. The leading case holding that a law firm may not be adverse to a current client even on a matter unrelated to the matter in which the firm is representing the client is *Cinema 5, Ltd., v. Cinerama, Inc.*, 528 F.2d 1384 (2d Cir. 1976). The court held the adverse representation "prima facie improper" and that to escape disqualification "the attorney must be prepared to show, at the very least, that there will be no actual or *apparent* conflict in loyalties or diminution in the vigor of his representation" (emphasis in original).

2. Lawyers may be prone to think that merely being a lawyer, coupled perhaps with a law school ethics class X years ago, will enable them to spot these issues and resolve them. Wrong. Just as an antitrust lawyer would not presume to advise on a client's tax or securities problem, neither should she advise herself on all but the most straightforward conflicts issue, especially as a mistake can harm not only her but her colleagues and firm as well. So either she does the research to find the answer — supported with authority — or she has recourse to an expert. Experts are better because the lawyer in this situation is, in a manner of speaking, a client of the advice, with an interest in an answer that will let her do what she wants to do. So increasingly, firms realize this, and the larger ones at least have someone in-house who concentrates in the field (sometimes called a *general counsel* or *ethics counsel*).

3. Model Rule (MR) 5.1. The New York rules impose parallel duties on the law firm as an entity: Rule 1.10(e).

4. *United States v. Carrillo*, 435 F.3d 767 (7th Cir. 2006) ("For purposes of criminal liability, deliberately avoiding knowledge of a criminal activity is the same thing as having actual knowledge of that activity").

5. *See, e.g., Bays v. Theran*, 639 N.E.2d 720 (Mass. 1994) (two or three brief telephone conversations were sufficient to create an attorney-client relationship for conflict purposes).

6. *IBM v. Levin*, 579 F.2d 271 (3d Cir. 1978), is a leading case on the concept. Although the law firm was not doing any work for IBM on the day it filed an antitrust complaint against the company, the court held that "the pattern of repeated retainers, both before and after the filing of the complaint, supports

the finding of a continuous relationship." MR 1.3 cmt. [4] provides that "[d]oubt about whether a client-lawyer relationship still exists should be clarified by the lawyer, preferably in writing. . . ." *See also Shearing v. Allergan, Inc.*, 1994 Westlaw 382450 (D. Nev. 1994) (representation intermittently over 13 years makes client a current client even though no work was done for more than a year).

7. *Jones v. Rabanco, Ltd.*, 2006 U.S. Dist. LEXIS 53766 (W.D. Wash. 2006).

8. D.C. Opinion 265 (1996).

9. *Restatement of the Law Governing Lawyers*, §128 cmt. [f].

~ 11 ~

Special Current Client Conflict Rules

Deals with Clients

Gifts from Clients

Money to Clients

Despite the elastic language in the general current client contact rule (Rule 1.7(a)(2)), the world of lawyer regulation recognizes some recurrent conflict situations where the text can be more specific in what it permits and forbids. We will look at three of these situations in some detail.

Deals with Clients and Adverse Pecuniary Interests
The law has long been suspicious of business or commercial arrangements between fiduciaries and their beneficiaries, and that includes (perhaps especially) lawyers and clients. The reason is simple. During the lawyer-client relationship, we assume that lawyers have an advantage when they make deals with their clients. They have access to the client's confidential information in a way that individuals in an arm's-length deal do not. They have the trust of the client, who may expect the lawyer to look out for the client's own interests

even over the interests of the lawyer. And very often lawyers are simply more sophisticated about business and financial matters. Even when they are not more knowledgeable about the economic aspects of a deal (or an industry), lawyers are more familiar with the various ways in which financial and legal arrangements can be described; particular language, which may appear mere boilerplate to a client, can favor one party or another depending on the words chosen. For these reasons, some courts say that a fiduciary's deal (or any kind of financial arrangement other than the most routine) with a beneficiary, which includes lawyer with client, if challenged, will be treated as presumptively improper or the product of overreaching, with the burden on the fiduciary to prove otherwise.[1]

In lawyer ethics rules, we see several ways in which a client's interests are protected when client and lawyer enter a financial arrangement or when the lawyer acquires a proprietary (or economic) interest adverse to the interests of the client, such as a security interest in the client's property, perhaps to secure payment of a fee. The protections apply even if the lawyer is not purporting to represent the client on the deal itself.[2] All that is required is that there be a current lawyer-client relationship, which we have seen may be true even if the lawyer is not doing work for the client at the very moment. The reason for a rule protecting clients even when the lawyer is not representing the client on the deal (and in fact even when the nature of the work the lawyer is doing for the client bears no relationship to the subject of the deal) is that clients are likely to trust their lawyers to watch out for the clients' interests. Cautions like "You understand I'm not your lawyer on this deal" may not alert a client to the fact that she is now supposed to be on guard and treat the relationship as, in effect, stranger to stranger. If the lawyer *is* representing the client (as well as himself) on the deal with the lawyer, then the general concurrent conflict rule applies as well as the specialized rule on lawyer-client deals. For then, the lawyer has a conflict between the lawyer's own interests and the interests of the client in the matter the lawyer is handling that creates a "significant risk" that the lawyer's representation will be "materially limited."

Procedural and Substantive Fairness When the protections do apply, the rules demand that the client be afforded both procedural and substantive protection. *Procedurally*, American Bar Association (ABA) Rule 1.8(a) requires the lawyer to advise the client in writing to get independent counsel on the matter and afford the client time to do so. It also requires that the terms of the transaction "are fully disclosed" to the client "in writing in a manner that can be reasonably understood by the client." The client must give "informed consent" in a writing the client signs, which must contain the "essential terms" and state whether the lawyer is representing the client in the matter. The Model Rules define "informed consent" to include an explanation of "the material risks . . . and reasonably available alternatives." All of these obligations are meant to ensure that the client understands the situation and the nature of the deal as well as the advisability of disinterested legal advice.

Substantively, even if the lawyer satisfies all of the procedural hurdles, ABA Rule 1.8(a) requires that the transaction also be "fair and reasonable to the client." That is, it will violate the ethics rules and will likely be declared void in court at the client's option, under the law of fiduciary duty — with the lawyer having the burden of proof — if the deal is not fair and reasonable to the client no matter how much the lawyer may have drummed home the substance of the deal and the lawyer's adverse interest. Fairness refers not only to the economic terms of the deal, where some clients may be even more sophisticated than the lawyer, but the non-substantive terms, too (the legal language), where the lawyer is the expert.

Indeed, in theory a deal can be voided in court and declared unethical if it is not fair and reasonable even if the client has independent counsel, although as a practical matter it would not be likely that with independent counsel a deal would be substantively unfair. Take note of the heightened level of court scrutiny here. In true arm's-length contracts, a court will not review the terms for fairness; the parties are stuck with the deal they make.

When Lawyers and Clients Have Adverse Interests The rules on lawyer-client deals apply not only to, say, decisions to invest together but also when a lawyer acquires an interest adverse to the client.[3] The most common example of this is when the lawyer tries to protect his ability to collect his fee by taking a security interest in a client's property, which the lawyer can foreclose and liquidate if the client fails to pay. Certainly, the rule applies when the security interest is taken once the professional (and therefore the dependency) relationship is in place. But perhaps it should apply where the interest is taken as part of the initial fee negotiation, even though the rule does not apply to a fee agreement reached before the lawyer is retained (and therefore before the fiduciary duty arises). This is because the security interest, if granted, will continue throughout the course of the lawyer-client relationship and introduce ongoing pecuniary adversity that will last until the fee is fully paid. At the same time, we saw in Chapter 8 that the courts do exercise oversight over fee agreements even without regard to Rule 1.8(a). Further, even if the rule does not apply to security interests taken before the relationship is formed, the general conflict rule protects the client thereafter if the lawyer's security interest conflicts with an interest of the client in the representation. For example, if the lawyer has a security interest in shares of a client's business, the lawyer may have a conflict when advising the client on whether to take a large loan for the business since that could reduce the value of the shares.

Investing in Clients   Many law firms have, or once had, rules against allowing their lawyers to invest with or in clients. They did so because they recognized that the rules here are strict. They knew that the arrangement could later be challenged in court as void and even lead to discipline. Some firms just thought it was a bad idea for a lawyer to invest in a client because, in a way, that makes the lawyer both a principal and an agent, as when the lawyer has a large stake in a client company. It opens the firm to malpractice or other civil claims based on the contention that advice was not really in the best interest of the company but rather in the best interest of investors with the lawyers' profile. Investing in clients, especially those that are publicly traded, runs the risk that the lawyer may be trading, or appear to be trading, on inside information either when she buys the interest or when she sells it.

While many firms still view investing in clients with suspicion, preferring to earn money the old-fashioned way, by practicing law, many other firms now allow their lawyers to do it, with supervision, and in fact some firms form investment pools through which partners can invest in or with clients. The reasons for the turnabout are simple. First, a lawyer can make a lot of money that way, as we saw in the Silicon Valley start-up days. Second, start-up clients often want their lawyers to take a piece of the equity in lieu of a cash fee both because it frees up capital for the client and because it is seen to signal the lawyer's commitment to and faith in the company. Further, once some law firms started to permit this activity, and especially if they do well financially, other firms will find it hard to resist their lawyers' eagerness to join the crowd.

Gifts from Clients[4]   For the same reasons that we view with concern deals between lawyers, we treat substantial gifts, including in a will or other instrument, from clients to lawyers (or a lawyer's relatives) the same way. The lawyer is in a unique position to take advantage of the client, so the rules and law operate from the perspective that we cannot encourage clients to trust and rely on their lawyers, and assure them that they are the sole focus of the lawyers' concern, on the one hand, and then fail to guard against the potential for abuse that dependence makes possible, on the other.

The rule forbids a lawyer to "solicit any substantial gift from a client" and forbids the lawyer to prepare "an instrument" making the gift (like a will). Someone else must prepare the instrument. But of course, some gifts can be made without an instrument (e.g., jewelry, money), and the lawyer is allowed to accept these so long as she does not "solicit" them, which might be difficult to verify, especially if the client is dead or no longer competent.

The situation here is a bit more nuanced, however, because a lawyer's client may be a relative of the lawyer and so naturally inclined to make a gift to the lawyer or the lawyer's relative (who might also be the donor-client's relative). If so, the prohibition in the rule does not apply. The rules also distinguish between gifts of modest worth and those of substantial value, yet the dividing line between the two is not self-evident, so cautious lawyers should resolve doubts in favor of compliance with the rule.

Even when the rule's restrictions are inapplicable because the donor is a relative of the lawyer, it will often be imprudent for the lawyer to accept a substantial gift, without independent counsel for the client, or personally to prepare the donative instrument. This is because the proscriptions in the ethics rule are not the only consideration a lawyer must weigh. There is also the danger that the substantive law will look with suspicion on the gift and require the lawyer to prove the absence of undue influence. Battles between relatives over a decedent's estate are not uncommon, after all; nor are challenges from one or more relatives who discover, after the fact and perhaps following the donor's death, that a common relative has made a sizeable gift to the lawyer (or the lawyer's immediate family) before death. The lawyer may then be in the position of having to disprove undue influence, a burden more readily surmountable if the client had independent counsel.

Giving or Lending Money to Clients   The first two categories of special current client conflicts and their policy underpinnings are pretty clear. This third category is clear, perhaps clearest of the three, but the policies behind it are cloudy and less defensible in the view of some. And unlike the first two categories, the prohibition against financial assistance to clients as described in the rule are not so easily explained as necessary or advisable to protect clients from lawyers' conflicted judgment or incentives. Further, they can result in great injustice to clients in some situations. Yet the category persists.

Essentially, the rule prohibits "financial assistance to a client in connection with pending or contemplated litigation" with exceptions discussed below.[5] First, take note of the fact that the prohibition on financial assistance applies only when the client is in or contemplates litigation. The rule does not apply to clients with transactional matters. Similarly, the separate prohibition against a lawyer acquiring a "proprietary interest" in a client's matter is limited to a "cause of action" or the "subject matter of a litigation" with exceptions for charging liens and contingent fees. For some reason, whatever conflict issues arise when lawyers lend or give clients money are seen to be absent, or at least less threatening, outside litigation.

The rule, however, creates an exception for "court costs and the expenses of litigation." These can be sizeable. They include court filing fees and the costs of discovery, investigation, tests (medical, laboratory), and expert witness fees (which can themselves be quite high). For a long time, the American Bar Association (ABA) rules required that the client accept ultimate legal responsibility for these expenses as well, win or lose. The lawyer could only *advance* them. In personal injury cases handled on a contingent fee basis, where advances were most prevalent, that meant that win or lose, the plaintiff would have to repay the lawyer for costs and expenses that could run into the many thousands (or tens of thousands) of dollars. Of course, if the plaintiff received a lot of money at trial or in settlement, repayment would not be an issue. But if the plaintiff lost or received very little compensation, the obligation to repay costs and expenses could be financially painful, even devastating. In reality, if the case were lost, lawyers rarely pursued recovery of their advances. No rule required them to do so. The rule only required that the client be obligated to repay. Lawyers might explain the distinction to new clients this way: "I have to tell you that you will be legally obligated to repay me win or lose, but I don't have to enforce that obligation if I lose and I have never tried to do so." The client would have to trust the lawyer not to enforce a claim in her case.

This was something of a charade and everyone knew it. What was the reason to require the client to be ultimately liable for costs and expenses? It was the view that if the lawyer could not look to the client for repayment even if he lost, the lawyer's judgment in litigating the case, and in particular in advising on whether to accept a settlement offer, might be influenced improperly. The lawyer might think, "This is an inadequate settlement offer for the client, but I have already sunk $10,000 into this case out of pocket, and if my client accepts the offer, I'll at least get that back, whereas if we go trial and I lose, I'll get none of it back." By making the client ultimately liable, the lawyer, it was assumed, would not be so influenced because he would be able to recoup his investment either way. The charade arises because clients often lacked the money to repay the lawyer if they lost their case, and lawyers in any event were quite disinclined to sue clients for costs and expenses after losing (bad for business). Another problem with ultimate client liability is that it gave lawyers a club to pressure the client to accept a settlement that the client might find inadequate. "You know, you can turn down the offer," a lawyer may say. "That's your right. But if we lose at trial, you'll owe me $_____ from your own pocket for expenses, plus whatever else I have to advance to try the case going forward."

Today, the rule most places, though by no means all, permits lawyers to make repayment "contingent on the outcome of the matter," which is in reality what happened most of the time anyway. Where the client is indigent, a further qualification allows, but not does not require, the lawyer to forgo recovery even if the client wins a pot of money. So, for example, if a big firm lawyer accepted the representation of an indigent person injured by her landlord's negligence and the lawyer won a $100,000 settlement, the rules do not require the lawyer to demand repayment of the out of pocket costs in prosecuting the action.

Two Justifications Offered for Limits on Financial Help to Clients

Now look at the financial assistance lawyers cannot give clients in litigation. They cannot give even small sums needed to enable the client to pay basic expenses (food, rent, medical bills). Again, in personal injury matters, clients may be financially desperate. Cases can take a long time to try or to settle. Insurance companies for defendants, recognizing the client's plight, can easily and lawfully exploit the delay, perhaps contributing to it by various motions and in extended discovery. The client may be able to borrow money or may have some savings, which can enable her to hang on for a while. But the client may also be broke (or eventually become broke). Depending on the nature of the injury, the client may not be able to work. What is the reason to forbid lawyers to provide even small amounts to tide the client over so he or she can tolerate the justice system's delay?[6]

Comment [10] to Rule 1.8 cites two reasons. First, permitting the forbidden advances can encourage clients to sue when they would otherwise not sue. But why should we discourage lawsuits? They are not bad in themselves. They are how people peacefully resolve their disputes. Perhaps the concern here is that a different rule would encourage meritless suits, which we do not want to do. But is there an empirical or even an intuitive basis for this conclusion? One would have to assume that in order to bring a meritless lawsuit, a lawyer would be prepared to give a client living expenses to get her to agree to be a plaintiff, which she would otherwise not do. In other words, one has to believe that lawyers would compete to buy meritless claims that they can sue on in the hope of winning some nuisance settlement that will at least be larger than the lawyer's investment of money and time in the case. That's hard to accept.

The second reason that comment [10] gives to forbid lawyers to give clients financial assistance is that lawyers would then have "too great a financial stake in the litigation." Presumably, that "stake" will skew their judgment. That is also hard to accept. As we see, lawyers can already advance substantial sums, which can run into the tens of thousands of dollars in some cases, in costs and expenses. Those advances could easily dwarf any assistance to a client to enable her to get food or medical care while she litigates her claim in the face of delay caused either by court congestion or a defendant's tactics. More important, the very reason the comment gives for tolerating the exception for costs and expenses of litigation — namely, that these advances are no different from the interest created by a contingent fee — also supports tolerating an exception for living expenses. We allow contingent fees in order to facilitate court access for persons unable to pay counsel. In other words, we want to make sure the courthouse doors are left open to injured persons who either cannot pay a lawyer or do not want to deplete savings to try to do so. But when the same clients are forced to settle early for inadequate sums because of the financial exigencies caused by the very injury for which they seek compensation in backlogged courts — where defendants can make valid use of procedural rules to delay judgment day — the ethics rules contribute to injustice. Further, the amounts that we would expect lawyers to provide in financial assistance will be a tiny fraction of their contingent fee (and time) investment in the litigation. And it is not as though lawyers would be allowed to buy clients in escalating and competitive bids. The amount of financial assistance can be capped at modest levels and limited to the necessities of life and medical help.

The absence of empirical support for the two reasons the rules give to forbid lawyers to advance money beyond court costs and litigation expenses raises a more fundamental question: Before ethics rules are used to forbid conduct *because of an assumption about harmful effects of that conduct,* shouldn't the profession and the courts be expected to support the assumption empirically or at least as intuitively probable? Shouldn't they especially be required to do so when the conduct if allowed could have beneficial effects, and where prohibition can lead to injustice, as is true here?

Another Reason to Forbid Living Expenses   A reason not offered in defense of the rule but which is worth evaluating is this: If lawyers can advance financial assistance to help plaintiffs meet acute needs and weather the delay in the administration of justice, isn't there a danger that clients will choose lawyers not based on their professional qualities but simply in response to the highest bidder? Let's assume that is a risk. The argument is overstated because clients might also choose lawyers based on price (fee) and we call that the market. But in any event, as stated, that risk can be minimized in two ways. First, we can limit the amount of money a lawyer can offer in financial assistance. Paying medical bills directly does that. Establishing a ceiling for basic needs is another way. A limit reduces the opportunity for a bidding war. Second, we can forbid lawyers from offering to provide financial assistance until after they are retained, as is true in California and elsewhere, which also requires the client to promise to repay the loan in writing.[7] True, these alternatives cannot wholly eliminate the possibility that a client will choose a lawyer for the wrong reasons, but they do reduce it while permitting the salutary objectives of financial assistance.

Why the Difference in Treatment for Litigation and Transactions? We began this discussion by noting that the prohibition against financial assistance (like the parallel prohibition against acquiring a "proprietary interest" in a client's case) is limited to clients with disputes that are in or headed to court (or other tribunal), but that neither prohibition applies to lawyers handling transactional matters. In the first category, we have a rule absolutely forbidding the activity; in the second we have the conditions on lawyer-client business or financial arrangements and the conflict rules, which if satisfied permit the activity. A lawyer may provide financial assistance to a client's business venture (that is, invest) subject only to the substantive and procedural requirements of a rule like Rule 1.8(a) and the general conflicts rule, Rule 1.7.

How do we explain the different treatment? Since one situation involves courts or other tribunals, or potentially does so, and the other does not, the explanation must in part be that the fact that a tribunal is (potentially) involved raises a public policy interest that warrants a total ban. That interest must be, in the language of comment [10] to Rule 1.8, the desire not to "encourage clients to bring lawsuits that might not otherwise be brought." Comment [16] refers to the common law doctrines of champerty and maintenance, doctrines which also had as their purpose avoiding (critics might say suppressing) litigation without distinguishing between frivolous and meritorious claims. Merely "stirring up" litigation, any litigation, was to be avoided. But the Supreme Court, in a case about lawyer advertising, refused to "endorse the proposition that a lawsuit, as such, is an evil." Rather, the Court called lawsuits a legitimate "means for redressing grievances, resolving disputes, and vindicating rights when other means fail."[8]

One wonders why the Model Rules choose to cite these ancient common law doctrines and their underlying policy, explicitly and unquestioned, as a reason to justify a ban on financial assistance to clients whose disputes are in or headed to court or other forums, despite the modern view that litigation is a valuable way to resolve grievances, not something to be shunned. Why not subject this kind of assistance to the same conflict rules that currently govern lawyers who invest in or with business clients? Perhaps there's a persuasive answer, but if so we haven't heard it.

ENDNOTES

1. In *Greene v. Greene*, 436 N.E.2d 496 (N.Y. 1982), the defendant lawyers drafted a trust agreement for the plaintiff that granted the lawyers certain advantages, including 10 percent of "profits from the sale of trust assets." When challenged by the plaintiff, the court held that her claim stated a cause of action, relying on the lawyer's fiduciary duty. Quoting precedent, the court said that the lawyers had the burden "to establish affirmatively that [the agreement] was made by the client with full knowledge of all the material circumstances known to the attorney, and was in every respect free from fraud on his part, or misconception on the part of the client, and that a reasonable use was made by the attorney of the confidence reposed in him." The agreement, the court said, might be invalid even absent fraud or undue influence if the attorney "got the better of the bargain," unless he could show that the client was fully aware of the consequences.

2. *Matter of Neville*, 708 P.2d 1297 (Ariz. 1985), dramatically illustrates this rule. Operating under the less demanding provisions of the Code of Professional Responsibility, the court nonetheless held that a lawyer violated his ethical obligations to his client in connection with a real estate deal where the lawyer was not representing the client. Equally dramatic, the court reached its result although the client was sophisticated in real estate matters and the lawyer was not.

3. This can happen if a lawyer serves both as a real estate broker and lawyer with regard to the client's effort to sell property. That is because, in the language of one court, the client's interest is "in selling the property as quickly as possible and at the most advantageous price." That can best be achieved through a multiple listing. But the lawyer will earn the most as broker if no other broker is involved. So lawyer and client have different interests in the transaction. In the particular case, the lawyer was disciplined. Matter of Lake, 702 N.E.2d 1145 (Mass. 1998).

4. The ABA rule is Rule 1.8(c).

5. The language in this paragraph is taken from ABA Rule 1.8(e) and (i), but, with some modest differences, it is broadly accepted nationwide.

6. A lawyer in Oregon was suspended for advancing $361 to a personal injury client who needed the money for living expenses. *In re Brown*, 692 P.2d 107 (Or. 1984). This is an unremarkable decision, but some courts have been willing to create a "humanitarian exception." That was true in *Florida Bar v. Taylor*, 648 So.2d 1190 (Fla. 1994), where the lawyer gave the client $200 for "basic necessities" with no expectation of repayment. Early drafts of the ABA Model Rules would have permitted "reasonable and necessary medical and living expenses" with repayment conditioned on the outcome of the matter. But the language never made it into the final document.

7. California Rule 4-210(A)(2) forbids lawyers to "pay the personal or business expenses of a prospective or existing client," but an exception states that the rule does "not prohibit" a lawyer "[a]fter employment, from lending money to the client upon the client's promise in writing to repay such loan."

8. *Zauderer v. Office of Disciplinary Counsel*, 471 U.S. 626 (1985).

~ 12 ~

Former Client Conflicts

Who Is a *Former* Client?

Protecting a Former Client's Confidences

Loyalty Obligations to Former Clients

The "Hot Potato" Rule

We have already seen that lawyers have duties to clients that survive the end of the professional relationship—namely, the duty not to reveal or adversely use the former client's confidential information (see Chapter 4) unless the information has become "generally known." But that prohibition is not seen as sufficient by itself to ensure that confidentiality will be respected. Nor is it seen as adequate to encourage clients to trust their lawyers and to provide them with information, especially harmful information. The rules here have two primary goals. The first goal is the actual protection of confidential information by forbidding revelation or adverse use after the professional relationship ends. It means to ensure that the information is not consciously or unconsciously abused. The second goal focuses on the client's behavior while the lawyer is working for the client. It means to ensure client candor. And there is yet a third, less prominent, interest. The rules recognize that lawyers have not only a duty of confidentiality to former clients but also a duty of loyalty. This third interest does not often surface because the concern for protecting confidentiality and encouraging candor are the main goals discussed in the primary and secondary authorities. But the duty of loyalty is also important and can provide an independent if limited check on the work a lawyer can accept after the termination of a professional relationship, as discussed below.

Former vs. Current Clients As discussed in Chapter 10, it can sometimes be a challenge to know whether a client is a current client or a former client. Of course, if work is incomplete, the client is a current client (at least on that matter) unless the lawyer has properly withdrawn. This is true even if only little remains to be done for completion of the work. Furthermore, as we also saw in the discussion of the episodic client in Chapter 10, a client may still be a current client even after the work is done, the bill paid, and the file sent to storage, simply because of the pattern of work for that client over time. And even if a client is not an episodic client — that is, even if it has retained the lawyer only once — the lawyer's or firm's behavior after completion of the work may signal to a court that the firm itself did not deem the relationship concluded, in fact wanted to encourage the view that it was still the client's law firm the better to get new work, in which case a court will accept the client's claim that it remained a current client. Indeed, we saw one case in which a client was held to be a current client three years after a dispute was settled because the firm was listed on the settlement papers to receive *copies* of notices, the firm stored the client's files from the matter, and the firm had not recorded the matter as closed in its own records. While this case may be extreme, and given the time gap perhaps wrongly decided, the factors the court cited to reach its result are unremarkable.[1]

You may ask: Why does it matter, at least for conflict analysis, whether a client is a current or former client? After all, lawyers have confidentiality and loyalty duties to both clients. The answer is that the scope of the loyalty duty to current clients is far broader than the scope of the loyalty duty to former clients. Much work will be foreclosed to the firm unless the client is deemed former, not current. In a sentence, the practical difference between the two kinds of conflicts is this: As we saw in Chapter 10, a law firm, without informed consent, may not be adverse to a current client on any matter (litigation or negotiation) regardless of whether there is a factual relationship between the adverse matter and the work the firm is then doing for the client (i.e., regardless of whether confidential information is at risk); but a law firm may be adverse to a former client on *any* matter except those matters that are, in the language of the doctrine, "substantially related" to the work the firm formerly did for the client. *That* limitation on adversity is comparatively narrow.[2] We discuss this standard — what has come to be known as the *substantial relationship test* — next.

The Substantial Relationship Test   Let's say a client is truly a former client. Should we allow its former law firm to sue or negotiate against it? A no answer may maximize the trust the client will be prepared to place in its counsel. "I will never be your enemy" may give clients a great deal of comfort. But that comfort will come at a large price. It will forbid firms to accept new matters adverse to a former client and therefore block the ability of other clients to hire the lawyers they want. It will lead to strategic behavior. Some clients will hire the best law firms (or the best firms that are possible future adversaries) at least once, thereby ensuring that those firms could never oppose them. So we don't forbid firms from ever acting adversely to former clients. The supposed tradeoff — increased client comfort — is not a sufficient reason to adopt a categorical prohibition, even assuming that the prohibition would indeed have any such benefit.

Shall we then say that a lawyer may act adversely to a former client on *any* matter — even a matter in which the information the lawyer learned when she previously represented the client could be used to the former client's disadvantage in the new matter — so long as the lawyer respects her duty to protect client confidences and honors the very narrow ongoing duty of loyalty to former clients (whose scope is discussed below)? We *could* say that. After all, revealing client confidences (or using them to harm the former client) could subject the lawyer to discipline and civil liability. We could say that these prospects are sufficient inhibitions — that is, sufficient to ensure that the lawyer behaves properly and sufficient to comfort the client that its confidences are not being abused.

But consider the situation from the client's point of view. If its former lawyer is now opposing it in a litigation or negotiation in which the former client's confidences are relevant, won't the lawyer be tempted to abuse those confidences? This can be a subtle influence. Let's say the lawyer knows fact X from the prior work and fact X is harmful to the former client in the new matter where the lawyer is working for the former client's adversary. The lawyer realizes that she cannot reveal or use fact X, at least not if her only source for knowing it is the prior work. So perhaps she tries to find an independent source for fact X — to "discover" it on her own, as it were.

If we let the lawyer oppose the former client in a matter in which confidences learned during the prior work are relevant, and could now be used against it, we are saying to the former client, aren't we, that you must trust your former lawyer to do the right thing. And ordinarily that's all the former client would be able to do. Trust the lawyer. After all, confidential informa-tion can be improperly exploited even if the lawyer never reveals it. How is the former client to know? The *new* work of the former lawyer is protected by attorney-client privileges and the work-product doctrine. It is performed in a sort of "black box." Indeed, the fact that policing compliance with confidentiality obligations is difficult or impossible may itself spur unscrupulous lawyers to cut corners. Remember, too, that the lawyer's new client may pressure the lawyer to "use what you know." The new client has no interest in safeguarding the former client's confidential information. The economic and reputational benefits to the lawyer of winning the new case or getting an excellent result in the negotiation may also encourage bad behavior. Or so the former client may fear.

This is where the substantial relationship test comes in. It is an effort to identify those adverse matters in which the former client's confidential information will be at risk, great enough risk so that the former lawyer must stay out of them. Applica-tion of the test almost always appears in litigation when the former client, now sued by former counsel, moves to disqualify the former firm on the ground that the former and current matters are substantially related. The name of the test, substantial relationship, is just a shorthand way of saying that when that kind of relationship between two matters is established — a substantial one — we presume that the former matter will have given the lawyer confidential information rel-evant to the new matter. A more precise term might be substantial *factual* relationship, because that is what we are protecting — confidential facts.

In deciding whether two matters are substantially related, a judge will ask whether, given the nature of the former matter, a lawyer will have acquired confidences that can be used to harm the former client in the new matter. The judge looks at the two matters, not the type of legal service that the lawyer performed. A lawyer may have given a company tax advice and later attempt to sue it for an antitrust violation. Tax and antitrust are different areas of law, but they have one big thing in common — financial information. So a judge would say that the two matters are substantially related because the lawyer would have been expected to get just the kind of information in the tax matter that he or she now has available to use against the former client in the antitrust matter.[3] The term "substantially related" is a label that is used when the judge reaches this conclusion.

Analyzing the issues this way carries risk of two errors: The judge may find a substantial relationship when in fact no information is at risk (*a false positive*); or a judge may not find a substantial relationship when in fact there is one (*a false negative*). These risks are present because the test we use is actually a proxy or a surrogate for close examination of the entire file in each matter, which the judge obviously has no time to do. Also, using a proxy relieves the former client from putting on the record the very confidential information it claims is at risk in the new matter and which it wants to protect. So the judge asks, first, what kind of information a lawyer would likely have acquired in the first matter and, second, whether it is the kind of information that would be helpful if used against the former client in the second matter.

The law firm whose disqualification is sought may insist that even though it looks like the answer should be yes, in fact if the court were to examine its entire file on the former matter, it would conclude otherwise (and thereby avoid a false positive). But the court cannot examine the entire file and must, simply as a matter of efficiency, use the proxy of the substantial relationship test. Judges don't have the time to do otherwise. Also, the conflict question ordinarily arises at the beginning of a matter, so even examining the whole file may be an inadequate tool because of uncertainty of precisely how the matter will develop.

As it happens, the danger of the false negative, unlike the danger of a false positive, can be avoided by examining just a very small part of a file, so small that there is only a slight intrusion on the court's time. The former client may say that although it looks like the two matters are *not* substantially related, in fact it can show that it gave its prior law firm just the kind of information that can now be used against it. It can ask the court to receive that information *in camera* (or ex parte) in order to avoid a false negative. Some judges have allowed this option.[4] We allow the former client to proceed ex parte so it does not have to reveal on the record the very confidential information it wishes to protect by making the disqualification motion in the first instance. Of course, if the two matters do appear to be substantially related, the former client will have no need and probably no interest in exposing its confidential information to the court, even ex parte, to avoid a false negative.

Loyalty to Former Clients   Lawyers have a continuing if modest duty of loyalty to a former client, not only a duty to protect former client confidences. The loyalty duty does not often appear in the case law. Yet if you read the one sentence test for former client conflicts contained in the American Bar Association (ABA) Rule 1.9(a), and common nationwide, you will see that the words *confidences* and *information* or variations on them nowhere appear. The test forbids opposing a former client in a substantially related matter. Full stop. Because the lynchpin is a substantial relationship — that is, an inquiry into factual overlap — it will *nearly* always happen that the new adverse matter puts the former client's confidential information at risk. This is why the case law on former client conflicts speaks about protecting confidential information.

But let us imagine a subsequent adverse representation in which no confidences are at risk. We can then see the role played by the duty of loyalty. Say Jones gets a big judgment against LMN Corp., which appeals and hires Sally to represent it to the state's intermediate appeals court. The only issue LMN wants Sally to argue is a question of law (let's say whether a state statute that is the entire basis for Jones's judgment violates the state constitution). Sally has no access to any LMN confidential information. Her entire case is based on the public record and her argument is purely a constitutional one. She wins. Then Jones asks Sally to represent him in a further appeal to the state's highest court. Can Sally do it? (I know this is unlikely ever to happen, but it is a useful hypothetical to isolate the duty of loyalty.) No confidential information is at risk. But none has to be. Sally would be adverse to LMN on the very same matter (and therefore, a fortiori, a substantially related one) as the matter on which LMN was her client.

The literal language of the former client conflict rules tells us Sally cannot do it. And that is how it should be. A lawyer should not be able to deprive a client of the specific objective that the client hired the lawyer to achieve for it. LMN hired Sally to free it from the judgment. She did. She should not now be allowed to represent LMN's opponent against it to reinstate the judgment. What's important here is that Sally would be undoing the very victory she was hired to win. But we have to be careful not to define this duty too broadly. The fact that it's the very same victory is key.

Here's another example. Say on behalf of EFG Corp., Max has successfully argued for a particular interpretation of a federal statute. Assume, like Sally, Max received no confidential information in doing this work. It was based entirely on public sources. A few years later, RST Co. wants to sue EFG for violating the same statute. RST wants to hire Max to argue for an interpretation of the statute contrary to the one he won for EFG. Perhaps the argument is based on some intervening federal case law or will be made to a court that is not precedentially bound by the earlier victory. So Max is now opposed to EFG over the meaning of the same statute. The duty of loyalty should not forbid Max to do this work. Nothing

Max does for RST will undo what he previously accomplished for EFG. The two matters are neither the same nor substantially related. Max has no duty to EFG never to advocate for a different legal position, even as against EFG itself. His only loyalty duty is not to do work adverse to EFG that deprives it of the decision he won.[5]

The "Hot Potato" Rule Because the lawyer conflict rules are more restrictive when the conflict concerns a current client than when it concerns a former client, a lawyer wishing to take a new matter will have greater freedom to do so if the client whose work presents the conflict is no longer a client. But what if it is still a client? Perhaps the lawyer can engage in a little self-help here by converting the current client to a former client, thereby freeing herself to accept an adverse matter that would otherwise be forbidden. The lawyer might do that by "firing" the client — that is, withdrawing from the representation. The client then becomes a former client and the lawyer can oppose it on any matter that is not substantially related to the work she had been doing for the client. What's wrong with that? It does seem pretty awful, doesn't it? Not the sort of crass opportunistic motive we expect (or hope to expect) from a member of a learned profession. But is it all right to do?

As it happens, the courts agree that this tactic is unworthy of respect and will not allow it as a way to avoid a current client conflict. The Ninth Circuit Court of Appeals criticized it long ago.[6] It said that it would refuse to view the fired client as a former client where the lawyer withdrew to be able to take on a new adverse matter. So for conflict purposes, the court said, it would treat the client as a current one, despite the lawyer's self-help tactic. Later, a federal district judge in Ohio gave this rule a name. She wrote that a "firm may not drop a client like a hot potato, especially if it is in order to keep happy a far more lucrative client."[7] And so was born the "hot potato rule." The rule protects the interests of a current client in the continuity of the professional relationship to its conclusion unless there are valid grounds to withdraw. The value, in other words, is the client's interest in staying with his lawyer to the end of the matter if he wants to do so. The economic interest of the lawyer in taking a new matter was not an acceptable reason to "fire" a client. The rule applies when a firm attempts to drop a client to accept a new client, to accept a new matter from a current client, or simply to achieve a firm merger or to hire a lateral lawyer where the firm could not do any of these things so long as the client remained a client.[8]

"Thrust Upon" Conflicts In one limited circumstance, courts will allow lawyers to escape from the rigors of the hot potato rule and withdraw from a representation to convert a current client to a former client in order to avoid a conflict. This is when the firm did nothing to create the conflict in the first place. Rather, it was "thrust upon" it. The two common thrust-upon situations are when an adverse party acquires or is acquired by a current client, so the firm suddenly finds itself in a concurrent client conflict situation, or when in the course of a litigation against a nonclient, a current client intervenes on the opposing side of the matter. Courts are disposed to let the firm decide which client to drop, but if one of the matters is in litigation, the court's interests are implicated and its permission required. In that event, the court might refuse to allow the lawyer to withdraw. Then, the other client will have the option of discharging the firm.[9]

ENDNOTES

1. *Jones v. Rabanco, Ltd.*, 2006 U.S. Dist. LEXIS 53766 (W.D. Wash. 2006).
2. *See* Model Rule 1.9(a). The substantial relationship test, at least in its modern articulation, was put forward by Judge Edward Weinfeld in *T.C. Theatre Corp. v. Warner Bros. Pictures, Inc.*, 113 F. Supp. 265 (S.D.N.Y. 1953). Since then it has been restated in essentially the same form, although from time to time courts will vary the language.

3. Tax advice followed by an antitrust action is exactly what occurred in *Analytica, Inc. v. NPD Research, Inc.*, 708 F.2d 1263 (7th Cir. 1983). There, Judge Posner defined the test as requiring the court to ask "if the lawyer could have obtained confidential information in the first representation that would have been relevant in the second." The answer was yes where the prior work was on a tax matter, followed by an adverse antitrust complaint.

4. *See, e.g., Decora, Inc. v. D.W. Wallcovering*, 901 F. Supp. 161 (S.D.N.Y. 1995).

5. In *In re American Airlines, Inc.*, 972 F.2d 605 (5th Cir. 1992), the court recognized that "the existence of a lawyer's duty of loyalty means that the substantial relationship test is not solely concerned with the adverse use of confidential information."

6. *United Sewerage Agency v. Jelco, Inc.*, 646 F.2d 1339 (9th Cir. 1989).

7. *Picker International, Inc. v. Varian Associates, Inc.*, 670 F. Supp. 1363 (N.D. Ohio 1987), *aff'd*, 869 F.2d 578 (Fed Cir. 1989).

8. *Truck Ins. Exch. v. Fireman's Fund Ins. Co.*, 8 Cal. Rptr. 2d 228 (Ct. App. 1992) (dropping one client to represent another current client adverse to the first client not permitted). In the *Picker* case, the source of the "hot potato" language, Jones Day represented Picker. It wished to acquire a boutique firm, MH&S. MH&S then represented Varian. But MH&S's work for Varian was on entirely unrelated matters so there was no risk to Varian's confidential information. Varian refused to waive the conflict. MH&S then withdrew from representing Varian and merged into Jones Day. Had MH&S not withdrawn, Jones Day, following the merger, would have been adverse to its own client. The district court refused to recognize Varian as a former client and disqualified Jones Day from representing Picker.

9. This is what happened in *Installation Software Technologies, Inc. v. Wise Solutions, Inc.*, 2004 Westlaw 524829 (N.D. Ill. 2004) (conflict created when *X*, client of firm *A*, acquired *A*'s litigation opponent; court rejects *A*'s motion to withdraw and says that *X* can choose if it wishes to terminate relationship with *A*).

～ **13** ～

Imputation of Conflicts

When and Why Are Conflicts Imputed?

When Can Screening Avoid Imputation?

The Special Case of Lateral Lawyers

Presumptions in Lateral Conflict Analysis

The idea of imputation is pretty easy to describe, but the policy justifications for it are a bit controversial, especially in the era of the huge, multi-office law firm. Imputation is a doctrine that says that the clients and former clients of one firm lawyer are also the clients and former clients of all of the other lawyers in the firm. So if the first lawyer cannot accept new work because it presents conflicts with other work he is then doing or has done, no other lawyer in the firm may do so either, unless the affected clients consent. Furthermore, if the first lawyer cannot accept work because the client's interests conflict with the lawyer's personal interests, then sometimes, though as we shall see not always, other lawyers in the firm cannot accept the work either, unless the affected client consents. One way to think of the imputation rule is to imagine that a law firm equals one lawyer, even a firm with 2,000 lawyers. There are different rules when the practice is in a government law office, but the imputation rules are the same for all private law offices, which includes law firms, corporate law departments, and institutional law offices (like legal services and legal aid offices), although some courts have created exceptions for some institutional law offices.[1]

Reasons for Imputation   We have seen that the rules credit a current client's interest in not having her lawyer oppose her on any matter (dispute or transaction) while he is representing her and also respect a former client's interest in preventing a former lawyer from opposing her on any matter substantially related to the work the lawyer did for the client. Other rules forbid a lawyer to represent a client when the conflicting interests are those of the lawyer himself or a third person to whom the lawyer may have allegiances or responsibility (like a relative). Yet other rules address certain recurrent situations by restricting the lawyer's behavior (e.g., business deals with clients) or forbidding the conduct outright (e.g., advancing living expenses to a litigation client). These rules mean to honor the lawyer's duties of loyalty or confidentiality or both.

So far so good. But why should we impute one lawyer's personal or professional disability to other lawyers in the same firm? (We can use *firm* broadly to refer to all nongovernment law offices recognizing that the greatest impact of the imputation rules is felt by private law firms.) The decision to do so reflects a basic policy—that is, the wish to encourage clients to have confidence and trust in their lawyers. Think of it from the client's point of view. Call him Mike. Mike's current lawyer, Jane, may not sue him, but isn't the harm to the professional relationship pretty severe if Jane's partner, Jody, brings the lawsuit? It may be an action for a large sum of money. Won't it affect Mike's ability to work with Jane if Jody is suing him? After all, even though Jane is his lawyer, her firm is "his" firm, or at least that's how Mike will think of it. Just to illustrate the concern a little more directly, imagine if Jane and Jody are the only lawyers in the firm. Similarly, if Mike is Jane's *former* client, will he be comforted to know that the lawyer suing him on a substantially related matter — that is, where the firm of Jane & Jody has Mike's relevant confidential information — is not Jane, but her partner Jody? Doubtful.

As with any policy decision, we could acknowledge that Mike won't be happy in this situation but choose not to impute Jane's conflict to Jody because of the same countervailing considerations that drive other policy choices in the conflict arena: a lawyer's career interest in developing her practice, another client's interest in retaining counsel of choice. We might even worry that some big clients, thinking strategically, will keep feeding good law firms small assignments for the express reason of conflicting all of the firm's lawyers from acting adversely to them ever. Of course, a firm can avoid imputation by declining work or by insisting on a waiver of any conflict the work would otherwise create (see Chapter 15).

Now look at the same question with a large law firm in mind. It's not the firm of Jane & Jody (or even Jane, Jody, and a half dozen other lawyers), but the firm of Global & Everywhere (G&E). It has more than 1,500 lawyers in 11 countries and 23 cities. Few lawyers know more than a tenth of the other lawyers in the firm, whose lawyer population changes monthly. At best, each lawyer knows (some of) the lawyers who practice in the same city or the same practice area. Now assume that Jack, in Tokyo, is advising Bigco on a trade issue. Jenya, in Chicago, is asked to represent XYZ in a negotiation with Bigco.

The matters are unrelated. No Bigco confidential information is at risk. Do we impute Jack's conflict (he cannot personally oppose Bigco in the negotiation without consent) to Jenya? We do. Of course, it is likely that Bigco will consent, but that's not the question. Does Jenya need consent? Can Bigco say that without its consent, it has a right not to see "its" firm on the other side of the table, even if the table is half a world away from where Jack is doing his work? The imputation rules do not differentiate between the law firm of Jane & Jody and the law firm of Global & Everywhere, but should they? (By the way, Jenya will also need consent from the client she is representing in the negotiation with Bigco. Do you see why? Under Rule 1.7(a)(2) there is a significant risk that Jenya's work will be materially limited by her reluctance to antagonize Bigco, which may be a big client of the firm.)

If we say that the rules should differentiate between smaller and larger firms, how do we do that? That is, where do we draw the line between a 2-lawyer firm and a 1,500-lawyer firm? Or do we draw the line between sophisticated and unsophisticated clients? Bigco can take care of itself, but maybe Mike, who rarely goes to a lawyer, does not know about imputation. So maybe the imputation rule should turn on the client's sophistication, not firm size. In this view, we would impute conflicts on Mike's behalf (i.e., imputation would be the default rule unless the law firm bargains to avoid it) but not on Bigco's behalf (i.e., no imputation would be the default rule unless Bigco bargains for it). Or should our default rule be a function of both variables — client sophistication and firm size (and geographical dispersion)? But then how do we capture the test for "sophistication" in the language of a rule? Remember that the language has to be sufficiently clear and predictable to let lawyers and clients plan.

You see the problem. Even if we decided that the proper default rule should accommodate these two variables (firm size and client sophistication), or either one of them, it would be a challenge to write a rule that provides adequate guidance to a firm as it decides whether it can accept a matter without consent. We need a bright-line rule that fits all situations, at least as a practical matter, leaving it to the firm or the client to negotiate for a different rule if so advised. And that's what we have: a single rule that imputes all current and former client conflicts throughout firms of any size. A rule that protects Mike also protects Bigco. (There is an exception for lateral lawyers in some jurisdictions, as discussed later.) That puts the onus on the firm to seek consent for a different rule, which it is well motivated to do, of course, because a more lenient rule frees it to accept new business that the default imputation rule might otherwise preclude. Large law firms, and even small ones, know (or should know) about the imputation rule and how to avoid it, whereas small clients often do not. Between client and lawyer, the rules operate from the assumption that if we need a single rule to apply to all situations, it is better to err on the side of protecting clients and requiring law firms to displace the rule with informed consent.

Not All Conflicts Are Imputed   We've been working with a fact pattern in which the conflict is between the interests of current clients or between the interests of former and current clients. And indeed the imputation rule operates to impute these client-client conflicts. But when we move from client-client conflicts to lawyer-client conflicts, the need for imputation to encourage client trust is often reduced. Not always, but sometimes. Imagine a firm of 100 lawyers. Sonya is retained to represent Realty in seeking a zoning change that will allow it to use a parcel of land for commercial purposes. Sonya's colleague Sam lives four blocks away and would not like to see Realty succeed. He likes his neighborhood residential. So perhaps Sam could not personally represent Realty because of his contrary interest, but should we impute Sam's conflict to Sonya? What questions would we ask? Maybe Sam is managing partner and Sonya is a senior associate or maybe the opposite is true. Will the zoning change significantly reduce the value of Sam's home or indeed have a measurable financial impact? Or is his interest aesthetic? Will Sam actively participate in a community effort to resist the zoning change so we can anticipate Sam and Sonya becoming vocal opponents at the meeting of the city planning commission?

For a long time, American legal ethics rules did not distinguish among sources of conflicts in applying the imputation rule. But today they do. In the language of Rule 1.10(a), a conflict will not be imputed if it is "based on a personal interest of the prohibited lawyer [Sam in our example] and does not present a significant risk of materially limiting the representation of the client by the remaining lawyers in the firm [like Sonya]." The questions posed in the prior paragraph are meant to identify whether there is a "significant risk." Variations on this hypothetical are many. Perhaps the effect of the zoning change will be to the home of Sam's brother, not Sam. Perhaps opposition to it from others ensures that Sam will not personally be opposing Sonya at the planning commission. Situations that would likely lead to imputation of Sam's conflict to Sonya are (1) where Sam is Sonya's boss and the zoning change would have a substantial effect on the value of Sam's home and (2) where Sam will personally appear in various forums to oppose the change with Sonya there to support it.

If the firm decides that the imputation rule will not apply, it may nonetheless choose to play it safe and tell Realty about Sam's interest. Notice I do not say that the firm needs Realty's consent, because if the conflict is not imputed there is nothing to which Realty has to give its consent. But it may make sense from a client relations and business perspective to tell Realty. Or a firm may ask for consent anyway just to inoculate itself against the possibility that a tribunal will later decide its analysis underplayed the "significant risk." The firm should in any event screen Sam from Sonya's work to assure Realty that none of its confidential information will fall into the hands of community groups opposing it.

One other example of a conflict that should not be imputed: Some lawyers draw the line at representing certain clients for ideological reasons.[2] I had a friend, a partner at a major firm, who would not personally represent tobacco companies because of the harm that cigarettes had caused members of his family. He was adamant that he would not and could not work for these companies on any matter at all, but he did not object if other firm lawyers wished to do so. His personal conflict did not create the triggering "significant risk" within the meaning of Rule 1.10(a). Indeed, it would not even have been necessary to tell a tobacco company client about my friend's position because there was not even the glimmer of a possibility that a judge might later find an imputable conflict. Incidentally, my friend also believed that the same position that prevented him from working for tobacco companies should lead him to decline any share of the firm's income derived from such work and he did (though no rule required it).

Screens   In a few words, screens, when allowed, avoid imputation that would otherwise occur; they thereby permit a lawyer or firm to escape a disqualifying conflict. The key phrase is "when allowed." Of course, just as a client can consent to a conflicted representation outright (see Chapter 15), so, too, can a client agree to let a firm use a screen to avoid imputation of a conflict that would otherwise restrict its work. Sometimes, indeed, clients will be willing to tolerate a conflict only if there is a screen. For example, in the situation with Jack and Jenya, Bigco might agree to let Jenya negotiate against it in Chicago while Jack represents it in Tokyo, but only if Jack is screened from the work Jenya is doing.

Of what substance are screens made?[3] There is no single formula. To answer this question we have to first ask what we are intending to protect with the screen. The ultimate goal is to erect intra-firm protocols to ensure that the two lawyers or two teams of lawyers have nothing to do with each other on the matters at hand. Sometimes a screen is used in a concurrent client conflict situation even though the two matters for the different clients are wholly (i.e., factually) unrelated, as is likely in the Bigco example. That is, Jack will not have acquired any confidential information about Bigco of use to Jenya's client as it negotiates (or even litigates) against Bigco. Then, the screen does not protect confidences but rather protects the trust necessary to the attorney-client relationship. Bigco can take comfort in knowing that Jack has nothing to do with — and is being kept from — the adverse matter Jenya is handling in Chicago. That comfort may not seem so important standing alone, especially if Jenya's matter is transactional, but it is a value nonetheless. It is the reason we require the firm to seek Bigco's permission for Jenya to take on her client. And if the Chicago work is a litigation, where ill feeling is more probable and where, unlike most transactions, no one can easily walk away from the table, it is easier to understand why Bigco would want the security of knowing that its lawyer, Jack, has nothing to do with case.

So where the only threat to the client is to trust in a lawyer's loyalty, a screen that simply ensures that the two (sets of) lawyers have nothing to do with each other on the matters should ordinarily be sufficient. Where, however, there is a substantial relationship between the two matters creating the conflict — say, Jack will receive Bigco's confidential information relevant to a negotiation or litigation Jenya is handling against Bigco — the company has the further interest in ensuring that the firm has taken steps to keep confidences from Jack's matter away from Jenya, assuming Bigco remains willing to consent. There is no single way to build a screen in this circumstance. At the very least, though, lawyers and support staff handling Jack's matter for Bigco must be told of the screen and the need to exclude lawyers and support staff on the other (i.e., Jenya's) matter from receiving any of Bigco's confidential information. Firms tend to give this instruction firm-wide to be extra safe. A firm may protect any such information in its database or file room with passwords or keys. If Jack and Jenya are in the same city, extra precautions are needed to avoid overlap in support staff.

As stated earlier, in the Jack and Jenya hypothetical, it is not only Bigco whose consent is required. Jenya's Chicago client, Bigco's adversary, must also be told of the conflict and consent. While its confidential information is not at risk in the work Jack is doing for Bigco in Tokyo, the fact remains that its lawyer's (Jenya's) firm also represents its opponent and that could influence the firm's (and Jenya's) willingness to really go after Bigco. Maybe Bigco is a big client of the firm. Maybe Jenya would not want to do anything, though legitimate, that would anger Bigco and cause it to withdraw business. Or maybe not. The point is that the client-client conflict encompasses both clients, and both have to consent to letting Jenya take the Chicago matter.

What we've said about conflicts between two current clients also applies to former client conflicts. Imagine that Jack has finished his work for Bigco and it is no longer a firm client. Then a new client, Upstart, seeks to retain Jenya to oppose Bigco in a negotiation or litigation. We know that she can take the matter if there is no substantial relationship between it and the work Jack did for Bigco. But what if there is a substantial relationship? Then, Jenya (and the firm) needs consent from Bigco. Bigco's recognized interest is in protecting confidential information in the firm's possession as a result of Jack's work and which, we're assuming, has relevance to Jenya's work against Bigco. Bigco might then agree to permit Jenya to accept the new matter (and is more likely to do so if the work is transactional, not litigation) so long as she and her team of lawyers and support persons are screened from the matter Jack handled. That means that neither Jack nor anyone on his team can work on the new matter against Bigco and that Jenya and her staff must be kept away from Bigco's confidential information. In addition, Upstart has to consent to the conflict. It needs to know that the firm has but may not use Bigco's confidential information relevant to the new matter. And it needs to know that Bigco was once a client because perhaps the firm has hopes of luring it back as a client, which may affect Upstart's view of the firm's willingness aggressively to represent Upstart against Bigco. Upstart, however, unlike Bigco, has no confidential information at risk.

A lurking question: Why would Bigco ever give its consent to let Jenya represent Upstart? After all, what does Bigco get out of it? The firm's work for it is done. It need not consent to the conflict as a condition of being able to hire the firm. Consent now would be entirely gratuitous. All true, and Bigco might not consent at this point, although if the matter is transactional (and so less adversarial) Bigco might actually be happy to see a lawyer from its former firm across the table, depending on its view of the firm's professionalism. We have been assuming that G&E, Jenya's firm, first seeks Bigco's consent after the work for it is over and Upstart seeks to retain it. That may not be so. G&E may have planned ahead. When Bigco first sought to hire Jack in Tokyo, G&E might have conditioned its willingness to accept Bigco's matter on Bigco's consent to screen other firm lawyers who might be asked to oppose Bigco in substantially related matters after the work for Bigco was over (or even if the work were still ongoing). G&E might or might not have been able to get that *advance consent*. It will depend on how badly Bigco wants to hire it. We discuss advance consents further in Chapter 15.

Lateral Lawyers   Much of the debate about screens has arisen in the context of lateral lawyers. A lateral (or migratory) lawyer is simply one who moves from one practice situation to another one — say, one private firm to a different private firm.

The lawyer may be an associate or partner. While job changes by young associates are nothing new, the last generation has seen a significant increase in the numbers of partners moving between private law firms. Not so very long ago, partnership was presumptively for life. Partners were not asked to leave, even if they were unproductive (although they may have suffered a decrease in income), and highly successful partners did not leave, even if they may have felt that their partnership share should be greater. That has all changed in our new "free agent" environment. Although some firms have managed to avoid it, it is now routine for partners to leave for more lucrative positions and for firms to fire unproductive partners. In fact, many firms, aiming to grow more quickly than is possible simply by hiring more new law graduates, look for lawyers at competing firms whom they can hire away. Sometimes a big firm will swallow a smaller one whole. Or two firms, large or small, might merge. (While we speak of partners, the same observations apply regardless of how a firm is organized. If it is in corporate form, we would simply substitute *shareholder* for *partner*.) But whatever the reasons for an increase in lateral movement, and whatever its scope, the conflict questions are the same. If a lawyer leaves firm A for firm B, what if any client conflicts does she bring to firm B? And will those conflicts be imputed to her new colleagues? If they are imputed, can the imputation be avoided with a screen?

The answer to the first question is easy enough. The lateral lawyer brings only those conflicts that are personal to her, not the ones that were merely imputed to her while she was at firm A.[4] If our lateral — let's call her Nina — worked for client Bigco on a matter while at firm A, then when she moves to firm B she brings this history with her. In effect, Bigco becomes the former client of firm B on Nina's matter for it. This happens instantly, as soon as Nina arrives. Firm B must put Bigco in its database of former clients. That means that unless a screen is allowed, the firm B lawyers will not be able to be adverse to Bigco on any matter substantially related to the one Nina handled for it at firm *A*. If firm *B* is then handling a substantially related matter adverse to Bigco, due diligence should discover that before Nina gets an offer and any offer will be conditioned on Bigco's agreement to let firm *B* screen Nina if agreement is required.

So much for the matters Nina personally handled at firm *A*. Once Nina leaves firm *A*, any conflict she labored under while at it *solely* because of the work of another firm *A* lawyer — that is, a conflict by imputation, not based on her own work — disappears with her departure. So if Nina's firm *A* colleague Charlie (but not Nina) did or does work for Bigco, conflicts arising out of that work are imputed to Nina while she is at firm *A*, but once she leaves, she sheds those imputed conflicts. So there is nothing to impute to the lawyers at firm *B* when Nina arrives. Both Nina and her new colleagues may be adverse to Bigco on any matter.

If Nina is *personally* conflicted because of work she did at firm *A* (or information she received about a firm *A* client even if she did not work for it), the second question we ask is whether firm *B* can avoid imputation of her conflict by screening her. As stated above, the answer is, of course, yes, with client consent. Imputation of any conflict that the lateral lawyer brings with her can be avoided with a screen just as imputation can be avoided with consent under other circumstances. Clients can agree to a screen. That's the easy part. The harder screening issue that arises in a lateral lawyer situation — the issue that gets a lot of attention — is somewhat different. It is whether client consent is needed at all. Here we are introduced to the concept of *nonconsensual screening*. Until now, our discussion has recognized screens as adequate to avoid imputation when the client consents to the screen. That's *consensual* screening. But in the lateral lawyer situation, should we allow the lawyer's new firm to screen the new lawyer without need for the former client's (Bigco's) consent, even over its objection?

The arguments in favor of allowing nonconsensual screening in this situation cite the legitimate career interests of lawyers. Young lawyers often change jobs and should not be unduly hampered in doing so. Older lawyers now move around quite bit, too, sometimes by choice, sometimes not. Proponents of nonconsensual screening argue that we should facilitate these job changes, that we can trust lawyers to honor their confidentiality obligations and trust their new firm colleagues not to importune them to do otherwise. Nonconsensual screening also enables a new client of the lawyer's new firm to hire the lawyer it wants.

The argument against nonconsensual screening is that it asks too much of the lateral lawyer's former client. Let's say while at firm *A*, Nina was an important strategist on behalf of Bigco in a litigation against it. Now she moves to firm *B*, which wants to screen her so it can represent an opponent of Bigco in that (or a substantially related) litigation. When we permit nonconsensual screening, we are asking Bigco to trust Nina not to reveal information that may give her new firm's client a real advantage in the matter. Bigco may complain that this is too much to ask it to do on faith, especially given the stakes in the litigation and the information Nina has. And it pretty much will be on faith, won't it? Bigco can't really police compliance with the screen. If the screen is violated, will Nina or other lawyers at firm *B* really come forward and confess?[5]

The committee that recommended changes to the American Bar Association (ABA) Model Rules in 2000 would have allowed nonconsensual screening of lateral lawyers, but the ABA House of Delegates rejected the proposal (one of the very few proposals from the committee that it did reject). However, in February and August 2009, the ABA reversed itself and revised Model Rule 1.10 to approve nonconsensual screening when lawyers change firms. The ABA added a requirement that the lateral lawyer and his or her new firm (Nina and firm *B*, in my example) certify the existence of and compliance with the screen, including after the matter has ended. Many states, either in their ethics rules or through court decision, have allowed law firms to screen lateral lawyers. These jurisdictions vary in how they do it. Some allow a firm to screen any lateral lawyer.[6] Some do the same, but to ensure compliance with the screen and allay the worry of the lateral lawyer's former client, they require the lateral lawyer and a lawyer at her new firm (firm *B*) to swear under oath that the screen has not been breached.[7]

Other jurisdictions adopt what we may call a middle position. They allow a new firm to screen a lateral only when the lateral lawyer does not have significant information about the matter creating the conflict. This is a sort of compromise.[8] The lawyer who may have spent a few hours on a matter at a prior firm, giving advice in the area of his expertise or researching a discrete and peripheral issue, can be screened, but the lawyer who was running (or helping to run) the matter cannot be screened. While this solution may make sense on paper as a compromise between no nonconsensual screening and unrestricted screening, it has limited value in practice. Come back to Nina, moving from firm *A* to firm *B*. As it happens, the two firms are opponents in *Blue v. Red*. Assume Nina is a third-year associate. The hiring partner at firm *B* knows, of course, that firm *A* represents Blue, so he asks Nina if she has done any work on the litigation. If not (and if she has received none of Blue's confidential information about the matter, even if she did not work on it), then of course there is no problem. She is not personally disqualified from acting adversely to Blue on the matter after she changes firms. She can do so and so can her new colleagues. There is no conflict to impute because Nina's conflict was solely a result of imputation while she was working at firm *A*. When Nina left firm *A*, her imputed conflict disappeared.

But let's say the conversation goes this way. Asked if she worked on *Blue v. Red*, Nina says, "Yes, I did a little work for Blue." What then? In a jurisdiction that subscribes to the middle position on nonconsensual conflicts, the hiring partner needs to know what "little" means. Was Nina exposed to significant and material information (or whatever may be the jurisdiction's test), or something less than that? So he asks her that question directly. What can she say? For one thing, she may not be able to describe the work, even generally, because that information may itself be confidential. Perhaps she could say how much time she spent on the matter, but a lawyer can acquire significant and material confidential information in five minutes, so time is not a sure proxy. And besides, will firm *B* be willing to let the prospective hire — here a third-year associate — decide for it whether she can be screened under the jurisdiction's test? Surely not. So Nina may not get hired because firm *B* will not relish the prospect, if it hires and screens Nina, of a motion to disqualify it from representing Red on the ground that Nina's participation in the case while at firm *A* was too substantial to permit screening to avoid her conflict.

Of course, firm *B* can always ask firm *A* to ask Blue to consent to letting it screen Nina regardless of what she knows (and Blue may agree). But that's not *non*consensual screening. No jurisdiction forbids consensual screening in this situation. So at the moment that it really matters — when a firm is deciding whether to take on a lateral lawyer and whether it can avoid imputation of her conflict with a screen — often it will have to guess. When it does have to guess, the firm will not likely be willing to take the risk of guessing wrong because the consequences include disqualification from a current matter and in all likelihood a very angry client. The lawyer in Nina's position would have to be a real star to cause the firm to take its chances, and even then it will hesitate.

Presumptions in Lateral Lawyer Conflict Analysis[9]   The world of lateral lawyer conflicts employs two presumptions to help identify whether a lawyer in Nina's position is personally disqualified or whether, instead, on leaving firm *A* she sheds any disability that was the product of imputation only. The first presumption is that Nina did receive confidential information about firm *A*'s client in the matter at issue — in other words, of Blue in the *Blue v. Red* litigation. Sometimes this presumption is counterintuitive. For example, Nina might be an associate in New York while the litigation is pending in California and handled by firm *A*'s Los Angeles office. Nina might even be in an entirely different department of the firm — tax, not litigation. Nonetheless, we have to begin somewhere, and Nina should know what she knows or doesn't know and what she did and did not work on (she should have access to her time records after all). This presumption is simply a way to put the burden on Nina and firm *B* — in the event of a disqualification motion from firm *A* — to prove that Nina has no confidential information from the matter. Often, that can be done with an affidavit and perhaps time records.

If Nina cannot rebut the presumption because she in fact did work on *Blue v. Red*, then we encounter a second presumption. It is that Nina will share what she knows with lawyers at firm *B* representing Red. In other words, harsh as it may sound, it appears to be a presumption that Nina will in fact violate her duty of confidentiality. Another, less cynical, way to look at it is to say that the rules do not actually mean to predict that Nina will in fact abuse Blue's confidential information. Rather, they simply accept Blue's anxiety that she will do so as sufficient to impute her conflict throughout her new firm. In jurisdictions that do not allow nonconsensual screening, that's the end of the matter. The presumption (which unlike the first presumption is about the future, not the past) is conclusive. It cannot be rebutted. In jurisdictions that allow nonconsensual screening, timely creation of the screen rebuts the presumption. But the screen must be in place when Nina arrives. The firm cannot get to it later, not even a short time later. If there is a lapse in time between Nina's arrival and creation of the screen, a court may not accept the belated screen as sufficient to rebut the presumption (and to provide comfort to Nina's former client, Blue).

ENDNOTES

1. The rule for private law offices is Model Rule (MR) 1.10(a). The rule for lawyers entering or leaving government law offices, whether or not their work in government is or was as a lawyer, is MR 1.11. For a case in which a judge refused to follow the usual imputation rules because the law firm was an institutional defender, *see United States v. Reynoso*, 6 F. Supp.2d 269 (S.D.N.Y. 1998). Taking the contrary view is *Duvall v. State*, 923 A.2d 81 (Md. 2007) (relying on §123 of the *Restatement of the Law Governing Lawyers*).

2. The example given in MR 1.10 cmt. [3] is in this category: "where one lawyer in a firm could not effectively represent a given client because of strong political beliefs . . . but that lawyer will do no work on the case and the personal beliefs of the lawyer will not materially limit the representation by others in the firm, the firm should not be disqualified." The comment contrasts the situation where the opposing party is owned by a firm lawyer. Then disqualification would be required if the loyalty of the other lawyers in the firm to that lawyer would materially limit their work.

3. For an example of a screen that satisfied a court, *see Cromley v. Board of Education*, 17 F.3d 1059 (7th Cir. 1994).

4. A leading case on this point is *Silver Chrysler Plymouth, Inc. v. Chrysler Motors Corp.*, 518 F.2d 751 (2d Cir. 1975).

5. As discussed in Chapter 14, the rule is different for lawyers who previously worked for a government body.

6. North Carolina's version of MR 1.10 retains the screening provisions that the ABA rejected in 2002.

7. *See, e.g.*, Oregon Rule 1.10(c) and Massachusetts Rule 1.10(e).

8. *See, e.g.*, Minnesota Rule 1.10(b), which requires that any "confidential information" possessed by the lateral lawyer "is unlikely to be significant in the subsequent matter." Minnesota based its rule on §124 of the *Restatement of the Law Governing Lawyers*. New York has achieved the same result through case law. *Kassis v. Teachers' Ins. & Annuity Assn.*, 717 N.E.2d 674 (N.Y. 1999).

9. For a description of the operation of presumptions in the Model Rules, see MR 1.9 cmt. [6]. This comment presumes that the lateral lawyer has confidential information but permits rebuttal. The lawyer or his/her new firm has "the burden of proof" on the question.

～ 14 ～

Lawyers in Government

Why the Rules Are Different

Confidential Government Information

Screening Former Government Lawyers

Successive Conflicts for Government Lawyers

Most of the rules that regulate lawyers for private clients also regulate lawyers who work for government. Loyalty and confidentiality duties are pretty much the same as are the other elements of the professional relationship covered in Chapter 6, but the conflict rules are notably different. Here we will look at important ways in which they are different and the reasons for the differences. Essentially, there are three reasons: to ensure that lawyers who work for government do not (and do not appear to) make decisions—choose their agenda—while in public office in order to enhance their employment prospects after they leave;

to facilitate the ability of lawyers who work for government to find private jobs after leaving government without scaring away prospective employers who fear imputation of conflicts; and to protect against abuse of a certain category of information, called confidential government information, that government officials are especially able to get because of the powers of their office. At the same time, we want to encourage lawyers to work for government despite what for many will be salaries that are substantially lower than in the private sector. And one inducement is experience they will get and which they can translate into responsible and remunerative private sector jobs.

Screening to Avoid Imputation of Conflicts As we saw in Chapter 13, the American Bar Association (ABA) Model Rules now recognize nonconsensual screening to avoid the imputation of a lateral lawyer's conflicts when the lawyer moves from one private practice setting to another. When the lateral lawyer is moving from government employment to private life, nonconsensual screening is also permitted. Indeed, the Model Rules long permitted nonconsensual screening of former government lawyers before it changed its rule in 2009 to allow the same for lateral lawyers from private practice. (Depending on the jurisdiction and the circumstances, the new firm may have to give the government notice of the screen and may need to exclude the former government lawyer from participating in the fee the firm earns for the matter from which he or she is excluded.) Even jurisdictions that do not allow for nonconsensual screening in other contexts do so for the former government lawyer in order to encourage lawyers to enter government service without fear that they will find it hard to get a job when they leave. Absent the authority to screen without first having to get permission from the government, a firm may refuse or be reluctant to hire a former government lawyer for two reasons. If the firm is then representing a client whom the former government lawyer could not represent by virtue of her government work, the lawyer's conflict would be imputed to the firm and it would have to withdraw. That is not an attractive prospect. Authority to screen without permission avoids this risk and encourages employment offers. Another concern of the prospective employer is whether the former government lawyer's work will prevent it from taking new matters after the lawyer arrives at the firm. If the firm knows it can screen the lawyer, it need not worry that it may be frozen out of new work by virtue of the lawyer's presence.

Take an example. People go to work for government to gain experience, often in a specialized area of law. Chet is interested in securities law and goes to work for the Securities and Exchange Commission (SEC), where he rises to a supervisory position. After five years, he decides to go back into private practice and looks for a firm with a vibrant securities practice. The firm he picks finds Chet to be a good prospect, specifically because of his SEC experience, which will also be attractive to prospective clients. But as we will see below, Chet's SEC work will prevent him from handling certain (perhaps many) cases. Some of those cases may now be at the firm and some others, which cannot be anticipated exactly, may emerge later. The firm does not want to lose current clients if Chet's conflict is imputed to it, and it does not want to have to turn away future clients for the same reason. The fact that Chet's government service has given him an enhanced specialty cuts two ways. It makes him more attractive to the firm, but if nonconsensual screening is not allowed, his government experience can be a business killer. If law firms could not screen lawyers like Chet without having to get the government to consent, Chet may never have chosen government work in the first place, for fear of shutting employment doors later. But we want lawyers to be willing to go to government, and so the rules do allow screening without the need for consent. Chet knows at the outset that he will not have to pay this price for taking a government job.

(Although the example uses the SEC, the rule applies to lawyers for local governments as well.)

When Is a Former Government Lawyer Conflicted?   So far, so good. We know that Chet can be screened if he has a personal conflict. But when will that be? The rules identify two situations: when the matter is one in which he "participated personally and substantially as a public officer or employee" and when he has "confidential government information" about the matter which he can use to the disadvantage of the subject of the information.[1] In the first instance, government consent will remove the conflict so that even Chet can work on the matter after leaving government; but government consent won't cure the second conflict.[2] We address the concept of *confidential government information* below (it's not the same as the *confidential information* protected by Rule 1.6). Here we analyze disqualification based on personal and substantial participation in a matter.

The first thing to notice about this restriction is that it applies to former government lawyers even if their government work was *not as a lawyer* but in some other capacity. That explains the reference to "public officer" in the language of the rule. So if the deputy undersecretary of the interior or the commissioner of transportation of Chicago is a lawyer, this rule would apply even though he or she was not working as a lawyer. The second thing to recognize about this rule is that it is not the exclusive limitation on a government employee's permissible work after leaving government. At the state and federal levels, there are statutes and regulations that constrain the postemployment work of government personnel, lawyers included. Here our concern is the ethics rules for lawyers only.[3]

Why do we forbid a former government lawyer from working on a "matter in which" he or she "participated personally and substantially"? Let's work with a hypothetical example that is quite close to an actual case. While at the SEC, Chet investigates Trading Co. for possible securities violations. The investigation takes a year or so and maybe charges are brought or maybe not. After Chet leaves, Vivian wants to hire him to sue Trading Co. for securities violations arising out of the same conduct that Chet investigated. The rule tells us that without the government's consent, he cannot accept the matter (and as we see in the next section, this may be a situation in which not even consent can cure the conflict). Government lawyers have a great deal of discretion, especially lawyers in a supervisory position. While their client may be the government, they (along with their office colleagues) are often on their own in deciding what to investigate, whom to charge, perhaps what rules to adopt. We don't want Chet while in government to choose his agenda based on his interest in post-departure work. That is, we don't want Chet choosing to investigate Trading Co. because that experience will later make him more desirable to private clients who may want to sue Trading Co. or, the converse, because the experience will increase the possibility that Trading Co. itself will hire Chet in private life to defend it against the kind of conduct Chet investigated while a government lawyer. The priorities Chet sets for his work should respond to the public interest only, not his interest after leaving his job. Of course, Chet gets a more general kind of experience by working for government whatever he does and he can exploit that experience in private life. In fact, we recognize that the opportunity for that kind of experience and the likelihood that it will help Chet get lucrative or rewarding private employment is a big reason that government is able to attract good lawyers in the first place, despite generally lower salaries for comparable work.

Where we draw the line, however, is with the particular "matters" Chet handles in government. In this hypothetical, the matter is the investigation of Trading Co. for certain behavior. Chet can't accept Vivian's (or Trading Co.'s) work in the area of his investigation without permission from his former office. In that way, the office is presumably in a position to guard against the loss of public confidence if Chet were free to continue his government work on behalf of Vivian or Trading Co. to his own advantage in private practice. It may seem unduly cynical to think that a government lawyer would choose his matters based on whether he thinks he will be able to exploit the work in the matter later for private gain, but the rule operates from a view of human nature that says it is certainly possible that that will happen. More important, the rule is concerned with the public's trust in the operation of government. Even if Chet never once thought of his postdeparture work when deciding to investigate Trading Co., the public (including Trading Co. if he then appeared against it for Vivian) may be suspicious of his motives. That is a result we wish to avoid.

The ability of the government to consent to Chet's post-departure work on behalf of Vivian (where consent is possible) or Trading Co. troubles some students of the rule. Who in government will make that decision? The answer is one or more government employees at the agency Chet left. But don't they have an interest in freely giving consent in anticipation of the day that they themselves will ask for consent for their own post-departure work? In other words, it may be seen to benefit agency personnel to establish a sort of common law of consent freely given. That is a danger.

As we've seen, if the government won't (or is not permitted to) consent to let Chet work on the matter, Chet's new employer can screen him to avoid imputing his conflict to his new associates.[4] This ability underscores the earlier discussion. If the new employer is already representing clients against Trading Co. on the same matter as the one Chet investigated, or if it is already representing Trading Co. on that matter, it can hire Chet without fear that it will thereby disqualify itself from current work unless the government consents. It does not need consent. And if it is not yet representing anyone in the matter, it can hire Chet secure in the knowledge that if such a client were to come along, it would not have to decline the work unless the government consents. Again, it does not need consent. That makes Chet more employable than he'd be if nonconsensual screening were not recognized.

Last, we should say something about the phrase "personally and substantially." Government employees may have different degrees of responsibility for a matter. The head of an agency is nominally responsible for all matters before her agency, but she may not do any work on, and be only dimly aware of, the great majority of them. The rule would not apply to her with regard to all of the agency's work, but it would apply to the assistant who is handling the matter on a daily basis and his direct supervisor who reviews the work. It's a question of degree. The rule does not prevent high officials who have little or no responsibility for a matter from working on the matter later, in private life. So broad a restriction would tend to discourage government employment and do little or nothing to advance the policy behind the rule — that is, to ensure that the officials making the important decisions about an agency's agenda have no incentive to choose based on their postgovernment career aspirations.

"Confidential Government Information" Government lawyers like other lawyers must respect their clients' and former clients' confidential information as described in Rules 1.6 and 1.9(c). But government lawyers' postemployment work is further restricted if they possess confidential government information. This term is defined in Rule 1.11 as "information that has been obtained under governmental authority and which, at the time this Rule is applied, the government is prohibited by law from disclosing to the public or has a legal privilege not to disclose and which is not otherwise available to the public." We can see the operation of this concept if we return to Chet and Trading Co. In his job at the SEC, Chet will have acquired information about Trading Co. and some of that information, perhaps most of it, will be information Chet was able to obtain because of the particular powers of government. These powers may include civil subpoena authority, grand jury process, or nonpublic filings a company or person is required to make.

Under the rule, Chet may not represent Vivian adverse to Trading Co. if the matter is one "in which the information could be used to the material disadvantage of" Trading Co. Nor may Chet's former agency waive this limitation. The rule is meant to protect Trading Co., which should not have to oppose a private litigant who has information about it (via Chet) that it (or others) were required to share with the government. This is not about the attorney-client privilege; the information is not within the attorney-client evidentiary privilege. True, the information is the government's confidential information under Rule 1.6 and, of course, a former client can waive the protection of Rule 1.6. But not here. By excluding the possibility of former client waiver in this situation, we mean to protect the interests of *nonclient* Trading Co. from a private opponent's adverse use of information acquired about Trading Co. because of the superior power of government to compel or elicit information.

This limitation is inapplicable if the information is available to the public anyway, as through a Freedom of Information Act (FOIA) request or because it has become known. The limitation is also inapplicable if the party wishing to hire Chet after he leaves government is not Vivian but Trading Co. That is because the information is *about* Trading Co., so Chet would not be representing a "private client whose interests are adverse" to Trading Co. within the language of the rule. But Chet would still be forbidden to represent Trading Co. in the matter unless the government consented because he will have participated "personally and substantially" in the matter while employed by the government.

As before, even if Chet is forbidden to represent Vivian against Trading Co. because he possesses confidential government information about it, his new firm may screen him and avoid imputation of his conflict. In that instance, we are asking the government and the opposing party (Trading Co.) to trust Chet not to reveal the information.

The Government's Claims as a Former Client We know that a lawyer may not be adverse to a former client on a substantially related matter. This is what Rule 1.9(a) and numerous cases say. But Rule 1.11 and comment [1] to Rule 1.9 make it clear that the analysis is different when the former client is the government. Rule 1.9(a) does not then apply. If there were nothing more, the former government lawyer would be able to act adversely to the government in a matter substantially related to the work he did for the government. But even though Rule 1.9(a) does not apply, the limitation in Rule 1.11(a), forbidding the lawyer to represent a private client "in connection with a matter" in which he "participated personally and substantially" does apply. And so it may seem that we reach pretty much the same result anyway, especially if we read the Rule 1.11(a) reference to "matter" to include not only the exact same matter but substantially related matters as well, which makes sense and which would seem to be the import of Rule 1.11 comment [10]. In fact, the disability in Rule 1.11(a) is in one way even broader than the language of Rule 1.9(a). Rule 1.11(a) would forbid the postgovernment work even if that work was *not* adverse to the government, the former client, whereas Rule 1.9(a) only forbids work on a substantially related new matter if the former client's interests are adverse in the new matter. Rule 1.9(a)'s prohibition against subsequent adverse representation on a substantially related matter would seem to be fully captured in the even broader language of Rule 1.11(a).

However, this is not exactly so because of the particular way that Rule 1.11(e)(1) defines *matter* solely for purposes of applying Rule 1.11. Specifically, it says the word includes "any judicial or other proceeding, application, request for a ruling or other determination, contract, claim, controversy, investigation, charge, accusation, arrest or other particular matter involving a specific party or parties." Not included in the definition is drafting a regulation or statute. A generic rule or statute does not "involv[e] a specific party or parties." And so Rule 1.11 would permit a lawyer who, for example, has drafted a regulation for a government agency to represent a private client in an effort to narrow the scope of the regulation or even have it declared void — for example, because the agency did not have the statutory authority to promulgate the regulation the lawyer drafted. This may sound strange to our "ethical ears." Can it be that a government lawyer can attack the validity if his own work product? The answer is yes when the work product is a statute or regulation that does not "involv[e] a specific party or parties." Obviously, a lawyer in private practice who negotiated a contract for a client could not thereafter challenge the (now) former client's interpretation of a provision of the contract, much less argue that the contract or a term of it is void as against public policy. That would violate Rule 1.9(a). But in the parallel situation, the government lawyer may do so when the issue is solely the validity of a generic rule or statute.

This is obviously a tradeoff. In favor of the rule is the fact that forbidding the former government lawyer from arguing against the government over the interpretation or even validity of a rule the lawyer drafted could seriously restrict the work the lawyer could accept in private practice, especially if the particular rule is in a special field in which the lawyer concentrates. The meaning of government rules and statutes is going to be litigated sooner or later by someone, probably often, so it is not as if the government will have to respond to a challenge that would not otherwise be made. And the government's confidential information (the information that Rule 1.6 protects) will not ordinarily be threatened by any challenge because resolution of the contest is not likely to depend in any way on the use of this information. Besides, Rule 1.9(c) *does* still bind the former government lawyer, and it forbids him or her to reveal or adversely use any confidential information that is not generally known.

The danger in permitting this post-departure adverse representation is one we addressed earlier — that is, that the cagey government lawyer will load up the rule or statute in such a way that makes it amenable to later challenge on behalf of a private client. The lawyer can then sell his or her services by touting special knowledge of where the rule or statute is particularly vulnerable. While this danger cannot be ignored — nor can we ignore the attendant risk that the public will suspect this behavior, even if incorrectly — it does seem remote. Whatever lawyer may bring a later challenge to the meaning or validity of the rule should be able to find the vulnerabilities nearly as quickly as the lawyer who drafted it. After all, that's what lawyers do. Furthermore, no single lawyer in government will ordinarily be the sole drafter of a rule or statute; rather, the drafting will go through a collegial process that includes many voices, thereby reducing the risk that one rogue lawyer can through clever drafting compromise the government's goals by including gaps that he or she can later exploit for a private client.

ENDNOTES

1. Model Rule (MR) 1.11(a) and (c).
2. MR 1.11(b) and (c).
3. *See, e.g.*, 18 U.S.C. §207 ("Restrictions on Former Officers, Employees, and Elected Officials of the Executive and Legislative Branches").
4. If Chet is screened, he may not participate in the fee the firm receives for the work. This is meant to deter Chet from benefiting from the work (and perhaps "helping" quietly). The prohibition against participating in the fee is something of a fig leaf. The loss to Chet can easily be compensated by increasing his salary or draw generally.

~ 15 ~

Consents to Conflict

What Conflicts Can Be Cured by Consent?

What Does Consent Permit the Lawyer to Do?

Who Must Consent?

The Mechanics of Consent

The conflict rules, it is often said (or at least I often say it), are mostly default rules, which means they are the rules that define the impermissible conflicts unless the lawyer or law firm and the client (or clients) agree otherwise. An agreement to displace the conflict rules does not necessarily make life easier for the lawyer. This is because clients may insist on rules that are *stricter* than the jurisdiction's default rule. So the words "consent to a conflict" can be misleading because they imply that any agreement will be in the lawyer's favor. Because the door swings both ways, the upshot is that whether an agreement displacing the conflict rules favors the client (by restricting the lawyer or firm further than would be true if the default governed) or favors the lawyer or firm (by freeing them from some of the constraints of the default rules) will depend on market power. Buyer meet seller. How badly does the lawyer want the work? A client with a lot of business to offer and a lot of firms from among which to choose can insist on more restrictive rules and get its way. Firms seeking the business may even be eager to promise greater restriction than the rules require. On the other hand, a firm that has a particular expertise of great value to a prospective client ("We have an office in Kazakhstan"; "The former chairman of the Securities and Exchange Commission has joined our firm") may be able to command consents to conflicts, current and future. This it will especially be inclined to do if it foresees that the client's work would otherwise foreclose it from accepting likely new (and lucrative) business. But despite this market view, my own experience tells me that if we were omniscient we would learn that when client and lawyer agree to abide by conflict rules different from those in the jurisdiction's rules, the substitute generally favors the law firm.

What Conflicts Can Be Cured by Consent? Short answer: Almost any current client conflict and any former client conflict can be waived with informed client consent,[1] assuming the client is not a government entity, where there are the limits we discussed in the prior chapter. Pause for a moment to acknowledge this reality. Doesn't it seem odd to talk about *ethics* in the context of the conflict rules when these rules can be so easily displaced by agreement? It can appear that there is not much "ethics" in these particular ethical rules. Rather, we draw the line where we do because we need to have a line somewhere, not because the place we draw it is inherently right. We then let the client and lawyer move the line in one direction or the other. But this is as it should be. The purpose of the conflict rules (determining where we draw that line) is to protect clients against the risk (or the apprehension) that an improper incentive will consciously or unconsciously influence a lawyer to fail properly to serve the client. Since the rules protect clients, why not let clients waive the protection so long as they are fully informed and competent to make the decision? And so, with narrow exception, we do.[2]

For current clients, the conflicts that cannot be waived are those where *the law* itself (apart from the ethics rules) may forbid waiver and, ethically, when the representation would require the lawyer or firm to assert a claim against another party represented by the same lawyer or firm "in the same litigation or other proceeding before a tribunal."[3] This is very narrow. For example, assume a firm represents two co-defendants in a civil litigation. The clients cannot agree to let the firm assert a cross-claim by one against the other. But if properly counseled, and if consistent with Rule 1.2(c), the clients can agree to forgo cross-claims and have the firm represent them both in their defense against their common enemy, the plaintiff. Rule 1.2(c) lets a client and lawyer agree to limit the scope of a representation so long as the limitation is "reasonable." The prohibition against waiver only applies to disputes before a tribunal.[4] It does not apply to transactional matters. So in a multiparty negotiation, two different lawyers at the same firm can each represent one of the parties with consent — and push for that client's position — even if their positions in the matter differ. Indeed, two lawyers in the same firm, with appropriate consent from sophisticated clients, can represent the buyer and seller of a property, respectively, although it is usually a bad idea if the transaction is at all complex or involves a lot of money.

Why make litigation adversity nonconsentable? Perhaps it is because litigation can be particularly nasty or because the tribunal, as a participant to the event, has an independent interest in a lawyer's undiluted commitment. Note, however, that the prohibition applies only if the firm represents the two clients in the *same* matter in which they are taking adverse positions. With consent, a lawyer can appear adverse to a party in a litigation where another lawyer in the firm represents that party *on a different matter*. A lawyer may represent Blue in

Blue v. Red, where Red is represented by a different firm, notwithstanding that Red may be a client of the lawyer's firm in another matter, even a factually related matter, although then the client, if it consents at all, is likely to insist on a screen between the two sets of lawyers.[5]

What Does Consent Permit the Lawyer to Do?　Lawyers can easily over-read the scope of a client's consent to allow a lawyer to do work that would otherwise be forbidden. That's a mistake. Translated, consent amounts to the client saying to the lawyer, "I understand the contrary influences on your loyalty, but I agree to trust you not to succumb to them." The consent is *not* a consent to violate any of the duties lawyers have to clients (as discussed in Part I). These continue undiluted. One exception to this arises when, in order to avoid a conflict, a client agrees to a limit on the lawyer's scope of work for that client. In other words, the retainer can sometimes carve out and exclude the part of the client's matter that creates the conflict. So, for example, a client may have a civil claim against five defendants. Her lawyer has a conflict with regard to one of them because a partner represents that defendant in an unrelated matter and that client either won't consent to let the firm sue it or the firm doesn't want to seek consent. So the lawyer may offer to sue four of the five defendants but not his firm's client. If the other four defendants are perfectly able to pay any adverse judgment and the loss of the fifth defendant does not significantly compromise the lawyer's ability to litigate the plaintiff's claim (and the fifth defendant is not an important source of discovery that may now be foreclosed), the lawyer can accept the client's consent to forgo suing the firm client.

Who Must Consent?　Depending on the situation, consent may be required from only one client or more than one client. For example, a firm may wish to act adversely to a current client whom it represents in an unrelated matter on behalf of a new client. The current client has a right not to see "its" firm acting adversely to it in any matter, and so the firm will need that client's consent. But the new client, whom the firm will be representing in opposition to the current client, must also consent because of a "significant risk" that the firm's unwillingness to antagonize its current client will dilute its efforts on behalf of the new client. If the new client consents, of course, it is not consenting to allow the firm to compromise efforts on its behalf. As another example, consider a firm that is asked to represent a new client adverse to a former client on a matter that is *not* substantially related to the work the firm did for the former client. No consent is required from the former client because the adverse work presents no conflict with it. But assume that the former client has been a good source of business and that the firm has been angling to get it to throw more business its way. Then, the new client should know about the former work and the firm's efforts to land more work from the former client because the new client may see these as a disincentive to do anything for the new client that might anger its opponent.

When Informed Consent Is Not Possible Sometimes, consent is impossible because the firm cannot tell the client from whom it would seek consent the information the client needs to know for the consent to be informed. The firm may not be able to impart this information because it is confidential. In that case, the conflict bars the work.

Take a lawyer representing Bank, which is about to make a large loan to Borrower. The lawyer's partner learns in otherwise unrelated work for Company that Borrower's finances are more risky than Bank realizes. Borrower may even have misrepresented its financial position. But that knowledge is a confidence of Company. Now, obviously, this information would be of great interest to Bank, which may then choose not to make the loan. So the firm is caught between its duty to reveal information to Bank (part of its professional obligation to keep its client informed; see Chapter 6) and its duty of confidentiality to Company (discussed in Chapter 4). It can ask Company for permission to reveal the information, but it probably then has to explain why it wants to do that in order to make a grant of permission informed. But the prospective loan from Bank to Borrower is a confidence of Bank, which the firm cannot reveal. The firm can ask Bank for permission to reveal the loan to another client in order to get the other client to agree to let the firm reveal the information to Bank, but perhaps Bank will want to know the identity of the other client, and in any event, even asking Bank for this permission can signal a problem that the firm knows about only because of a client confidence. Things can get really complicated.

One thing the firm cannot do at the time the dilemma arises is ask Bank to waive the firm's duty to inform Bank of important information bearing on the loan because that waiver can hardly be informed if Bank doesn't know what it is agreeing not to know. On the other hand, could a firm include in its retainer letter a client's agreement that the firm has no duty to inform the client of information learned while representing other clients, even if directly relevant to the client's matter and even if the lawyer handling the client's matter happens to learn that information from a firm lawyer representing another client? This is a hard question. In my judgment the answer is no, even though *at the time* of retainer, there may be no prospect that the situation will ever arise. Because we cannot know what the information is or how central to the client's matter it may be, this is an advance consent that is far too broad for me. And I doubt it would offer much protection if, as in the example here, the lawyer representing the lender learned confidentially that the borrower was facing bankruptcy and then let the lender go through with the loan anyway in reliance on such an advance consent from the lender.

It may be that the firm can find a way to steer around this problem and get the permissions it needs to extricate itself without violating a duty of confidentiality. But probably it cannot, and if it cannot, it has only one option — namely, to withdraw from representing Bank. Of course, even doing that (without explaining why) could tip Bank to a problem, but the alternative of continuing with the loan work while saying nothing about the borrower's financial distress is certainly unacceptable. Sometimes the best way out of a dilemma is not perfect, only the least imperfect.[6]

I've skipped over one difficulty in describing this issue. I've tacitly assumed that the lawyer representing Bank *knows* what the lawyer representing Company has discovered or, alternatively, that the lawyer for Company knows about the work her colleague is doing for Bank. It would hardly be fair to fault the lawyer for Bank for continuing with the loan if she doesn't know what lawyer for Company knows or to fault the lawyer for Company if she doesn't know about the work for Bank. In other words, the law firm's conflict between the duty to inform and the duty of confidentiality arises for the firm (which represents both clients) only if someone at the firm is aware of the situation. In even moderately sized firms, this will often not be so. And it is even less likely to be so in large firms with many offices. We can't impute the knowledge of any single lawyer throughout a firm. Unlike imputation of clients for conflict purposes, information cannot be stored with a tag in a firm's database, available for easy retrieval every morning to see if it creates a problem. And firms, even small ones, receive vast amounts of information daily. It is only when a lawyer at the firm (the one who is working for Bank or the one working for Company or someone else) has actual knowledge of what Company's lawyer knows and what Bank's lawyer is doing that the firm's duty to obtain consent or withdraw should arise.

ENDNOTES

1. I'm going to use *waiver* as a synonym for *consent*. Some may see them as distinct, with consent being a conscious decision to allow conduct and waiver being the legal consequences of action or inaction. For example, a party who is

not permitted to object to representation on conflict grounds may be found to have waived its right to complain because of delay, even though it has not given informed consent to the conflict. For discussion, *see Alexander v. Primerica Holdings, Inc.*, 822 F.Supp. 1099 (D.N.J. 1993).

2. For convenience, I list here each of the conflict rules that have express provision for removal by consent: Model Rule (MR) 1.7(b)(4) and cmt. [18-20]; MR 1.9(a) and (b) and cmt. [9]; MR 1.10(c) and cmt. [6]. Rule 1.8(a), concerning lawyer-client financial arrangements, also has a consent provision. Consent for former government lawyer conflicts was discussed in Chapter 14. The Model Rules require that consent to a conflict be "confirmed in writing," which means that the client doesn't have to sign anything. The consent can be memorialized in a letter or e-mail from the lawyer. Some jurisdictions do not require a writing at all, and some require a writing signed by the client.

3. MR 1.7(b)(2) and (b)(3).

4. "Tribunal" includes more than courts. The terminology says it

denotes a court, an arbitrator in a binding arbitration proceeding or a legislative body, administrative agency or other body acting in an adjudicative capacity. A legislative body, administrative agency or other body acts in an adjudicative capacity when a neutral official, after the presentation of evidence or legal argument by a party or parties, will render a binding legal judgment directly affecting a party's interests in a particular matter.

5. *See, e.g., Visa U.S.A., Inc. v. First Data Corp.*, 241 F.Supp.2d 1100 (N.D. Cal. 2003) (upholding an advance consent for adverse litigation).

6. These facts are based loosely on *Bank Brussels Lambert v. Fiddler Gonzalez & Rodriguez*, 305 F.3d 120 (2d Cir. 2002), where in doing work for a different client, a firm discovered a serious problem with a client's prospective borrower but confidentiality rules prevented it from telling the lender. It allowed the loan to close and the lender eventually lost a lot of money. It sued the firm, among others. The court ruled (on a jurisdiction challenge) that if confidentiality rules prevented the firm from telling the lender, it should have withdrawn. It was a jury question whether withdrawal would have resulted in the lender not making the loan (because its suspicions would be sufficiently aroused).

part III
Rules for
Trial Lawyers

~ 16 ~

Ethics in Advocacy

The Client's Interests vs. Duty to the Tribunal

Do Rules Differ When the Client Is a Criminal Defendant?

Special Rules for Prosecutors

A paradox.

Ethical quandaries facing trial lawyers (or litigators, to use the broader term) get more attention from popular culture than any other issue surrounding the behavior of lawyers. It's not hard to see why. Film companies, book publishers, and television producers are fascinated by trial lawyers who, as myth (at least) would have it, live by their wits, have to think fast, and are expected at the last possible moment, either through brilliant strategy or logical deduction invisible to lesser mortals, to change entirely the perception of the case and win for the client, who is usually either a (falsely accused) criminal defendant or the state that brought the (valid) prosecution. Much less attention is paid to those civil litigators whose work life is mostly spent fighting discovery battles and making motions than is paid to real trial lawyers, men and women who actually stand up before juries and put their credibility on the line. The fact that trials end in verdicts (most of the time) adds to the popular attraction because it creates suspense and because a verdict promises closure of a sort.

Now here's the paradox: In fact, most lawyers are not trial lawyers, are not even litigators. What's more, most trial lawyers and litigators will live their entire professional lives without encountering the moral dilemmas that populate the popular culture's portrayal of them. These dilemmas rarely occur in the stark way that popular entertainments present. Still, they do absorb us.

It is not only the popular culture that is fascinated by the lawyer as courtroom warrior. Lawyers are as well, including lawyers who do not try cases. We can all venture a guess as to why this is so. My guess is that the particular moral challenges that can confront a trial lawyer, especially (but not only) a criminal defense lawyer, somehow crystallize the unavoidable discrepancy between duties of the professional role and the demands of justice, or justice as some, including lawyers, might see it. Most lawyers would probably say that so long as a lawyer energetically fulfills his or her professional duty, the result is justice, by definition. This is a "justice as process" view. By definition, it holds, justice is the result of a process in which a lawyer is devoted to the goals of a client and behaves lawfully and ethically. At least, that will be so in a constitutional democracy with an independent judiciary.

But this position, whether right or wrong, doesn't address an antecedent question, which for our purposes is this: What limits should and does the adversary system impose on trial lawyers and litigators? There must be *some* limit on what these lawyers can do for a client. It may, for example, benefit litigants to have lawyers who will suborn perjury, lie to a judge, or forge a document, but we don't let them do these things. And even after we answer this question, non-lawyers and many lawyers, too, will continue to find it fascinating that a lawyer will work hard within the rules we set down to win for a client *without regard* to the justice of the situation, indeed even if her work produces injustice and she knows it. Those who view justice as process may acknowledge the apparent contradiction but respond somewhat like this: "If a lawyer's advocacy produces what some consider an unjust result, that's simply not the lawyer's problem. Perhaps in some cosmic sense the result is truly unjust (although often one would have to be omniscient to know). But if so, blame the rules that govern the conduct of the trial, including the lawyer's behavior, or blame the law, or blame the judge or the jury for doing a poor job, but don't blame the lawyer who has scrupulously obeyed the (perhaps) imperfect rules as she found them. And if a lawyer can't live with contradiction between what the rules describe as her duty to her client and what she may view as the unfair consequences of obeying that duty in a particular matter, which is perfectly understandable, the solution is to decline work on the matter, or even to find a field of practice where that contradiction is absent."

Duty to Client, Duty to Court   From the perspective of the individual lawyer representing a client before a court, there is no contradiction between duty to client and duty to court. If a rule requires the lawyer to protect the court (against fraud, say), then the lawyer must do that even if it harms the client. If not, not. The lawyer follows the rules. But from the perspective of the rules (or those who draft them), there are inconsistent interests that must be reconciled somehow. The rules must define the scope of the duty to the court, which can in turn detract from what lawyers may or may not do for a client. For example, if a lawyer is required to tell the judge when she knows that her client or one of the lawyer's witnesses has lied under oath, it will hurt the client but protect against fraud on the court. We have to choose which result — protecting the court or the client — we value more. Once we decide, the lawyer is obligated to comply. Or a lawyer may know of a witness whose testimony would harm the client's case but whom the opposing lawyer has not discovered. If we require the lawyer to tell her opponent about the witness, we further the cause of truth in some way (or so it may be argued) but we require the lawyer to do something that harms her client. So for each dilemma, which will it be?

About some issues there is little or no debate. A lawyer cannot act illegally to achieve the client's goals, even laudable goals. A lawyer can't break the law or help someone else do so. That takes a lot off the table. But it leaves a lot on it, too. Consider again the lawyer who learns that a client or one of her witnesses has lied under oath — in deposition, affidavit, or on the witness stand — and assume that the trial has either not begun or has started but is ongoing. Now, the lawyer did not break the law because she did not know about the lie when it was told, but she knows now. Ordinarily, people have no legal duty to report a criminal act, but sometimes they do (e.g., emergency room doctors may have to report suspected child abuse or a gunshot wound). What should we require the lawyer to do, if anything? To complicate the matter further, assume the lawyer learns of the lie because of a confidential (perhaps even a privileged) client communication (see Chapter 4 for the difference between the two). In fact, we can assume that as a practical matter when the lawyer learns about the lie it will always be a client confidence (and possibly privileged, too) given the breadth of that category. Which is more important, client confidentiality or protecting the court?

Before attempting to answer that question, let me identify a subtle but necessary ambiguity in the text so far. I have used the words *court* and *tribunal* interchangeably. They are not synonyms. All courts are tribunals, but not all tribunals are courts. Administrative agencies conduct hearings that render decisions that have legal effect. Arbitrations do the same. So may legislative bodies. The Model Rules would make all three entities tribunals when they act in an "adjudicative capacity," which the rules define to occur "when a neutral official, after the presentation of evidence or legal argument by a party or parties, will render a binding legal judgment directly affecting a party's interests in a particular matter."[1] Model Rule 3.3 is the American Bar Association (ABA) rule that attempts to identify the proper dividing line between a lawyer's duty to adjudicative bodies and her duty to clients. It uses the word *tribunal*, not *court*, so even when I use the word *court*, everything here applies equally to the broader category of tribunal as defined in the Model Rules, so far as the ABA is concerned.

Now back to the open question: Which is more important, duty to the tribunal or duty to client? If the former, on the simple facts posed above, the lawyer would have to warn the tribunal even if the client refused to let him do so; if the latter, the lawyer would remain silent but do nothing to exploit the fraud on the court (i.e., the lawyer would not help the client take advantage of it) because that would be criminal. As we'll see, it's not so easy to remain silent if you're in the middle of litigation, especially if the case is on trial, but for the moment, let's focus on the two options. For many years, the ABA and many U.S. jurisdictions took the position that the lawyer must remain silent, that client confidentiality is more important than protecting the tribunal from fraud, even a fraud the lawyer may have assisted, though unwittingly because she did not know at the time that the testimony was false.[2] But a majority of jurisdictions favored protecting the court even at the expense of client confidentiality. So for a long time we had this stark division in American legal ethics.

Then, with the adoption of the Model Rules, the ABA reversed the priorities. The Model Rules provide that if other "remedial measures" are unavailable to protect the court — as rarely they will be — lawyers *must do so* even if that means revealing confidential information. Rule 3.3(a)(3) states that "if a lawyer, the lawyer's client, or a witness called by the lawyer, has offered material evidence and the lawyer comes to know of its falsity, the lawyer shall take reasonable remedial measures, including, if necessary, disclosure to the tribunal." This is a mandatory rule. The triggering events are limited to false testimony (or other false evidence, like a false document) by the lawyer, the client, or other witness called by the lawyer. Notice that the words are "false evidence." The code used the word "fraud," a narrower category. Evidence may be false even though no one has lied. The witness may simply have been wrong, as the lawyer soon learns. Of course, often the witness who gives false testimony *is* lying. But lie or not, the rule requires the lawyer who called the witness to act even if all she knows is that the testimony (or document) is false.

Rule 3.3(b) goes further. It states, "A lawyer who represents a client in an adjudicative proceeding and who knows that a person intends to engage, is engaging or has engaged in criminal or fraudulent conduct related to the proceeding shall take reasonable remedial measures, including, if necessary, disclosure to the tribunal." This provision broadens the circumstances requiring ameliorative action to include misconduct by anyone, not merely the lawyer's client and her witnesses. If "criminal or fraudulent conduct" in Rule 3.3(b) is read to include giving "false evidence," it's hard to figure out why we would need both this provision and Rule 3.3(a)(3). But apparently the drafters had different conduct in mind in drafting Rule 3.3(b). Comment [12] identifies the following conduct as within this part of the rule:

> bribing, intimidating or otherwise unlawfully communicating with a witness, juror, court official or other participant in the proceeding, unlawfully destroying or concealing documents or other evidence or failing to disclose information to the tribunal when required by law to do so.

Putting aside for a moment the lawyer for a criminal defendant, who may be seen to present a special case, what options do the Model Rules now leave the lawyer whose witness has given false testimony or where the lawyer has knowledge of any of the other events that trigger the Rule 3.3 remedial duty? If the lawyer is a prosecutor, the rules, echoing the Constitution, will require correction.[3] So let us focus initially on civil litigators whose client (or whose witness) has lied in discovery or at trial or who learns about the type of "criminal or fraudulent conduct" described in Rule 3.3(b). The first thing to recognize is that the lawyer has no duty to do anything under the rules unless he or she *knows* of the lie or other event. Suspicion, even strong belief, is not enough to require correction (although it may lead to reconsideration of strategy). Knowledge is a high standard, but not impossible. Further, the rule tells us that even though the words *knowledge* and *know* denote "actual knowledge of the fact in question," knowledge "may be inferred from the circumstances."[4] That's another way of saying that despite a lawyer's claim that the evidence available to him was insufficient to show actual knowledge of a fact — perhaps at most only a likelihood of the fact, which is not the same as knowledge — a judge or jury may conclude the opposite from the same evidence. Furthermore, lawyers cannot consciously avoid knowledge to escape from the obligations of Rule 3.3. As is often said, the conscious avoidance of knowledge is knowledge. In sum, the lawyer is not the final arbiter of his own knowledge.[5] It behooves him to predict accurately what others might conclude.

If our civil litigator does know of a triggering Rule 3.3 event — and for simplicity let us deal here with a lie by the client although the triggering events are much broader than that — the lawyer must take "remedial measures." What measure short of disclosure can remedy that situation? The client can be encouraged to confess, or (more likely) perhaps the lawyer may be able to find a way to withdraw the false statement without the client having to admit that it was knowingly false. If so, fine. But if not?

The lawyer can't settle the case with the lie in the record (and we are assuming that the statement is "material"). Settling without correction would help the client exploit the fraud. The opponent may have altered its settlement posture because of the false testimony, not knowing it was false. Perhaps the lawyer could settle on the express understanding that the opponent is not relying on all or a designated part of the client's testimony, but it will be the rare adversary who doesn't smell blood in the water when asked to make that agreement. The lawyer can't argue the lie in summation for the same reason — it exploits the perjury. If the lie occurred during discovery, the lawyer might be inclined to think that she's all right so long as she doesn't introduce the lie in evidence at trial. Not necessarily. The statement might have affected how the opponent has chosen to try his case. Perhaps the lawyer can avoid any problem just by withdrawing from the matter. Perhaps. The comments recognize that possibility, but they don't say that withdrawal will always be sufficient. Rather, if withdrawal "will not undo the effect of the false evidence, the advocate must make such disclosure to the tribunal as is reasonably necessary to remedy the situation."[6] And withdrawal may not be possible. A lawyer who has appeared in a matter needs a judge's permission to withdraw, which becomes increasingly unlikely as the case gets closer to trial and almost certainly will not be allowed if the case is actually on trial.[7]

So when all else fails, the lawyer will have to remedy the situation by revealing the false statement to the court as an express exception to the duty of confidentiality. Of course, that is the remedy lawyers most hate. It goes against the grain to blow the whistle on your client at any time, but here it's worse because the lawyer is telling the court (and perhaps the prosecutor) that his client committed perjury. But it also goes against the grain for a profession to assist a client's crime or fraud, even if only indirectly. State courts over the years, in adopting ethics rules, have had to choose whose grain they prefer to go against, and the ABA and state bar groups have had to decide what rule to ask those courts to adopt. It is perhaps no wonder that today courts have decided that protecting themselves (and the mission of the justice system) is more important than confidentiality. Reasonable people may disagree over how we should resolve these competing interests, but those who favor confidentiality then have to offer an alternative. They need to offer another exit strategy for lawyers whose clients lie or suborn lies. This need has been most acute where the client is a criminal defendant because they, unlike other litigants, have a constitutional right to counsel[8] and to testify in their own behalf.[9] Should that matter? Should it lead to a different rule? And if so, what should that rule say?

When the Client Is a Criminal Defendant   The legal profession has had the most trouble dealing with the apparent conflict between client confidentiality and protecting the court when the lawyer's client is a criminal defendant. There are good reasons for this. As stated, the criminal defendant has a constitutional right to testify in his defense, even over his lawyer's caution that doing so is a really bad idea. Also, the criminal defendant has a Sixth Amendment right to the effective assistance of counsel, which necessarily encompasses a right to confer with counsel in confidence.[10] These differences have led two law teachers to argue forcefully that if a defense lawyer cannot dissuade her client from taking the stand and committing perjury, the unhappy but only recourse is to let the lawyer call the defendant, question him, and argue his testimony even if the lawyer knows the testimony or parts of it are false and her conduct will help the client benefit from the lie. The alternatives — revealing the client's lies or encouraging lawyers to remain ignorant of the facts so as not to *know* when a client has lied — are viewed as worse in this view. This position has some serious problems, and no court decision has accepted it.[11]

Early on, some courts and commentators sought to reconcile the competing values by devising what has become known as the narrative method. Before we describe it, we should recognize that the defense lawyer's quandary can arise at two different times during a trial. First, the defense lawyer may know even before the client takes the stand that he intends to commit perjury. He knows because the client told him as much but has insisted on his constitutional right to testify. The lawyer tries to dissuade the client, without success. What should the lawyer do then? Alternatively, the defense lawyer may not know when he calls the client to testify that the client plans to lie, but then the client lies while on the stand and the lawyer knows it; or the lawyer learns after the testimony (but during the trial) that the client lied. What should the lawyer do?

The narrative method can appear to be an attractive remedy at first blush. If the evil we most want to prevent is putting the lawyer in the position of consciously assisting a client's fraud on the court, the narrative method satisfies this goal by instructing the lawyer to remain passive, not to assist the fraud. If the lawyer knows before calling the client to testify that he will lie, the narrative method instructs the lawyer to question the client about those matters that the lawyer does not know are lies (if any) and then say something like this: "Now, Mr. Defendant, I understand that there are other things you wish to tell the jury, so why don't you go ahead and do that." Then the lawyer sits down. In this way, the lawyer does not aid the client through questioning, and of course the lawyer will have refused to help the client prepare the false testimony in advance. The client is on his own. At summation, the lawyer does not mention the testimony she knows is false. She just ignores it and thereby does not help the client take advantage of the perjury through her argument.

When the lawyer has called the client without knowing in advance that the client plans to lie but the client then does lie, the narrative method must be modified slightly. If the lawyer realizes during the testimony that the client is lying, she immediately stops the Q&A and invites the client to continue in a narrative. And whether the lawyer recognizes the lie during or after the testimony, she does not argue it in summation.[12]

Proponents of the narrative method say that it honors the constitutional right to testify without forcing the lawyer to suborn or assist perjury. They also expect that a client who is told that his lawyer will use the method will back down and not lie (this is only possible if the lawyer knows in advance of the false testimony). And they say that the client will not likely benefit from the lie in any event because the lawyer's passivity during the client's narrative will alert the jury that the testimony has a problem. Last, of course, the judge will know exactly why the lawyer is using the narrative method so if the client is convicted, he may "pay" for his perjury with a heightened sentence. All in all, this is offered as a perfect solution (or as close to perfect as the situation permits) because every interest is given its due. Right?

Not necessarily. First of all, if the defense lawyer doesn't *know* the client will or has lied, the narrative method violates the client's constitutional rights. The client is entitled to be defended in the usual way, with questions and answers and argument. The narrative method (though not it alone) makes the lawyer the judge of the client's truthfulness. What happens when the client challenges the defense lawyer's conclusion about what he or she claims to know? Who resolves that dispute? The trial judge? Another judge? Can the lawyer reveal the defendant's confidences to support her conclusions of intended or concluded perjury? Is the defendant entitled to an independent lawyer to represent him in this dispute with his own trial lawyer? Or should the judge simply defer to the lawyer's conclusion that the client will lie or has lied, without inquiry? These are hard questions. They arise not only when the jurisdiction's solution is the narrative method but also when the jurisdiction adopts the ABA solution as well. If the jurisdiction requires the lawyer to report the false testimony to the court, we also make the lawyer the judge of the client's truthfulness and must also figure out what to do if the client challenges the lawyer's conclusion.

But let us assume that sometimes (if rarely) lawyers do *know* that clients will lie or have lied. If in fact, the client intends to lie, his constitutional right to testify is gone, isn't it? There is no constitutional right to testify falsely, only to testify.[13] So another problem with the narrative method is that it is too generous to the defendant who intends to commit perjury. The lawyer who knows this should decline to let him testify. That violates no rights of the client.

Where the lawyer recognizes the perjury during or after the testimony, it is too late to prevent the client from testifying. Then the considerations differ, and matters become more complex. If the lawyer recognizes the perjury during the testimony, she can just refuse to continue to question the client without inviting a narrative because, again, the client has no right to continue with his lies even in narrative. She can just say "no further questions." She won't argue the lies to the jury because that would assist the client's fraud. Should she reveal the lies to the court? This is a delicate question, because the lawyer who does so will be implicating the client in a further crime. If it were a civil case, as we've seen, the lawyer would be required to reveal the fraud to the court (assuming no other remedial measure sufficed to undue the harm). Why not here? It would not violate a constitutional right of the defendant for a lawyer to reveal the client's perjury to the court. As an ethical matter, the ABA would require it. Rule 3.3 recognizes no difference between the civil case client and the criminal defendant. And the same duty to reveal would arise if the lawyer first learns about the perjury after the testimony is concluded. But obviously, we've upped the ante. When a lawyer refuses to call the client intent on committing perjury, the lawyer is merely preventing a criminal act. No one needs to know more. It's a private decision. When a lawyer reveals completed perjury to a court, the lawyer is exposing a criminal act by her own client even more clearly than is implicit when the lawyer employs the narrative option. Maybe that goes too far. Maybe, in that situation, the narrative method is the better, though not a happy, solution. Maybe that is why some states continue to embrace it.

ENDNOTES

1. Model Rule (MR) 1.0(m).
2. DR 7-102(B)(1), ABA Code of Professional Responsibility; ABA Opinion 341 (1975).
3. MR 3.8(d); *Brady v. Maryland,* 373 U.S. 83 (1963).
4. MR 1.0(f).
5. *See, e.g., United States v. Lizardo*, 445 F.3d 73 (1st Cir. 2006).
6. MR 3.3 cmt. [10].
7. MR 1.16(c).
8. U.S. Constitution, 6th Am.
9. *See, e.g., United States v. Mullins*, 315 F.3d 449 (5th Cir. 2002).
10. *Neku v. United States*, 620 A.2d 259 (D.C. 1993).
11. Monroe Freedman & Abbe Smith, *Understanding Lawyers' Ethics* 159-95 (3d ed. 2004). For criticism of this argument, see Stephen Gillers, *Monroe Freedman's Solution to the Criminal Defense Lawyer's Trilemma Is Wrong as a Matter of Policy and Constitutional Law*, 34 Hofstra L. Rev. 821 (2006).
12. For discussion of the narrative method in the case law, *see Commonwealth v. Mitchell*, 781 N.E.2d 1237 (Mass. 2003); *People v. DePallo*, 754 N.E.2d 751 (N.Y. 2001); *State v. McDowell*, 681 N.W.2d 500 (Wis. 2004). A broad-ranging discussion of the options appears in *People v. Johnson*, 72 Cal. Rptr.2d 805 (Cal. App. 1998).
13. The leading Supreme Court case is *Nix v. Whiteside*, 475 U.S. 157 (1986), a homicide prosecution. Whiteside's lawyer told him that if he planned to testify to the false fact that the victim had what looked to Whiteside like a gun, the lawyer would have to advise the court that the testimony was false. Whiteside did testify but omitted the (false) fact and was convicted. The Supreme Court held that Whiteside was not denied the effective assistance of counsel because of his lawyer's threat.

⌒ 17 ⌒

Special Rules for Real Evidence

What Is Real Evidence?

Real Evidence and Ethics

Real Evidence and Criminal Law

Real Evidence and Privilege

The discussion in the prior chapter focused on potential conflicts between duty to client and duty to a tribunal. We discussed how different jurisdictions approach these conflicts and the particular issues confronting lawyers for criminal defendants. In our discussion, we assumed that the lawyer's knowledge of fraud on the tribunal will have come in the form of communications, written or oral, from the client or from others to whom the lawyer (or her investigator) might talk in the course of a factual investigation. In this chapter, we look at a different contest between the interests of a client and the interests of the justice system. Sometimes, a lawyer will discover or be given a thing (as good a word as any in this context) that has evidentiary value. The thing might be a document that proves the client's civil or criminal culpability. It might be the stolen bank money or the robbery victim's wallet.

It might be the gun used in the homicide. It might be the client's laptop with a file containing the plan for the crime that the client is now charged with having committed. Or it might be something as modest as the client's (or its officer's) handwritten notes, which are probative of civil liability because they show that the author was aware of a fact or instigated an unlawful plan.

Now that you know what the thing can be, we can use the somewhat more technical term *real evidence* to refer to things that tend to prove or disprove an element of a claim, charge, or defense. The real evidence itself is not a communication, nor is it confidential or within the attorney-client privilege. But a client's act of *delivering* the real evidence to a lawyer *is* communicative. The client is saying, in effect, "Look, I have this." We must separate the *act of delivery* from the item itself, which will be the focus here. The duty of confidentiality does not play a prominent role in this chapter. On the other hand, the real evidence may be harmful, even devastating, to the client if it gets into the hands of the adversary. So we might view any act of the lawyer in producing the item, or even in revealing its existence, as a supreme act of *disloyalty*, especially if it was the client who gave it to the lawyer or told her where to find it. But it cannot be disloyal if the law or ethical rules leave the lawyer no choice but to give the real evidence to the court or his adversary. And that's the question, or one of them.

When does a lawyer have no choice? When must she reveal or turn over real evidence that comes into her possession? A second (and overlapping) question this chapter considers is the relationship between real evidence and privilege. Although the real evidence is itself not privileged, can the lawyer be required to say where or from whom he got it? What if it came from the client? These are difficult but fascinating questions with which the profession has grappled for some time. As with the conflict between duty to client and court discussed in the last chapter, the issues addressed here do not often arise, but they get a lot of attention because resolving them forces us to grapple with the American lawyer's place in our system of adversary justice. And as in the last chapter, the issues in this one almost always seem to arise — or at least they are almost only discussed — in the context of criminal investigations and prosecutions. So that's the context we will use here, but it is important to remember that obstruction-of-justice statutes and ethical rules do not distinguish between civil and criminal matters.[1]

Real Evidence and Legal Ethics   Ethical rules do not require lawyers to take control of items of real evidence and turn them over to the authorities. The rules don't transform the lawyer for a private client into an arm of the state. But they do become relevant if the lawyer in fact takes possession of the item. Before we see how, do not assume that the entire problem can be resolved simply by a lawyer leaving a piece of incriminating real evidence where she found it. Sometimes, she can (and perhaps she should), but it's not always possible.

Richard Ryder was a criminal defense lawyer and had been an assistant U.S. attorney.[2] A man named Cook was suspected of having robbed a bank and hired Ryder. Cook had marked money from the robbery in his possession but claimed he won it gambling. Later, urged to tell the truth, Cook told Ryder that someone gave him $500 to put a package in Cook's safe deposit box. Ryder didn't believe him. Ryder got a power of attorney from Cook, went to the box, and found a bag of money and a sawed-off shotgun. He put both items in his own safe deposit box. Eventually, the FBI searched Ryder's box and found the items. Ryder was charged with misconduct and the court suspended him from practice for 18 months. (He was lucky, actually, that he wasn't charged with obstructing justice.)

Ryder's conduct violated the predecessor to Model Rule 3.4(a), which forbids a lawyer to "unlawfully obstruct another party's access to evidence or unlawfully alter, destroy or conceal a document or other material having potential evidentiary value." Lawyers are also forbidden to "counsel or assist another person" to do these things. In one sense, Rule 3.4 is pretty useless because it forbids only what the law forbids. If it's *unlawful*, it's unethical; if not, not. So why do we need the rule? Looked at another way, however, the rule is broad because it incorporates by reference all law addressing obligations with regard to real evidence, including discovery rules and obstruction of justice statutes, and that law (as we shall see) is quite extensive. What that means is that if destruction, alteration, or concealment of real evidence is "unlawful," disciplinary authorities have a basis for punishing a lawyer like Ryder for violating a rule like Rule 3.4, even if he is never prosecuted for obstruction.

In Ryder's case, the court said that taking possession of the money and gun was unlawful because (1) the money was not his, so he was in possession of stolen property, and (2) it was illegal to possess a sawed-off shotgun. Ryder claimed he was going to return the money to the bank once the case was over. The court believed him, but that didn't give him the right to conceal it. The court said Ryder "allowed the office of attorney to be used in violation of law." It rejected Ryder's theory that he could legitimately do this in order to break the *chain of custody* of the money and gun — that is, their connection to his client — so the authorities would be unable to use these items to prove guilt when the client's lockbox was searched, as Ryder expected it would be. Ryder's theory seems to have been that the attorney-client privilege would operate to make the gun and money inadmissible against the client if they were found instead in Ryder's lockbox. This is nonsense. Ryder did exactly what the penal law declared illegal. He hid evidence. That was his sole admitted motive. And the privilege has nothing to do with it. The privilege does not convert admissible evidence into inadmissible evidence simply because it is given to a lawyer. Otherwise, law offices would become repositories for stolen goods, contraband, evidence of crimes, and so on. So Ryder was suspended.

The lesson here is that unlawful conduct can become unethical conduct and punished as such. Ryder would have been safe if after seeing the gun and money in Cook's box, he left them there. (He might have wanted to take a look, and would have been justified in looking, just to make sure that Cook was telling the truth and not delusional.) Ryder had no duty to remove the items and turn them in. He had no duty to help the authorities. Quite the opposite. His problem was that he *hindered* the authorities — briefly, to be sure. But it could have been otherwise. Discovery of Ryder's lockbox, as the court noted, was not inevitable. He could have gotten away with it.

Passivity — that is, leaving the real evidence where a lawyer finds it — will not always be so easy. What if a client walks in with a dangerous instrumentality? Say a slightly deranged client comes to your office with a loaded gun or a mean-looking hunting knife that he says was used in a criminal act. Will you let him walk out with it? You won't get much comfort from the proposition that you have no legal duty to disarm your client. The last thing you want is for your client to leave armed and hurt someone. Yet if you take the gun or knife into your possession, aren't you in Ryder's position? You can examine the weapon briefly, but if you hide it in your office safe, you may be in trouble with the criminal law and therefore with the ethical rules. In the language of the obstruction statutes, you may have concealed evidence of a crime. If you tell your client to get rid of the gun or knife, aren't you in violation of the part of the rule that says you cannot "counsel or assist another person to do" what you cannot? You might try to avoid these problems by delivering the weapon to the police. At trial, you would then argue that the state cannot tell the jury that you were the source of the weapon, which carries the obvious (and intended) implication that they came from your client. Even if you won that argument, and perhaps you would,[3] the weapons themselves may still be incriminating. They almost certainly contain your client's fingerprints, which you must take pains not to remove because doing that would be destroying evidence. The police may also be able to tie the weapons both to the crime and your client in other ways, too (e.g., ballistics tests, witnesses).

You might think that the problem goes away if the real evidence in your possession is not the weapon used in the crime but merely some proof of your client's culpability that is not unlawful to possess, unlike the gun and money that Ryder put in his lockbox. What if all you have are your client's handwritten plans for the crime? That's what Cline, an Alaska public defender, had.[4] Cline was assigned to represent Morrell, who was charged with kidnapping. Morrell was in jail. Morrell's friend Wagner was staying at Morrell's apartment and using his car with Morrell's permission. Wagner cleaned the car and found what appeared to be a plan for the crime in Morrell's handwriting. He gave it to Cline. Cline tried to give it back to Wagner, who wouldn't take it. So after seeking advice from other lawyers, Cline gave the plan to the authorities and withdrew as Morrell's counsel.

Obviously, this evidence was devastating. After conviction, Morrell claimed that Cline's conduct denied him the effective assistance of counsel promised by the Sixth Amendment. The Alaska Supreme Court wrote an ambiguous opinion that said one of two things (it's ambiguous because we don't know which): Either the state's obstruction of justice statute required Cline to give the kidnap plan to the authorities, or, alternatively, Cline "reasonably could have concluded" that the statute required him to do so. These are different statements, but either could be seen as sufficient to reject Morrell's claim that Cline was constitutionally ineffective. If Cline was required to, or just reasonably concluded that he had to, deliver the plan, he cannot be constitutionally ineffective. Now, of course, the kidnap plan, unlike the gun and money that Ryder held, is not illegal in itself to possess. It just proves the crime, rather powerfully. But the state supreme court found no constitutional impediment to a law that required (or could be read to require) a defense lawyer to give the police evidence of a crime that has come into the lawyer's possession.

You can see that we are inching our way over to the criminal law, which is inevitable because the ethical rule incorporates the criminal law, although it imposes an independent (ethical) duty to accompany the penal one. Ryder's concealment of the gun and money was illegal. The attorney-client privilege would neither excuse what Ryder did nor enable the client to block proof that the gun and money came from his safe deposit box. For his part, Cline would have (or could reasonably have believed he would have) violated Alaska's penal law if he had kept the kidnap plan. Now we turn to the criminal law directly.

Real Evidence and the Criminal Law   Since the law defines the scope of the ethical rule, it behooves us to take a look at the law on obstruction of justice. The federal obstruction statutes are particularly broad. They figured in the criminal prosecution of the auditing firm Arthur Andersen (whose conviction was reversed on a narrow ground having to do with the judge's instructions to the jury), Martha Stewart, and I. Lewis Libby, Vice President Cheney's chief of staff. Following the corporate scandals of recent years, Congress further broadened the obstruction statutes when it passed the Sarbanes-Oxley Act (SOX). The obstruction laws punish alteration, concealment, or destruction of real evidence or attempts to do so even if unsuccessful. They also punish the act of inducing (or attempting to induce) others to do so (even if they don't realize what they're doing), where in either case the intent is to keep the item from an "official proceeding," a term that includes pending or merely foreseeable agency hearings as well as civil or criminal court proceedings.[5] This book is not a criminal law treatise, so it is not the place to get into the interstices of the federal or state obstruction statutes. But I reprint one small part of one section of the federal law (which SOX added) to give you the flavor of what we're talking about:

> 18 U.S.C. 1512 . . . (c) Whoever corruptly — (1) alters, destroys, mutilates, or conceals a record, document, or other object, or attempts to do so, with the intent to impair the object's integrity or availability for use in an official proceeding; or (2) otherwise obstructs, influences, or impedes any official proceeding, or attempts to do so, shall be fined under this title or imprisoned not more than 20 years, or both.

Another provision says that the "record, document, or other object need not be admissible in evidence or free of a claim of privilege" for the conduct to be a crime.[6] In other words, the defendant can't say "no harm, no foul because the file I shredded would have been inadmissible anyway." While lawyers are rarely prosecuted in federal court for obstruction of justice in the representation of their clients, it does happen.[7]

Real Evidence and the Attorney-Client Privilege The connection between the attorney-client privilege on one hand and real evidence on the other can be a little confusing. But there are a few simple rules, recognized in most jurisdictions, and one big exception.

Rule #1: The real evidence itself — the stolen money, the document detailing the crime plan, the weapon, the drugs — is not privileged. (Oral and written communications between lawyer and client are privileged, however, so if a lawyer asks a client to "write down what you remember and send it to me," or if a client does that without being asked, the letter will be privileged even though it is a physical object.) This means, of course, that Ryder's belief that by taking the money and gun into his possession, the government would be prevented from offering them in evidence against Cook, his client—that is, that by taking possession Ryder could legitimately break their connection to Cook's safe deposit box through operation of the attorney-client privilege—was ridiculous. It also means that a statute requiring lawyers along with everyone else not to conceal, alter, or destroy real evidence is not a violation of the privilege or the right to counsel. And that in turn means that if a lawyer comes into possession of real evidence, he may have an obligation to turn it over to the authorities (otherwise he'd be concealing it) unchanged (otherwise he'd be altering it), assuming he is unable to give it back (which if possible would probably be a safe response because then the lawyer would not have altered the status quo) or doesn't want to give it back (because, for example, it's a dangerous weapon and the client is a dangerous person).

Rule #2: The fact that that a client gives a piece of real evidence to a lawyer is likely to be communicative and privileged (assuming the prerequisites to privilege are otherwise present), even if the thing turned over is not privileged. The lawyer probably cannot be forced to reveal the source when the source is the client.[8] That may be small comfort to the client if the thing itself must be turned over and can implicate the client in a crime (e.g., if it's the victim's wallet containing the client's fingerprints). But the client's delivery to the lawyer is a product of the trust relationship between lawyer and client and will be protected. In other words, it is a communication within the privilege.

Rule #3: If someone other than the client gives the lawyer a piece of real evidence, the source is not going to be privileged and the lawyer may be required to reveal the source even if the identity of the source focuses the authorities' attention on the client, as it would if, for example, the source were a close relative of the client. Cline, our Alaska public defender, got

Morrell's handwritten kidnap plan from Wagner, Morrell's friend. If the authorities wanted to know who gave the kidnap plan to Cline, he'd have to tell them it was Wagner since Wagner was not Cline's client. In the actual case, of course, the plan itself was highly incriminatory regardless of source since it was in the client's handwriting.

Now the exception. In a famous California case, a client (Scott) participated in a murder and took the victim's wallet, which he eventually threw in the trash bin behind his own house.[9] After Scott was arrested for the murder, he told his lawyer (Schenk) about the wallet and its location. Schenk understandably wanted to confirm Scott's story so he sent an investigator (Frick) to Scott's house, and, sure enough, the wallet was in the trash bin just as Scott had said. Frick brought the wallet to Schenk, who gave it to the police after examining it briefly. It had no fingerprints, probably because Scott had tried to burn it. Now without prints, the wallet was of no particular evidentiary value to the prosecutor. What was of evidentiary value, however, was the fact that Frick had found the wallet in the trash bin behind Scott's house. In other words, the evidence connecting the wallet to Scott was *its location*. But Schenk, via Frick, had "destroyed" the location by removing the wallet. No one blamed Schenk. Schenk may have thought that he was fulfilling his obligations by giving the wallet to the police. (He couldn't keep it until the case was over for the same reason that Ryder could not keep the bank money. It wasn't his, and it was evidence of the crime.)

The question for the court was whether Schenk (or successor counsel) had to make the prosecutor "whole" by either testifying — or having the investigator testify — to the location of the wallet or by stipulating to the location. What Scott told Schenk about where to find the wallet would ordinarily be privileged. It was a communication. The question the court had to answer was whether to create an exception to the privilege because the evidentiary value of the wallet — its location—had been destroyed, even if with good intentions. The court said it would create an exception. It rejected as too speculative the argument that the state should be required to prove that the police would have found the wallet in the trash bin had it been left there. So the exception might be stated this way: A lawyer's knowledge of the location or even the existence of incriminating real evidence is privileged if the knowledge comes from a client communication, but the privilege is lost if the lawyer defeats the state's ability to discover or to make evidentiary use of the evidence. Removing the evidence as Frick did is one act that will destroy the privilege. Wiping off the client's fingerprints (even unintentionally) would be another.

If Frick had simply left the wallet in the bin, or if Scott had replaced it after examining it, the client would have been better off, all in all. Sure, the police might have found it in the trash bin, but they might also have failed to find it. We can be confident that after this case was decided, lawyers in the same situation will now leave the wallet where they found it. But leaving the real evidence where it was found is not always possible. It wasn't possible for Cline to return the kidnap plan in the Alaska case, and he had (or reasonably could have concluded that he had) no alternative but to turn it in to the authorities. That's what the court eventually held.

In another famous case, a murder defendant told his lawyers that he had killed two young women in addition to the person he was charged with killing.[10] He told the lawyers that he had buried the bodies under leaves and told them where to look. The lawyers checked, and sure enough, they found the bodies. They photographed the bodies but left them where they found them. The lawyers told no one, not even the families of the missing young women, who were searching for their relatives. Eventually the story came out but only because the lawyers decided to use the fact of the additional murders to bolster the client's insanity defense. The public was outraged that the lawyers had not told the families of the young women sooner, but the lawyers believed that they had no choice. Their knowledge of the location of the bodies came from a client communication and was, in their view, confidential as well as privileged. Although a local prosecutor charged one of the lawyers with the obscure state law misdemeanor of failing to ensure a proper burial for one of the young women, the courts threw out the charge and endorsed the lawyers' view that their knowledge of their client's murders and the location of the bodies were confidential. In this case, the lawyers left the evidence where they found it and escaped legal sanction. It is what Ryder should have done with the bank money and sawed-off shotgun.

ENDNOTES

1. The federal obstruction of justice chapter is found at 18 U.S.C. §§1501 et seq. The provisions apply to obstruction of both civil and criminal matters.

2. The case is *In re Ryder*, 263 F.Supp. 360 (E.D.Va. 1967), *aff'd* 381 F.2d 713 (4th Cir. 1967).

3. *State v. Olwell*, 394 P.2d 681 (Wash. 1964) (lawyer required to turn over real evidence, but state could not cite lawyer as its source).

4. *Morrell v. State*, 575 P.2d 1200 (Alaska 1978).

5. 18 U.S.C. §§1512(f)(1), 1515(a)(1).

6. 18 U.S.C. §1512(f)(2).

7. *See, e.g., United States v. Kloess*, 251 F.3d 941 (11th Cir. 2001).

8. *See, e.g., Hitch v. Pima County Superior Court*, 708 P.2d 72 (Ariz. 1985). Because we are dealing here with privilege law, which may vary from place to place, some jurisdictions might have a contrary view. However, the rule in *Hitch*, that if the client is the source that fact is privileged seems to be the dominant view. *See also Rubin v. State*, 602 A.2d 677 (1992) (prosecutor cannot introduce proof that lawyer's investigator found incriminating evidence in client's handbag, but the evidence itself is not privileged).

9. *People v. Meredith*, 631 P.2d 46 (Cal. 1981).

10. *People v. Belge*, 372 N.Y.S.2d 798 (County Ct. 1975), *aff'd* 376 N.Y.S.2d 771 (4th Dep't 1975), *aff'd* 359 N.E.2d 377 (1976). This case has become known as the "Buried Bodies Case."

~ 18 ~

The "No-Comment" Rule

Public Comment About Pending Cases

Where Does a Lawyer's Duty End?

Public Relations and Privilege

Lawyers try cases in court, or at least those few cases that don't get settled or plea bargained before trial (as most do). Think trial lawyer and you picture a courtroom. But there is another court: the court of public opinion. A small number of cases get "tried" there, too. Therein lies a problem, or at least an issue. But first some background.

First of all, we are talking about very few cases indeed. In the civil arena, it is rare for a litigation to be interesting enough to capture the attention of the media. When one is, it is likely to involve celebrities, often a divorce or an allegation of improper (perhaps sexual) behavior. Or it may be a big class action or tort case charging a manufacturer with putting a dangerous product on the market, especially if many users may be harmed. But even then, media attention is sporadic and, in the case of celebrity litigants, largely confined to tabloids and talk shows. The public's penchant for voyeurism is not long piqued by the travails of drug companies or automakers. Rarely if ever do these cases involve "personalities" or particularly intriguing facts, at least not ones that the public can or is willing to spend time absorbing. So what we're really talking about are criminal cases. And those fall into two categories. First, the case may involve a famous person, preferably someone from the entertainment world, like Michael Jackson or O. J. Simpson, or perhaps a defendant from the political world. Criminal cases without celebrities may draw media attention if the facts are especially interesting (a sexual angle helps), even gruesome. The trial of Scott Peterson for killing his wife, Lacey, and their unborn child is an example. No need to list others.

Then there is the press — the tabloid media, the talk shows, and even the more responsible press. They can be all over a story if the public is curious enough or if its curiosity can be encouraged. And there is no end to those willing to speak or be quoted — most notably, former law enforcement individuals, lawyers generally, and anyone with even a passing relationship to an accused or victim ("Now we'll have an exclusive interview with the sister of the defendant's former next-door neighbor"). To one extent or another, the talking heads will offer their opinions or recollections of the accused. The lawyers may even evaluate the odds of conviction and the skills of the prosecutors and defense lawyers (or their lack of skills). Often, these contributions are little better than guesswork. Sometimes, the comments are inflammatory efforts to get attention (ratings! ratings!) and irresponsible. The commentators are not generally privy to inside information, but that might not discourage speculation. The more provocative they are willing to be, the more likely that Greta or Larry or Nancy will invite them back on the show. They then become celebrities by association.

Fairness and the Perception of Fairness While very few court cases draw the attention of the national media, less prominent contests may attract local television and newspaper coverage. And for our purposes, that is as important as the national stories, because behind the rules we here address is the assumption that airing the purported facts and progress of a case publicly can sometimes threaten the integrity of the eventual trial, if there is one. Or if not the actual integrity of the trial, then the appearance of its fairness to the public and the parties ("They convicted her in the press before they convicted her in court"). A trial, with its rules of evidence, is meant to resemble a laboratory, at least metaphorically. The judge as gatekeeper decides what the jury may hear and how it may use what it hears. If the jurors are, before selection, exposed to a good deal of pretrial publicity, including information that the judge and rules of evidence would exclude from the courtroom, we might say the trial is contaminated (to continue the laboratory trope). The antiseptic premise of the process — that the verdict must be based only on what the judge allows the jury to hear as evidence — may be compromised. On the other hand, not everything that the media might report will threaten the perception of the trial's fairness. Some of it — probably most of it — will be harmless, especially if it is reported long before trial. So one issue is this: How do we separate the harmless from the harmful? And then what do we do to minimize trial taint or the perception of it?

The First Amendment   Then, there's a second issue, or more accurately a fact of life and law. We have a First Amendment. In the United States, the judge cannot forbid the press to cover an investigation and trial. On a proper showing, a judge can seal court documents,[1] but he cannot forbid journalists from tracking down and talking to potential witnesses or others who may have interesting information about the defendant, the witnesses, or the alleged act. This is information that the journalist's public will pay or tune in to learn (or so his editor might believe, and editors are paid to be right). This reporting then gets published or broadcast and, if juicy enough, is repeated endlessly. Blogs help here. Some of it may be wrong or inadmissible in court. Much of it will be speculative. Some of it may be inflammatory. What can be done about this threat? Nothing much. This is a reality that the law must abide. In a contest between the interests of the courts and press freedom protected by the First Amendment, the press usually wins. Of course, the fact that the media can report facts, even explosive ones — or what it claims are facts — doesn't mean it is required to do so. But journalism is a competitive business, the Internet has added many new sources of information, and so self-restraint will never be a solution.

Remedies   But the justice system is not helpless. It has some tools to diminish, if not eliminate, the risk that pretrial publicity will (or will be seen to) compromise the fairness and accuracy of the trial. I mentioned a jury trial. Some trials go before judges (though that is less likely for the kinds of high-profile criminal cases that generally raise the issues here discussed). Pretrial publicity, however lopsided, unfair, inaccurate, or even incendiary is — or should be — less likely to influence a judge than a jury. Also, when a judge will try a case, he or she will ordinarily know of that possibility long in advance (the case may be assigned to that judge when it enters the court system), so the judge can be expected to avoid publicity about the case. Jurors are not picked for a case until immediately before trial and have no reason to avoid publicity. The chance of ending up on a particular jury is miniscule.

If the trial is to a jury, *voir dire* questions — the process by which a jury is chosen — can inquire into each potential juror's exposure to pretrial publicity and whether the exposure has given the juror a view of the case (i.e., whether it has biased him in one direction or the other). If the juror equivocates, or even if she denies it, she can be asked if she will in any event promise to decide based solely on the evidence at trial and the court's instructions. This is not a perfect solution. Jurors may lie about the extent of their exposure to press reports. They may lie about their views of the case or their ability to put those views aside. Or they may not lie, but they may be wrong about their capacity to "forget" (to be unswayed by) what they know and to consider only the evidence the judge admits. But though not perfect, the voir dire questions aimed at eliminating jurors who cannot decide solely based on the evidence and the law as the judge explains it afford at least a partial remedy and cannot be discounted.

Next, in an extreme case, a state court judge might move the case from one county to another; or within the federal system a case can be moved from one state to another, even clear across the country if need be. Changes in venue will not much help if a prosecution has attracted national attention, like the homicide trial of O. J. Simpson, but it can help where the publicity is mainly local or regional.

And finally — the subject of this chapter — the rules governing lawyers can and do command lawyers who are appearing in, or who are associated with, a case to refrain from making certain public comments about the case. Violating the professional conduct rules can subject a lawyer to discipline.

Gag Orders   The professional conduct rules do not apply to non-lawyers, like law enforcement personnel, but a judge can issue an order, usually called a "gag order," that does apply to non-lawyers.[2] A gag order can forbid non-lawyers (as well as lawyers) associated with a case, or who have access to court or law enforcement information about it, to comment about it publicly. That would include the police and others in law enforcement. However, gag orders have limited utility. It is near to impossible to identify the source if the order is violated by a person deep in law enforcement who may have no publicly known role in the case and who speaks to the press without attribution. This is one of the problems that criminal defense

lawyers face. There are many more people on the law enforcement side who can feed stories to reporters than there are on
the defense side, which generally consists solely of the accused
and his counsel, and perhaps an investigator. A separate rule
requires prosecutors to "exercise reasonable care to prevent"
persons in law enforcement from making statements that
the prosecutor may not make under the professional conduct
rules.[3] But prosecutors have limited ability actually to control
members of police departments and law enforcement agencies.

Making matters a bit more complicated is the fact that
many lawyers do not accept the proposition that a lawyer's
arguments must occur exclusively in the courtroom, and not
in the media, at least not in all cases all the time. Among
the proponents of a broader responsibility — a responsibility
to represent clients in the court of public opinion when
warranted — are four Supreme Court Justices. Their remarkable view appears in a plurality opinion written by Justice
Kennedy in *Gentile v. State Bar of Nevada*.[4] Justice Kennedy
wrote:

> An attorney's duties do not begin inside the courtroom door.
> He or she cannot ignore the practical implications of a legal
> proceeding for the client. Just as an attorney may recommend a
> plea bargain or civil settlement to avoid the adverse conse-
> quences of a possible loss after trial, so too an attorney may
> take reasonable steps to defend a client's reputation and reduce
> the adverse consequences of indictment, especially in the face
> of a prosecution deemed unjust or commenced with improper
> motives. A defense attorney may pursue lawful strategies to
> obtain dismissal of an indictment or reduction of charges,
> including an attempt to demonstrate in the court of public
> opinion that the client does not deserve to be tried.[5]

With such an endorsement of the propriety of the conduct, if
not a duty to employ it, it should be clear that absent a gag
order — a direct order from a judge to say only "no comment"

when questioned by the press — a lawyer has a great deal of room to defend his or her client outside the courtroom. Exactly how far he or she may go remains unclear. What we do know, however, is that a state's ethics rules do not in fact forbid any and all comments and after *Gentile* (discussed further below), they could not do so. But they can forbid some comments. Which ones? The challenge here is to identify the appropriate boundary between the permitted and the forbidden, vague though that boundary must be.

The No-Comment Rule The American Bar Association (ABA) Model Rules offer a general test to determine whether a public comment is permitted. The rule is addressed only to a lawyer who "is participating or has participated in the investigation or litigation of a matter."[6] The rule does not bind other lawyers who comment, whether to print journalists, on talk shows, on blogs, or in articles they write themselves. The idea behind the distinction is that only those lawyers who are or were associated with the matter will have or appear to have inside information — will be publicly presumed to know things about the matter that the public, including other lawyers, do not know — and given this presumption, the biasing effects of their comments are of special concern. It is also doubtful that the First Amendment would tolerate a limitation on the speech of unassociated lawyers any greater than it would tolerate limitation on the speech of nonlawyers.

The ABA rule applies to civil and criminal matters equally, at least on its face, although the test the rule sets out is more likely to be an issue in criminal cases, if only because they are more likely to attract media attention. Here is the rule.

> A lawyer who is participating or has participated in the investigation or litigation of a matter shall not make an extrajudicial statement that the lawyer knows or reasonably should know will be disseminated by means of public

communication and will have a substantial likelihood of materially prejudicing an adjudicative proceeding in the matter.[7]

The rule applies when the lawyer "knows" the effect his or her speech will have or "reasonably should know," so even a well-intentioned lawyer who wrongly evaluates the biasing effects of a statement can be found in violation. The key phrase is "substantial likelihood of materially prejudicing an adjudicative proceeding." It is not immediately clear what the adverb *materially* adds to the meaning that *substantial* does not independently achieve. The likely answer is that *substantial* refers to the degree of risk and *materially* refers to the degree of harm if the risk comes to pass. But how likely must the likelihood be in order to be substantial? How does a lawyer know? We don't have a clear answer to either question, so to some extent a lawyer who talks publicly about his or her matter may invite discipline. But, of course, most public comments will be so innocuous that this danger will be nil. Still, there is a murky middle area where the lawyer can't be sure. Notably, the test is not as protective of speech as a "clear and present danger" test would be. It is something less than that. But the rule is much more protective of speech than the rule in the old Code of Professional Responsibility, which had no test at all. It prohibited all public comment without regard to risk of prejudice, except for certain narrowly defined safe harbors.[8]

A Right of Reply   The current rule has safe harbors, too, and they fall into two categories. The first category consists of a fairly narrow list of topics on which a lawyer may speak (ten in all, of which four pertain to criminal cases only).[9] A second category recognizes a right of reply. It permits a lawyer to make a statement that *does* create the forbidden "substantial likelihood" but only as reasonably required in order to reply to adverse publicity generated by others (not necessarily the opponent). This provision states:

> Notwithstanding paragraph (a), a lawyer may make a statement that a reasonable lawyer would believe is required to protect a client from the substantial undue prejudicial effect of recent publicity not initiated by the lawyer or the lawyer's client. A statement made pursuant to this paragraph shall be limited to such information as is necessary to mitigate the recent adverse publicity.[10]

The fact that the "right of reply" rule does not turn on the source of the original comment that the lawyer means to neutralize bears emphasis. The rule recognizes that a client's interest in a fair trial may be compromised by publicity from third parties or the media's own investigations and ruminations. The opposing side may have had nothing to do with it. This truism is often overlooked. Many lawyers will insist that they do not want to "try their cases" in the media. They will honestly insist they prefer that the case go unnoticed by anyone beyond the immediate participants. The less attention to the case, they may say, the better it will be for their client (especially if the client is a criminal defendant). That's not always so, of course, but it is often so. No matter. Public attention may be thrust on even these lawyers if the case is deemed newsworthy and the press gets on the trail. If that happens, it will be hard for the lawyer constantly to say "no comment" when questioned for a story. "I'm getting creamed in the tabs," the client might complain, "and all you say is 'no comment.' Can't you offer them more than that?"

Defining the Test   The nub of the issue remains. What is the meaning of "substantial likelihood of materially prejudicing"? Questions one might ask in deciding whether a particular comment violates this test are these: What was actually said?

How inflammatory is it? Will the revealed information be admissible in the eventual trial anyway? How far in advance of trial was the comment made (the longer, the less chance of prejudice because people forget)? Can we have confidence that voir dire of prospective jurors will eliminate any bias the comment may have engendered?

The facts in *Gentile* are about as good a place to begin the analysis as one could hope. Gentile, an experienced criminal defense lawyer in Las Vegas, was representing Grady Sanders, who was charged with various crimes, including theft of cocaine and travelers' checks from a safe deposit box. (The events occurred before either the ABA or Nevada had adopted a safe harbor for a right of reply.) News reports prior to the indictment cast increasing suspicion on Sanders while relying on unnamed police sources to exonerate others who had also fallen under suspicion, including persons in law enforcement. Following indictment, Gentile researched the Nevada "no comment" rule (based on ABA Rule 3.6 as it then read). He then held a press conference and protested the innocence of his client. He also suggested that witnesses against his clients were liars and suggested possible motivations. He said that a police detective was criminally responsible for the thefts attributed to his client. This is not the place to reprint the entire transcript of Gentile's press conference, which can be found in Appendix A to the plurality opinion, but a few paragraphs from his prepared remarks will give you the flavor:

> When this case goes to trial, and as it develops, you're going to see that the evidence will prove not only that Grady Sanders is an innocent person and had nothing to do with any of the charges that are being leveled against him, but that the person that was in the most direct position to have stolen the drugs and money, the American Express traveler's checks, is Detective Steve Scholl.

There is far more evidence that will establish that Detective Scholl took these drugs and took these American Express traveler's checks than any other living human being.

And I have to say that I feel that Grady Sanders is being used as a scapegoat to try to cover up for what has to be obvious to people at the Las Vegas Metropolitan Police Department and at the District Attorney's office.

Now, with respect to these other charges that are contained in this indictment, the so-called other victims, as I sit here today I can tell you that one, two–four of them are known drug dealers and convicted money launderers and drug dealers; three of whom didn't say a word about anything until after they were approached by Metro and after they were already in trouble and are trying to work themselves out of something.

Now, up until the moment, of course, that they started going along with what detectives from Metro wanted them to say, these people were being held out as being incredible and liars by the very same people who are going to say now that you can believe them.

The Court narrowly reversed Gentile's discipline. Four justices, in the opinion by Justice Kennedy, thought that the "substantial likelihood" test required a showing of "speech that creates a danger of imminent and substantial harm" in order to comport with the First Amendment. They concluded that Gentile's statement did not create such a danger. The trial was at least six months away. The jury pool was large. In the event voir dire revealed that Gentile's remarks had biased some prospective jurors, other jurors would be available to replace them. As it happened, when the trial began, none of the prospective jurors recalled Gentile's press conference. Gentile's client was acquitted of all charges.[11]

In dissent, four justices believed that the "substantial prejudice" standard did not require a showing of "a danger of imminent and substantial harm" to satisfy the First Amendment.

Something less was acceptable. And they explained why Gentile's statement, in their view, did create the prejudice the rule was intended to avert. The ninth justice, Justice O'Connor, sided with the dissent on this issue, which means it was the majority view. She did not believe that the First Amendment required "imminent and substantial harm." Nevertheless, she voted to reverse Gentile's discipline because she concluded that one of the "safe harbors" in Nevada's rule (drawn from the ABA rule) was vague. The Kennedy plurality also cited the vagueness of the safe harbor as an independent basis to reverse the discipline. So vagueness is the precise reason for the Court's judgment. A majority of the Court upheld the Nevada rule's description of the forbidden risk, which remains the description in the ABA rule.

Where was the vagueness that gave Gentile his victory? At the time, the Nevada and ABA provision allowed comment despite the general prohibition in the rule — that is, despite a "substantial likelihood of materially prejudicing" the trial — but only to the extent of allowing Gentile to state "without elaboration . . . the general nature of the . . . defense." The Kennedy plurality opinion concluded that the words *elaboration* and *general* offered "insufficient guidance" to a lawyer wishing to stay within the rule. Gentile could not know how broadly or narrowly these words should be read. Justice O'Connor agreed. She was also impressed that Gentile had researched the meaning of the rule and its exceptions before speaking and had tried to conform his comments to fall within the exception. Regardless of whether Gentile was right or wrong, his interpretation was "valid," making discipline constitutionally improper. The vagueness of the language meant that Gentile did not have the constitutionally required notice of the forbidden conduct. After the Court's decision, the ABA changed the language of the safe harbor to eliminate the words *elaboration* and *general*. Today, a lawyer is told only that she "may state . . . the claim, offense or defense involved."[12]

There is something of a disconnect between the "no-comment" rule, on the one hand, and real life, on the other. Lawyers talk to the press all the time, and nothing happens to them. It is rare for a lawyer to face discipline for public comments about pending cases, although he may encounter judicial displeasure, which might be seen as worse. Some lawyers never talk to the press as a matter of policy. They don't see an advantage in it. Also, there's an art to talking to reporters. Public relations specialists are skilled in that art. Trial lawyers, strangely enough, often are not, even though much of what they do for a living is talking to judges and juries. For many lawyers, the best advice is don't talk to the media, not because it's forbidden or will be punished, but because, while it may make their clients feel good, it's more likely to harm their clients' cause than help it.

ENDNOTES

1. *See, e.g., Globe Newspaper Co. v. Superior Court*, 457 U.S. 596, 603 (1982) (holding that it was "firmly established . . . that the press and general public have a constitutional right of access to criminal trials"); *Publicker Indus., Inc. v. Cohen*, 733 F.2d 1059, 1071 (3d Cir. 1984) (the "public and the press possess a . . . common law right of access to civil proceedings").

2. *See, e.g., United States v. Brown*, 218 F.3d 415 (5th Cir. 2000); *United States v. Cutler*, 58 F.3d 825 (2d Cir. 1995) (holding lawyer in contempt for violating gag order).

3. Model Rule (MR) 3.8(f) instructs prosecutors to "exercise reasonable care to prevent investigators, law enforcement personnel, employees or other persons assisting or associated with the prosecutor in a criminal case from making an extrajudicial statement that the prosecutor would be prohibited from making under Rule 3.6 or this Rule."

4. 501 U.S. 1030 (1991) (Justices Brennan, Marshall, and Stevens joined this opinion, which will be further discussed later in the text).

5. *Id.*

6. MR 3.6(a).

7. *Id.*

8. The various paragraphs of DR 7-107 forbid extrajudicial statements in civil, criminal, or administrative matters, with a few narrow exceptions. The rule does not have language equivalent to the "substantial likelihood" language in Rule 3.6(a).

9. MR 3.6(b). So for example, a lawyer may state "a request for assistance in obtaining evidence and information necessary thereto." MR 3.6(b)(5). And in a

criminal case, a lawyer (most likely the prosecutor) may state "the identity, residence, occupation and family status of the accused." MR 3.6(b)(7)(i). A further safe harbor is identified in the discussion of the *Gentile* case.

10. MR 3.6(c).

11. The plurality also credited as appropriate a secondary goal Gentile offered for his decision to hold a press conference. In addition to avoiding trial prejudice from press reports harmful to his client, Gentile explained that "the investigation had taken a serious toll on his client. Sanders was 'not a man in good health,' having suffered multiple open-heart surgeries prior to these events."

12. MR 3.6(b)(1).

part IV

Other Special Rules and Relationships

～ 19 ～

Transactional Lawyers

The "Bad Client" Problem

Noisy Withdrawals

Permissive and Mandatory Exceptions to Confidentiality

One of the reasons lawyers sometimes get into trouble is that they get mixed up with a bad client, by which I mean someone who, unknown to the lawyer, is using the lawyer's services to advance criminal or fraudulent conduct.[1] Maybe that wasn't the client's plan at the outset, but then the client starts to cut legal corners during the representation. The lawyer may not realize it until the matter is over, or perhaps there are warning signs during the work. The lawyer's headache may then appear in the form of a lawsuit by the people who have lost money as a result of the client's allegedly unlawful scheme. The client may be broke by then, so the lawyer and her firm (and perhaps other professional service firms, like accountants) are all that remain to sue. Even if the client is also the target of a lawsuit, the lawyer and firm will have some money and maybe even a (large) malpractice insurance policy. So they get sued, too. Later in this book

(Chapters 21 and 24), we look at the legal theories that can create lawyer liability to third parties in these situations, but here we look at the ethical rules governing the contest between the duty of loyalty and confidentiality, on one hand, and, on the other, the duty or authority to protect third persons from a bad client whose scheme a lawyer learns he has unwittingly assisted. The two subjects — the ethical rules and the civil liability theories — are related, because if the rules *permit* a lawyer to protect a person who, as the lawyer knows or has good reason to believe, has been or may be harmed by the client's conduct, even if a warning hurts the client, the lawyer is at greater risk of civil liability if he fails to do so. Of course, if the rules *require* the lawyer to protect innocent third parties, there is nothing to discuss. The lawyer must do so. We saw such a requirement in our discussion of fraud and candor to tribunals (Chapter 16). Now, not a tribunal but another person or entity is the victim.

Consider a jurisdiction whose ethical rules say that a lawyer *cannot* warn a third-party victim of client wrongdoing by revealing client confidences but must instead protect even the bad client's confidences and probably withdraw to avoid illegal assistance thereafter. A lawyer who was sued for assisting a client's fraud (by failing to warn when he learned the truth) could then cite his ethical duties in defense. "I would have loved to alert you," the lawyer might say, "but the court's confidentiality rules said I was forbidden to do so." That defense might or might not work. (For example, it would not work if substantive law overrides the ethical rule, which may be so if the claim against the lawyer is based on federal law and the lawyer in defense cites a state ethics rule.) If, however, the ethical rules do *not* forbid the lawyer to protect the third party, but allows her to do so, this defense evaporates. And that's what the Model Rules sometimes allow when a lawyer discovers client fraud that may cause or has caused substantial financial harm to others. I say "sometimes" because permissive disclosure of client confidences in this circumstance also depends on other conditions, as we saw in Chapter 4. This is a permissive authority only, not a mandatory one (although some states have amended their version of the rule to make it mandatory).[2] But there's more. As we'll shortly see, when two different rules are read together, the Model Rules, which appear to permit but not require warning, may actually require a lawyer to blow the whistle on his transactional client. These rules can sound quite complicated, and they are. So we should proceed to unpack them. That in turn requires a little history.

The O.P.M. Case[3]   In the 1970s and early 1980s, two New York businessmen, Goodman and Weissmann, ran a company called O.P.M. The company leased very large computers to businesses. (This was at a time when all computers were very large.) O.P.M. had credit with banks. The collateral for the credit consisted of the cash flow from the leases O.P.M. had with big companies that were O.P.M.'s customers. Banks were happy to lend money because the leases would mean that O.P.M. had a reliable source of funds to pay the interest on the loans. O.P.M.'s law firm was called Singer Hutner. Professor Susan Koniak describes what happened:

> For the entire span of the fraud, [Singer Hutner] handled O.P.M.'s transactions, papering and closing lease deals and providing legal opinions to lenders vouching for the soundness of the security for the loans — the underlying leases. By early 1979, if not earlier, the law firm had plenty of reasons to suspect that fraud was afoot, and those reasons multiplied in 1980. . . . Then, in June 1980, O.P.M.'s chief financial officer resigned and sent the law firm a letter stating that he had discovered that a substantial number of O.P.M.'s loans had been obtained through fraud. Lawyer Hutner of

Singer Hutner, who received that letter, later claimed that O.P.M.'s Goodman had snatched the letter away from him before he had a chance to read it. Nothing terribly suspicious about that! Later, however, Hutner met with the chief financial officer's lawyer, who told him that his client . . . had evidence of a "multimillion-dollar fraud, . . . that [Singer Hutner's] opinion letters . . . had been based upon false documents," and that O.P.M. could only survive by continuing to engage in fraud. . . . Faced with the near certainty that its work had been used (and was still being used) by its client to defraud O.P.M.'s lenders, and that its client had no intention of rectifying its ongoing crimes or refraining from committing new ones, Singer Hutner was apparently unsure about what, if anything, the law required it to do. [I]t hired two experts to advise it on legal ethics. . . . [4]

In New York at the time, the Code of Professional Responsibility said that a lawyer could not reveal a client's fraud on a court or person if the lawyer's knowledge was protected under the New York Code of Professional Responsibility as a "confidence" or a "secret."[5] The ethics experts — a law school dean and a practicing lawyer — told the firm that it could not warn the lending banks. While a New York Code exception to confidentiality allowed lawyers to reveal a client's *future* crimes, no exception permitted them to reveal past misconduct, the experts said. The firm was also told that while it could not reveal what it knew, it could not assist the fraud. That would seem to indicate that it had to withdraw from the representation. But the experts said the firm had another option. It could keep silent and continue to represent O.P.M. *if* the client assured the firm that the fraud had stopped. The client gave the assurance. As Professor Koniak tells us, eventually the firm learned that the assurance was false and the fraud continued, probably because the company depended on the fraud even to survive. Fraud was built into its business model. So finally the law firm withdrew, but even then it remained silent. It did not tell O.P.M.'s successor law firm, Kaye Scholer, why it withdrew, not even after a partner there asked to know the reason. After the fraud unraveled, O.P.M. collapsed, and some of its principals went to prison. Singer Hutner paid the defrauded banks $10 million to settle claims against it (others contributed an additional $55 million).[6] Because of the settlement, the opinion of the ethics experts was never tested in court.

While the O.P.M. case is history (and Singer Hutner has long since gone out of business, although not because of this event), the fallout has persisted for decades and remains influential today in professional debates about the proper way to frame the duty of lawyers who learn of a transactional client's illegal conduct. The initials O.P.M. are permanently embedded in the archeological history of U.S. legal ethics. (Indeed, as the story has it, and it's a detail that rings true, the initials O.P.M. stood for "Other People's Money.") Singer Hutner believed, on advice of counsel, that between warning its client's victims of a fraud that the firm had unwittingly assisted and keeping its client's secrets, it was obligated to do the latter under the New York Code. But then it got sued anyway and settled for millions. So could it be that a law firm might be civilly liable for aiding fraud through silence even though silence is itself ethically mandated by court rule? If Singer Hutner had warned the bank — or gone to the district attorney — and revealed what it knew, it might have escaped civil liability, but would its lawyers then be subject to professional discipline for breaking a client's confidence? How can we fairly place lawyers in this dilemma? How are they supposed to choose?[7]

Noisy Withdrawal[8]   The New York State Bar Association believed that lawyers should not be required to choose between these alternatives, that the confidentiality rule had to be changed so that a future law firm in Singer Hutner's position would have the option to warn the client's victim and thereby avoid the conflict between professional duty and exposure to civil liability. The bar proposed, and the New York courts accepted, a new exception to confidentiality, which says that a lawyer may reveal

> [c]onfidences or secrets to the extent implicit in withdrawing a written or oral opinion or representation previously given by the lawyer and believed by the lawyer still to be relied upon by a third person where the lawyer has discovered that the opinion or representation was based on materially inaccurate information or is being used to further a crime or fraud.[9]

The first thing to notice here is that the exception does not actually allow the lawyer to reveal a client's confidences. It only allows the lawyer to withdraw or retract anything the lawyer wrote or said in the circumstances described. Of course, retraction will *implicitly* reveal a confidence. The drafters wanted to go only so far as necessary to protect the lawyer — and indirectly the intended victim — and no further. Protecting the victim seems, in fact, to be a fortunate byproduct. Under the new rule, Singer Hutner would have been allowed (and possibly required) to tell the lawyers for lending banks that it was withdrawing from representing O.P.M. and also retracting any opinions it had given or representations it had made to the banks in connection with loan closings, but that's all it would have been allowed to say. It could not recount the facts that led it to this decision. The facts remain confidential. But the lawyers for the banks would immediately realize there was a serious problem with the loan and presumably act to protect their clients.

The second thing to notice about this provision is that the authority is only available where there is something for the lawyer to withdraw — an oral or written opinion or representation. It has no value if the lawyer learns that he has assisted a client's fraud without having given an opinion or made a representation. And the final thing to notice is that the authority to withdraw the opinion or representation is created if the lawyer *either* learns that that it was based on "materially inaccurate information" *or* if someone (not necessarily the client) is using the opinion or representation to "further a crime or fraud."[10]

A lawyer in this situation might prefer to withdraw from representing the client and thereby do nothing to further assist the fraud, but she also might prefer not to withdraw an opinion or representation. A lawyer may certainly do that, because the authority in the new rule is likely permissive only.[11] But that kind of *quiet* withdrawal may not alert the client's victim, and so the lawyer has not reduced the risk of civil liability. The lawyer is safer if, when she withdraws from representing the client, she concurrently withdraws any oral or written opinion or representation, if there are any. That kind of withdrawal from a representation has been given a name. It is called a *noisy withdrawal*, as opposed to a quiet one, where you just kind of slink away.

In a different form, the idea of the noisy withdrawal also found its way into the comments to the Model Rules when they were adopted in 1983. The comment purported to make it clear that disaffirmance of a lawyer's prior statements did not violate the lawyer's confidentiality obligations. Some observers thought that putting this authority in a comment, rather than in the rules themselves as in New York, gave it too little recognition. Also, inconsistencies between the comments and the rules must be resolved by favoring the rule.[12] So there was a danger that a court that found inconsistency would ignore the comment. But for better or worse, the comments were where the authority was placed and where it has remained to this day, although it has been moved from the comment to Rule 1.6 to the comments for Rules 1.2 and 4.1.

Two decades after the American Bar Association (ABA) adopted the noisy withdrawal comments in 1983, it adopted an amendment to Rule 1.6 that broadened the permissive confidentiality exceptions. The amendment, which had been proposed but rejected several times beginning as far back as 1983, overlaps (and is broader than) the noisy withdrawal authority, but it is not identical. So sometimes a noisy withdrawal will be a lawyer's only option, and at other times a lawyer might choose it over the 2003 authority because he finds that it offers sufficient protection against civil liability while minimizing the extent to which the lawyer needs to reveal a client's confidential information, something lawyers hate to do.

The 2003 Confidentiality Exceptions What then were the two new exceptions to confidentiality in Rule 1.6(b)? One of them says that a lawyer may reveal a client's confidences

> to the extent the lawyer reasonably believes necessary . . .
> (2) to prevent the client from committing a crime or fraud that is reasonably certain to result in substantial injury to the financial interests or property of another and in furtherance of which the client has used or is using the lawyer's services. . . .

Under this authority, the lawyer acts in order to "prevent" a crime or fraud. But to use this authority, the lawyer must be able to support his belief that disclosure is "reasonably necessary," the harm has to be financial and substantial, and the lawyer's services had to have been used in committing or attempting to commit the illegal or fraudulent act.[13] If any of these conditions is absent, the lawyer may still be able to use the noisy withdrawal authority in the comments to the rules.

The second addition to Rule 1.6(b) permits revelation

> to the extent the lawyer reasonably believes necessary . . .
> (3) to prevent, mitigate or rectify substantial injury to the financial interests or property of another that is reasonably

certain to result or has resulted from the client's commission of a crime or fraud in furtherance of which the client has used the lawyer's services. . . .

This provision is dramatically more expansive than the first one and greatly increases the ability of lawyers to protect third parties from the unlawful conduct of clients. The same level of confidence is required ("reasonably believes necessary"), the same harm is identified ("substantial injury to . . . financial interests"), and as before the lawyer's services had to have been used in committing the wrong. But this exception operates on the assumption that the crime or fraud (or some part of it) has already occurred. No longer is the lawyer revealing confidential information to prevent it. Instead, revelation now works to "prevent, mitigate or rectify" the "injury" from the crime or fraud. The word *prevent* is prospective, and so to that extent the aim of this exception, like the first one, is to keep something from happening, but now that something is *the injury*, not the act. By contrast, the words *mitigate* and *rectify* have a retrospective dimension. They assume that the injury has already occurred (or is occurring) but can be reduced or undone. A lawyer might be able to reveal a client's confidences weeks or even years after the work is done if the lawyer then learns that his services were used to commit the crime or fraud.

This more expansive exception is likely to arise in one of two ways. First, the lawyer may learn about a completed crime or fraud shortly after doing the work. The injury has occurred and may be ongoing but can be stopped and possibly reversed (as by getting the money back). This is the situation in which Singer Hutner seems to have found itself. When it first learned about the client's fraud, it may have been possible, through immediate revelation, to get back some of the loan money, and it would certainly have been possible to "mitigate" the injury by shutting down the line of credit. And of course, the firm may have been encouraged to do just that to avoid its own liability for failure to warn when warning could have done some good. This is probably the circumstance in which Rule 1.6(b)(3) is most likely to be used.

The new authority could also become important if a former client is sued and the plaintiff seeks information from its former lawyer, either formally in a deposition or simply in an informal interview. Let's say that the lawsuit (or the phone call about its likelihood) is the lawyer's first indication that the client's conduct was fraudulent. Ordinarily, when a lawyer is asked about communications with a client or former client, her duty is to refuse to answer because the inquiry seeks confidential information. If ordered to answer, the lawyer should assert privilege unless and until a judge rules that the privilege does not apply and orders the lawyer to disclose. On these facts, a judge is likely to reject a privilege claim because of the exception to privilege when the client's purpose in using a lawyer is criminal or fraudulent (see Chapter 4). What the new exception to the duty of confidentiality does is allow the lawyer to reveal information she received from or in the representation of a client without awaiting a judicial ruling on privilege. (Recall from Chapter 4 that privilege and confidentiality describe different doctrines.) A lawyer may choose not to do that, preferring the greater security of a judicial decision rejecting any claim of privilege and ordering her to reveal, but the new exception does not require the lawyer to wait.

Rule 4.1 and Mandatory Disclosure Although the new Rule 1.6 exceptions are permissive only, Rule 4.1 is mandatory, applies to transactional lawyers, and could convert the permission to disclose in Rule 1.6 into an obligation to do so. No one can be quite sure how the two rules will operate together. Rule 4.1(b) provides:

> In the course of representing a client a lawyer *shall not* knowingly ... (b) *fail to disclose* a material fact to a third

> person when disclosure is necessary to avoid assisting a criminal or fraudulent act by a client, unless disclosure is prohibited by Rule 1.6.

The text creates a mandatory duty ("shall not . . . fail to disclose") when the client has, for example, lied about a material fact in the course of a negotiation ("There have never been termites in this house"; "The company has no unrecorded debt"). But the exception seems to destroy the duty because the duty disappears if the lawyer's knowledge of the crime or fraud is a client confidence within Rule 1.6, as it almost always will be, given the breadth of that term. So between confidentiality and protection of fraud on a third party, the confidentiality obligation may be seen as superior. (Recall in Chapter 16 that we learned that if the fraud is on a court or other tribunal, not a person, the confidentiality duty is subordinate to the duty to remedy the fraud on the court.)

Not so fast. It turns out that it's all an illusion. Confidentiality is not superior after all. The amendments to Rule 1.6(b) just discussed mean that when their conditions are present, disclosure is not "prohibited by Rule 1.6" within the meaning of Rule 4.1, and if disclosure is not prohibited, the final clause of Rule 4.1(b) (beginning with "unless") is eliminated and we are left with the mandatory duty ("shall not . . . fail"). So, for example, if a client has used a lawyer's services to commit a fraud causing substantial financial harm, the lawyer is not "prohibited by Rule 1.6" from revealing confidential information. The lawyer is then commanded by Rule 4.1 to disclose her client's material false statements of fact *if* failing to do so means the lawyer will be "assisting" the client's crime or fraud within the meaning of Rule 4.1(b), a distinct legal question under the substantive law. Will the lawyer's silence be assisting? This is all terribly dense, but that conclusion seems to be the upshot of the interplay between the two rules. This is the sort of textual complexity that only a lawyer could love, and maybe not even a lawyer.

Comment [3] to Rule 4.1, which follows, is a bit confused on this issue and not particularly helpful. I've put a boldfaced letter before each sentence in the comment to facilitate the discussion:

[**A**] Under Rule 1.2(d), a lawyer is prohibited from counseling or assisting a client in conduct that the lawyer knows is criminal or fraudulent. [**B**] Paragraph (b) states a specific application of the principle set forth in Rule 1.2(d) and addresses the situation where a client's crime or fraud takes the form of a lie or misrepresentation. [**C**] Ordinarily, a lawyer can avoid assisting a client's crime or fraud by withdrawing from the representation. [**D**] Sometimes it may be necessary for the lawyer to give notice of the fact of withdrawal and to disaffirm an opinion, document, affirmation or the like. [**E**] In extreme cases, substantive law may require a lawyer to disclose information relating to the representation to avoid being deemed to have assisted the client's crime or fraud. [**F**] If the lawyer can avoid assisting a client's crime or fraud only by disclosing this information, then under paragraph (b) the lawyer is required to do so, unless the disclosure is prohibited by Rule 1.6.

Sentences A and B are unremarkable restatements of the requirements of Rule 1.2 as applied in this context. Sentence C predicts that withdrawal will "ordinarily" avoid the problem of assisting client fraud. That view of the substantive law may be overly optimistic. The sentence doesn't address the problem that can arise if the lawyer has already unwittingly assisted the fraud, especially if documents the lawyer prepared, and which may have the lawyer's name on them, are still being used (or relied upon) to accomplish the fraud. Will mere withdrawal suffice then? Will mere withdrawal without warning protect the lawyer from civil liability? Ethics rules cannot determine what a court will say as a matter of substantive law. Suggesting perhaps that the answer to both questions will sometimes be no, sentence D offers the option of a noisy withdrawal.

But none of this explains why the lawyer isn't obligated to go even further and reveal client confidences to prevent the fraud or its injury when revelation is not "prohibited" by Rule 1.6. For one thing, a noisy withdrawal will not have much value if the lawyer has given no "opinion, document [or] affirmation" that he can withdraw. And even if he has, full disclosure is more likely to stop the mischief than is a coded reference. So the last two sentences, E and F, anticipate that the substantive law, if not the rules themselves, may in fact require disclosure to avoid liability for assisting the crime or fraud. But then sentence F seems to say that regardless of substantive law, Rule 1.6 limits what the lawyer can say even if silence equals assistance.

Of course, that can't be true. The ethical rules are about ethics, not law. They don't purport to define substantive law duties. And the substantive law may override what an ethical code says. But we need not have that debate because yet another new confidentiality exception makes it moot. It would seem to make the requirements of substantive law superior to the duty of confidentiality. It says that a lawyer may reveal confidential information "to comply with other law or a court order."[14] So it's pretty clear that the confidentiality obligation is subordinate to the requirements of substantive law. The "unless" clause in sentence F is therefore of little consequence in the face of a legal duty to disclose.

Other Rules for Transactional Lawyers   We have focused on the "bad client problem" and the interplay between the confidentiality rule and the rule forbidding assisting client fraud, on one hand, and the substantive law of civil liability, on the other.[15] Of course, transactional lawyers are governed by all of the same rules and duties that govern lawyers in other areas of practice, including the rules against contacting another lawyer's client in the matter (Chapter 7), the client-centered duties studied in Chapters 3-6, and the conflict-of-interest rules. Other rules that constrain transactional lawyers (along with others) are worth mentioning. Lawyers are forbidden to make false material statements of fact or law,[16] with the implication that if a lawyer has done so unaware of the falsity, she must correct the error, but again subject to the (illusory) constraints of the confidentiality rule. A special rule governs what lawyers may say in communicating with unrepresented persons.[17] And transactional lawyers, like all others, may not use means lacking "a substantial purpose" if these "embarrass, delay, or burden a third person."[18] The key adjective in the last sentence is *substantial*. The fact that a lawyer can conceive of a justification for offensive conduct does not mean the conduct serves a substantial purpose.

It is, however, the phenomenon of the bad client—the client bent on illegal conduct who is using the lawyer to achieve his or her unlawful goals — that has drawn the greatest attention in discussions of the duties of transactional lawyers. Although bad client problems also arise in litigation, litigation is overseen by a judge or other "neutral." Transactions happen in private. In litigation, also, parties and opponents have recourse to court process to discover information. Not so in transactional matters. And it is rare that an injured party sues a litigator based on a client's misconduct in a litigation. But transactional lawyers have increasingly had to face such actions, sometimes resulting in large judgments or (more likely) settlements. These differences, and the facial difference between the rules depending on whether the client's misconduct harms a tribunal or a person, make the bad client problem particularly thorny for transactional lawyers who try to steer their way between the duty of confidentiality, preventing harm to a third person, and avoiding their own civil liability.

ENDNOTES

1. If the lawyer knows about the crime or fraud, then the reason for the trouble is the lawyer's stupidity. And of course, it would violate Model Rule (MR) 1.2(d).

2. *See, e.g.*, New Jersey Rule 1.6(b).

3. Much has been written about the O.P.M. case. A good discussion of that case and the broader issues it raises, including discussion of other frauds in which lawyers were implicated, can be found in Susan Koniak, *When the Hurlyburly's Done: The Bar's Struggle with the SEC*, 103 Colum. L. Rev. 1236 (2003); Stuart Taylor, Jr., *Ethics and the Law: A Case History*, N.Y. Times, Jan. 9, 1983, §6 (Magazine), at 31.

4. Koniak, *supra* n.3 at 1260-1264.

5. This was based on the language of DR 4-101 of the ABA's Code of Professional Responsibility.

6. The $10 million figure comes from Stuart Taylor's article, *supra* note 3. Some report a higher payment.

7. Was Singer Hutner an innocent victim of poor advice? Some, including Professor Koniak, have cited facts that imply that the firm intentionally avoided learning too much so it could keep a lucrative client.

8. Noisy withdrawal was introduced briefly in Chapter 4.

9. DR 4-101(C)(5). It is now numbered MR 1.6(b)(3).

10. It's worth noting, too, that the level of confidence required to trigger the rule is not clear. It suffices that the lawyer "believes" that a third person still relies on an opinion or representation, but the rule also requires that the lawyer have "discovered" something. Does "discovered" mean that the lawyer's conclusion must be right? What if the lawyer discovers that an opinion was based on false information, but the lawyer turns out to be wrong after the client's deal capsizes as a result of the lawyer's decision? Is the lawyer liable or subject to discipline? We don't know.

11. I say "possibly permissive" because under the old New York Code, there was an argument that the noisy withdrawal authority was required when its preconditions were satisfied. It is not worth walking through this argument any longer because it is no longer available after the New York rules were amended effective April 1, 2009.

12. See Model Rules, Scope cmt. [22] (comments are "guides to interpretation, but the text of each Rule is authoritative").

13. We might ask the reason for the last requirement. Why shouldn't lawyers be permitted to act whether or not their services have been utilized in committing the crime or fraud? Some states do not include this last requirement. *See* Massachusetts Rule 1.6(b)(1), which allows revelation to prevent substantial financial harm.

14. MR 1.6(b)(6).

15. Everything said here could equally well apply to exposure to criminal liability.

16. MR 4.1(a).

17. MR 4.3. Lawyers cannot "state or imply that [they are] disinterested." A lawyer who "knows or reasonably should know that the unrepresented person misunderstands the lawyer's role" must try to correct the misunderstanding. And lawyers are forbidden to "give legal advice to an unrepresented person, other than the advice to secure counsel," when the interests of an unrepresented person and the client's interests "are or have a reasonable possibility of being in conflict."

18. MR 4.4(a).

～ 20 ～

Lawyers for Organizations

The Lawyer's Role

Reporting Up and Reporting Out

Changes in Corporate Control

The Lawyer's Role When the Client Is an Organization[1]
Lawyers for organizations — whether retained or employed —
labor under an additional set of circumstances. Specifically,
their client is the organization, which may be a company, a
partnership, a labor union or trade association, a not-for-profit
entity, or something else. But their client can't tell them what
to do because it is not real. It is a construction of the law, a legal
fiction or idea, if you will. So the lawyers must take instruction
from, and fulfill the rest of their client obligations through,
other agents of the client. In the case of a company, which
will be our main focus in this chapter, those agents will usually
be officers, managers, and directors. The triangular nature of
this situation (client, agent, and lawyer at each of the corners)
need not create problems and as a rule will not. The agents
through whom the lawyer works for the client also have
fiduciary obligations to the client. Presumably, lawyer and nonlawyer agents are interested in the best possible outcome for

the client. The lawyer's assignment is the law, not business strategy; the businesspeople have the opposite responsibility. This triangular structure is not, of course, limited to organizational clients. A biological client may deal with his or her lawyers through agents and employees as well, but the triangle is unavoidable when the client is an organization.

It follows that the agents or employees (a particular type of agent) of the organizational client are not the lawyer's clients even though they are working for the same company as is the lawyer. The client is the organization unless something else is said or done to create a professional relationship with the agent. The American Bar Association (ABA) Model Rule 1.13(a) makes this clear when it states that a "lawyer employed or retained by an organization represents the organization acting through its duly authorized constituents." The term "duly authorized" is also important. It tells us that the lawyer takes direction from and gives her advice to the persons at the client who are empowered to give or receive the instruction or advice. How does the lawyer know who that is? The organization has a governance structure (usually found in its bylaws and board resolutions) that should identify who may speak and act for it and in what contexts. The lawyer's job is to recognize the structure, identify the right people, and, as a rule, unless something irregular is happening (see below), treat them as the living embodiment of the client.

So far so good. A second attribute of entity representation requires the lawyer to remember her place. She's the lawyer for the organization. Her role is not to make business decisions. She may be asked her advice about these, of course, and an employed lawyer who knows her company well is especially likely to be a source of advice on non-legal decisions. But business is not the domain of a lawyer. The businesspeople run the business. The lawyer has no duty and no right to seek to countermand a lawful business decision even if she thinks it happens to be wrongheaded. Even when a business decision may subject the organization to liability because it is unclear whether the company can engage in the contemplated conduct, as is often true in a complicated regulatory environment, the job of the lawyer is to advise the client, through its constituents, on the risks associated with a particular decision. The businesspeople can then choose to take those risks once properly counseled so long as there is a legitimate basis for concluding that the conduct is lawful. But this assumes that the law is unclear.

Now, it sometimes happens that an employed lawyer will have a second title. Vice president and general counsel are not uncommon. Sometimes the duties associated with the vice president title will include business decisions. That's fine; however, the lawyer must be aware, and must make others in the organization aware, that when operating under the separate title — or even without that title, when performing business tasks — communications with the lawyer will not enjoy the attorney-client privilege.[2] Of course, it won't always be clear in which role the lawyer is working. Since anyone claiming the privilege has the burden of proving the elements of the claim,[3] the lawyer with two titles should take care to clarify when she is working in her legal capacity and to be able to prove it. Ambiguity will work against the company.[4]

Representing Entity Constituents   As stated, a lawyer for a company or other organization does not thereby represent its constituents. Usually, this will be clear to everyone. Sometimes, however, it may not be clear. Those times cannot be defined precisely, so judgment is required and appropriate warnings issued when they arise. Warnings are needed to avoid the situation where a constituent of a company can make a plausible claim that the company's lawyer was his lawyer, too, if not by virtue of an express agreement then by implication.

Separately, warnings may be required simply as a matter of fairness so that an employee or officer is duly warned about whom the lawyer represents (not them). Of course, it may be that the lawyer has chosen to represent both the entity and the constituent on a matter, as when a company is sued along with an officer because of conduct alleged against the officer and imputed to the company. Joint representation makes it easier to coordinate the defense and it saves money. When a lawyer, with approval from her regular client, the company, chooses joint representation, she should make it clear that neither client will enjoy privilege for communications with the lawyer in the event of a later dispute between them[5] and that confidential information learned in the representation will be shared with both clients (see Chapter 21).[6] The lawyer may also want to ask the officer for advance consent to continue to represent the company in the event the lawyer chooses to withdraw from representing the officer because of a perceived conflict of interest as the work develops (see Chapter 15).

But this is the easy part, because everyone is focused on the decisions, which are express. The danger zone is when the lawyer does not decide to represent the officer or employee along with the company, indeed does not want to do so, but the circumstances are murky enough so that the officer or employee may later claim that he was also a client, a claim which if credited may hurt the company in several ways. First, it may disqualify the lawyer from continuing to represent the company if its interests and those of the officer become adverse.[7] Second, it may prevent the company from sharing information the lawyer obtained from the officer (and is therefore privileged to him) with third parties if the company decides it is in its interest to do so.[8] Third, because of the duty to keep a client informed about a matter (see Chapter 6), it will entitle the officer to information the lawyer received from others in the company in the (implicit) joint representation with the company.

Miranda Warnings To avoid these and other dangers, as briefly signaled in Chapter 5, company lawyers may choose to give what have come to be known as corporate Miranda warnings, a concept that takes its name from the Supreme Court's *Miranda* decision, which requires police to give certain warnings to persons under arrest. Those warnings may go something like this: "You understand that only the company is my client and I'm working for it. I don't represent you. While your communications with me are privileged and confidential, it is the company, not you, that controls the privilege and confidentiality. And the company can choose to waive protection for our communications and reveal them without your permission."[9] The precise language will vary, but this is essentially what a lawyer would say. Of course, giving such warnings may cause the officer to clam up depending on his perception of his own legal exposure. But that's a price the lawyer may sometimes need to pay in order to avoid an implicit professional relationship with the officer.

In fact, the lawyer may be bound to give this warning even if there is no obvious confusion about the lawyer's true client. In the interest of fairness, ABA Model Rule 1.13(f) provides:

> In dealing with an organization's directors, officers, employees, members, shareholders or other constituents, a lawyer shall explain the identity of the client when the lawyer knows or reasonably should know that the organization's interests are adverse to those of the constituents with whom the lawyer is dealing.

And Rule 4.3, which would seem to operate in tandem, provides:

> In dealing on behalf of a client with a person who is not represented by counsel, a lawyer shall not state or imply that the lawyer is disinterested. When the lawyer knows or reasonably should know that the unrepresented person misunderstands the lawyer's role in the matter, the lawyer shall

make reasonable efforts to correct the misunderstanding. The lawyer shall not give legal advice to an unrepresented person, other than the advice to secure counsel, if the lawyer knows or reasonably should know that the interests of such a person are or have a reasonable possibility of being in conflict with the interests of the client.

Notice that Rule 1.13(f) requires the warning whenever the interests of the officer and company "are adverse." Unlike Rule 4.3, the Rule 1.13 mandate does not depend on whether the officer "misunderstands the lawyer's role in the matter," as Rule 4.3 does. Rule 1.13(f), as an ethical rule, is meant to ensure that the officer is treated fairly. He may realize the lawyer is not his lawyer but may not realize that he is at risk and that his statements may hurt him. For example, it may come to pass that the company chooses to share what the officer tells the lawyer with the government in order to minimize harm to itself from an enforcement action or to head off an indictment. But sharing the officer's information may subject him to serious penalty. Separately, the officer may tell things to the company lawyer that leads the company to fire him or even sue him.

As stated, however, the lawyer may choose to give the warning for the very practical reason that under the circumstances she is worried about an implication that the officer is a client. What circumstances will support that implication? Among them is a course of dealing between the two that might have encouraged the officer to view himself as a client of the lawyer and the fact that the lawyer may have done and may be doing private legal work for the officer (with the company's permission). If the constituent is not an officer but a low-level employee of the company, his lack of sophistication in dealing with lawyers may lead him to assume the company's lawyer also represents him.

The Third Circuit (upholding a test devised by the trial court) endorsed five factors company constituents must prove to establish a professional relationship with company counsel:

> First, they must show they approached [counsel] for the purpose of seeking legal advice. Second, they must demonstrate that when they approached [counsel] they made it clear that they were seeking legal advice in their individual rather than in their representative capacities. Third, they must demonstrate that the [law firm] saw fit to communicate with them in their individual capacities, knowing that a possible conflict could arise. Fourth, they must prove that their conversations with [counsel] were confidential. And, fifth, they must show that the substance of their conversations with [counsel] did not concern matters within the company or the general affairs of the company.[10]

Reporting Up   Suppose a lawyer for a company learns in the course of the representation that a constituent is violating the civil or criminal law, or intends to, either by committing an act that harms or will harm the company (like stealing or self-dealing) or by directing the company to commit an illegal act against others and that could subject the company to liability (like violation of a regulatory statute or the antitrust law). Assume, too, that the unlawfulness of the conduct is clear and that the harm to the company can be significant. What should the lawyer do?

Obviously, the lawyer must take steps to protect her client, the company. That's easy, but how? If the lawyer is a subordinate lawyer in the general counsel's office or a junior lawyer in an outside law firm, he will go to his boss. If he's the outside lawyer in charge of the client's matter, he will go to someone high up in the general counsel's office, maybe to the general counsel. And whoever he is, if he can't get satisfaction and the harm or potential harm to the company is serious enough, he will need to go higher. This is called *reporting up*, because that is what the lawyer is doing—reporting up the chain of authority—and it is required because the lawyer's duty is to protect his client against harm caused by the unlawful behavior of others (whether or not they are the client's officers and employees). While none of this should be seen as controversial, it is also true that often reporting up is not going to be easy. The in-house lawyer may be going above the head of his boss and above the head of his boss's boss, and so on. From the lawyer's point of view, this is really unpleasant. Who knows what will be the consequences to the lawyer's career and position within the company? And yet the lawyer cannot simply ignore the bad conduct and leave the client unprotected. If he did that and the client suffered serious harm, what could he say when asked why he didn't pursue the issue higher and higher within the company, even as high as the board of directors itself, to protect his client? Not much really.

At this point we should draw a few distinctions. First, Rule 1.13 (as originally adopted and today) gives the lawyer a duty to report up only if the lawyer "knows" of illegality and only if the conduct is "in a matter related to the representation." That means that as far as the ethics rule is concerned, the lawyer has no obligation if he only *believes* there is illegality or if he knows there is but the misconduct is not "related" to his work for the client. However, while the absence of either factor (knowledge or relatedness) might remove the ethical problem, it will not absolve the lawyer of the risk of civil liability for malpractice. In other words, Rule 1.13's demanding preconditions to the obligation to report up will not necessarily be the measure of the lawyer's civil law duties as a professional charged to protect his client.

Now back to the ethical duty, and let us assume that the lawyer does have knowledge, that the illegality is related to his representation, and that the prospective injury is serious. What exactly does reporting up consist of?

When the ABA Model Rules were first adopted in 1983, Rule 1.13(b) required a rather weak response by the lawyer. After the introductory sentence (essentially unchanged since 1983) spelling out the knowledge and relatedness requirement and describing the nature of the illegality that requires response, the paragraph continued:

> In determining how to proceed, the lawyer shall give due consideration to the seriousness of the violation and its consequences, the scope and nature of the lawyer's representation, the responsibility in the organization and the apparent motivation of the person involved, the policies of the organization concerning such matters and any other relevant considerations. Any measures taken shall be designed to minimize disruption of the organization and the risk of revealing information relating to the representation to persons outside the organization. Such measures may include among others:
>
> > (1) asking for reconsideration of the matter;
> >
> > (2) advising that a separate legal opinion on the matter be sought for presentation to appropriate authority in the organization; and
> >
> > (3) referring the matter to higher authority in the organization, including, if warranted by the seriousness of the matter, referral to the highest authority that can act in behalf of the organization as determined by applicable law.

While some believed that this instruction was an inadequate resolution of the lawyer's duty in these unfortunate circumstances, it certainly made life easier for the lawyer (at least ethically) than would a more demanding reporting-up obligation. The need for a change appeared around the time of the millennium, and the change can be directly attributed to the corporate scandals that hit America (think Enron, WorldCom, Tyco, and Arthur Andersen). Today, in place of the portion of Rule 1.13(b) just quoted, we have the following directive:

> Unless the lawyer reasonably believes that it is not necessary in the best interest of the organization to do so, the lawyer

shall refer the matter to higher authority in the organization, including, if warranted by the circumstances, to the highest authority that can act on behalf of the organization as determined by applicable law.

This language creates a presumptive obligation to report up, perhaps to the company's highest authority, "[u]nless the lawyer" can establish that he "reasonably believe[d]" it was not necessary to do so to protect the client. This language gives the lawyer the burden of justifying *a failure* to report up, all the way to the top "if warranted by circumstances."

Reporting Out   Reporting up is done within the company. No exception to confidentiality is needed because even if the lawyer reports to the highest authority in the organization, usually a board of some kind or a board committee, she is still talking *to the client itself*, not outsiders. The reporting up duty is premised on the lawyer's obligation to inform and protect her client within the sphere of her representation. *Reporting out*, by contrast, does mean that the lawyer will be revealing a client's confidences to outsiders and therefore needs an exception to Rule 1.6. Depending on the situation, there may be an exception in Rule 1.6(b)(2) or (b)(3), whose focus is preventing a crime or fraud that will cause substantial financial injury to another or preventing, mitigating, or rectifying the injury to another from a completed crime or fraud, if in either event the lawyer's services have been used to commit the crime or fraud. Or substantive law may require reporting out, in which case Rule 1.6(b)(6) supplies an exception to the confidentiality duty. (See generally Chapters 4 and 5 on these exceptions.)

The Rule 1.6(b)(2) and (b)(3) exceptions do not require that the lawyer "know" the facts establishing their preconditions. It is enough that the lawyer "reasonably believes" the facts. Further, these exceptions (unlike Rule 1.13(b)) do not require that the circumstances be "related to the representation," although they likely will be if the lawyer's services were used to commit the crime or fraud. Sometimes, therefore, the information that a lawyer might want to report out will fall within the permissive authority of the Rule 1.6(b) exceptions.[11] But not always. For example, the illegality may be directed at the organization itself and not, as required by Rule 1.6, "another" person. Or the illegality may not have benefited from the lawyer's unwitting assistance, as the two Rule 1.6(b) exceptions require.

At the expense of some redundancy, which is not always a bad thing, Rule 1.13 contains its own exception to confidentiality, which, like the Rule 1.6 exceptions, is permissive, not mandatory. The Rule 1.13 exception was adopted in 2003 at about the time the Securities and Exchange Commission (SEC) was gearing up to issue final rules of conduct for lawyers practicing before it. Adoption of the exception was an obvious effort to keep the SEC's rules as weak as possible while complying with the congressional mandate in Sarbanes-Oxley that the SEC adopt rules.[12] That's not only because lawyers feared a more stringent rule, but also because lawyers prefer to have their respective state courts, not the federal government, define the profession's ethics rules. The Rule 1.13 confidentiality exception provides:

> (c) Except as provided in paragraph (d),[13] if
>
> (1) despite the lawyer's efforts in accordance with paragraph (b) the highest authority that can act on behalf of the organization insists upon or fails to address in a timely and appropriate manner an action, or a refusal to act, that is clearly a violation of law, and
>
> (2) the lawyer reasonably believes that the violation is reasonably certain to result in substantial injury to the organization, then the lawyer may reveal information relating to the representation whether or not Rule 1.6

permits such disclosure, but only if and to the extent the lawyer reasonably believes necessary to prevent substantial injury to the organization.

While Rule 1.13 does create authority for reporting out, notice the rather demanding preconditions. First, the lawyer must have gone to the highest authority without success. The illegal conduct must be "clearly a violation of law." The lawyer must be "reasonably certain" that the organization will suffer "substantial injury." Even then, the reporting out is limited to that which is "reasonably necessary to prevent" the injury. Since the authority is permissive only, it will be rare that a lawyer invokes it, especially considering the effect of such conduct on her standing in the organization (read job security and chances of promotion).[14] The greatest incentive to invoking the authority will be the avoidance of personal liability if the lawyer remains silent when the rules permitted her to speak. Think of a lawyer who learns that the client's consumer product, already on the market, poses significant danger to the safety or health of the public.

Changes in Corporate Control   Every organization has a governance structure (or should). Lawyers must look to it to know from whom to take instructions — that is, to identify the person or persons empowered to make decisions that clients are entitled to make. In battles for control, it is especially important for the company's lawyer to stay neutral, meaning that he or she is not supposed to favor one faction over another. The lawyer has no interest as a lawyer in who controls the company or a particular decision except in so far as the law mandates certain procedures or forbids certain actions. Lawyers who take sides in control fights, more likely in small companies than large ones, put themselves at risk.[15]

Those in control of the company are also in charge of its privilege and the decision whether to waive it. This became abundantly clear in *CFTC v. Weintraub*,[16] where the Supreme Court held that for the federal privilege, the trustee in bankruptcy (as the new control person) had the power to waive the company's privilege over the objection of its former officers. *Weintraub* has been influential in state courts. It follows that those in control according to the governance structure or law also have the power to decide whether to waive protection for confidential information, something they may choose to do for the good of the organization even if it is not good for the former officers and directors.

The holding in *Weintraub* should not be a surprise, and the rule it adopts is completely straightforward and easy to apply. More complex and intellectually interesting is how the conflict rules and the confidentiality rules play out when the owners of a company sell the company, either through a sale of stock or an asset sale. This envisions not the sale of some property (a plant, a building, even a division) but of the entire company or something close to it.

Consider this situation: The owners of a successful company decide to sell it to another company. They structure it as an asset sale for tax purposes, meaning the owners are selling everything the company owns but not the company as such, which will immediately cease to exist after the sale. However, our analysis would be the same if they were selling their equity interest (their stock) in the company. The buyers form a shell company to acquire the assets, and after the deal is closed they may change the name of the shell company—perhaps they even give it the same name as the company (now defunct) whose assets they have purchased. Indeed, the right to do so is likely to be part of the sale. As far as the world is concerned, from outward appearances nothing at all has changed. Except for top management, everything is the same, and, indeed, even some of top management may be the same. The owners, however, are different.

Because the selling company is going to dissolve, the buyer wants the selling shareholders (which may be a parent company or individuals) to stand behind (guarantee) the warranties in the buy-sell agreement, and they do. Down the road, the buyer claims that the seller breached one of the warranties and brings a claim against the guarantors, who show up with the law firm that has long represented their former company and that represented it and them in the negotiations of the sale of the company's assets. As it happens, the claim of breach identifies a particular facility that was part of the sale and alleges that, contrary to the warranty, it is not operating in accordance with the law (zoning, environmental, safety requirements, whatever). Or maybe the claim is that a document filed with a government agency was inaccurate (say, a tax return) and negligently prepared, resulting in additional payments and penalties. And the final fact: The law firm that now defends the breach of warranty claim happens to have done the legal work to bring the facility within the requirements of the particular law or it prepared the document filed with the government.

While the facts in this hypothetical — which is based on an actual case[17] — may not often arise, the situation is quite useful in understanding how conflict and confidentiality doctrines work in the corporate setting. And as an added bonus, one of the key lessons can be immensely useful to lawyers and their clients when selling a business. Here's why.

In the real case, the buyer moved to disqualify the law firm that showed up to represent the guarantor (a man named Tang, who was the sole shareholder of the selling company) in the arbitration over the claimed breach of warranty. The buyer made a pretty straightforward argument. The company that had acquired all of the assets of Tang's former company, and which kept the same name, was in effect *the former client* of the firm now representing Tang. True, the buying company did not exist at the time the firm did its work for the predecessor company, including on the subject of the alleged breach of warranty, but as a practical matter the new company *inherited* the rights of the former company to the loyalty and confidentiality duties of the law firm. In other words, although it was legally a new company, for purposes of deciding to whom the firm owed professional duties, it was still the same company as when Tang owned it. The duties of confidentiality and loyalty were incidents of the sale that traveled to the new owners with the other assets — no different from the real estate and the accounts receivables.

The New York Court of Appeals accepted this argument — to a point. First, the court agreed that the new company was, as a practical matter, the same as the old company notwithstanding that the sale took the form of a transfer of assets, not stock, which meant that technically the old company, having dissolved following the sale, no longer existed. The court emphasized the practicality of the situation — the reality — not the formality. Second, the court applied the substantial relationship test discussed in Chapter 12 and concluded that the firm was now opposing its former client (in the shape of the new company) on a warranty claim that centered on the very work the law firm had performed for the predecessor version of the client a few years earlier. In the actual case, that work, and the subject of the warranty claim, was to bring a plant of the company into compliance with local environmental laws. These findings necessarily meant that the firm's appearance adverse to the new company was forbidden as a former client conflict, requiring disqualification.

The new company also argued that it had inherited the law firm's duties arising out of the work the law firm did in negotiating the asset sale itself. If so, the buyer as the former client would be entitled to the law firm's files on that work and would be owed the law firm's duties of confidentiality and loyalty for the work. The court rejected that claim. When it came to the asset sale itself, it was clear to all that Tang and the selling company were adversaries of the buyer, and therefore on the buy-sell they were the true clients of the law firm. The files and the law firm's duties arising out of the buy-sell negotiation remained with Tang.

The lesson for lawyers engaged in the purchase and sale of going companies—whether through stock sales or asset sales—is clear. If you have represented the seller on matters that antedate the sale, and your client wants to be able to use your services in the event of any dispute with the buyer arising from those matters, your duties to the company under conflict and confidentiality rules will transfer to the buyer, who will become your former client with regard to those matters, unless something is said to prevent that. To be blunt, ethical and fiduciary duties are a commodity that can be purchased or withheld as part of a sale of the entity client. The inference will likely be that if nothing is said, these duties transfer to the buyer, at least in so far as they arise from work prior to the negotiations of the sale. If the seller doesn't want this to happen—and presumably its lawyer doesn't want it either, because it can mean that he or she will not be permitted to represent the seller in any dispute with the buyer—the seller must insist that the buy-sell agreement state that the seller retains the lawyer's ethical and fiduciary duties. The buyer will not then inherit them. Of course, the buyer may balk at the demand or may insist on some concession. But then it simply becomes a bargaining chip, with each side evaluating the relative worth relative to what is demanded in return.

ENDNOTES

1. In Chapter 5, we addressed the operation of the privilege in entity representation.

2. *Georgia-Pacific Corp. v. GAF Roofing Mfg Corp.*, 1996 Westlaw 29392 (S.D.N.Y. 1996) (privilege denied for communications between lawyers and officers because lawyer "was acting in a business capacity" when he negotiated the environmental terms of an agreement).

3. *Restatement of the Law Governing Lawyers* §86(3).

4. Lawyers may "paper" the situation with use of legends like "Privilege and Confidential: Attorney-Client Communication." That's fine, even advisable, but lawyers take a risk if they use this label for everything they write. It will then have much less credibility.

5. *Restatement of the Law Governing Lawyers* §75(2). The *Restatement* concludes that the clients can agree otherwise.

6. *Restatement* §60 cmt. *l*. *See also* ABA Model Rule (MR) 1.7 cmt. [31], which says that lawyers "at the outset . . . advise each client that information will be shared and the lawyer will have to withdraw if one client decides that some matter material to the representation should be kept from the other."

7. *Id.* at cmt. [29] and cmt. [30].

8. *Restatement* §75(1) (in co-client situation, party who is the source of information controls the privilege for the information as against third parties).

9. Some commentators have called this an *Upjohn* warning, after *Upjohn v. United States*, discussed in Chapter 5. I don't think this label fits. *Upjohn* upheld a company's claim of privilege for information received from corporate constituents. It did not concern whether the communication with the constituent made the latter the lawyer's client. Perhaps these commentators use *Upjohn* rather than *Miranda* simply because they don't like to use the name of a case that implies criminal wrongdoing.

10. *Matter of Bevill, Bresler & Schulman Asset Mgmt. Corp.*, 805 F.2d 120 (3d Cir. 1986).

11. Sometimes, the lawyer will be able to use the "noisy withdrawal" authority in the comments to MR 1.2 and 4.1 (see Chapter 19).

12. *See* generally Roger Crampton, George Cohen, & Susan Koniak, *Legal and Ethical Duties of Lawyers After Sarbanes-Oxley*, 49 Villanova L. Rev. 725 (2004).

13. Paragraph (d) deals with the situation where a lawyer is hired specifically to investigate or defend an alleged violation of law.

14. While a lawyer who is fired or denied advancement because she has fulfilled her ethical or legal duties to the client may have a retaliatory discharge claim, and while such a claim is better than no recourse at all, all in all lawyers would prefer to stay on target in their careers than bear the expense and trauma of having to sue a former client, perhaps while also looking for a new job. On retaliatory discharge claims for employed lawyers, *see Crews v. Buckman Laboratories Intern'l, Inc.*, 78 S.W.3d 852 (Tenn. 2002).

15. *Granewich v. Harding*, 985 P.2d 788 (Or. 1999) (upholding claim against company lawyer who allegedly helped two of three shareholders freeze out the third shareholder).

16. 471 U.S. 343 (1985).

17. *Tekni-Plex, Inc. v. Meyner & Landis*, 674 N.E.2d 663 (1996).

~ 21 ~

Virtual (or Vicarious) Clients

Who Is a Virtual Client?

What Duties Does a Lawyer Owe a Virtual Client?

As mentioned in Chapter 2, courts will sometimes treat a person (including an entity) as entitled to one or more of the duties lawyers owe current or former clients, even though that person is not a client in the traditional sense because he did not retain the lawyer to perform a legal service, nor did a court assign the lawyer to represent him. I quoted Judge Sprecher's observation in 1978 that the "client is no longer simply the person who walks into a law office." The Second Circuit has used the term "vicarious client" to refer to one type of client in this category—namely, a member of a trade group where the lawyer's traditional client is the trade group itself.[1] Whatever the label, lawyers must understand the concept because the presence of a current or former virtual client can boot a lawyer off a case or subject a lawyer to liability for negligence just as though the client were a traditional client. I identify seven types of virtual clients below. Not every type is established in the case law of every jurisdiction, but each has some recognition somewhere, and some are acknowledged in many jurisdictions. The most frequent consequence of a finding that a person is a virtual client will be disqualification of the lawyer because of a conflict. However, status as a virtual client may also create malpractice liability.

Common Interest Arrangements The concept here is simple. Two or more clients, represented by two or more lawyers, have a common legal interest. The most frequent example is of two or more people facing indictment or criminal trial, each with his or her own counsel. They have a common interest (avoiding conviction) and a common enemy (the prosecutor).[2] Because this is the most frequent example, the doctrine is sometimes mislabeled the joint defense privilege. But the doctrine does not protect defendants only (let alone solely defendants in criminal cases). Plaintiffs can claim it, too.[3] And some courts have allowed the doctrine's protection where there are no plaintiffs or defendants because the matter is entirely transactional, so long as the common interest is legal, not commercial.[4] Other courts have refused to go that far.[5] The label "joint defense privilege" is incorrect in a more fundamental way. The doctrine does not create a privilege. It describes a rule that avoids loss of a privilege that is otherwise present. Lawyer-client communications ordinarily lose their privilege if a third person who is not reasonably necessary to the professional relationship is present. Absent the common interest rule, the presence of another lawyer's client, or the other lawyer, would defeat privilege for the communication. The rule avoids that result so long as one of the lawyers in a valid common interest arrangement is a party to the communication.[6]

A complication arises if one client in the common interest arrangement claims that by virtue of it another client's lawyer owes him or her a duty of some kind. For example, Lawyer *A* and Client *A* may have a common interest arrangement with

Lawyers *B* and *C* and their clients (*B* and *C*). Whether an arrangement is explicitly described as among the clients only or also includes the lawyers need not concern us. Client *A*'s interests may become adverse to those of Clients *B* and *C*.[7] Lawyer A may then find herself in the position of either asserting claims against or having to cross-examine Clients *B* and *C*. Can she do so? Or will her prior participation in the common interest arrangement preclude this? Perhaps she learned confidential information in the common interest arrangement that she can now use to their disadvantage. Is she obligated to protect that information? Does the existence of the common interest arrangement create fiduciary duties to clients of other lawyers? Does it turn them into traditional clients? To the extent that the answer to any of these last three questions is yes, the consequences to the lawyer's work, including her (and her firm's) ability to continue to represent her client, can be significant. That prospect raises a fourth question: Can the members of the common interest arrangement displace the law's default rule by agreement?

Courts have given lawyers in common interest arrangements fiduciary duties to the clients of other lawyers, and at least some courts have gone further, holding that lawyers in a common interest arrangement have an "implied" attorney-client relationship with clients of other lawyers.[8] The consequence is likely to be disqualification from representation of the lawyer's traditional client.[9] Liability for malpractice or breach of fiduciary duty would be a doctrinally modest extension.

In re Gabapentin Patent Litigation[10] is an example of the duties a lawyer (and therefore his entire firm) might unwittingly assume by virtue of a common interest arrangement, despite seemingly sensible precautions that the court ruled were inadequate. We can benefit from examining its facts and the court's analysis. Attorneys Lindvall and Clarke had represented IVAX, a defendant in *Gabapentin*, while at the firm Darby & Darby. That representation ended in June 2003, although IVAX remained a party. In March 2005, Kaye Scholer was contemplating offers to Lindvall and Clarke. But at the time, Kaye Scholer was representing Pfizer, the plaintiff in *Gabapentin*, in another matter in the same court. The firm anticipated that Pfizer might ask it to substitute in as its counsel in *Gabapentin*. Obviously, if Lindvall and Clarke were then working at Kaye Scholer, the firm would be in the position of being adverse to the two lawyers' former client IVAX in the very same litigation in which they had represented IVAX. And the firm would expect that the Lindvall and Clarke conflict would be imputed throughout Kaye Scholer unless nonconsensual screening were permitted, which was not likely.

So the firm conditioned offers to Lindvall and Clarke on IVAX's consent to screen them from the representation of Pfizer adverse to IVAX if they joined Kaye Scholer. IVAX gave consent and the lawyers went to work at the firm. Kaye Scholer then appeared for Pfizer in *Gabapentin*.

But then IVAX's co-defendants moved to disqualify the firm. The question before the court was whether Lindvall and Clarke, and by imputation Kaye Scholer, had any duty to IVAX's co-defendants and if so its nature. The court held that they did have a duty because of a joint defense agreement (JDA) among IVAX and its co-defendants. "In assessing this position, the Court must consider whether the JDA (and actions taken pursuant thereto) created a fiduciary relationship or implied attorney-client relationship among all the parties thereto and their respective counsel, thus placing the co-defendants in a position to seek disqualification of Kaye Scholer," wrote the court.[11] It looked at the JDA and inferred a duty to the co-defendants:

> An examination of the terms of the JDA reveals a clear intent that any voluntarily-shared information would remain confidential and be protected by the attorney-client privilege.

For example, the JDA states that the signatories are required to "take all steps necessary to maintain the privileged and confidential nature of the information."[12]

This and other language permitted the court "to conclude that an implied attorney-client relationship arose between Mr. Lindvall and Ms. Clarke, as counsel for IVAX, and the other [defendants] by virtue of their joint participation in the defense of the *Gabapentin* matter."[13] While the court's conclusion prevented Kaye Scholer from representing Pfizer, the opponent in the litigation, its analysis is potentially more consequential. One wonders if the court realized as much. No lawyer for any of the parties to the joint defense agreement would be able to continue to represent his or her client in the event adverse positions emerged between or among the parties to the agreement. That conclusion necessarily follows from the decision to label the relationship between any lawyer and another lawyer's client as an "implied attorney-client relationship." So, for example, if it came to pass that there was adversity among all the co-defendants — as might happen if it became necessary to allocate responsibility for each defendant's proportionate share of damages — they would each have to get new lawyers.

Gabapentin's holding depends on a finding that Lindvall and Clarke had an implied attorney-client relationship arising out of the JDA. That finding was necessary to the court's further conclusion that their conflict would be imputed to the lawyers at Kaye Scholer under Rule 1.10(a). But what if the court found only a contractual duty of confidentiality or even a fiduciary duty between the two lawyers and the other defendants? In that instance, the court would not be able to use Rule 1.10(a)'s imputation rule, which presumes an attorney-client relationship. Only the two lawyers would then be sidelined and, if screened (even without consent), their disability would not be imputed to the firm.

Affiliates of a Corporate Client Recurring questions for lawyers whose corporate clients are members of a family of companies are as follows: When does the representation of one corporate family member create duties to other members of the corporate family? And what is the nature of those duties? Do they encompass the entire package of duties subsumed in the attorney-client relationship or something else? For example, a lawyer may represent one subsidiary of a corporate parent. Does she thereby have duties to the parent or to its other subsidiaries, and if so, what are they? This is a sensitive subject because an affirmative answer, depending on its breadth, can have significant consequences to the work of a lawyer, especially when the traditional client is in a family with dozens or hundreds of affiliates, whose identity may change monthly. The broader the duties and the larger the population of corporate family affiliates to whom they are owed, the greater will be the potential exposure to civil liability and also to exclusion of the lawyer — and because of the imputation rule, exclusion of the lawyer's colleagues — from other representations.[14] Answers here are not entirely clear. Bar opinions and courts have stated various tests for determining what, if anything, a lawyer owes a client's corporate affiliates.

American Bar Association (ABA) Opinion 95-390[15] concluded that the representation of one company will make its corporate affiliate a client only under limited circumstances. Certainly if the law firm and the client agree that affiliates of the client will (or will not) be deemed clients of the law firm, that may end the matter. Beyond agreement, which may be implicit, the ABA opinion concluded that an affiliate of a client will be deemed a client if the two companies operate as alter egos, if the two companies have integrated operations and management, if the in-house legal staff handles legal matters for both the affiliate and the client, or if representation of the client has provided the law firm with confidential information about the affiliate that would be relevant in a matter in which the firm has appeared adverse to the affiliate.[16]

The ABA opinion attempted to put one issue to rest, but it has resurfaced in the *Restatement of the Law Governing Lawyers* and some cases. Its resolution can have significant consequences when law firms represent a member of a corporate family. Suppose a firm represents Parent in several matters. It is then retained to bring a claim against Subsidiary. Assume the claim is factually unrelated to any work the firm does for Parent. And assume that none of the tests in the ABA Opinion would make Subsidiary the client of the firm for any purpose. What if the action against Subsidiary involves a great deal of money? Perhaps it could put Subsidiary out of business. That in turn may cause Parent substantial harm. Should the fact that the action could have a serious financial effect on the firm's client prevent the firm from acting adversely to non-client Subsidiary? On the one hand, much that a law firm may do for one client could have harmful economic consequences to another client, yet ordinarily that alone will not create a conflict. Firms may even represent economic competitors.[17] Similarly, it would not ordinarily be disloyal to real estate client *A* for its law firm to represent client *B* in a distinct and unrelated effort to win an interpretation of the tax code that will, as it happens, increase *A*'s income taxes. But is the situation different when a lawsuit against a client's affiliate could cause the client substantial financial injury?

The ABA Opinion concluded that the answer was no.[18] Economic adversity, standing alone, would not create a conflict. But the *Restatement of the Law Governing Lawyers* appears to disagree. It states the general rule that when a lawyer represents Corporation *A*, the company "is ordinarily the lawyer's client; neither individual officers of Corporation *A* nor other corporations in which Corporation *A* has an ownership interest, that hold an ownership interest in Corporation *A*, or in which a major shareholder in Corporation *A* has an ownership interest, are thereby considered to be the lawyer's client."[19] So far, so good. But the comment then goes on to say that in some situations this will not be true, such as "where financial loss or benefit to the nonclient person or entity will have a direct, adverse impact on the client."[20] The comment then gives this example:

> Lawyer represents Corporation A in local real-estate trans-actions. Lawyer has been asked to represent Plaintiff in a products-liability action against Corporation B claiming substantial damages. Corporation B is a wholly owned subsidiary of Corporation A; any judgment obtained against Corporation B will have a material adverse impact on the value of Corporation B's assets and on the value of the assets of Corporation A. Just as Lawyer could not file suit against Corporation A on behalf of another client, even in a matter unrelated to the subject of Lawyer's representation of Cor-poration A (see §128, Comment e), Lawyer may not repre-sent Plaintiff in the suit against Corporation B without the consent of both Plaintiff and Corporation A under the limita-tions and conditions provided in §122.[21]

Members of a Lawyer's Trade Group Client   A law firm may pursue the interests of clusters of companies organized in a trade association. The association is the traditional client, but its purpose is to protect the common interests of its members. It may not have interests of its own except as they inure to the benefit of the members, although it will need legal help to function as an organization (e.g., real estate, contract, and employment law advice). What, then, does the firm owe the membership? The answer to this question may influence the responsibilities in other cluster situations — for example, asso-ciations of individuals, a syndicate of banks participating in a loan, and joint ventures — but here my focus is trade associa-tions. (Corporations embody clusters, too, of the shareholders who own them, but corporate representation has spawned an independent body of rules.)[22] Courts have recognized that the client of a lawyer for a trade association is the association itself, not its members.[23] But if the members have provided (or are likely to have provided) the lawyer with confidential information to enable the lawyer to advance the interests of the association and therefore its members, the lawyer will not be permitted to act adversely to the source of the information in a matter where the information is relevant. To this extent, the members are virtual clients.[24]

The Second Circuit's analysis in *Glueck* supports the "information overlap" basis for finding client identity, but it is actually more subtle than that. Philips Nizer represented the Apparel Manufacturer's Association, of which Jonathan Logan was a member, in labor negotiations. It then sued Jonathan Logan in a labor matter. The Court wrote:

> Disqualification will ordinarily be required whenever the subject matter of a suit is sufficiently related to the scope of the matters on which a firm represents an association as to create a realistic risk either that the plaintiff will not be represented with vigor or that unfair advantage will be taken of the defendant. Moreover, once that risk appears, it is appropriate to assess the risk that prosecution of a plaintiff's lawsuit by an association's law firm will inhibit the free flow of information from the defendant to the firm that is necessary for the firm's proper representation of the association.[25]

We see here several concerns beyond the most obvious one — that is, that the association's law firm will in fact have received information from the defendant, a member, that can be used to the member's disadvantage in the current action. First, there is the concern that the representation of the association may lead the law firm to compromise its "vigor" on behalf of the plaintiff against the association's member. The worry is that the firm will not wish to unduly antagonize the association, which may be an important client. This was particularly a concern here because an executive vice president of the Apparel Manufacturer's Association, and a member of its negotiating committee, was president of a division of Jonathan Logan, the adverse party in the lawsuit. Philips Nizer would then be in a position as counsel to the association to work with this person in its representation of the association, while also acting adversely to the company of which she was an officer.[26] As such, the firm might qualify its zealousness. But that is a problem for the plaintiff, not the association or its member, who may have been willing to waive the conflict.

A second concern reflected in the excerpt from the court's opinion is the "risk . . . that unfair advantage will be taken of a defendant"—here, Jonathan Logan. Reference to "risk" broadens the scope of potential disqualification. The member would not have to prove that in fact the law firm had received relevant information from the member. It was sufficient that the firm represented the association in the same area of law as the litigation adverse to Jonathan Logan. Or, to put it another way, the court created a conclusive presumption that Jonathan Logan will have given the firm information in the area of labor relations that could now be used against it. Then the court broadened the scope of the unacceptable risk even further when it wrote that the pendency of the lawsuit might inhibit Jonathan Logan from providing the law firm with information it needs to properly represent the association. All of these threats, at least in combination, supported disqualification of the firm.

The Principal of an Agent-Client (or Beneficiary of a Fiduciary Client) Who Has Hired the Lawyer to Assist in Protecting the Principal (or Beneficiary)   Agents hire lawyers to assist them in work for their principals within the scope of their agency.[27] The agency relationship is by definition fiduciary,[28] although not all fiduciaries are agents.[29] In some jurisdictions, a lawyer (like anyone else) who knowingly assists an agent's or fiduciary's act of disloyalty may be jointly liable to the principal for harm done.[30] The trickier questions are these: Does a lawyer have an affirmative duty to the agent-client's principal or the fiduciary's beneficiary by reason of the professional relationship? For example, if the lawyer discovers the agent's or fiduciary's breach of fiduciary duty to which the lawyer may or may not have provided unwitting assistance, what does the lawyer owe the principal or beneficiary? Or if the lawyer commits malpractice in his or her work for the agent or fiduciary that injures the principal or beneficiary, to whom is the lawyer liable?

Cases are inconsistent on these questions. An Arizona opinion held that "when an attorney undertakes to represent the guardian of an incompetent, he assumes a relationship not only with the guardian but also with the ward." Consequently, if the attorney "knew or should have known that the guardian was acting adversely to his ward's interests, the possibility of frustrating the whole purpose of the guardianship became foreseeable as did the possibility of injury to the ward." The court "upheld" the denial of the lawyers' summary judgment motion, finding "a legal relationship and concomitant duty to the ward."[31] Taking a contrary view is *Angel, Cohen & Rogovin v. Oberin Inv., N.V.*[32] The ABA has concluded that the Model Rules do not give a lawyer any greater obligation to the beneficiary of a fiduciary client than the lawyer has to any other third party.[33] This opinion construes the Model Rules only. The committee has no authority to construe the law of fiduciary duty. *Trask v. Butler,*[34] after setting out a balancing test, concluded that a trustee or the executor of an estate owes no duty to beneficiaries in the performance of his task. But *Leyba v. Whitley*[35] reaches a different conclusion where the fiduciary was a child's personal representative in a wrongful death action, distinguishing a trustee:

> A trustee in the traditional sense has broad discretionary powers over the estate assets and must make difficult investment and distribution decisions. The attorney for the

trustee must assist the trustee to make these discretionary decisions. A personal representative under the Wrongful Death Act, by contrast, must simply distribute any proceeds obtained in accordance with statute and has no discretionary authority.

That distinction lead the court to find a duty to the beneficiary of the personal representative.[36]

Intended Third-party Beneficiaries of a Legal Service Performed for a Client

This category resembles the prior one, but it differs in this way: Here, the client is not an agent or fiduciary but is instead hiring the lawyer to perform a service with the intention of benefiting a third party, possibly along with the client. Unlike a client who is an agent for another, the client here has no fiduciary duty to the third party. The classic example is the testator who instructs her lawyer to include a bequest to another. The lawyer forgets to include the bequest. The testator dies and, of course, her intention is frustrated. She is no longer able to sue. Can the third-party beneficiary of the testator's instruction sue the lawyer for negligence? Surely, there was negligence. If the beneficiary cannot sue, perhaps the executor of the estate may do so, which can have the same consequence. Courts are divided on whether an intended beneficiary has standing to sue the testator's lawyer for malpractice.[37] Although the will cases are perhaps the most common example for this category, the paradigm can fit elsewhere. For example, a separation agreement may require the husband to maintain an existing life insurance policy on which his children are beneficiaries. The wife's lawyer may then forget to notify the insurance company that the beneficiaries cannot be changed. The now former husband eventually changes the beneficiaries to his children from his second marriage. (People do things like that for reasons of their own.) The change is discovered on his death. Do the children of the first marriage have a claim for the lost insurance against their mother's lawyer because he forgot to notify the insurer?[38]

A Third Party Who Gives a Lawyer Confidential Information to Assist in Providing Legal Services for a Traditional Client Because of the Nature of the Relationship Between the Source and the Traditional Client This category, perhaps the least refined, presents a variation on the corporate family and trade group issues described above. There is no overarching entity. We saw that a lawyer for one member of the corporate family can acquire duties to an affiliate that gives the lawyer information to assist her in providing legal services to the client.[39] The difference here is that the source of the information is not a member of a client's corporate family, nor is she a member of a trade group client, which presents a similar but distinct situation. At the same time, of course, a lawyer does not, and could not be expected to, have a duty to every source that provides the lawyer with information for use in representing a client. Rather, there must be a relationship of some sort between the source and the client, as there is in the corporate family or trade group context, which induces the source to give the lawyer its information. But what kind of relationship will suffice? Two appear influential.

As might be expected, the first is when the lawyer's work for the traditional client will directly benefit the source of the information, thereby providing the source with an incentive to share the information in the first place. The position of the source, then, may be seen roughly to approximate the position of a traditional client and create a duty not to appear adversely to the source in a matter in which the information can be used to its detriment. But for this principle to hold, the benefit must be particular to the source of the information and derive from the source's relationship to the traditional client. It cannot be a benefit enjoyed generally or by many. For example, in seeking a zoning variance that will allow a client to open a retail business in a particular neighborhood, area property owners who support the change (perhaps it will make their lives easier) may provide the lawyer with information about their own property and needs. That help should not be sufficient to create a duty to the neighbors.

Contrast *Analytica, Inc. v. NPD Research, Inc.*[40] Malec was an employee of NPD between 1972 and 1977. He had two shares, or 10 percent, of NPD's stock. During the course of his employment, his two co-owners wished to give him an additional two shares of stock as compensation for his services. They told him to find "a lawyer who would structure the transaction in the least costly way." Malec hired Richard Fine, a partner in Schwartz & Freeman, and Fine devised a plan for the transfer of the stock. Because the stock had to be evaluated, NPD gave Fine information on its financial condition, sales trends, and management. Several months later, Malec left NPD and formed Analytica to compete with it. He then hired Fine's law firm to represent Analytica in an antitrust action against NPD, which moved to disqualify Fine's firm.

The firm argued that NPD had never been its client. Malec, it said, was the only client. The court thought otherwise, but it also wrote that the issue was immaterial. "If NPD did not retain Schwartz & Freeman [Fine's firm]—although we think it did—still it supplied Schwartz & Freeman with just the kind of confidential data that it would have furnished a lawyer that it had retained; and it had a right not to see Schwartz & Freeman reappear within months on the opposite side of a litigation to which that data might be highly pertinent."[41]

The second type of relationship between a traditional client and a source of information that may create duties to the source is not commercial but personal or familial. Cases here are few. Suppose a young woman is charged with driving under the influence of alcohol. Her mother hires a lawyer. The client is the driver, not the mother, who is paying the fee. The mother may also provide the lawyer with confidential information about the family, including financial information, to assist in the representation. The daughter may not herself know all of the information. The parent directly benefits from the lawyer's goal on behalf of her daughter, although not economically, as in *Analytica*. But neither is the benefit incidental and shared by many, as would be true for the property owners in the neighborhood of the client who seeks a zoning variance. So far as the legal service is concerned, the mother and daughter share what we might call legal identity in seeing the justice system deal least harshly with the daughter, just as the owners of NPD Research and Malec shared a legal identity in achieving the most tax advantageous stock transfer.

The familial context is rare, but one example is *Hornish v. Hoffer*, which tells an unhappy tale.[42] Hornish sued Hoffer, her former boyfriend, and Hoffer appeared through the Moots law firm. Hornish claimed that she and Hoffer had an agreement that she would help him build a house on the understanding that she and her children could live in it. She claimed that she had spent more than 1,000 hours in the construction of the house, and that on completion Hoffer would not allow her and her children to live in it. Hornish moved to disqualify the Moots law firm on the ground that it had "previously represented her minor son in a criminal matter" in which Hoffer was the alleged victim.[43] She argued successfully that disqualification was necessary because her son's criminal action and the present action had "the relationship between herself and the defendant" in common.[44] The Moots law firm claimed that it had never had an attorney-client relationship with Hornish and therefore she could not seek its disqualification.[45] The court held:

> The case presents a unique situation, in which the plaintiff was not a client of [the Moots firm], but rather participated in discussions with them in which she revealed confidential

information about her relationship with the defendant while they were representing her minor son. [The disqualification rule] applies in this case because "[t]he issue is whether plaintiffs' counsel derived confidential information from [his] former representation . . . which may disadvantage the defendant in this case." Clearly, though the plaintiff was not the true client of [the firm], she was, in a significant manner, in the role of their client as she acted as guardian for her minor son. The plaintiff has stated that in the course of that representation, she revealed to the attorney information regarding her relationship with the defendant, which she claims could be used to her detriment in the current action.[46]

A Third Party That, as the Lawyer Does or Should Realize, Will Rely on the Accuracy of the Lawyer's Factual Assertions for a Traditional Client A lawyer represents a defendant charged with negligence for failing to safely maintain the pavement in front of his property as a city ordinance requires. The plaintiff is seeking $250,000. The lawyer tells plaintiff's counsel that the defendant is insured for only $100,000. The lawyer believes this is so because he has seen the insurance policy with that limit. The plaintiff settles for the policy limit and provides a general release. Later, it transpires that the defendant had a second policy for $300,000, which was available to the lawyer among the defendant's papers but which the lawyer failed to discover. He was wrong in what he told the plaintiff, but he believed that what he said was true. The plaintiff may or may not have further recourse against the settling defendant personally. Our question is whether the plaintiff can now sue the lawyer for negligent misrepresentation or a different tort.

These facts are a variation of those in *Slotkin v. Citizens Casualty Co.*[47] A child's parents brought a medical malpractice action against the hospital in which the child was born and others, alleging that the child suffered neurological and brain damage as a result of professional negligence at his birth.[48]

While the trial was in progress, but before a verdict, the parties settled for $185,000.[49] Counsel for the hospital made certain representations to counsel for the plaintiffs.[50] On one occasion, the hospital's lawyer said that he "knew" the hospital's insurance coverage was only $200,000.[51] On another occasion, he said that this was so "to the best of [his] knowledge."[52] In agreeing to the settlement, the plaintiffs relied on these statements. It later transpired that the hospital had a separate insurance policy for $1 million in addition to the $200,000 policy to which its counsel was referring.[53] Its counsel had documents in his file (of which he claimed to be unaware) revealing the excess coverage.[54] After the settlement and after the plaintiffs learned about the additional insurance coverage, they sued the hospital's counsel, among others, alleging fraud and related claims. Judgment against the hospital's lawyer was upheld:

> [His] insistence that the policy limit was $200,000 . . . renders him liable under the New York definition of scienter as reckless indifference to error, a pretense of exact knowledge, or (an) assertion of a false material fact susceptible of accurate knowledge but stated to be true on the personal knowledge of the representer.[55]

This category should be distinguished from formal opinion letters that a lawyer writes to a third party to assist a client's objectives. For example, in a Colorado case, a borrower's law firm sent an opinion letter to the lending bank, stating the signator's "opinion that the Town and the Authority have adopted the Urban Renewal Plan in accordance with requirements of the laws of the State of Colorado and the Charter of the Town," and that allegations in a pending lawsuit against the town were therefore "without merit."[56] The court held that this language created a duty to the lending bank that could support its action for negligent misrepresentation.[57] The difference between this case and *Slotkin* or *Rubin* is the formality of the representation. *Slotkin* and *Rubin* (cited in Note 55) arose out of statements casually made in negotiation, whereas statements in the Colorado case were formalized in a letter to the bank lending money to the lawyer's client.

ENDNOTES

1. *Glueck v. Jonathan Logan, Inc.*, 653 F.2d 746 (2d Cir. 1981).

2. Of course, their interests may not be identical because either may have a factual or legal defense that is of no help to the other or may even harm the other. *See, e.g., Griffin v. McVicar*, 84 F.3d 880 (7th Cir. 1996), where the two homicide defendants had a common enemy — the prosecutor; but one also had a defense (present at the crime but not a participant) that was factually unavailable to the other, who had to rely on alibi and mistaken identification.

3. This is clearly explained in *United States v. Schwimmer*, 892 F.2d 237 (2d Cir. 1989).

4. *In re Regents of the University of California*, 101 F.3d 1386 (Fed. Cir. 1996).

5. *Aetna Cas. & Sur. Co. v. Certain Underwriters at Lloyd's of London*, 676 N.Y.S.2d 727 (Sup. Ct. N.Y. Co. 1998), *aff'd* 692 N.Y.S.2d 384 (1st Dept. 1999).

6. *See, e.g., Volpe v. Conroy, Simberg & Ganon, P.A.*, 720 So.2d 537 (Fla. App. 1998).

7. For example, Client A may settle with the common opponent and agree to testify for it. This is most common in criminal cases where one of several defendants reach a plea bargain in exchange for testimony — *see, e.g., United States v. Stepney*, 246 F.Supp.2d 1069 (N.D. Cal. 2003) — but it can also happen in a civil case.

8. In *United States v. Henke*, 222 F.3d 633 (9th Cir. 2000), the court held that a "joint defense agreement establishes an implied attorney-client relationship" between a lawyer for one defendant and the co-defendant. As a result, when the co-defendant plead guilty and appeared as a prosecution witness against the lawyer's client, the lawyer's motion to withdraw to avoid cross-examining the co-defendant should have been granted. *United States v. Almeida*, 341 F.3d 1318 (11th Cir. 2003), reaches a contrary result, concluding that by deciding to cooperate and testify against former co-defendants, a government witness has waived the privilege for communications with the lawyers of the co-defendants. In *United States v. Stepney*, supra, Judge Patel, perhaps impelled by *Henke*, required lawyers in a multi-defendant drug and weapons conspiracy case to put all joint defense agreements in writing and submit them to the court. After reviewing the submissions, the judge concluded that the agreements had to be redrafted. In doing so, she read *Henke's* reference to an "implied attorney-client relationship" to be limited to the creation of a duty of confidentiality only, not a duty of loyalty, to the clients of other lawyers. Furthermore, she required that the agreements before her specifically waive this duty of confidentiality. In effect, Judge Patel required the defendants to give up the protection that she read *Henke's* default rule to provide.

9. *In re Gabapentin Pat. Lit.*, 407 F.Supp.2d 607 (D. N.J. 2005).

10. *Id.*

11. *Id.* at 611.

12. *Id.* at 613.

13. *Id.* at 614. The court also found a fiduciary relationship. *Id.* at 615. The fact that Lindvall and Clarke were screened did not change the result. The New Jersey professional conduct rules recognize screening of lateral lawyers without consent but only if those lawyers did not have "primary responsibility" for the matter at their prior firm. New Jersey Rule 1.10(c)(1). But Lindvall and Clarke did have primary responsibility.

14. For example, in 1996, a district judge, ruling on a motion by Sprint to disqualify Jones Day because the law firm represented another company in the Sprint family, denied the motion, pointing out that Sprint had "over 250 subsidiaries and affiliated entities," while Jones Day had "1098 attorneys spread over 20 world-wide offices." *Rueben H. Donnelly Corp. v. Sprint Publishing and Advertising, Inc.*, 1996 Westlaw 99902 (N.D. Ill. 1996). Ten years later, Jones Day had nearly doubled its lawyer population to 2,136 lawyers. American Lawyer, May 2006.

15. ABA Opinion 95-390.

16. In addition, a law firm will have a conflict if the representation adverse to one member of a corporate family will be compromised by its reluctance to antagonize the client member of the corporate family. In that instance, the conflict is one that affects the adversary of the non-client affiliate and its consent will remove the conflict.

17. "[S]imultaneous representation in unrelated matters of clients whose interests are only economically adverse, such as representation of competing economic enterprises in unrelated litigation, does not ordinarily constitute a conflict of interest and thus may not require consent of the respective clients." Model Rule (MR) 1.7 cmt. [7].

18. ABA Opinion 95-390.

19. *Restatement of the Law Governing Lawyers* §121, comment d.

20. *Id.*

21. *Id.* Interesting though this issue may be, when economic effect appears in the corporate family context, there is generally a whole lot more going on that would independently support disqualification. *See, e.g., JP Morgan Chase Bank v. Liberty Mutual Ins. Co.*, 189 F.Supp.2d 20 (S.D.N.Y. 2002), where the action against the non-client subsidiary if successful would have a profound effect on the parent, a client of the firm. The parent owned 95 percent of the nonclient, which accounted for 90 percent of the parent's business. The court emphasized this fact. However, the case also involved common management and headquarters, among other factors. Where a firm has a conflict because its work against Subsidiary will financially harm its client Parent, Subsidiary does not become a client. Rather the firm is seen as acting adversely to its own client, Parent.

22. MR 1.13(a) specifically instructs that a "lawyer employed or retained by an organization represents the organization acting through its duly authorized constituents." Any other rule would create a potential for paralyzing conflicts between the organization's lawyers and its constituents (board members, officers, employees, and agents). Information an organization's constituents provide to the entity lawyer is the entity's information. The lawyer's duties of confidentiality and

loyalty, as well as the right to assert privilege, run to the entity. *Commodity Futures Trading Comm'n v. Weintraub*, 471 U.S. 343 (1985). See Chapter 5.

23. This would seem to be true by definition. See, *e.g.*, Glueck v. Jonathan Logan, Inc., 653 F.2d 746 (2d Cir. 1981).

24. *Id. Glueck* uses the term "vicarious client." *Id.* at 749.

25. *Id.* at 750.

26. *Id.* at 748.

27. Most obviously, lawyers for organizations, including corporations, are necessarily hired by their agents.

28. *Restatement of Agency*, 2d, §1.

29. For example, doctors have fiduciary duties to patients but are not thereby agents of the patient. *Moore v. Regents of University of California*, 271 Cal. Rptr. 146 (Cal. App. 1990); *Taber v. Riordan*, 403 N.E.2d 1349 (Ill. App. 1980).

30. See Chapters 19 and 24.

31. *Fickett v. Superior Court of Pima County*, 558 P.2d 988 (Ariz. App. 1976). *See also Albright v. Burns*, 503 A.2d 386 (N.J. App. 1986) (lawyer "had reason to foresee the specific harm which occurred").

32. 512 So.2d 192 (Fla. 1987) (negligently helping fiduciary violate trust does not state claim).

33. ABA Opinion 94-380.

34. 872 P.2d 1080 (Wash. 1994).

35. 907 P.2d 172 (N.M. 1995).

36. *Id.* at 178.

37. *Compare Needham v. Hamilton*, 459 A.2d 1060 (D.C. 1983) (will beneficiary has standing), and *Blair v. Ing*, 21 P.3d 452 (Hawaii 2001) (standing for trust beneficiaries) with *Taylor v. Maile*, 127 P.3d 156 (Idaho 2005) (denying standing to residuary trust beneficiaries).

38. This was the situation in *Pelham v. Griesheimer*, 440 N.E.2d 96 (Ill. 1982), where the court declined to find that the attorney for the mother had accepted a duty to the children. For such a duty to exist, the court wrote, "there must be a clear indication that the representation by the attorney is intended to directly confer a benefit upon the third party." *Id.* at 99. Elsewhere the court wrote that "the nonclient must allege and prove that the intent of the client to benefit the nonclient third party was the primary or direct purpose of the transactional relationship." *Id.* at 98. In subsequent cases, courts in Illinois have had to analyze the client's "primary" purpose. *See, e.g., McLane v. Russell*, 546 N.E.2d 499 (Ill. 1989).

39. See text accompanying notes 23-25 *supra*.

40. 708 F.2d 1263 (7th Cir. 1983).

41. *Id.* at 1269. The court cited *Westinghouse Electric Corp. v. Kerr-McGee Corp.*, 580 F.2d 1311 (7th Cir. 1978), a trade association case in which Judge Sprecher's observation quoted at the top of this article appears. There, the court had disqualified Kirkland & Ellis as counsel for the plaintiff because the firm, in its representation of the American Petroleum Institute, had received Kerr-McGee's "confidential information . . . in connection with the law firm's work for the Institute." 708 F.2d at 1268.

42. 2006 Westlaw 696542 (Superior Ct. Conn. 2006).

43. *Id.*
44. *Id.*
45. *Id.*
46. *Id.*
47. 614 F.2d 301 (2d Cir. 1979). This case and the underlying doctrine are also discussed in Chapter 24.
48. *Id.* at 305.
49. *Id.* at 304.
50. *Id.* at 307.
51. *Id.*
52. *Id.*
53. *Id.* at 304.
54. *Id.* at 307.
55. *Id.* at 314. Although the court characterized the lawyer's conduct as fraud, *Id.* at n.20, in fact it should be seen as recklessness, not lying. Today, the plaintiffs would be likely to sue for negligent misrepresentation because 13 years after *Slotkin*, the New York Court of Appeals recognized such a third-party claim against a lawyer. *Prudential Insurance Co. of America v. Dewey, Ballantine, Bushby, Palmer & Wood*, 605 N.E.2d 318 (1992). The *Restatement (Third) of the Law Governing Lawyers* §51(2) (2000), would also recognize this claim. *See also Rubin v. Schottenstein, Zox & Dunn*, 143 F.3d 263, 270 (6th Cir. 1998) (*en banc*). *Rubin* was an action for a securities fraud and common law fraud against a borrower's attorney, who defended on the ground that the lender's attorney had no right to rely on the borrower's attorney's factual statements. *Id.* at 265. The court responded:

> That principle . . . is limited to reliance on the opinions or research of the other party's attorney on points of law . . . . The theory is that one's own lawyer ought to be able to detect and cure misleading statements of law from the other side. Extending the principle to factual representations would put an investor in far greater peril in speaking to an issuer's counsel than in speaking with the president of the company. In short, it would allow an attorney to mislead investors with impunity. We cannot endorse this perverse result.

Id. at 270. Although the basis for liability here was securities and common law fraud, the court wrote more broadly about duty. An attorney in "a securities transaction may not always be under an independent duty to volunteer information about the financial condition of his client, [but] he assumes a duty to provide complete and nonmisleading information with respect to subjects on which he undertakes to speak." *Id.* at 268.

56. *See, e.g., Mehaffy, Ryder, Windholz & Wilson v. Central Bank of Denver, N.A.*, 892 P.2d 230, 237-238 (Colo. 1995).
57. *Id.*

~ 22 ~

Judges

Recusal for Conflicts

Discriminatory Conduct or Memberships

Campaign Contributions

Campaign Speech

In 2007, the American Bar Association (ABA) adopted a Model Code of Judicial Conduct. This was its third iteration of such a code. Earlier codes had been adopted in 1972 and 1990. As with the Model Rules, the document is a "model" only. It is offered to state courts as a guide, but as with the Model Rules, the ABA codes have been widely adopted, though often with changes. It is not only the states that have judicial conduct codes. The federal bench below the Supreme Court is governed by a Code of Conduct for United States Judges, promulgated by a committee of the Judicial Conference of the United States and available online. The Code of Conduct for U.S. Judges also closely tracks the ABA Model Code, although it omits the rules addressing judicial campaign conduct because federal judges do not run for election. The Code of Conduct for U.S. Judges does not bind

Supreme Court justices because it is promulgated by lower court judges and apparently it is deemed unseemly for lower court judges to make rules that control the behavior of the justices. However, from time to time, justices say they will voluntarily comply with the code.

In addition to the various codes of conduct, judges in all states are governed by statutory law, most prominently laws that may require a judge to disqualify (or recuse) himself or herself because of a conflict of interest or for some other reason, rules requiring annual financial disclosure statements, and other rules. In the federal system, the recusal statute is 28 U.S.C. §455. Key portions are set in endnotes.[1] The language of this statute tracks the 1972 ABA Code, after which it was modeled. But it is very close to the 2007 ABA Code, too, because few significant changes were adopted between the two codes on the recusal issue. The codes of conduct are much more detailed than statutory law because they cover many aspects of a judge's professional conduct, not just recusal.

It is not possible or productive to address all the ways in which judges are regulated. We would need a separate book for that. But four issues deserve discussion. First are rules governing disqualification because of conflicts of interest or other reasons. This is the most important category because it is the most litigated and because litigants correctly view the identity of the judge who hears their matters as influential in determining the outcome. This is necessarily true because law is an art, not a science, and although many legal questions suggest only one right answer, many others invite disagreement. Besides, judges make many discretionary decisions in the course of a trial, decisions that are quite often unreviewable, and different judges will exercise their discretion differently. Disqualification is also an important issue because, as stated, it is governed not only by the judicial conduct codes but many places, as in the federal system, by a statute, too.

Another question, which is related to disqualification based on a statute or ethics rule, is the extent to which the Due Process Clause of the U.S. Constitution forbids a judge to sit in a matter. This issue was prominent on the Supreme Court's docket in the 2008 Term.

The other two subjects in the world of judicial ethics that we will address are bias or the public perception of bias on or off the bench and judicial campaign speech. The latter topic asks what limitations, consistent with the First Amendment, a state may impose on what a person running for judicial office may say about his or her views on subjects likely to come before the court to which the candidate seeks election.

Disqualification In endnote 1, I printed the text of the recusal provision of the United States Code that is most often cited as the basis for judicial disqualification. Footnote 2 contains the equivalent language from Rule 2.11 of the current ABA Model Code.[2] You can see the similarity — that is, the ABA's influence on Congress. The most frequently cited basis for disqualification is the very first one — that the judge's "impartiality might reasonably be questioned." The allegation under this provision is not that the judge is partial but that the public, including one or more of the litigants, might think he or she is partial. Obviously, that states a standard the application of which calls for a large dose of judgment. The other bases for disqualification, by contrast, offer (comparatively) bright-line categories. If a judge is in one of those categories, he or she must step aside unless the litigants affirmatively consent to let the judge stay (where consent is allowed as it mostly is in Rule 2.11(C).)) or the conflict is waived because the litigants do not seek the judge's removal. (A party with a basis to disqualify a judge cannot remain mum and then make the motion later when the case seems to be going against him.[3] Once the litigant knows or reasonably should know the basis for disqualification, he has to speak up or lose the chance.)

327

"Impartiality Might Reasonably Be Questioned." This test may seem easy to meet. You might think it enough that a party can show a reason to question the judge's impartiality. Let's say the judge once worked with one of the lawyers for one of the parties before her. Many nonlawyers would question whether that judge could be impartial under those circumstances. And they would point to the word *might* as the operative word. Surely, it sets a low bar. Not, mind you, that our hypothetical nonlawyers would predict partiality in fact. Rather, they would say there is enough there to question whether the judge *might* be partial and so the judge, if asked, should step aside.

But this statutory and code language (it appears in both places) is not quite so easy to satisfy. The operative word turns out to be *reasonably*, not *might*. And more than that, the courts have said that the issue assumes a person who knows all the facts and is not given to unfounded suspicion.[4] Will that person reasonably question the judge's impartiality? Another line of cases tells us that a judge's *remote, contingent,* or *speculative* interests will not suffice to warrant removal. There must be a *direct* connection between the alleged interest to disqualify and the claim of partiality.[5] So the fact that a party to a matter is the cousin of the judge's next-door neighbor would not be direct, assuming that's all there was. To say that this connection to the judge warrants questioning his impartiality on those facts is speculative. On the other hand, the fact that the judge dated the litigant exclusively for 3 years after law school, although that was 15 years ago, would be seen as a direct connection to the judge that "might reasonably" question his impartiality. Then, there is not only a personal relationship, but a close one. You see the difference between the two situations. But there is no bright line separating one from the other. We can hypothesize intermediate situations. At some point, many people would say that there is no basis for recusal, while others will disagree. As we weaken the link, more and more people will find no basis until the link is so loose that it is no longer possible reasonably to question the judge's impartiality.

Other Bases for Recusal   The remaining bases for recusal in the code and federal law are different in kind. Unlike recusal when impartiality might reasonably be questioned, the other reasons define specific categories. In effect, they tell the judge that if he or she is in one of those categories, it is not permissible to sit unless the conflict is waived, where waiver is allowed. These other bases fall into two situations — the financial interests of the judge or certain of his or her relatives, either in a party or in the result of the litigation, and the judge's past or present relationships with lawyers or parties, including while the judge was in law practice.

Let's use the ABA Code to illustrate, while recognizing that the language here may differ from the parallel language in state codes or statutory law. If a judge is actually biased in favor or against a party or a lawyer, she cannot sit. Nor may she sit if she has knowledge of any disputed fact. (In the latter instance she might have to be a witness.) These grounds for recusal cannot be waived by party consent.

But there's an important caveat here. A judge may become biased or prejudiced for or against a party because of the evidence the judge hears, not because of any inclination or view the judge may have had before the case started. Does a disqualifying bias have to be based on an extrajudicial source — that is, information the judge receives out of court? Or can a judge's disqualifying bias be based on what he or she hears when judging? For a long time, it was thought that the bias must be extrajudicial. After all, we want the judge to form opinions based on the evidence. That's what judging is all about. Judges have to rule, and that requires them to have a point of view about the facts.

In one case, however, the Supreme Court said that a judge could become so emotionally or irrationally disposed toward a party based on the evidence that the judge will not be able to rule fairly. In other words, some evidence in some cases may hit a nerve with certain judges and undermine their ability to be objective.[6] This will be exceedingly rare.

A judge can't sit if the judge or certain relatives have more than a *de minimis* interest in the outcome that could be "substantially affected" by it. Nor may the judge sit if certain close relatives are parties or lawyers in the proceeding or have officer positions in a party. These bases for recusal can be waived under the ABA Code but not under the federal statute. Admittedly, the terms *de minimis* (which is defined as "insignificant") and *substantially* are somewhat elastic. Reasonable people will sometimes disagree, but not as often as they will over the "might reasonably be questioned" language.

Other provisions may disqualify the judge if she or close relatives have "economic interests" (itself defined to require that they be greater than de minimis) in a party or the subject matter of the proceedings or if the judge or her former law firm while she was at it represented a party. Judges who once worked for the government cannot sit in matters where they had "participated personally and substantially" in the matter as a government lawyer or official. These bases for recusal can also be waived under the ABA Code but not under the Code for U.S. Judges.[7]

Duty to Be Aware and to Reveal   In order to step aside when required, judges have to stay aware not only of their own financial and other interests but also of those of relatives whose interests can trigger recusal. The ABA Code and the Code for U.S. Judges say as much. And because information that may justify recusal may not be known to the litigants, the judge has a duty to inform them of it. The judge must do this even if the judge does not believe the facts warrant recusal, so long as a plausible argument can be made to the contrary. That enables the litigants to decide whether to make a disqualification motion if they choose to do so. Even if the judge does not believe the facts warrant recusal, the parties may change the judge's mind through argument. In any event, the parties can preserve the issue for an appellate court if necessary.[8]

Whether a conflict exists will often depend on the facts, and sometimes the judge is the only one with the facts. That is not always so. Judges file financial disclosure forms, and these contain a lot of information about the judge's sources of income, gifts to the judge, and holdings and those of the judge's spouse and minor children as well. Litigants do check these if they think they may describe a basis for recusal.

A judge is required to step aside under the "impartiality might reasonably be questioned" standard even if he is unaware of the facts that could support questioning his impartiality. The provision does not require knowledge. Wait a minute. How can that be? How can you take action based on knowledge you don't have? The issue arose in a famous Supreme Court decision. Justice Stevens said that, of course, the judge in that case could not have been expected to recuse himself based on facts that he did not at the time recall. But later he did recall facts that put his impartiality in question while the matter was not yet final. At that time, the Court held, he was required to step aside, even though the matter was nearly over. And he was also required to undo what he had done before he recalled the disqualifying facts. The reason: The public may not believe that he didn't know what he should have known. (The Court may not have believed the judge's claim either, if you read between the lines.)[9]

Lawyers think, with justification, that many judges take umbrage when they ask the judge to step aside because of a disqualifying conflict. However, that request, unless based on a charge of actual bias, is not personal. It says nothing harsh about the judge. And since in nearly all courts, except certain state high courts and the Supreme Court, another judge can replace the judge who steps aside, what's the big deal? I don't mean to say that judges should remove themselves from cases just for the asking. A lawyer should be required to put forward a solid case. But if he does, why not resolve serious doubts (if there are serious doubts) in favor of recusal? It fosters public confidence and does not in the least suggest the judge's inability to rule fairly.

Campaign Contributions and Due Process State high courts decide issues that can have enormous economic consequences for vested interests. These decisions often involve no federal issues. Consequently, they are final and not subject to U.S. Supreme Court review. They define, for example, the scope of tort liability, rules of evidence, the permissible size of punitive damages, and the availability of various defenses. Of late, repeat litigators (that is, moneyed interests that are often sued in state courts) have tried through campaign contributions to influence state high court elections (entirely legally). The question has arisen: When is it a violation of a litigant's due process rights to be required to appear before a judge who has received very high campaign contributions from the litigant's opponent and little or none from the litigant?

Before coming to that question and the case that presented it to the Supreme Court in the 2008 Term, we need a quick review of some older precedent. The Court had long ago held that a defendant was denied due process if the judge hearing the case would financially gain from a conviction and fine.[10] For example, the judge's salary may depend on the amount of fines collected. The unfairness here may seem obvious now, but it was not always so clear. The conflict need not be quite so dramatic. In 1986, the Court held that a defendant (Aetna) did not get due process in a civil case where legal questions before the Alabama Supreme Court in Aetna's case were also present in an otherwise unrelated pending case brought by one of the judges on that court, Justice Embry. Justice Embry wrote the majority opinion affirming a $3.5 million judgment against

Aetna by a 4-3 vote. He then settled his own case. The Supreme Court held that "Justice Embry's opinion . . . had the clear and immediate effect of enhancing both the legal status and the settlement value of his own case." The Embry vote was decisive to Aetna's loss, and this fact was decisive to the Court.

So even though the Alabama court's opinion did not enhance Justice Embry's finances quite as directly as in the earlier cases where a judge's fines determined his income, still the perception of a causal connection was too great to withstand due process analysis. The Supreme Court stressed that it was not saying that Justice Embry was biased. Rather, it held that his interest meant that the result did not "'satisfy the appearance of justice'" (quoting precedent).[11]

The campaign contribution issue is a bit harder. For one thing, the contribution will already have been made *before* the judge rules. The ruling doesn't produce the contribution in the same way as the *Aetna* decision prospectively benefited Justice Embry's claim. But what if the contribution is very large and is also a substantial portion of the candidate's campaign fund? That was the issue before the Supreme Court in *Caperton v. Massey Coal Co*. The certified question says it all:

> Justice Brent Benjamin of the Supreme Court of Appeals of West Virginia refused to recuse himself from the appeal of the $50 million jury verdict in this case, even though the CEO of the lead defendant [a man named Blankenship] spent $3 million supporting his campaign for a seat on the court — more than 60% of the total amount spent to support Justice Benjamin's campaign — while preparing to appeal the verdict against his company. After winning election to the court, Justice Benjamin cast the deciding vote in the court's 3–2 decision overturning that verdict. The question presented is whether Justice Benjamin's failure to recuse himself from participation in his principal financial supporter's case violated the Due Process Clause of the Fourteenth Amendment.

Shall we say that Justice Benjamin's participation falls so far short of *Aetna*'s insistence on the "appearance of justice" that it violates due process without regard to whether the judge was actually biased in favor of Massey Coal? On June 8, 2009, the Supreme Court reversed the West Virginia Supreme Court's decision in a 5-4 ruling with Justice Kennedy writing the majority opinion. The Court focused on the particular sums involved in this case. The Court did not purport to identify dollar amounts (or percentages) that would presumptively violate due process standards generally. Influential, too, the timing of the contribution—while Massey's appeal was pending.

Justice Kennedy wrote:

> We turn to the influence at issue in this case. Not every campaign contribution by a litigant or attorney creates a probability of bias that requires a judge's recusal, but this is an exceptional case. We conclude that there is a serious risk of actual bias—based on objective and reasonable perceptions—when a person with a personal stake in a particular case had a significant and disproportionate influence in placing the judge on the case by raising funds or directing the judge's election campaign when the case was pending or imminent. The inquiry centers on the contribution's relative size in comparison to the total amount of money contributed to the campaign, the total amount spent in the election, and the apparent effect such contribution had on the outcome of the election.
>
> Applying this principle, we conclude that Blankenship's campaign efforts had a significant and disproportionate influence in placing Justice Benjamin on the case. Blankenship contributed some $3 million to unseat the incumbent and replace him with Benjamin. His contributions eclipsed the total amount spent by all other Benjamin supporters and exceeded by 300% the amount spent by Benjamin's campaign committee. Caperton claims Blankenship spent $1 million

more than the total amount spent by the campaign committees of both candidates combined. . . .

The temporal relationship between the campaign contributions, the justice's election, and the pendency of the
case is also critical. It was reasonably foreseeable, when
the campaign contributions were made, that the pending
case would be before the newly elected justice. The $50
million adverse jury verdict had been entered before the
election, and the Supreme Court of Appeals was the next
step once the state trial court dealt with post-trial motions.
So it became at once apparent that, absent recusal, Justice
Benjamin would review a judgment that cost his biggest
donor's company $50 million. Although there is no allega-
tion of a quid pro quo agreement, the fact remains that
Blankenship's extraordinary contributions were made at a
time when he had a vested stake in the outcome. Just as
no man is allowed to be a judge in his own cause, similar
fears of bias can arise when — without the consent of the
other parties — a man chooses the judge in his own cause.
And applying this principle to the judicial election process,
there was here a serious, objective risk of actual bias that
required Justice Benjamin's recusal.[12]

Bias Generally As we've seen, actual bias will lead to
recusal. Now we leave the recusal rules and discuss bias
from a wholly different perspective. Here the issue is the
judge's conduct, on and off the bench, that may lead the
public to believe that the judge is biased against particular
segments of the population or at least insensitive to
difference. This behavior may sometimes violate a provision
of the judicial conduct code. On the other hand, some conduct may, in the view of some, simply be in bad taste. Telling
an off-color joke to a friend? What about telling an off-color
joke at a bar association meeting to an audience of 300
lawyers? I suppose it would depend on how off-color it is

and who is the target. The lines here are not easy to draw. Judges don't give up their private lives when they become judges. And most of us do tell off-color jokes now and then, or at least willingly listen to them. And yet . . . to some extent, judges cannot do that, at least not in some circumstances. *When* is the question.

Biased Comments on the Bench   Location matters. We will be much less tolerant of sexist or homophobic language on the bench — when the judge is being a judge — than at a dinner with friends, which is not to say it is acceptable there either. It will depend. A federal trial judge who while presiding in court made disparaging references about Hispanics was censured even though he made them off the record in a note to his court clerk. (He wrote: "It smells like oil in here — too many greasers." The defendants were Hispanic.)[13] An even milder ethnic reference caused a circuit court to remand a case for resentencing. The judge, in sentencing a man from Guinea, said he wanted to deter others from Guinea from committing the same crime.[14] And a state judge was sanctioned when, asked to approve an abortion for a minor, was reluctant to do so, but then added that one circumstance where he might do so was if a black man raped a white girl.[15] Commenting on the appearance of a female litigant or lawyer is unacceptable. Comments that reveal stereotypical thinking about particular groups will lead to appellate criticism and reversal, discipline, or both.[16]

At a trial, I once questioned a witness who identified a lawyer by name. To make it clear to whom the witness was referring, I said "Is that the young woman sitting at counsel table?" There was only one woman at the table. She was young, sort of, and certainly younger than the men at the table. The judge told me that no one is young or old in court and I should not thereafter refer to age when describing others unless it was relevant to the issues. Oh, well. Anyone can make a mistake.

Was it a mistake? What if there were two women at the table and she was the younger one?

Biased Comments off the Bench   Racist, sexist, and other unfortunate comments off the bench are less often the subject of inquiry, perhaps because they are not discovered. But sometimes they are, as when a judge gives an interview to a newspaper. A state appellate judge from Florida, in the course of a long media interview, said "Girls are wearing panty hose and miniskirts that would make a guy my age chase them down the hallway. . . . And that's also causing the blacks, the blacks are playing with those white girls, with the white girls' consent. . . ." He was reprimanded and removed as chief judge of the court. There were other unacceptable comments in the media interview, and it seems to me the judge should have been removed.[17]

Membership in Discriminatory Organizations   Although it took many years to reach the point, it is now the rule both in the ABA Code and the Code of Conduct for U.S. Judges that a judge cannot be a member of a discriminatory organization. But there are stark differences between the two documents. The ABA Code is much more demanding. The Code for U.S. Judges, though revised after the ABA Code was published, is more tolerant of such memberships.

The 2007 ABA Code forbids a judge to be a member of an organization that "practice[s] invidious discrimination on the basis of race, sex, gender, religion, national origin, ethnicity, or sexual orientation" (Rule 3.6). Ethnicity, gender, and sexual orientation were not included in the 1990 code. The code language is mandatory. It says that a "judge shall not hold membership" in such an organization. Furthermore, a judge who discovers that he or she is a member of such a club "must resign immediately."

The Code for U.S. Judges retains the original 1990 list. It does not add the three discriminatory bases that the ABA added in 2007. Furthermore, the Code for U.S. Judges says only that a judge "should not" belong to such an organization, not that he or she "shall not." Elsewhere in the code, judges are told what they "must not" or "may not" do. Last, the Code for U.S. Judges does not require immediate resignation if a judge learns the organization discriminates based on a forbidden category. The commentary instead says that

> the judge is permitted, in lieu of resigning, to make immediate and continuous efforts to have the organization discontinue its invidiously discriminatory practices. If the organization fails to discontinue its invidiously discriminatory practices as promptly as possible (and in all events within two years of the judge's first learning of the practices), the judge should resign immediately from the organization.

Again, we see that the verb phrase is "should resign," not "must resign." So unless the authors of the code intended the word *should* to be mandatory (in law, it is usually only aspirational), a federal judge can join and remain a member of an organization that invidiously discriminates based on, say, race or gender, so long as the membership restriction is not illegal.

What Is "Invidious" Discrimination?   A separate question is this: When is discrimination "invidious"? People in a beach community might form a beach club limited to residents of the community. If the community happens to be nearly all white, does the club invidiously discriminate? Or consider women all of whom attended a college that admits only women. They wish to form an alumna organization. Obviously, no men are eligible. Does the club invidiously discriminate based on sex or gender? The answer to both questions is no.

Antidiscrimination law cannot constitutionally reach purely private organizations. If an organization has a constitutional right to discriminate, as do the Boy Scouts when it does not let gay men become Scout leaders, is membership in it forbidden?[18] Or, to put it another way, can we require a person who becomes a judge to give up at least some of his or her constitutional rights including the right to belong to a purely private club that discriminates based on, say, sex or national origin? Here's how the ABA comment to Rule 3.6 tries to identify the boundary, recognizing that it will not always be clear.

> An organization is generally said to discriminate invidiously if it arbitrarily excludes from membership on the basis of race, sex, gender, religion, national origin, ethnicity, or sexual orientation persons who would otherwise be eligible for admission. Whether an organization practices invidious discrimination is a complex question to which judges should be attentive. The answer cannot be determined from a mere examination of an organization's current membership rolls, but rather, depends upon how the organization selects members, as well as other relevant factors, such as whether the organization is dedicated to the preservation of religious, ethnic, or cultural values of legitimate common interest to its members, or whether it is an intimate, purely private organization whose membership limitations could not constitutionally be prohibited.

Notice that this comment does not answer the important question: If an organization has a constitutional right to discriminate on one of the forbidden bases, does it mean that it does not do so "invidiously"?

The fact is that judges *do* give up some constitutional rights when they become judges. For example, all of us have a First Amendment right to say what we like about a pending court case. But a judge does not have the same right. Judges cannot make public comments "that might reasonably be expected to affect the outcome or impair the fairness of a matter pending or impending in any court. . . ." (Rule 2.10(a)). As for the Boy Scouts, on the one hand it can discriminate based on sexual orientation but it would not ordinarily be called "an intimate, purely private organization." So is membership allowed? We don't know.

Campaign Speech Most state court judges are elected. They run, sometimes every six years, in contested elections (which means there is an opposing candidate) or for "retention" following a period of service, which means voters simply say yes or no. What can a candidate for a judgeship (who may or may not already be a judge) tell the electorate about his or her legal views? Of course, candidates can say they will work hard and that they value justice and fairness. They can offer their biographies (Such and Such Law School, This and That Law Firm) and distribute pictures of themselves in family settings. *Yada yada yada*.

Everyone can say and do such things. But if we're asking voters to choose between Tweedle Dee and Tweedle Dum for a judicial post, don't they have an interest in knowing how, if at all, the candidates differ, at least in the general orientation and perspective, on the important legal questions they will be asked to decide on the bench? If the candidates were running for town supervisor or the county legislature, you bet voters would want to know these things and the candidates would want to say (or be pressed to say) how they differed from their opponents on important policy questions. Even more so if the contest is for governor or U.S. senator. So it would seem that voters also have an interest in the same kind information from judicial candidates. Indeed, that interest will be at its peak if the position is on the state's highest court, where state law questions are finally decided.

Often decried is the apparent lack of interest in judicial elections. But maybe that's because, traditionally, candidates were not allowed to tell voters their views on the legal questions likely to come before them on the bench. In other words, if we silence the candidates, they can look like Tweedle Dee and Tweedle Dum. It can be a bit insulting to tell a voter he or she has to make an important decision about who will be a judge but all he can know about the candidates is biographical facts.

I recall one judicial race in New York where, as elsewhere, the candidates tried to use visual metaphors to telegraph their views on crime. They were both "tough on crime" of course. But they wanted to do more than just say so. So one candidate produced a television commercial in which a prison cell door slammed shut. The other candidate, not to be outdone, then broadcast a commercial in which a more imposing prison door slammed shut with greater force and louder, and the image was repeated several times during the commercial. Message: My door is stronger than his door, and I have more of them, so I'll be tougher on crime.

On the other hand — there is always another hand in these matters — judges are not governors or senators. The job is different. A judge is supposed to have an open mind when deciding how to rule, with no commitment and without pre-dilection. Right? A candidate for state senator can promise to vote for a bill, but a judicial candidate can't promise to vote for the plaintiff in a pending case. The judge does not *represent* the voters. A legislator or executive does. Nor can a judge promise to vote in a particular way when a particular question comes before her on the bench ("I promise to vote that our state constitution does not require that the state recognize same-sex marriage" or "I promise to hold that our constitution does protect the right to abortion.") A judge who made such a commitment may be disqualified from then sitting on the case that raises the question.

Here was the problem: A judicial candidate very likely does have views on some issues likely to come before her court, though certainly not all. If we forbid the candidate to say what they are, it is not as though we've erased them. They are there anyway. We have simply denied ourselves information. We will have chosen to keep ourselves ignorant. What value does that serve? Well, at the very least, if the candidate does not lock herself into a position with a promise, she is (more) free to change her mind without breaking her promise.

Telegraphing how you'll vote on a particular question encourages you to do so or to accept charges that you betrayed the voters.

Just to make this a little harder, the candidate may, prior to becoming a candidate, already have expressed her views on those very hot-button issues. She may have done that in a law journal article or in a speech to a bar group. Alternatively, she may be a sitting judge running for reelection or election to a higher judicial post and already have written or joined in opinions on the hot-button issues in her current job. In other words, we may know her views in any of these other ways. So what do we gain by refusing to let her restate them on the stump? Furthermore, her opponent may not have expressed his views on the same issues (or on some of them), in which case, unless we let him do so in the campaign, voters will have only one candidate's position.

The Announce Clause For a long time, judicial ethics codes in the United States limited the speech of judicial candidates. The language varied, but in essence it addressed two kinds of speech. A candidate could not "announce his or her views on disputed legal or political issues." This was called the Announce Clause. Another clause, called the Pledges and Promises Clause, said a candidate could not make "pledges or promises of conduct in office other than the faithful and impartial performance of the duties of the office." These two clauses, but especially the Announce Clause, practically ensured that candidates for judicial election could not say much more than biographical facts or in some subtle way try to imply a difference between herself and her opponent (the slamming jail cell doors). Of course, some biographical facts could be good clues to positions on the bench ("a member of Planned Parenthood" or "an avid collector of firearms") and so attitudes, at least, could be suggested in this coded way. But the candidate took risks if she said that in her view the state constitution protected reproductive freedom or that she had doubts about the legality of laws limiting gun ownership.

The Announce Clause came before the Supreme Court in 2002 in a challenge by a judicial candidate for a seat on the Minnesota Supreme Court.[19] By the time the case reached the high Court, however, lower federal and state supreme courts had narrowed the scope of the clause. It was now said to reach only "disputed issues that are likely to come before the candidate if elected judge." In addition, "general discussions of case law and judicial philosophy" were allowed. (These quotes and those below come from the Supreme Court's opinion in *Republican Party of Minnesota v. White*.) In a 5-4 decision, the Court struck down the state's prohibition even as narrowed.

For starters, the clause limited the *content* of speech, so under long precedent, the limit had to satisfy the Constitution's requirement of strict scrutiny. Minnesota had to show that the clause was "(1) narrowly tailored, to serve (2) a compelling state interest." The compelling state interest was said to be judicial "impartiality." In his opinion for the Court, Justice Scalia said that "one meaning of 'impartiality' . . . is the lack of bias for or against either party to the proceeding." But the Announce Clause was not "narrowly tailored to serve impartiality (or the appearance of impartiality) in this sense" because it limits speech for or against "particular issues," not "particular parties."

Another meaning of *impartiality* may be "lack of preconception in favor or against a particular legal view." The Court said that this interest was not "compelling." By the time candidates get to an age where they can compete for judicial election, it will be "virtually impossible to find a judge who does not have preconception about the law." Avoiding "judicial preconceptions on legal issues is neither possible nor desirable [so] pretending otherwise by attempting to preserve the 'appearance' of that type of impartiality can hardly be a compelling state interest either."

A final meaning of *impartiality* might be "open-mindedness." The Court said the Announce Clause was not narrowly tailored to advance this goal. A candidate was free to say whatever he wished "up until the very day before he declares himself a candidate." He could also say the same thing after winning and until actual litigation is pending. Consequently, this defense of the clause was "so woefully underinclusive as to render belief in that purpose a challenge to the credulous."

The Court further rejected the dissent's claim that strict limits on judicial campaign speech were justified because the judicial and legislative functions are different, warranting the greater restrictions. The differences weren't as clear as the dissent maintained. State judges "possess the power to 'make' common law," and "they have the immense power to shape the States' constitutions as well." In other words, judges make law, too.

The upshot of *White* is that the Announce Clause failed the strict scrutiny test. The Court did not also have to address the Pledges and Promises Clause, which was not before it. It would be harder to invalidate a rule that prohibited candidates for judicial office from promising to vote a particular way on a particular case or a particular issue. Indeed, the very promise to decide an *issue* a particular way would likely disqualify the judge, if elected, from sitting on that issue. Similarly, a promise to decide a *case* in a particular way would certainly disqualify the judge from sitting on that case. Nonetheless, in the fallout from *White*, we still do not know the ultimate fate of the Pledges and Promises Clause. The answer to that question will turn on how broadly it is read.

Since judicial elections are not going away, the Court will eventually have to deal with these issues again. They are profoundly important in part because state high court elections, once sleepy affairs that were ignored by the public (except in so far as candidates outdid each other in their promises to be "tough on crime"), have become expensive contests. And some candidates will always see advantage in being able to signal to voters how they approach particular legal questions. We can be sure that the First Amendment's boundaries will be tested.

The ABA's Reaction After *White*, the ABA amended its 1990 Model Code of Judicial Conduct to comport with the holding. When it adopted a new code in 2007, the ABA largely adhered to its post-*White* changes with some drafting modifications. Today, there is no Announce Clause in the ABA Code. There is a Pledges and Promises Clause. It provides (Rule 4.1(A)(13)) that a judicial candidate (whether via election or appointment) shall not "in connection with cases, controversies, or issues that are likely to come before the court, make pledges, promises, or commitments that are inconsistent with the impartial performance of the adjudicative duties of judicial office." And Rule 2.11(A)(5) requires a judge to step aside if the

> judge, while a judge or a judicial candidate, has made a public statement, other than in a court proceeding, judicial decision, or opinion, that commits or appears to commit the judge to reach a particular result or rule in a particular way in the proceeding or controversy.

The Code defines *impartial* to mean "absence of bias or prejudice in favor of, or against, particular parties or classes of parties, as well as maintenance of an open mind in considering issues that may come before a judge."

In short, the ABA's solution can be read to say that the state's interest in avoiding recusal is a compelling state interest and that, therefore, a rule can constitutionally forbid a judge from making any commitment that under the state's ethics rules would in fact warrant disqualification.

ENDNOTES

1. (a) Any justice, judge, or magistrate judge of the United States shall disqualify himself in any proceeding in which his impartiality might reasonably be questioned.

(b) He shall also disqualify himself in the following circumstances:

(1) Where he has a personal bias or prejudice concerning a party, or personal knowledge of disputed evidentiary facts concerning the proceeding;

(2) Where in private practice he served as lawyer in the matter in controversy, or a lawyer with whom he previously practiced law served during such association as a lawyer concerning the matter, or the judge or such lawyer has been a material witness concerning it;

(3) Where he has served in governmental employment and in such capacity participated as counsel, adviser, or material witness concerning the proceeding or expressed an opinion concerning the merits of the particular case in controversy;

(4) He knows that he, individually or as a fiduciary, or his spouse or minor child residing in his household, has a financial interest in the subject matter in controversy or in a party to the proceeding, or any other interest that could be substantially affected by the outcome of the proceeding;

(5) He or his spouse, or a person within the third degree of relationship to either of them, or the spouse of such a person:

(i) Is a party to the proceeding, or an officer, director, or trustee of a party;

(ii) Is acting as a lawyer in the proceeding;

(iii) Is known by the judge to have an interest that could be substantially affected by the outcome of the proceeding;

(iv) Is to the judge's knowledge likely to be a material witness in the proceeding.

(c) A judge should inform himself about his personal and fiduciary financial interests, and make a reasonable effort to inform himself about the personal financial interests of his spouse and minor children residing in his household.

(d) For the purposes of this section the following words or phrases shall have the meaning indicated: . . .

(4) "financial interest" means ownership of a legal or equitable interest, however small, or a relationship as director, adviser, or other active participant in the affairs of a party . . .

(e) No justice, judge, or magistrate judge shall accept from the parties to the proceeding a waiver of any ground for disqualification enumerated in subsection (b). Where the ground for disqualification arises only under subsection (a), waiver may be accepted provided it is preceded by a full disclosure on the record of the basis for disqualification.

2.   (A) A judge shall disqualify himself or herself in any proceeding in which the judge's impartiality might reasonably be questioned, including but not limited to the following circumstances:

(1) The judge has a personal bias or prejudice concerning a party or a party's lawyer, or personal knowledge of facts that are in dispute in the proceeding.

(2) The judge knows that the judge, the judge's spouse or domestic partner, or a person within the third degree of relationship to either of them, or the spouse or domestic partner of such a person is:

(a) a party to the proceeding, or an officer, director, general partner, managing member, or trustee of a party;

(b) acting as a lawyer in the proceeding;

(c) a person who has more than a de minimis interest that could be substantially affected by the proceeding; or

(d) likely to be a material witness in the proceeding.

(3) The judge knows that he or she, individually or as a fiduciary, or the judge's spouse, domestic partner, parent, or child, or any other member of the judge's family residing in the judge's household, has an economic interest in the subject matter in controversy or is a party to the proceeding.

(4) The judge knows or learns by means of a timely motion that a party, a party's lawyer, or the law firm of a party's lawyer has within the previous [insert number] year[s] made aggregate. Contributions to the judge's campaign in an amount that [is greater than $[insert amount] for an individual or $[insert amount] for an entity [is reasonable and appropriate for an individual or an entity].

(5) The judge, while a judge or a judicial candidate, has made a public statement, other than in a court proceeding, judicial decision, or opinion, that commits or appears to commit the judge to reach a particular result or rule in a particular way in the proceeding or controversy.

(6) The judge:

(a) served as a lawyer in the matter in controversy, or was associated with a lawyer who participated substantially as a lawyer in the matter during such association;

(b) served in governmental employment, and in such capacity participated personally and substantially as a lawyer or public official concerning the proceeding, or has publicly expressed in such capacity an opinion concerning the merits of the particular matter in controversy;

(c) was a material witness concerning the matter; or

(d) previously presided as a judge over the matter in another court.

(B) A judge shall keep informed about the judge's personal and fiduciary economic interests, and make a reasonable effort to keep informed about the personal economic interests of the judge's spouse or domestic partner and minor children residing in the judge's household.

(C) A judge subject to disqualification under this Rule, other than for bias or prejudice under paragraph (A)(1), may disclose on the record the basis of the judge's disqualification and may ask the parties and their lawyers to consider, outside the presence of the judge and court personnel, whether to waive disqualification. If, following the disclosure, the parties and lawyers agree, without participation by the judge or court personnel, that the judge should not be disqualified, the judge may participate in the proceeding. The agreement shall be incorporated into the record of the proceeding.

3. *Summers v. Singletary*, 119 F.3d 917 (11th Cir. 1997).

4. *Cheney v. U.S. District Court for the District of Columbia*, 541 U.S. 913 (2004).

5. *United States v. Morrison*, 153 F.3d 34 (2d Cir. 1998) ("[W]here an interest is not direct, but is remote, contingent, or speculative, it is not the kind of interest which reasonably brings into question a judge's impartiality") (internal citations omitted).

6. *Liteky v. United States*, 510 U.S. 540 (1994).

7. Unlike the ABA Code, the federal disqualification statute and the Code of Conduct for U.S. Judges disqualify a judge who has a "financial interest in the subject matter of the proceeding or in a party to the proceeding" regardless of the size of the financial interest.

8. ABA Code Rule 2.11 comment [5]. *Liteky v. United States, supra.*

9. *Liljeberg v. Health Services Acquisition Corp.*, 486 U.S. 847 (1988).

10. *Tumey v. Ohio*, 273 U.S. 510 (1927).

11. *Aetna Life Ins. Co. v. Lavoie*, 475 U.S. 813 (1986).

12. *Caperton v. A.T. Massey Coal, Co. Inc.*, 129 S.Ct. 2252 (2009).

13. See Stephen Gillers, *Regulation of Lawyers* 624 (8th ed. 2009).

14. *United States v. Kaba*, 480 F.3d 152 (2d Cir. 2007).

15. *Matter of Bourisseau*, 480 N.W.2d 270 (Mich. 1992).

16. *In re Marriage of Iverson*, 15 Cal. Rptr. 2d 70 (Ct. App. 1992).

17. Gillers, *supra* note 12, at 625.

18. *Boy Scouts of America v. Dale*, 530 U.S. 640 (2000).

19. *Republican Party of Minnesota v. White*, 536 U.S. 765 (2002).

part V
Quality Assurance

~ 23 ~

Admission to the Bar

Geographical Requirements

Education, Bar Examination, and Character Inquiries

Temporary Presence "in" a Jurisdiction (Cross-border Practice)

It comes as no surprise, of course, that the right to practice law requires a license. In the United States, bar admission is decentralized. It is the prerogative of each state (including the District of Columbia, Puerto Rico, the Virgin Islands, and Guam) to license lawyers to practice *in* their territory and to identify the criteria for getting a license (subject to constitutional constraints). Take note of the italicized preposition in the prior sentence — *in* — about which we will have more to say below; but here it is worth mentioning that the suggestion of physical presence that *in* implies has a certain unreality in an age when a person anywhere can do much in the way of law practice anywhere else, via fax, e-mail, telephone, express mail, video conferencing, and who knows what miracles technology may yet offer, without ever or hardly ever physically leaving home.

First, back to basics. To practice anywhere, a license is needed, and in our federal system, the states do the licensing.

Federal courts admit lawyers, too, but there is no elaborate federal admissions pathway — no bar examination, no character committee. It is the states that prescribe the educational, testing, and character criteria for a law license. The federal courts mainly piggyback on state admissions. If you're admitted to a state court, you can apply (perhaps after a waiting period) to the federal court in the state. (Discipline is different. A federal court will not automatically impose the same or any discipline on a lawyer whom the state disciplines.)[1]

Where Do You Live?   Kathryn Piper lived in Vermont, 400 yards from the border with New Hampshire. She wanted to take the New Hampshire bar examination as a prelude to gaining admission to its bar and practicing law there. We can imagine that the 400-yard "commute" would not have discouraged her. But New Hampshire said no. Under a state supreme court rule, Piper could not be a New Hampshire lawyer unless she lived in the state. New Hampshire thought it had a legitimate basis for wanting its lawyers to be New Hampshire residents, at least when they first joined the bar. The state did not strip its lawyers of their law licenses if they moved away, say to Vermont, a fact that left the rule underinclusive and harder to defend. Piper went to federal court and eventually all the way to the Supreme Court to get the right to join the New Hampshire bar.[2]

In its 8-1 opinion (Justice Rehnquist dissenting), the Court relied on the Constitution's Privileges and Immunities Clause, which states that the "Citizens of each State shall be entitled to all Privileges and Immunities of Citizens in the several States." In other words, unless justified, a state cannot treat its own citizens more favorably than it treats another state's citizens. This requirement of "equal treatment," as the Court called it, recognizes that the clause "was intended to create a national economic union." The clause "guarantees to citizens of State A [the privilege] of doing business in State B on terms of substantial equality with the citizens of that State."[3] The Court viewed the practice of law as a "privilege," one that it said was "important to the national economy," indeed "a fundamental right."[4] But more than that, law practice also had a "noncommercial" dimension — the representation of "persons who raise unpopular federal claims . . . . The lawyer who champions unpopular causes surely is as important to the 'maintenance or well-being of the Union,'" as were the purely commercial occupations protected in earlier cases.[5]

But that was not enough to win the day for Piper. The clause's guarantee is not absolute. A state may discriminate against nonresidents if "there is a substantial reason for the difference in treatment" and if "the discrimination practiced against nonresidents bears a substantial relationship to the State's objective." To meet this burden, the New Hampshire Supreme Court identified the following objectives served by its rule. Nonresident bar members, it said, "would be less likely (i) to become, and remain, familiar with local rules and procedures; (ii) to behave ethically; (iii) to be available for court proceedings; and (iv) to do pro bono and other volunteer work in the State." The U.S. Supreme Court rejected each reason.[6]

> There is no evidence to support appellant's claim that nonresidents might be less likely to keep abreast of local rules and procedures. Nor may we assume that a nonresident lawyer — any more than a resident — would disserve his clients by failing to familiarize himself with the rules. . . .
>
> We also find the appellant's second justification to be without merit, for there is no reason to believe that a nonresident lawyer will conduct his practice in a dishonest manner. The nonresident lawyer's professional duty and interest in his reputation should provide the same incentive to maintain high ethical standards as they do for resident

lawyers. A lawyer will be concerned with his reputation in any community where he practices, regardless of where he may live. Furthermore, a nonresident lawyer may be disciplined for unethical conduct. The Supreme Court of New Hampshire has the authority to discipline all members of the bar, regardless of where they reside.

There is more merit to appellant's assertion that a nonresident member of the bar at times would be unavailable for court proceedings. In the course of litigation, pretrial hearings on various matters often are held on short notice. At times a court will need to confer immediately with counsel. Even the most conscientious lawyer residing in a distant State may find himself unable to appear in court for an unscheduled hearing or proceeding. Nevertheless, we do not believe that this type of problem justifies the exclusion of nonresidents from the state bar. One may assume that a high percentage of nonresident lawyers willing to take the state bar examination and pay the annual dues will reside in places reasonably convenient to New Hampshire. Furthermore, [the] trial court, by rule or as an exercise of discretion, may require any lawyer who resides at a great distance to retain a local attorney who will be available for unscheduled meetings and hearings.

The final reason advanced by appellant is that nonresident members of the state bar would be disinclined to do their share of pro bono and volunteer work. Perhaps this is true to a limited extent, particularly where the member resides in a distant location. We think it is reasonable to believe, however, that most lawyers who become members of a state bar will endeavor to perform their share of these services.[7]

Dissenting, Justice Rehnquist cited a state interest that hadn't occurred to the New Hampshire Supreme Court.

Put simply, the State has a substantial interest in creating its own set of laws responsive to its own local interests, and it is reasonable for a State to decide that those people who have been trained to analyze law and policy are better equipped to write those state laws and adjudicate cases arising under them. The State therefore may decide that it has an interest in maximizing the number of resident lawyers, so as to increase the quality of the pool from which its lawmakers can be drawn . . . . Since at any given time within a State there is only enough legal work to support a certain number of lawyers, each out-of-state lawyer who is allowed to practice necessarily takes legal work that could support an in-state lawyer, who would otherwise be available to perform various functions that a State has an interest in promoting.

Nor does the State's interest end with enlarging the pool of qualified lawmakers. A State similarly might determine that because lawyers play an important role in the formulation of state policy through their adversary representation, they should be intimately conversant with the local concerns that should inform such policies. And the State likewise might conclude that those citizens trained in the law are likely to bring their useful expertise to other important functions that benefit from such expertise and are of interest to state governments — such as trusteeships, or directorships of corporations or charitable organizations, or school board positions, or merely the role of the interested citizen at a town meeting.[8]

Although Rehnquist's argument did not win the day, or indeed any day thereafter, it does represent a perspective that must be taken seriously. Take an extreme case. Assume that after *Piper*, lawyers living in or around Boston take the New Hampshire bar while remaining in Massachusetts. They then use their license to "cherry-pick" the most profitable client matters from New Hampshire. That will reduce the economic base of New Hampshire lawyers and perhaps, therefore, make them less amenable to spend spare time doing pro bono or other volunteer civic work. The pool of New Hampshire lawyers will shrink because the work, especially the most profitable work, will decline — that is, much of it will have been outsourced to Boston. Yet the state relies on its bar members to serve on boards, as a source of talent for government jobs, and so on. An even more compelling description of these risks can be made on behalf of New Jersey, which has New York City lawyers to the north and Philadelphia lawyers to the south. Why can't a state like New Hampshire or New Jersey legitimately apprehend these consequences and protect against them by requiring lawyers to reside in their states?

The Rehnquist argument makes empirical assumptions without an empirical study, but are the assumptions so improbable? If the assumptions are rational and the state expects them, what business is it of the federal courts to substitute different expectations? Now, as it happens, Rehnquist's predictions have not come to pass so far as anyone has shown, but that's not the question. The question is whether the risk of them doing so was great enough to entitle a state not to take a chance that they would occur. The Court said no, at least not without some proof, and New Hampshire had no proof. No surprise since, as stated, it didn't even rely on this argument. The Court's conclusion necessarily rests on the fact that a constitutional right was at issue and on the fact that the state had not met its burden of proof on the empirical assumptions advanced in the dissent.

Where Do You Work? The Court extended *Piper* a few years later when a lawyer who lived in Maryland but worked in Virginia sought to gain admission to the Virginia bar "on motion," which means without having to take the bar examination. At the time, about half the states allowed experienced lawyers to bypass the examination and join the state's bar subject only to a character examination. A state did not have to do this, but many did. Myra Friedman's application for motion admission was denied because Virginia required state residence for motion admission. Virginia required in addition that the lawyer practice full time in the state, but Friedman did that, so the validity of this requirement was not before the court. Virginia offered two reasons for its rule:

> First, they contend that the residence requirement assures, in tandem with the full-time practice requirement, that attorneys admitted on motion will have the same commitment to service and familiarity with Virginia law that is possessed by applicants securing admission upon examination. Attorneys admitted on motion, appellants argue, have "no personal investment" in the jurisdiction; consequently, they "are entitled to no presumption that they will willingly and actively participate in bar activities and obligations, or fulfill their public service responsibilities to the State's client community." Second, appellants argue that the residency requirement facilitates enforcement of the full-time practice requirement . . . .[9]

Using the same analysis as it did in *Piper*, and written by the same justice (Kennedy), the Court found "each of these justifications insufficient to meet the State's burden of showing that the discrimination is warranted by a substantial state objective and closely drawn to its achievement."[10] But when a Virginia resident who worked in Washington, DC (the converse of Friedman's situation) sought admission by motion, he lost. The Fourth Circuit upheld Virginia's other condition for admission — full-time work in the state — which the challenger could not satisfy.[11] Other courts have also upheld restrictions on motion admission that required applicants to work in the state or, in one case, spend more than half of their professional time working for in-state clients.[12] *Friedman*, like *Piper*, turns on the unconstitutionality of a state treating a nonresident differently from its treatment of a resident.

Education, Examination, and Character Nearly all states require graduation from an American Bar Association (ABA)-accredited law school as a precondition to taking the bar examination. Some states allow graduates of state-approved law schools that are not ABA accredited to take the bar; some states still allow law office study of specified duration as sufficient to qualify an applicant to take the bar. There are other variations. This is not the place to identify them, but anyone interested can find them on the ABA Web site in a publication called *Bar Admission Requirements*. It is published annually by the ABA and the National Conference of Bar Examiners. It can also be purchased in book form. Go to *http://www.abanet.org* and search for "Bar Admission Requirements."

The same publication contains a chart on the scope and nature of the character and fitness inquiry in U.S. jurisdictions. All states make this inquiry.[13] Examining character rests on two policies. First, bad character may predict future misconduct as a lawyer. Lawyers must be trustworthy and honest. They receive client confidences and hold client property. Whether such a prediction from past behavior to future conduct as a lawyer is possible to make — or possible to make with sufficient confidence that anything as important as bar licensure should be allowed to depend on it — has been questioned. Nonetheless, character inquiries are not going to go away, although over the years courts have limited the kinds of questions that can be asked. The second justification for character inquiries, apart from their predictive value, if any, is the state's interest in assuring public confidence in the bar. If anyone who passes a bar examination after a legal education can become a lawyer regardless of past behavior or even criminal activity, the public may be expected to put little faith in the fact of a law license as a credential encouraging clients to repose trust in those who hold one. Nonetheless, do not conclude that applicants who have blemished pasts are automatically excluded. Even applicants with felony convictions may be able to gain admission to the bar in all but a half dozen American jurisdictions. See the ABA publication cited here for a list.

Temporary Practice There was surely a time, though long ago, that lawyers rarely traveled for professional reasons. Practices were confined to the city, town, or county in which the lawyer had an office. Over time, several factors combined to change that: The nation expanded, travel became easier, and the nature of clients' problems changed so that lawyers had to go to meetings or do work outside their communities. Other developments also made it easier for lawyers to ignore the traditional boundaries. Among these are the increasing homogenization of the law, meaning that some areas of law are pretty much the same everywhere, or at any rate variations can be readily identified, and of course federal law is *identical* everywhere. Also, discovery of the law of other jurisdictions became much easier with the advent of legal databases. No longer was an extensive library required to know the rule on subject X in a distant state. Last, specialization by lawyers made it sensible for clients to hire lawyers from other areas of the nation who were expert in some narrow legal field. A lawyer in Chicago whose area of concentration is antitrust law with reference to a particular industry, or tax law as it affects multinational banks, will be attractive to clients with problems in her area of concentration wherever the client may be. Indeed, there may be no lawyer in the client's part of the country with quite the same depth of expertise. So lawyers got on trains and planes and in cars and worked for clients in other states or worked for home-state clients whose matters required their temporary presence elsewhere.

As time passed, it often became unnecessary to get on the train or plane or in the car. Modern communications — telephone in the early years, then express mail, fax, and e-mail — made it easy to do business a thousand or more miles away without leaving your desk. Conferences via audio, then video, among lawyers and clients in different cities (or even countries) became possible via satellite transmission.

True, use of these facilities can be costly, but they are a whole lot cheaper than paying for a lawyer's time on the road, while often permitting participants to achieve the same goals as in a live, in-person meeting.

There was just one problem. Every jurisdiction has laws forbidding persons who are not lawyers in their jurisdictions to practice law *in* them. Some of these laws provide criminal penalties. And professional conduct rules everywhere forbid a lawyer to engage in unauthorized practice or to help someone else do so. Now, of course, a lawyer licensed in New York, say, is not a lawyer in New Jersey or Florida. So when that New York lawyer travels down to Florida to meet with a prospective client or to negotiate for a client back home, is she violating the Florida rules on unauthorized practice of law (UPL)? On the one hand, she is not a layperson, either. She is trained in the law and admitted to a bar somewhere. On the other hand, she is not admitted to the bar in Florida. And what if she doesn't actually travel to Florida but simply communicates with individuals in Florida, using e-mail, fax, and satellite conference facilities, while never leaving New York? Has she thereby practiced law in Florida *virtually* in violation of its UPL rules? Does the answer depend on whether the particular matter involves Florida law or a Florida client? Complicating the answer to all of these questions is the fact that so long as that New York lawyer stayed in New York and didn't enter Florida physically or virtually, she could give advice on the law of Florida or any other place in the world if competent to do so. Only if she did the same things *in* Florida — physically or virtually — would she risk a UPL violation. That's not ideal for Florida residents who want to call upon the special expertise of a lawyer practicing elsewhere. They would need to travel to the lawyer's office to get her advice.

As it happens, no one much thought about these questions because rarely were lawyers charged with UPL based on their presence in another state; and when they were, it was for truly egregious conduct, like appearing in another state's court without seeking permission to do so, or opening a law office in another state without bothering to gain admission to its bar. Meanwhile, as travel and communication became easier, and as clients' problems increasingly required cross-border practice, lawyers behaved as though the regulatory framework was rational, which meant that so long as their presence in another jurisdiction was temporary or incidental (indefinite terms), not prolonged or indefinite, they figured they were safe. And mostly they were safe. But the regulatory framework was not entirely rational, as it happens. It was historical. Or to put it another way, it was rational, but for nineteenth-century America, not twenty-first-century America. It showed little awareness of how life had changed in the intervening century.

But even if the regulatory framework did not explicitly allow for the realities of modern practice, at least those charged with enforcing it — courts and disciplinary authorities — could exercise good judgment and try not to use outdated doctrines to pounce on lawyers who travel away from home for a week of meetings. And overwhelmingly good judgment is what we got, which further encouraged lawyers to get on the planes and trains and venture out of their home states.

Furthermore, as an additional safety valve, lawyers who go to court could apply to a judge in jurisdictions in which they were not admitted for *pro hac vice* ("for this turn") status, allowing them to try a single case in those courts. Pro hac vice admission was only a partial solution, however. It would not protect transactional lawyers. And it would not even protect litigators who went into a new state before an action was filed there, and therefore before there was opportunity to seek pro hac vice status, or litigators who went into a state to do work in connection with a matter filed (or to be filed) in a different state. Nor would it protect litigators who were going to try their cases in arbitration or in another form of alternate dispute resolution tribunal, which do not generally have the authority to admit lawyers pro hac vice.

Enforcing UPL in Fee Disputes As it happens, enforcement of UPL against lawyers from outside a jurisdiction has mainly occurred not through discipline or prosecution but in fee disputes. Clients who were unhappy with their lawyer's work (or who just saw the opportunity to avoid paying the bill) might defend against a firm's action for payment of fees by claiming that the lawyer's practice "in" the jurisdiction was unauthorized and that therefore the court should not enforce the fee agreement as a matter of public policy.[14] (Clients might then throw in a malpractice counterclaim for good measure, which is one reason that law firms think twice before suing for fees.) Courts accepted the public policy argument, even when the client knew the lawyer's jurisdictional limitations. Courts explained that because of the state's overriding interest in the policies underlying its UPL rules, clients could not waive them. But these decisions were rare, or narrow, or from courts that did not seem to be influential.

The Birbrower Decision Then, in 1998, in *Birbrower, Montalbano, Condon & Frank P.C. v. Superior Court*, a case that stunned American lawyers, the California Supreme Court dropped a doctrinal bomb. The California Supreme Court *is* influential. But more than that, its holding was quite broad. It ruled that New York lawyers would be guilty of practicing law "in" California for work they did while *physically in New York* "by advising a California client on California law in connection with a California legal dispute by telephone, fax, computer, or other modern technological means." They could not get paid for this work because it was "virtually" in California. The court also held that the lawyers could not get paid for the work they did during three trips to California of a few days each in order to prepare for an arbitration in which they had been retained to represent the client. But the lawyers could get paid for work they did exclusively in New York and not virtually in California.[15] One could hardly write a stranger opinion, an opinion less in tune with the reality of modern legal life.

Birbrower led to the creation of an ABA commission to study the problem of cross-border practice or, to put it more starkly, to figure out the best way to accommodate the fact that the United States admits lawyers locally (state by state) while, increasingly, lawyers, even lawyers in smaller firms, practice regionally and nationally and that they do so both by traveling to other jurisdictions and virtually — through various forms of communication that are only going to get easier, faster, more reliable, and cheaper. The commission proposed amendments to Rules 5.5 and 8.5 (among other solutions) in order to make cross-border practice easier while protecting the interests of state regulators. Rule 5.5 appears in note 16. Its key paragraph is (c), which identifies the circumstances in which a lawyer from one jurisdiction can practice "temporarily" in another jurisdiction. Rule 5.5(d)(1) contemplates a special admission rule for lawyers employed by organizations, including companies, and who may be assigned to places in which they are not admitted to practice.[16] The amendment to Rule 8.5 makes it easier for a jurisdiction into which a lawyer temporarily travels (physically or virtually) in representing a client (sometimes called a "host" jurisdiction as opposed to the lawyer's "home" jurisdiction) to discipline that lawyer if he or she violates the professional conduct rules of the host jurisdiction or indeed another jurisdiction in connection with the work in the host state.[17]

Whether Rules 5.5 and 8.5 are *the* solution to the problems raised by local licensure cannot be known.[18] They may only be a stopgap. Some lawyers believe that the solution we will ultimately need to embrace must include a form of national licensure, whether through a federal bar examination (highly improbable at the moment) or a rule that allows a lawyer admitted anywhere, perhaps after several years of active practice, to relocate anywhere else, temporarily or permanently. In other words, law licenses would become transportable, recognized as valid everywhere. Whether this will come to pass is anyone's guess. Time will tell.

ENDNOTES

1. *Theard v. United States*, 354 U.S. 278 (1954).
2. *Supreme Court of New Hampshire v. Piper*, 470 U.S. 274 (1985).
3. *Id.* at 280.
4. *Id.* at 281.
5. *Id.*
6. *Id.* at 285. One interesting angle here is that we are dealing with empirical inferences. Why is one court better positioned than another to reach these? There was no record evidence either way. The case could have been decided on the ground that New Hampshire did not meet its burden of proof, but the Supreme Court went further and found the empirical assumptions wrong in fact.
7. *Id.* at 285-287.
8. *Id.* at 292.
9. *Supreme Court of Virginia v. Friedman*, 487 U.S. 59 (1988).
10. *Id.* at 68.
11. *Goldfarb v. Supreme Court of Virginia*, 766 F.2d 859 (4th Cir. 1985).
12. *Scariano v. Supreme Court of Indiana*, 38 F.3d 920 (7th Cir. 1994) (Indiana rule allowing motion admission only for candidates who "predominantly [practice] in Indiana" upheld even though the rule was satisfied by representing Indiana based clients from a law office elsewhere).
13. States may not deny admission to otherwise qualified applicants who are not U.S. citizens. *In re Griffiths*, 413 U.S. 717 (1973).
14. As the estate of one did successfully in *Ranta v. McCarney*, 391 N.W.2d 161 (N.D. 1986) (Minnesota lawyer advising North Dakota client on federal tax matters could not get paid for work he did while in North Dakota).
15. 949 P.2d 1 (Cal. 1998).
16. Rule 5.5 Unauthorized Practice of Law; Multijurisdictional Practice of Law

> (a) A lawyer shall not practice law in a jurisdiction in violation of the regulation of the legal profession in that jurisdiction, or assist another in doing so.
> (b) A lawyer who is not admitted to practice in this jurisdiction shall not:
> > (1) except as authorized by these Rules or other law, establish an office or other systematic and continuous presence in this jurisdiction for the practice of law; or
> > (2) hold out to the public or otherwise represent that the lawyer is admitted to practice law in this jurisdiction.

(c) A lawyer admitted in another United States jurisdiction, and not disbarred or suspended from practice in any jurisdiction, may provide legal services on a temporary basis in this jurisdiction that:

(1) are undertaken in association with a lawyer who is admitted to practice in this jurisdiction and who actively participates in the matter;

(2) are in or reasonably related to a pending or potential proceeding before a tribunal in this or another jurisdiction, if the lawyer, or a person the lawyer is assisting, is authorized by law or order to appear in such proceeding or reasonably expects to be so authorized;

(3) are in or reasonably related to a pending or potential arbitration, mediation, or other alternative dispute resolution proceeding in this or another jurisdiction, if the services arise out of or are reasonably related to the lawyer's practice in a jurisdiction in which the lawyer is admitted to practice and are not services for which the forum requires pro hac vice admission; or

(4) are not within paragraphs (c)(2) or (c)(3) and arise out of or are reasonably related to the lawyer's practice in a jurisdiction in which the lawyer is admitted to practice.

(d) A lawyer admitted in another United States jurisdiction, and not disbarred or suspended from practice in any jurisdiction, may provide legal services in this jurisdiction that:

(1) are provided to the lawyer's employer or its organizational affiliates and are not services for which the forum requires pro hac vice admission; or

(2) are services that the lawyer is authorized to provide by federal law or other law of this jurisdiction.

17. For an analysis of *Birbrower* and a review of the commission's work see Stephen Gillers, *Lessons from the Multijurisdictional Practice Commission: The Art of Making Change*, 44 Ariz. L. Rev. 685 (2002).

18. As of April 2009, 40 jurisdictions have adopted Rule 5.5 or a variation of it.

～ 24 ～

Lawyer Liability

Liability to Clients for Malpractice or Breach of Fiduciary Duty

Causation Requirements

Fee Forfeiture and Disgorgement

Liability to Third Parties

Like other professionals, lawyers may face financial liability arising out of their work for clients. The liability may be, and traditionally has been, to the client. Sometimes, as discussed in Chapter 21, a lawyer may face liability to someone who is not a traditional client but is recognized as one for purposes of this liability. An example of the latter in some jurisdictions is the client's intended beneficiary in an estate plan. The lawyer may negligently fail to follow the client's instructions, the beneficiary may then not inherit on the client's death, it is too late to correct the error, and so the beneficiary sues the lawyer. She alleges that but for the lawyer's negligence, she would have inherited; and that she has standing to bring the claim, though not a traditional client, because the traditional client intended that she benefit from the work the client had hired the lawyer to do. Some jurisdictions recognize this claim, and others do not.[1]

Apart from liability to clients, lawyers also may face liability to third persons who are injured because of the conduct of the client in which the lawyer provided assistance. For example, a client (say, a company) may be guilty of fraud in connection with a deal. The lawyer may be ignorant of the fraud (if he is not ignorant and helps the client commit the fraud knowingly, he may be liable for aiding the fraud just like anyone else who knowingly aids a fraud).[2] The plaintiff may claim that the lawyer should have known about the fraud, or that he consciously disregarded warning signs, or that in any event once having learned about the client's misconduct he had a duty to warn the victims to help them to avoid its consummation or minimize the harm. We saw some of these issues play out in Chapter 21 on transactional lawyers.

Whether any of these theories are recognized will depend of course on the statutory and (more likely) the common law of the jurisdiction whose law applies. But we have seen in the last 25 years an increasing willingness of courts to entertain theories of lawyer liability to third persons (i.e., not a client or someone who could stand in the shoes of a client like the beneficiary of a will). In fact, this trend probably began (or at least got a solid doctrinal boost) in the 1950s in California and gradually spread to other states. Where accepted, lawyer liability to third persons rejects what had long been a defense that lawyers successfully raised when sued by nonclients. That defense relied on the lack of privity between the lawyer and the plaintiff, which is just another way of saying that only clients could sue lawyers in these circumstances because only clients were in privity with — that is, had a professional relationship with — the lawyers, which entitled them to demand a certain level of professional conduct.

The privity doctrine was not, as we might initially be inclined to believe, simply a way to protect lawyers. It had (and to some extent retains) a sensible policy goal. It was meant to ensure that lawyers would be able to concentrate on their duty of loyalty to and zealous representation of clients without having to worry that their actions would subject them to potential legal exposure to others arising out of their work, a worry that might compromise the quality of that work. The doctrine also took account of the adversary system. The lawyers for other parties to a litigation or transaction would be there to protect those parties, so there was no felt need to give opposing lawyers duties to their clients' adversaries other than the duty not to assist a client's crime or fraud knowingly. The weakening (though not the disappearance) of the privity requirement reflects judicial recognition that in some instances the requirement overprotects lawyers without corresponding gains. Sometimes, in other words, legal rules that create potential lawyer liability to third persons will not interfere with a lawyer's lawful and zealous representation of clients. At the same time, the risk of liability may encourage lawyers to take care not to do things that facilitate their client's harmful and unlawful conduct. Furthermore, reliance on the adversary system to protect third parties, while often sensible, is far from foolproof even when there is another lawyer in the picture. And sometimes, there isn't, as when a lawyer is merely advising on the legality of contemplated conduct (say, introduction of a new financial or consumer product), where the advice if wrong can injure purchasers. We discuss third-party liability more fully at the end of this chapter. First, though, is liability to clients.

Malpractice   The very word *malpractice* signifies the existence of a professional of some kind—for example, doctor, architect, lawyer, accountant. When a person not traditionally viewed as a professional makes an error that causes harm— say, an electrician or a bus driver—we may say they were negligent or that their conduct failed the "reasonable person" test, but we don't call it malpractice. This is true even if the defendant is highly skilled — a ship's captain, for instance. Nonetheless, when we get deeper into the meaning of malpractice, we see that at bottom, negligence is the touchstone.

A preliminary word now about breach of fiduciary duty. Unlike malpractice, which presumes a professional, any agent may breach fiduciary duty, because all agents are fiduciaries.[3] Partners are fiduciaries of each other, the executors of an estate are fiduciaries to the estate, and so on. Ordinary life is full of fiduciaries, although lawyers are sometimes said to be the, or among the, highest,[4] assuming we can calibrate degrees. No fixed boundary separates malpractice from breach of fiduciary duty. It can sometimes seem that a court will use the labels interchangeably. Unless the statutes of limitations differ depending on which category is used, or unless the amounts or kinds of damages vary, or unless the elements of one claim can more readily be proved than the elements of another, it shouldn't much matter what theory a client sues under as long as it uses the label the particular jurisdiction requires for the particular conduct (if it requires any). For purposes of this discussion, we will use *malpractice* to mean professional negligence and treat *breach of fiduciary duty* separately later on. This is a defensible distinction, even though (beware) it is not necessarily one that every court would make. But it is useful for our purposes.

Lawyers, as we know from Chapter 3, have a duty of competence. That duty appears in rules of professional conduct as an ethical matter, and it is also a requirement of civil law. Disciplinary committees do not generally enforce the duty of competence. They have more important things to do, like go after liars, thieves, and attorneys who take money and do no work (itself a kind of thievery). So when competence is challenged, it will almost always occur in a malpractice action or in a challenge to a conviction based on ineffective assistance of counsel. Courts define the civil law standard as requiring lawyers to exercise the degree of *care, skill, and knowledge* (or perhaps courts will add or substitute the words *judgment, diligence,* or *prudence*) that lawyers in the same community bring to bear in such matters.[5] This is negligence measured by professional standards (as opposed to the reasonable person standard in the law of torts). So let's use the term *negligence* or *professional negligence.* If the lawyer holds herself out as a specialist (probably charging more because of her expertise), she will have to satisfy the presumably higher standards of specialists in the field.[6] The community is commonly the state in which the lawyer practices.[7] That "state" standard will be difficult to apply, and may in fact be largely irrelevant, in some instances, because of the growth of national law firms, the fact that increasingly lawyers practice across state lines, and the fact that some legal specialties are truly national (or international), requiring any sensible evaluation of a lawyer's conduct to be measured by lawyers in the same (perhaps arcane) specialty in other jurisdictions. While the state standard may not soon yield to a national standard on paper, we may see that courts will sometimes have to look to out-of-state practitioners to figure out what the state standard of care should be.

If a lawyer's work in a particular matter is negligent, then the client will have a malpractice claim. It does not mean, it is important to add quickly, that the lawyer is incompetent, only that her work was below par *in the particular matter.* (To collect damages, the client will have to prove other things, too, as discussed below.) The malpractice claim may be based on a contract theory (you made a contractually binding promise to do X and you did it negligently or didn't do it) or a tort theory (you undertook to do X and you did it poorly or negligently).[8] The line between the two is not entirely clear; nor will it much matter unless, again, limitations periods vary depending on which theory is used or unless one theory, probably tort, will permit damages (say for emotional injury or punitive damages) that a contract theory will not.

Now we need to make an important distinction. A lawyer is not a guarantor of success. The fact that a lawyer does not succeed in achieving the client's goal (lost the case, couldn't get the contract term the client wanted, etc.) doesn't mean the lawyer is liable to the client. In fact, a client cannot win simply because her lawyer chose strategy *AB* over strategy *XY*, and now, with the benefit of hindsight, the client is prepared to prove that strategy *XY* would have succeeded. We are all smarter in hindsight. But as long as the lawyer's care, skill, diligence, and knowledge were up to the standards for lawyers in the state, the lawyer will not be liable. Of course, the very premise — that the lawyer chose between two strategies — necessarily implies that the lawyer was mindful that both existed. So a lawyer whose research identifies various options — each with advantages and disadvantages — and who then chooses one after exercising a considered and reasonable judgment (and when required, checked with the client) will have acted properly. But a lawyer who pursues the *same* option without even having done the minimal factual or legal research to discover the other options (and who by definition therefore does not *choose* between them) may have acted unreasonably.[9] Alternatively, a lawyer whose research has identified various options and whose choice among them is unreasonable — that is, negligent under the malpractice standard — will also be liable for any damages.

Proximate Cause   Which brings us to the interesting policy issues surrounding the question of proximate cause. Whether malpractice is viewed as a breach of contract or a tort, the malpractice plaintiff must prove that the lawyer's failure resulted in damages and the amount of those damages. Malpractice that produces no harm is not compensable. This is not a rule special to malpractice. It is the rule in any breach of contract or tort claim. The plaintiff must show that *but for* the lawyer's malpractice, she would have been better off. What does that mean — "better off?"

Let's take a simple and recurring situation. An injured person hires a lawyer to sue the person who caused her injury (maybe the other driver, or the doctor who treated her, or a company that defrauded her). The lawyer neglects the case, the statute of limitations expires, and the plaintiff can no longer sue. Or consider a variation on this situation that is popular in legal ethics classes. A lawyer concludes, without doing any factual or legal research, that a prospective client has no case. The client then goes away and learns only many months later that she really did have a case, but the limitations period has expired. The lawyer in each of these situations is guilty of malpractice. That's the easy part. But to win a judgment the plaintiff must prove that *but for* the professional negligence, she would have won the underlying case. So in addition to and as part of proving the "outer" case, as it's sometimes called — the one against the lawyer for legal malpractice — she will also have to prove the "inner" case, the one the lawyer should have brought but didn't. She'll have to win both cases. But how can she do that? The original defendants cannot be sued because the claim is no longer timely. That means (and this can be rather strange) that the negligent lawyer must defend not only the legal malpractice case against him, but also the inner case that he was originally asked to bring. In other words, a lawyer who is retained to sue X and who neglects the assignment now stands in the shoes of X, the party that the lawyer failed to sue, a kind of role reversal. The lawyer needs to mount any defense that X might have mounted if the lawyer had done the right thing. And the jury hearing the *legal malpractice* case must decide not only that case (was the lawyer negligent?), but also what the result in the inner case would have been had it been brought (would the lawyer have won the case against X?).[10]

We have been assuming that the lawyer failed to bring a proper case, but the same analysis obtains if the lawyer brings the case but prosecutes it negligently, with the result that the client loses or does not win as much as she would have secured absent the negligence. Perhaps the lawyer failed to call an obvious witness whose absence made a difference. Perhaps the lawyer missed a legal theory that would have supported (a greater) recovery. And the same principles apply if the lawyer represents a defendant who, because of the lawyer's negligence, winds up having to pay a judgment, or a larger judgment, than would have otherwise been true.

Burden of Proof   The burden of proof belongs to the malpractice plaintiff for both the outer case and the inner case (assuming it was there to begin with). This can seem unfair. Once the malpractice plaintiff proves the lawyer's negligence, we could, as a matter of policy, require the lawyer to prove that the plaintiff would have lost the inner case had it been filed timely. That's an interesting idea, but I am not aware that any jurisdiction has adopted it. (The idea has more appeal when the "inner case" is a transactional matter, given what may be the greater difficulty of proof, as discussed below.) Furthermore, not only does the malpractice plaintiff have to prove two cases, but she is at a further disadvantage for at least two reasons. First, in the nature of things, the legal malpractice case will be tried later than the inner case would have been tried had it been timely brought. This delay hurts the plaintiff because memories fade and witnesses are harder to find. Second, as we saw in Chapter 4, the defendant-lawyer is permitted to use confidential information gained in his representation of the plaintiff (or in the preliminary interview that didn't lead to a retainer) in self-defense. In other words, the lawyer will have access to and can use information (oral or written) that would have been unavailable, or not as easily available, to the original defendant — the one whose conduct caused the plaintiff to consult the lawyer in the first place.[11]

One variation on a case-within-a-case requirement deserves mention. The malpractice plaintiff may contend not that she would *necessarily* have won the inner case, but rather that the inner case, had it been brought, would have settled. She might point to the fact that in the particular jurisdiction a very high percentage of civil cases settle, including civil cases like hers. She might introduce expert testimony on the settlement value of her claim. Some courts will allow this alternate theory of damages instead of or in addition to the claim that the inner case if tried would have been won.[12]

We've been assuming that the inner case was a dispute that should have been filed but was not because of a lawyer's neglect or alternatively was filed but badly handled or defended negligently. In a way, that's the easier model because, as stated, the malpractice jury, if it finds the lawyer negligent, can then simply be asked to do the job that a jury in the inner case would have been asked to do if that case had been properly tried. Or if the inner case would have been to a judge, a jurisdiction might give the decision on the outcome of the inner case to the judge. Similarly, if the legal malpractice was not a failure to file a case at all, but a failure to file a timely appeal or a failure to raise key arguments in the appeal, the question would then be what an appellate court would have done if an appeal had been filed or competently argued. There, too, the answer will be for the judge, not a jury, because a judge (or judges) would have given the answer about the appeal in the underlying matter.[13]

Malpractice in Transactions   But what if the inner case is not a dispute or an appeal but a transaction? Say lawyer Bob represents Company *A* in negotiating a deal. Say Company *A* tells Bob that it wants clauses protecting it in certain ways, and Bob forgets to bargain for these clauses. Or perhaps Company

A doesn't really know the standard protections that a company in its situation should bargain for and relies on lawyer Bob to know these things, inform it, and bargain for them. But it turns out Bob doesn't know, either, or that for some other reason he fails to get the standard protections. Assume in any of these situations, Bob's conduct is malpractice. The company sues him when, after the contract is signed, it discovers that it is not protected in ways it thought it would be or should be. For example, maybe the company discovers that it gave away more rights than it intended or needed to give away and that the loss of those rights has a price tag. "We could have sold the television rights to someone else for big dollars, but Bob didn't reserve them for us as we told him to or as he should have done even without being told."

At first blush, this sounds pretty easy. The client says that Bob's negligence resulted in the loss of a right having a particular value (and the company is prepared to prove that value). But it's not always so easy for this reason. Assume Bob's negligence was his failure to negotiate for television rights. Even if Bob had asked for these rights, the opponent might have said no. The company has to prove that Bob could have won that right if he had pursued it, as he should have, not merely that he was negligent for failing to pursue it. If he would not have won the rights anyway, his negligence did not produce harm. We can call this the "better deal" scenario. The company claims and is prepared to prove that it would have gotten a better deal (the rights) absent the negligence. Or the company might say that if Bob had explained to it that the deal did not reserve television rights, the company would not have done the deal at all because no deal would have left it better off than the deal it got. We can call this the "no deal" scenario. So if the company wishes to collect for Bob's malpractice (assuming it can prove malpractice), it must prove that Bob's negligence contributed to its inability to get a better deal or that it would have been better off with no deal.

Viner v. Sweet   Notice the words *contributed to* in the prior sentence. I did not write that the company must prove these consequences *but for* Bob's negligence. Does the "but for" test also apply where the malpractice occurs in transactional work? Should it? Or should there be a less demanding proximate cause test? Some judges and commentators have advocated a lesser standard. Perhaps the plaintiff need only prove that the lawyer's negligence was "a substantial factor" in the client's injury, in this view. They make this argument because, unlike negligence in the context of litigation, they see "but for" causation as too great a burden to impose on a transactional malpractice plaintiff. Here are the reasons an intermediate California appellate court (the Court of Appeal) gave for lightening the proximate cause burden in this situation. The court had affirmed a judgment (in part) where the trial judge's instructions only required the plaintiff to prove that the malpractice was a "substantial factor in bringing about" the harm, not a "but for" factor. The following description of the appellate court's reasons appears in a later opinion of the state Supreme Court in the same case:

> The Court of Appeal distinguished transactional malpractice from litigation malpractice, in which the plaintiff is required to prove the harm would not have occurred without the alleged negligence, and it offered three reasons for treating the two forms of malpractice differently. First, the court asserted that in litigation a gain for one side is always a loss for the other, whereas in transactional work a gain for one side could also be a gain for the other side. Second, the court observed that litigation malpractice involves past historical facts while transactional malpractice involves what parties would have been willing to accept for the future. Third, the court stated that "business transactions generally involve a much larger universe of variables than litigation matters." According to the Court of Appeal, in "contract negotiations the number of possible terms and outcomes is virtually

unlimited," and therefore the "jury would have to evaluate a nearly infinite array of 'what-ifs,' to say nothing of 'if that, then whats,' in order to determine whether the plaintiff would have ended up with a better outcome 'but for' the malpractice."[14]

The California Supreme Court rejected the lower court's approval of a relaxed burden of proof on proximate cause in transactional cases. "We see nothing distinctive about transactional malpractice," it wrote, "that would justify a relaxation of, or departure from, the well-established requirement in negligence cases that the plaintiff establish causation by showing either (1) but for the negligence, the harm would not have occurred, or (2) the negligence was a concurrent independent cause of the harm." The Court then explained its different view of the empirical and proof issues:

> In litigation, as in transactional work, a gain for one side does not necessarily result in a loss for the other side. Litigation may involve multiple claims and issues arising from complaints and cross-complaints, and parties in such litigation may prevail on some issues and not others, so that in the end there is no clear winner or loser and no exact correlation between one side's gains and the other side's losses. In addition, an attorney's representation of a client often combines litigation and transactional work, as when the attorney effects a settlement of pending litigation. The "but for" test of causation applies to a claim of legal malpractice in the settlement of litigation even though the settlement is itself a form of business transaction. . . .
>
> Nor do we agree with the Court of Appeal that litigation is inherently or necessarily less complex than transactional work. Some litigation, such as many lawsuits involving car accidents, is relatively uncomplicated, but so too is much transactional work, such as the negotiation of a simple lease or a purchase and sale agreement. But some litigation, such as a beneficiary's action against a trustee challenging the trustee's management of trust property over a period of decades, is as complex as most transactional work. . . .

It is true, as the Court of Appeal pointed out, that litigation generally involves an examination of past events whereas transactional work involves anticipating and guiding the course of future events. But this distinction makes little difference for purposes of selecting an appropriate test of causation. Determining causation always requires evaluation of hypothetical situations concerning what might have happened, but did not. In both litigation and transactional malpractice cases, the crucial causation inquiry is what would have happened if the defendant attorney had not been negligent. This is so because the very idea of causation necessarily involves comparing historical events to a hypothetical alternative.[15]

The plaintiffs (the Viners) had also argued that it would be harder to prove what the result would have been — how the parties would have behaved — if the lawyers in the case had sought to include the contract terms whose omission the plaintiffs claimed constituted the professional negligence. The Supreme Court described this argument and rejected it:

> [Plaintiffs] argue that proving causation under the "but for" test would require them to obtain the testimony of the other parties to the transaction, who have since become their adversaries, to the effect that they would have given the Viners more favorable terms had the Viners' attorneys not performed negligently. Not so. In transactional malpractice cases, as in other cases, the plaintiff may use circumstantial evidence to satisfy his or her burden. An express concession by the other parties to the negotiation that they would have accepted other or additional terms is not necessary. And the plaintiff need not prove causation with absolute certainty. Rather, the plaintiff need only " 'introduce evidence which affords a reasonable basis for the conclusion that it is more likely than not that the conduct of the defendant was a cause in fact of the result.' " In any event, difficulties of proof cannot justify imposing liability for injuries that the attorney could not have prevented by performing according to the required standard of care.[16]

We might question how a plaintiff could *circumstantially* make the proof that it would have gotten a better deal. What evidence would it offer? The fact that others in comparable negotiations had achieved the particular terms doesn't even begin to prove what the result would have been in the plaintiffs' deal, assuming that there even are comparable deals. Of course, if the other side to the deal were to say, "Sure, we would have given them that provision," that could do it, but how likely and how credible will such an admission be? Is it credible that the other side would have conceded a valuable provision in the negotiation — and it must be valuable or the plaintiff would not be bringing a malpractice claim for failure to get it — without having expected something equivalent in return? And anyway, this would not be circumstantial proof but direct proof.

On the other hand, it should be easy to prove that without the omitted terms the plaintiffs would have walked away from the deal (if they knew the terms were missing). They can offer their own testimony on that point, and the jury might believe them. But then they would still have to prove that "no deal" would have been better than the one they got, which should be a little easier to do with direct proof.

If a lawyer *does* successfully negotiate for a particular provision but then drafts it ineffectively so its value is lost, the plaintiffs' proof (assuming it cannot get reformation of the contract) will be to show the worth of the provision had it been competently drafted.

The "but for" test in transactional matters is most sensible and easy to satisfy when the transaction is simple and common (a separation agreement, a contract to sell a home, a routine employment contract) and also where the lawyer has failed to include a provision that would have protected his client against ensuing harm and which is customary in such agreements or to which the opposing party had already agreed. It is harder to prove but for causation where the deal is complex. That doesn't mean that we should create exceptions to the test in complex transactions (and anyhow, how would we would define *complexity*?). These are important policy issues, which the California Supreme Court has now resolved in favor of a single test for proximate cause regardless of the nature of the underlying legal service.

Fee Disgorgement and Forfeiture Forfeiture and disgorgement of a lawyer's fee is a remedy a court might impose if the lawyer has violated a duty to the client. Forfeiture occurs when the lawyer is denied part of or the entire fee. Disgorgement means she has to return all or part of what she got. The doctrine derives from agency law, long established, that holds that a disloyal (or otherwise misbehaving) agent is not entitled to compensation. The denial of compensation is meant to recognize that the agent has failed to give the principal (or client) the service that the law required, a failure of consideration for the agent's compensation. A disloyal agent by definition has denied the principal her due because principals (clients) are entitled to loyalty. The agent has not delivered and so the principal can deny compensation. As originally applied, and still in some jurisdictions, the loss of compensation is total. The client need not show any further damage. She need not show that the disloyalty or other professional transgression caused her to be "worse off," which is of course what the client would have to show in a civil action. The professional misconduct standing alone is the predicate for the loss of fee.

The doctrine can be a little extreme, can't it? For the lawyer, it can be a whole lot worse than loss of a civil claim. The lawyer may have spent much time on the matter. The client may actually have benefited from the lawyer's work overall, especially the work the lawyer did before the professional lapse. The lawyer's misconduct may be modest and unintentional, perhaps a conflict the lawyer failed to notice. The upshot is that the operation of the doctrine can result in a windfall to the client if the doctrine is strictly applied. So of late, some authorities have said that while the doctrine remains available as a general matter, the *amount* of forfeiture or disgorgement should not necessarily be total. Factors to consider are the degree of harm to the client as a result of the misconduct; the seriousness of the misconduct; whether the client has benefited from the lawyer's work, whether done before or after the lawyer's violation of duty; and whether loss of less than the entire fee can still have a deterrent effect (where deterrence is seen as a legitimate byproduct of the doctrine). Some courts have said that with a flexible approach, the lawyer may not lose any fee at all, although the lawyer may be subject to other sanctions, like disqualification or even discipline.[17]

Third-party Liability   As introduced above, not so very long ago, lawyers were largely protected against liability to third parties (that is, those persons who were not clients or former clients of the lawyers) by the doctrine of privity. This doctrine said, essentially, that whatever a lawyer did or failed to do as a professional, while potentially creating liability to clients, could not create liability to non-clients because they were not "in privity" with the lawyers. That was just another way of saying they were never the lawyer's client and what followed was that the lawyer owed them no duty as a professional. There were exceptions to the privity requirement, or perhaps it is more accurate to say that there were theories of liability for which privity or the lack of it was irrelevant. For example, lawyers would not escape liability, the same as anyone else, if they helped a client commit a fraud or a crime. That exception was noncontroversial.

The beginning of the demise (though certainly not the death) of privity might be traced to a decision of the California Supreme Court in 1958. Although others might reasonably identify a different birthplace and time, the court's decision in *Biakanja v. Irving*[18] was certainly an important development.

Oddly, the defendant was not a lawyer, but a notary public, sued by the intended beneficiary of a testator who charged that the notary had negligently drafted the will to exclude his bequest. The *Biakanja* court said that whether a person in the notary's position would be liable to a nonclient for negligence would turn on a "balancing of various factors." Upholding liability (while also chastising the notary for unauthorized law practice), the court wrote:

> The determination whether in a specific case the defendant will be held liable to a third person not in privity is a matter of policy and involves the balancing of various factors, among which are the extent to which the transaction was intended to affect the plaintiff, the foreseeability of harm to him, the degree of certainty that the plaintiff suffered injury, the closeness of the connection between the defendant's conduct and the injury suffered, the moral blame attached to the defendant's conduct, and the policy of preventing future harm. Here, the "end and aim" of the transaction was to provide for the passing of Maroevich's estate to plaintiff. Defendant must have been aware from the terms of the will itself that, if faulty solemnization caused the will to be invalid, plaintiff would suffer the very loss which occurred. As Maroevich died without revoking his will, plaintiff, but for defendant's negligence, would have received all of the Maroevich estate, and the fact that she received only one-eighth of the estate was directly caused by defendant's conduct.

Inevitably, the court's decision appeared in cases in which nonclients sued lawyers. The Washington Supreme Court among others has attempted to give greater content to the California doctrine:

> Absent privity of contract, two tests were previously applied in Washington to determine whether an attorney owes a duty to a nonclient: the California "multi-factor balancing" test and the Illinois "third party beneficiary" test. . . .

The multi-factor balancing test involves analysis of the following six factors:

(1) the extent to which the transaction was intended to affect the plaintiff;

(2) the foreseeability of harm to the plaintiff;

(3) the degree of certainty that the plaintiff suffered injury;

(4) the closeness of the connection between the defendant's conduct and the injury;

(5) the policy of preventing future harm; and

(6) the extent to which the profession would be unduly burdened by a finding of liability.[19]

One nice thing about a privity requirement is that it is eminently predictable. No privity, no liability for professional (mis)conduct. End of story. There might be the occasional remote exception, but lawyers pretty much knew there was a bright line that protected them so long as they remained on the correct side of it. A balancing test does not offer the same sense of security. By definition, a balancing test tells us the line is not bright but will depend on variables stated in pretty general language.[20] Over time, with enough cases conducting the "balance" in particular and recurrent fact patterns, the line will become brighter for *that* fact pattern, which offers some predictability if not solace. But it is in the very nature of balancing tests that they are open-ended. A new situation or circumstance may come along and surprise the unwary lawyer. You just can't be sure.

But privity, at least as an absolute precondition for liability, is dead most places.[21] What has replaced it? Giving a right of action to a client's intended third-party beneficiary is perhaps most consistent with established legal principles, but that will only be a small population of plaintiffs. So the process of "balancing" has, over time, led to certain categories in which lawyers are liable to third parties. Most notable, perhaps, is liability based on negligent misrepresentation of a fact. A lawyer represents that a fact is true, perhaps his client's insurance limits, a non-client (the opponent) reasonably relies on it, and the representation turns out to be false and negligently or recklessly made, subjecting the lawyer to liability.[22] This is different from intentional misrepresentation, which is closer to fraud, and fraud does not require privity.[23] But negligent misrepresentation punishes negligence and is closer to malpractice. Negligent misrepresentation should also be distinguished from opinion letters given to an opposing client. Such letters are formal affairs, not casual remarks, in which a firm consciously represents that a fact or legal position is true (e.g., that its client observed all corporate formalities and is legally authorized to enter the particular agreement).[24] Violation of certain statutes (like consumer protection laws or the securities laws) or common law torts (malicious prosecution or abuse of process) can also lead to liability to nonclients.[25]

It is not possible to catalog all the situations in which lawyers may be liable to nonclients beyond the traditional liability based on aiding fraud. But two circumstances in which lawyers will not be liable, though their clients may be, should be identified. First, a lawyer may advise her client to break a contract because the damages she will have to pay will be preferable to the consequences of not breaking the contract (perhaps the market has changed significantly). The client will have to pay damages but the lawyer cannot be sued for inducing the breach of contract even though someone else who did the same thing and who is not the client's lawyer could be sued. The reason: We want lawyers to be able to give this advice; the client has a legitimate interest in getting it. The lawyer is not an interloper, a mischief maker.[26] The second situation, somewhere between aiding fraud and advising a client to breach a contract, is where a lawyer aids a client's breach of fiduciary duty to another for which the client will be liable (as a competent lawyer would have to advise). Breach of fiduciary duty is a tort, and therein it is not like breach of contract, which though actionable is not a tort. One might argue that, unlike the breach of contract situation, protecting the confidential relationship of lawyer and client should not require immunizing lawyers who aid fiduciary duty breaches. Yet some courts have chosen otherwise.[27]

ENDNOTES

1. *See, e.g., Blair v. Ing*, 21 P.3d 452 (Haw. 2001) (collecting cases). Other jurisdictions reject the claim. *DiStefano v. Milardo*, 886 A.2d 415 (Conn. 2005). Even jurisdictions that reject the claim may allow the executor, rather than the beneficiary, to sue. *Belt v. Oppenheimer, Blend, Harrison & Tate, Inc.*, 192 S.W.3d 780 (Texas 2006).

2. *JPMorgan Chase v. Winnick*, 406 F.Supp.2d 247 (S.D.N.Y. 2005).

3. *Restatement of Agency* 3d, §1.01.

4. *Milbank, Tweed, Hadley & McCloy v. Boon*, 13 F.3d 537 (2d Cir. 1994) (lawyers occupy a "unique position of trust and confidence").

5. A typical description of the standard appears in *Russo v. Griffin*, 510 A.2d 436 (Vt. 1986) ("the appropriate standard of care to which a lawyer is held in the performance of professional services is 'that degree of care, skill, diligence and knowledge commonly possessed and exercised by a reasonable, careful and prudent lawyer in the practice of law in this jurisdiction' ") (internal citation omitted).

6. *Walker v. Bangs*, 601 P.2d 1279 (Wash. 1979).

7. *Chapman v. Bearfield*, 207 S.W. 3d 736 (2006).

8. The Minnesota Supreme Court identified the distinction in *Togstad v. Vesely, Otto, Miller & Keefe*, 291 N.W.2d 686 (Minn. 1980), as follows: "Under a negligence approach it must essentially be shown that defendant rendered legal advice (not necessarily at someone's request) under circumstances which made it reasonably foreseeable to the attorney that if such advice was rendered negligently, the individual receiving the advice might be injured thereby. . . . A contract analysis requires the rendering of legal advice pursuant to another's request and the reliance factor, in this case, where the advice was not paid for, need be shown in the form of promissory estoppel."

9. *See, e.g, Meyer v. Wagner*, 709 N.E.2d 784 (Mass. 1999) (negligence to recommend acceptance of a settlement without doing the factual and legal research necessary to evaluate it).

10. *Frazier v New Jersey Mfg. Ins. Co.*, 667 A.2d 670 (N.J. 1995) ("In order to recover against an attorney for missing the time-bar, a client must establish the recovery which the client would have obtained if malpractice had not occurred. . . . [T]he measure of damages is ordinarily the amount that the client would have received but for his attorney's negligence. Such damages are generally shown by introducing evidence establishing the viability and worth of the claim that was irredeemably lost. This procedure has been termed a suit within a suit.") (internal citations omitted).

11. These disadvantage are identified in *Garcia v. Kozlov, Seaton, Romanini & Brooks, P.C.*, 845 A.2d 602 (N.J. 2004).

12. *Id.*

13. *Daugert v. Pappas*, 704 P.2d 600 (Wash. 1985).

14. *Viner v. Sweet*, 70 P.3d 1046 (Cal. 2003).

15. *Id.*

16. *Id.*

17. *See, generally, Restatement of the Law Governing Lawyers* §37, which reveals the agency law predicate for the forfeiture and disgorgement rule. The *Restatement* takes the position that whether fees should be lost and if so the amount if not all depends on multiple factors, including the seriousness of the lawyer's misconduct, whether the client is harmed, when in the representation the misconduct occurred, and whether the client enjoyed any benefit from the lawyer's services. *See also Burrows v. Arce*, 997 S.W.2d 229 (Tex. 1999); and *Hendry v. Pelland*, 73 F.3d 397 (D.C. Cir. 1996), for court treatment of the doctrine. *Phansalkar v. Andersen Weinroth & Co., L.P.*, 344 F.3d 184 (2d Cir. 2003), discusses the "faithless servant doctrine" and its operation.

18. 320 P.2d 16 (Cal. 1958).

19. *Trask v. Butler*, 872 P.2d 1080 (Wash. 1994). Cases in this part of the chapter and the underlying doctrine are also discussed in Chapter 21. A leading Illinois case utilizing a third-party beneficiary test is *Pelham v. Griesheimer*, 440 N.E.2d 96 (Ill. 1982).

20. Where the test instead is the third-party-beneficiary test adopted in *Pelham v. Greisheimer, supra*, prediction is easier. Then the question is whether the client retained the lawyer at least in part to benefit the third party who later shows up as a plaintiff against the lawyer. *Id.*

21. Even New York, a privity-loving state if ever there was one, has partly rejected it. *Prudential Ins. Co. of America v. Dewey, Ballantine, Bushby, Palmer & Wood*, 605 N.E.2d 318 (N.Y. 1992), is a case that recognizes that a lawyer may be liable to an opposing party for negligent representation where the lawyer has given the opponent an opinion. The court, however, found that the alleged misrepresentation was not actionable on the facts before it. *Restatement of the Law Governing Lawyers* §51 also rejects privity.

22. *See, e.g., Slotkin v. Citizens Casualty Co.*, 614 F.2d 301 (2d Cir. 1979) (representation of insurance coverage recklessly made); *Greycas, Inc. v. Proud*, 826 F.2d 1560 (7th Cir. 1987) (representation of no prior liens). *Slotkin* was decided before New York abandoned strict privity in *Prudential, supra* note 21. Consequently, the court upheld the jury's verdict on the ground that the lawyer's "reckless" misstatement that he knew the insurance was limited to a particular sum amounted to fraud even if the lawyer actually believed it.

23. *Fire Ins. Exchange v. Bell*, 643 N.E.2d 310 (Ind. 1994) (false representation of insurance coverage is actionable as a matter of law).

24. *Mehaffy, Rider, Windholz & Wilson v. Central Bank of Denver, N.A.*, 892 P.2d 230 (Colo. 1995).

25. *Guenard v. Burke*, 443 N.E.2d 892 (Mass. 1982) (consumer protection laws); *Rubin v. Schottenstein, Zox & Dunn*, 143 F.3d 263 (6th Cir. 1998) (en banc) (securities law and state common law fraud); *Seltzer v. Morton*, 154 P.3d 561 (Mont. 2007) ($11 million malicious prosecution judgment against Gibson, Dunn & Crutcher).

26. *Los Angeles Airways, Inc. v. Davis*, 687 F.2d 321 (9th Cir. 1982).

27. *Reynolds v. Schrock*, 142 P.3d 1062 (Or. 2006) (analyzing the policy reasons to reject lawyer liability). *But see Albright v Burns*, 503 A.2d 386 (N.J. App. 1986). It may be that whether a lawyer's assistance of a breach of fiduciary duty is actionable will come to depend on the particular facts. In *Albright*, the lawyer was alleged to have helped a fiduciary steal from an estate. In *Reynolds*, the lawyer allegedly assisted the client in violating a fiduciary duty to a former business partner by selling some property, among other things. The court held that "a lawyer may not be held jointly liable with a client for the client's breach of fiduciary duty unless the third party shows that the lawyer was acting outside the scope of the lawyer-client relationship." It may be that the Oregon court would hold that helping an executor steal estate assets is always "outside the scope of the lawyer-client relationship." *Thornwood v. Jenner & Block*, 799 N.E.2d 756 (Ill. App. 2003), upheld a firm's liability to a plaintiff for allegedly aiding a client's breach of fiduciary duty.

～ 25 ～

Discipline

When Lawyers Can Be Disciplined

Procedures

Sanctions

Rules of legal ethics or professional responsibility (or whatever the name) would not mean much if lawyers could violate them without consequence. Of course, as comment [20] in the Scope section of the American Bar Association (ABA) Model Rules acknowledges, and as many courts have held, violation of a rule "may be evidence" that a lawyer has violated "the applicable standard of conduct" under substantive law. And as we saw in Chapter 24, unethical conduct can be the basis for loss of some (or all) of a lawyer's fee, even if the client suffers no other injury. The rules can also be the basis for disqualification of a law firm from a matter based on a conflict of interest (see Chapter 12).

But every jurisdiction also has a disciplinary system that can impose sanctions on lawyers who violate a legal ethics rule. Disciplinary systems operate under the authority of the jurisdiction's courts. The courts admit lawyers to practice, and the courts have the authority to throw them out (to disbar them) or to impose a lesser sanction. The operation of disciplinary systems varies from place to place—that is, in how they are organized, in who staffs them, in their use of volunteer lawyers and nonlawyers, and in their procedures. One common feature for all disciplinary systems is that they are seriously under-funded. They cannot effectively police the behavior of all law-yers in the jurisdiction. So they mostly pursue the low-hanging fruit, the thieves, the lawyers who neglect client matters, the lawyers who commit crimes. That is not to say that that is *all* they do, but it is the very great part of their inventory.

Despite variations in how disciplinary systems operate, they must all accord certain due process rights to any lawyer who is charged with misconduct. These rights include notice of the charges, the right to be represented by counsel (although there is no right to free counsel), the right to summon witnesses in the lawyer's behalf, the right to confront witnesses, and the right to an impartial tribunal.[1]

Most states require the disciplinary authority to prove a violation by clear and convincing evidence, which is a higher burden than the preponderance of the evidence but not so high as the criminal standard of proof beyond a reasonable doubt. A minority of states requires only proof by a preponder-ance of the evidence, a test that has withstood challenge on constitutional grounds.[2]

Nearly all states make the early stages of a disciplinary investigation secret. The idea here is that the investigation may go nowhere (it's so easy for an unhappy client or adversary to complain; they just write a letter), yet the fact of an investi-gation alone may harm a lawyer's reputation. Most states, however, then open the process to public view if the disciplinary body finds probable cause to charge misconduct. The public may then go to any hearing, although most people would find most hearings rather boring, just as most trials in court are boring except to the parties. A few states maintain secrecy for the process unless and until a court orders public discipline.

A disciplinary proceeding, like a criminal prosecution (with which discipline has been compared), is generally divided into two parts: a hearing to determine the facts and to decide if they show a violation of a rule; and if they do show a violation, there is a separate hearing to determine appropriate sanction, which may include additional evidence, much as a sentencing hearing may follow a criminal conviction.

It is not profitable to get too deep into the details of the various state procedures except to know that they do vary and that they must all comport with constitutional due process guarantees.

Reasons for Discipline   In theory, any violation of a rule in the jurisdiction's professional conduct rules can support discipline. But as a practical matter, that doesn't happen. Certain transgressions have not been the focus of disciplinary committees. For example, absent a truly egregious situation, discipline has not been used to punish incompetence, even though competence is an ethical obligation (*see* Model Rule 1.1). Rather, we leave it to the civil courts to remedy incompetence in actions for malpractice or challenges to convictions based on ineffective assistance of counsel. Furthermore, the fact that a lawyer has been proved negligent on a particular occasion is not reason to conclude that the lawyer poses a danger to clients across the run of matters. That is, there is no reason to think that he or she is "walking malpractice," as the saying goes. We all err, and sometimes we pay a price, but that doesn't mean we're fundamentally rotten, professionally speaking.

Violation of conflict-of-interest rules are also mostly left to the courts to remedy through disqualification of a lawyer or law firm, at least where the conflict is not blatant. This is because many conflicts are technical (even in the view of some, hypertechnical) and do not lead to worries about the conflicted lawyer's professionalism. There are exceptions, of course, where the conflict is obvious and the lawyer appears to have been motivated by self-gain to the self-evident disadvantage of the client.

The benefit of leaving competence and conflicts to the courts to police in civil and criminal cases is that it frees up disciplinary committee time to go after lawyers whose violations are particularly heinous and who do pose serious dangers to the public. In this category are lawyers who have taken (or "borrowed") money from a trust account. Doing so, even if the lawyer intends to pay it back and even if he or she has paid it back, is uniformly viewed as requiring serious discipline, often disbarment or long suspension.[3]

Also in this category are lawyers who neglect a client's matter (or many clients' matters) after accepting the client and, usually, taking money as a retainer. In other words, these lawyers are not negligent in how they perform. They do nothing at all or nearly at all to advance the client's goals. This is a frequent reason for complaint to the disciplinary authorities.

In many jurisdictions, conviction of a crime, especially a felony, will demand the attention of disciplinary committees, even if the crime is unconnected to law practice, but certainly if it is connected. Billing fraud — whether the victim is a client or the lawyer's firm — will, once detected, end in discipline. Deceit — lying to a tribunal or even another lawyer — will support discipline. Less frequently but still of interest to disciplinary committees is sexist or racist behavior in law practice.[4]

Also, in the last several decades and increasingly, lawyers have been disciplined for commencing sexual relations with clients during the representation, even if the client "voluntarily" engaged in the relations (and certainly if the client was told that "playing ball" will make the lawyer more willing to spend time on her matter). A sexual relationship with a client is seen as inimical to the professional relationship. It could, for example, undermine a divorce client's legal position with regard to support or child custody. Indeed, most of the disciplinary cases involving sexual relationships with clients have arisen out of matrimonial matters.[5]

Sex with clients can also lead to civil liability for breach of fiduciary duty if the court concludes that the lawyer took advantage of the client's dependency or his knowledge of confidential information.[6] While there may be risks to a client who has a preexisting sexual relationship with his or her lawyer, when the relationship first begins only after the professional relationship has begun, there is the added danger that the client is not truly free to say no and that the lawyer will be able to take advantage of the client's dependency on him and perhaps confidences about the client learned in the professional relationship. The ABA and many states have a rule addressing this issue (*see* Model Rule 1.8(j)).

If, however, I were pressed to identify the three most common reasons lawyers get disciplined, they would be the abuse of trust or escrow money, neglect of client matters, and conviction of serious crimes.

Mitigating Factors   So, then, what happens to a lawyer who is found guilty of violating a disciplinary rule? The first thing that happens, of course, is to hold a hearing to determine the sanction. At it, the tribunal will take evidence on any mitigating factors it (or the courts) should weigh. The most common mitigating factor is the lawyer's "unblemished" record. *Unblemished* is a word that seems, in law, almost exclusively to appear in disciplinary opinions. But it makes sense. If the lawyer has been practicing for some time and has no prior discipline, the immediate transgression may be viewed as aberrational. That won't mean that the lawyer escapes all sanction; it will only influence what the sanction will be.

Other mitigating factors include the lawyer recognizing his or her violation and is contrite, the lawyer self-reporting (turned herself in), the lawyer being dependent on (not necessarily illegal) drugs or on alcohol, and the lawyer suffering from some mental strain or syndrome.[7] Depression often gets mentioned, but other psychological explanations also appear. If the lawyer has taken money, he might show that he repaid it. In other words, at this stage, the tribunal takes the full measure of the lawyer's character along with his or her misconduct on the particular occasion.

Sanctions[8]   The most frequent justification for sanctioning lawyers who violate professional conduct rules is, it is said, protection of the public. Surely, this is prominent, especially when the sanction is disbarment. Retribution, deterrence, and rehabilitation are rarely if ever mentioned, although they are factors that play into determination of criminal sentences. However, we would be blind not to realize that retribution and deterrence, at least, are also influential here. Why else suspend a lawyer from practice for, say, 30 days? It does not protect the public except for those 30 days, which is no protection at all. Or why else publicly reprimand a lawyer, but allow him or her to continue to practice without interruption? The explanation can only be that the transgression calls for some official response in the form of punishment, however mild, and the wish to deter other lawyers from conduct that might lead to whatever humiliation accompanies a public reprimand.

Here you begin to see the possible sanctions. They range from the most minor — a private reprimand or a public one (discoverable on line), suspension from anywhere between 30 days and five years — to disbarment. Disbarment is not forever most places. A lawyer can apply for readmission after some period of time, generally measured in years. Readmission is not guaranteed and, in some states, is very difficult to achieve. A few states treat disbarment as permanent. "Don't come back" is the message.

This is snapshot of the sanction universe. There will be particular variation from place to place.

ENDNOTES

1. Leading Supreme Court cases on a lawyer's rights in discipline are *In re Ruffalo*, 390 U.S. 544 (1968); and *Willner v. Committee on Character and Fitness*, 373 U.S. 96 (1963).

2. *In re Barach*, 540 F.3d 82 (1st Cir. 2008).

3. *See, e.g., In re Munsiff*, 871 N.Y.S.2d 257 (2d Dept. 2008) (disbarment for violating escrow duties).

4. *In re Kahn*, 791 N.Y.S.2d 36 (1st Dept. 2005).

5. *Matter of DiSandro*, 680 A.2d 73 (R.I. 1996).

6. *McDaniel v. Gile*, 281 Cal. Rptr. 242 (Cal. App. 1991).

7. The lawyer in *People v. Lujan*, 890 P.2d 109 (1995), escaped disbarment by proving that her thefts were motivated by a compulsion to shop.

8. The ABA has attempted to identify what might be called "sentencing guidelines" keyed to the kinds of rule violations a court might find. See its publication *Standards for Imposing Lawyer Sanctions* on the Web site of the ABA Center for Professional Responsibility: *http://www.abanet.org/cpr*.

~ 26 ~

Restrictions on Advertising and Solicitation

How Do They Differ?

Limits on Regulation of Content

Noncontent-based Regulation

Greater Protection for Public Interest Lawyers

Most people reading this book will have no memory of the day that lawyers were forbidden to advertise or publicly promote their credentials. Extremely limited exceptions allowed for law lists like Martindale-Hubbell, assuming that these could even be called exceptions. Those readers will have no memory of a time when ads for legal services were banned from television and radio, the Yellow Pages, buses and subways, newspapers, and billboards — in short, from just about every means a lawyer might wish to use to make his or her services known to the general public or particular segments of it. Readers may wonder why that was ever the rule. What purpose was served by the near total ban? What values did it mean to protect? What were courts (and many lawyers) afraid of?

Even after these questions are answered, readers who came of age after 1977, the year of the Supreme Court opinion liberating lawyer commercial speech, may continue to wonder what all the fuss was about. Were the evils the ban was meant to prevent really so dire? Have they since proven so? Was the loss of information to consumers of legal services even worse?

Before 1977, and still for a sizeable if declining number of lawyers, legal advertising, which includes solicitation, was and remains a very bad thing. The practice, they say, emphasizes the commercial aspects of the profession, a profession that is supposed to put public service above desire for private gain. Indeed, critics maintain, lawyer advertising actually encourages (inflames?) the bar's commercial impulses, which might otherwise lie dormant. Beyond that, they charge, legal advertising and solicitation encourage disputes and lead to excess litigation, too often for the greater benefit of lawyers, not clients. And clever marketing causes unsophisticated clients to choose counsel based on the quality (if not the flamboyance) of Madison Avenue tricks, rather than the quality of the lawyer. And so on.

But that was yesterday's war. Legal advertising is here to stay, made exponentially easier and more efficient with the advent of the Internet. The only question is how much a state (through its courts) may regulate it. The answer is not much at all, as we shall see. And just in case one were to infer, based on the most visible ads, that this is all about high-volume lawyers trolling for personal injury clients — well, it is about that, of course; but legal advertising has infiltrated all rungs of the profession, except the name of the activity changes as you move up the food chain. At the top of the profession, in the precincts of the big law firms, it is in the domain of the marketing department. Recently, I learned that the New York office of an international law firm had a staff of 30 in its marketing department. Thirty. In New York City alone. These are not lawyers. Their job is to promote the firm and help its lawyers get business. Even prominent firms advertise in a fashion — by contributing to public television and radio (with on-air acknowledgments), by underwriting museum exhibits (same), or by taking out tasteful (always tasteful) full-page display ads in select publications likely to include potential clients among their readership.

Bates   Monday, June 27, 1977. That is the date that the Supreme Court's 5-4 decision in *Bates v. State Bar of Arizona*[1] unshackled legal advertising from the constraints of state ethics rules. The newspaper ad in *Bates* was modest by any standards and certainly in comparison to what we see today. Extremely modest. If you wanted to bring a test case, you could hardly have asked for a less intrusive ad. The ad listed some run-of-the-mill legal services (uncontested divorce, wills, adoption, uncontested bankruptcy) and the cost of each ($250 was the top price). The ad had no illustrations, no graphics except the scales of justice, no pictures or endorsements. Just type, comprising a menu of services and their prices.

In disciplining the lawyers, Arizona made a series of arguments. Legal ads, the state explained, had an "adverse effect on professionalism" and encourage "commercialization," were inherently misleading, would stir up litigation, would increase the cost of legal services, would encourage shoddy work, and were difficult to monitor against abuse. The Court rejected each of these claims and, most notable for this topic and others, has since gone on to emphasize that encouraging litigation is not always a bad thing.[2] Litigation is the civilized way to settle disputes. It beats the alternatives (violence or accepting injustice). The Court did allow that a state could ban misleading or false ads. A state could also require disclaimers to ensure that ads were not misleading (e.g., "no recovery, no fee" alone does not tell the client that she may have to pay court costs, win or lose).[3] And a state might be able to restrict claims of quality because quality is hard to measure (e.g., "one of the best lawyers in Greenville").[4]

Of all the arguments Arizona advanced, the claim that legal advertising undermines the professionalism of the bar is still heard today, but the debate is mainly occurring in the profession, less so in the courts. The *Bates* holding that a perceived threat to professionalism could not justify a ban on lawyer commercial speech remains the law. The claim is, in any event, intuitive or anecdotal. It would be hard if not impossible to construct an experiment that tested the broad claim empirically.[5] And absent that proof, at least, the matter would seem settled. Interference with free speech, even commercial speech, requires not just the assertion of a countervailing state interest but some demonstration that the interest is threatened and that the restriction is narrowly tailored to protect it.[6]

Of course, the Court could change its mind about all this at any time. It almost did in the 1980s, when some dissenting justices argued for a return to the pre-*Bates* era expressly because of the danger of commercialization of law practice and a state's wish to avoid it. Or at least those justices were willing to defer to a state's perception of the existence of that danger without any solid proof. But today, more than three decades after *Bates*, and with other lawyer advertising cases affirming it, reversal of course is improbable. Further, whole industries have grown up to help lawyers trumpet their skill and availability. It is doubtful that the Court will do a U-turn and shut down that industry. Further, the Supreme Court has no role here unless a state court first promulgates a rule that directly confronts *Bates*, and, as time passes, the likelihood of that happening decreases.[7]

A Dissenting View Justice O'Connor has advanced the most eloquent judicial plea that legal advertising harms professionalism. In a 1985 opinion (joined by Chief Justice Burger and Justice Rehnquist), she dissented in a case that upheld constitutional protection for targeted direct mail advertising. A targeted ad is one that is aimed at persons known to need specific legal help as opposed to advertisements (mail or print) that appeal to the public generally. The lawyer in *Shapero v. Kentucky Bar Association*[8] wanted to write to individuals facing mortgage foreclosure, offering his professional aid. He was able to learn the recipients' names and addresses from court records. The Kentucky (and American Bar Association [ABA]) rule at the time prohibited targeted mail. The state high court upheld the validity of the rule. The Supreme Court reversed. The plurality concluded that the state's legitimate goals could be met with something less than a categorical ban on the practice.[9] Justice O'Connor in dissent wrote:

> *Bates* was an early experiment with the doctrine of commercial speech, and it has proved to be problematic in its application. Rather than continuing to work out all the consequences of its approach, we should now return to the States the legislative function that has so inappropriately been taken from them in the context of attorney advertising. . . .
>
> Imbuing the legal profession with the necessary ethical standards is a task that involves a constant struggle with the relentless natural force of economic self-interest. It cannot be accomplished directly by legal rules, and it certainly will not succeed if sermonizing is the strongest tool that may be employed. Tradition and experiment have suggested a number of formal and informal mechanisms, none of which is adequate by itself and many of which may serve to reduce competition (in the narrow economic sense) among members of the profession. A few examples include the great efforts made during this century to improve the quality and breadth of the legal education that is required for admission to the bar; the

concomitant attempt to cultivate a subclass of genuine scho-
lars within the profession; the development of bar associations
that aspire to be more than trade groups; strict disciplinary
rules about conflicts of interest and client abandonment;
and promotion of the expectation that an attorney's history
of voluntary public service is a relevant factor in selecting
judicial candidates.

Restrictions on advertising and solicitation by lawyers
properly and significantly serve the same goal. Such restrictions act as a concrete, day-to-day reminder to the practicing
attorney of why it is improper for any member of this profession to regard it as a trade or occupation like any other.

One must appreciate Justice O'Connor's longing for the
profession she describes in this excerpt and elsewhere, while
also recognizing that the description is, today, somewhat
quaint and historical. Whatever the value of the kind of bar
Justice O'Connor prefers, and there are some who would say it
was elitist and unresponsive to the needs of ordinary clients,
that bar is long gone. The exceedingly dim prospect of over-
ruling *Bates* or any of the decisions solidifying its place in
commercial speech jurisprudence will not quell the still ongoing debate over professionalism and the corrosive effects (as
some see it) of so-called commercialization, a debate that continues within the profession and occasionally beyond.

Post-Bates Cases   In the decades since *Bates*, the Court has
rejected nearly all efforts to restrict the content of lawyer
commercial speech or the way the message is delivered, so
long as the speech is not false, misleading, or deceptive.
Most of the cases that have helped define the scope of protection for legal advertising arose in the dozen years following
Bates. Of late, the Court has been silent in this area. So, for
example, the Court has protected the right of lawyers to place
newspaper advertisements aimed at clients with particular
claims against identified defendants.[10] It follows, of course,

that lawyers can sponsor Web sites that seek to attract clients with specific claims or needs (who may discover the Web site through Internet searches). As stated above, in *Shapero*, the Court protected the right of lawyers to send direct mail advertisements targeted at potential clients proposing to represent the recipients in a specific matter or type of matter. And while the Court has never had to identify the limits a state might impose on the use of electronic media and the Internet, there can no longer be any doubt (as there might have been immediately after *Bates*) that lawyers may employ both vehicles to attract clients. No state's rules forbid use of electronic media, although they vary in the degree of control they seek to impose.

The Court's protection has extended to both advertising and, if a distinction can be drawn, solicitation. The line between advertising and solicitation is a matter of interpretation and not, as a practical matter, all that important. One distinction that makes sense is to view advertising as appeals to potential clients generally, as through a television or a newspaper advertisement, while solicitation focuses on a specific population of potential clients with identified needs. So a letter to individuals who the lawyer has discovered have been arrested for drunk driving, offering to represent them, would be solicitation, as would an advertisement appealing to all users of an identified product. Or we may further refine the distinction by using solicitation only where the lawyer's appeal is to a very small group of individuals — say, the dozen injured in a building collapse — rather than to a large group but much smaller than the public generally (the thousands who may have been harmed by a drug's side effects).

In only two post-*Bates* cases has the Court upheld significant state limitations on lawyer advertising or solicitation. One addressed limits on the *method* of a communication, and the other addressed the *timing* of a communication. Neither sought to limit content. A year after *Bates*, the Court (9-0) upheld a state rule that prohibited lawyers from soliciting business in person from a stranger (i.e., prospective clients who are not relatives, friends, or former clients of the lawyer).[11] That case involved a lawyer who approached a personal injury client shortly after the accident giving rise to her claim and when she might be expected still to be shaken by the event. Further, the potential client was wholly unsophisticated in the retention of lawyers. It is doubtful that the Court would tolerate a categorical ban on all in-person solicitation of business clients.[12] The context matters: here, an unsophisticated person was recently in an accident.

Separately, the Court (5-4) upheld a Florida law forbidding direct mail solicitation of potential personal injury clients or their survivors for 30 days after the event causing the harm.[13]

Aside from these two situations — in-person solicitation and a brief prohibition on direct mail contact following an injury — the scope of state regulation seems likely to be restricted to ensuring that content is not false or misleading, to rules that impose recordkeeping and filing requirements, and to directions to include specific language in lawyer ads in order to avoid misunderstanding.

Public Interest Lawyers Public interest lawyers enjoy greater First Amendment protection than do lawyers in private practice. In 1973, Edna Smith Primus, a South Carolina lawyer cooperating with the American Civil Liberties Union (ACLU), wrote to a woman who had been sterilized, allegedly as a condition of receiving welfare payments. Primus offered to represent the woman in a lawsuit against the doctor who had performed the operation. Today, that targeted direct mail solicitation would be protected as commercial speech under *Shapero*, but at the time of the Supreme Court decision in Primus's case (1978), protection for targeted direct mail was still an open question. So the case proceeded on the assumption that the First Amendment would not protect a lawyer *in private practice* who sent the same letter. The question for the Court was whether Primus enjoyed greater First Amendment protection because she was a public interest lawyer and was not offering to take the case for a fee. Or, to put it another way, was Primus's speech "commercial," or did the absence of a monetary incentive mean that it enjoyed greater First Amendment protection?

On the same day that it upheld *Ohralik*'s discipline for in-person solicitation of an accident victim, the Court (8-1) overturned Primus's discipline.[14] Its conclusion rested on the ACLU's particular reasons for petitioning the courts and on a factual difference between Primus's motives and those of lawyers in private practice. First, the Court described the role litigation played in the ACLU's mission. It compared the ACLU's activities with those of the National Association for the Advancement of Colored People (NAACP), whose practice of soliciting clients to bring school desegregation cases the Court protected in *NAACP v. Button* 15 years earlier.[15]

> From all that appears, the ACLU and its local chapters, much like the NAACP and its local affiliates in Button, "[engage] in extensive educational and lobbying activities" and "also [devote] much of [their] funds and energies to an extensive program of assisting certain kinds of litigation on behalf of [their] declared purposes." The court below acknowledged that " 'the ACLU has only entered cases in which substantial civil liberties questions are involved. . . . ' " It has engaged in the defense of unpopular causes and unpopular defendants and has represented individuals in litigation that has defined the scope of constitutional protection in areas such as political dissent, juvenile rights, prisoners' rights, military law, amnesty, and privacy. For the ACLU, as for the NAACP, "litigation is not a technique of resolving private differences"; it is "a form of political expression" and "political association. . . ."
>
> South Carolina's action in punishing appellant for soliciting a prospective litigant by mail, on behalf of the ACLU,

must withstand the "exacting scrutiny applicable to limitations on core First Amendment rights. . . ." South Carolina must demonstrate "a subordinating interest which is compelling" and that the means employed in furtherance of that interest are "closely drawn to avoid unnecessary abridgment of associational freedoms."

The state argued that it had a supervening interest in preventing misconduct by lawyers and that this interest justified its antisolicitation rule and Primus's discipline. The Court disagreed. Primus was not motivated by money but by vindicating the civil rights of her potential client. The absence of a pecuniary motive reduced the risk of lawyer overreaching, conflict of interest, and undue influence. Avoiding these harms was, to be sure, a legitimate state goal, but when the lawyer's motive is not monetary, the chance of their occurrence is reduced, even if not eliminated. Nor did this analysis change because the court was empowered to award the ACLU counsel fees if the suit succeeded, thereby introducing a monetary, if not the usual commercial, motive. "It is conceded that [Primus] received no compensation for any of the activities in question. It is also undisputed that neither the ACLU nor any lawyer associated with it would have shared in any monetary recovery by the plaintiffs. . . ."

In other words, because the danger of lawyer misconduct was reduced by the absence of a pecuniary motive and because Primus's communication enjoyed core, not commercial, First Amendment protection as "political expression," the state's rule, though at the time valid to restrict the commercial speech of the private bar, was unconstitutional as applied to a public interest lawyer. As the Court concluded:

> At bottom, the case against appellant rests on the proposition that a State may regulate in a prophylactic fashion all solicitation activities of lawyers because there may be some potential for overreaching, conflict of interest, or other

substantive evils whenever a lawyer gives unsolicited advice and communicates an offer of representation to a layman. Under certain circumstances, that approach is appropriate in the case of speech that simply "[proposes] a commercial transaction." In the context of political expression and association, however, a State must regulate with significantly greater precision.

ENDNOTES

1. 433 U.S. 350 (1977).

2. *Zauderer v. Office of Disciplinary Counsel*, 471 U.S. 626 (1985) ("we cannot endorse the proposition that a lawsuit, as such, is an evil. Over the course of centuries, our society has settled upon civil litigation as a means for redressing grievances, resolving disputes, and vindicating rights when other means fail.").

3. *Id*.

4. The *Bates* Court wrote, "[W]e need not address the peculiar problems associated with advertising claims relating to the quality of legal services. Such claims probably are not susceptible of precise measurement or verification and, under some circumstances, might well be deceptive or misleading to the public, or even false. [The State Bar] does not suggest, nor do we perceive, that appellants' advertisement contained claims, extravagant or otherwise, as to the quality of services."

5. In *The Florida Bar v. Went For It, Inc.*, 515 U.S. 618 (1995), discussed below, the Court did uphold a ban on mail solicitation of accident victims within 30 days of the cause of an injury in part based on a survey that purported to show that the practice harmed the bar's reputation.

6. *Central Hudson Gas 7 Elec. Corp. v. Public Service Commn. of New York*, 447 U.S. 557 (1980).

7. At the margins, short of direct confrontation with *Bates*, state courts will occasionally adopt rules that a lawyer will challenge. *See, e.g., Ficker v. Curran*, 119 F.3d 1150 (4th Cir. 1997) (30-day waiting period to contact arrested persons held invalid). But neither this case nor any other of recent vintage requires reexamination of the underpinnings of the *Bates* holding.

8. 486 U.S. 466 (1988) (O'Connor, J., dissenting).

9. The state argued, for example, that the ban was necessary to avoid misleading communications that would otherwise go undetected. The four-justice plurality concluded that this could be avoided by requiring lawyers to file their direct mail advertisements with a regulator. Two other justices concurred in part and dissented in part.

10. *Zauderer v. Office of Disciplinary Counsel*, 471 U.S. 626 (1985). *Zauderer* also upheld the right of lawyers to include illustrations in their print advertisements.

11. *Ohralik v. Ohio State Bar Assn*, 436 U.S. 447 (1978) (in-person solicitation of accident victim is "inherently conducive to overreaching and other forms of misconduct" and lawyer's conduct "virtually immune to effective oversight").

12. *Compare Edenfield v. Fane*, 507 U.S. 761 (1993). In rejecting a categorical ban on in-person solicitation by accountants of potential business clients, Justice Kennedy's opinion for the Court made it "clear that a preventive rule was justified only in a situation 'inherently conducive to overreaching and other forms of misconduct.'" Justice Kennedy wrote that a CPA, unlike a lawyer, was not "trained in the art of persuasion" and that "Fane's prospective clients are sophisticated and experienced business executives," whom the Court then distinguished from the accident victim in *Ohralik*.

13. *The Florida Bar v. Went For It, Inc.*, 515 U.S. 618 (1995).

14. *In re Primus*, 436 U.S. 412 (1978). Justice Rehnquist, dissenting, thought that the rule should be the same for public interest lawyers as for lawyer in private practice.

15. 371 U.S. 415 (1963).

Index